Pioneer Efforts
in Rural Social Welfare

Pioneer Efforts in Rural Social Welfare

Firsthand Views since 1908

Emilia E. Martinez-Brawley

Editor

Foreword by Leon H. Ginsberg

The Pennsylvania State University Press

University Park and London

I am indebted to many gracious people without whose help this book
would not have been completed. I want to thank the Administration
and Grants Committee of La Salle College, Philadelphia, whose
support was crucial to the completion of the initial research. I
thank Georgette Most and Helen Wall of the La Salle Library for
their help in securing many rare books. I am grateful to my former
student and capable assistant, Russ Hartman, who typed the initial
manuscript. I appreciated the encouragement of David Bast of the
University of Wisconsin and Leon Ginsberg of the West Virginia
Department of Welfare during the beginning stages of preparation of
the manuscript. I am grateful for the support and cooperation of
Dr. Roland Pellegrin, Chairman of the Sociology Department, and of
Dean Thomas Magner of the Liberal Arts Research Office at the
Pennsylvania State University for their support during the final
stages of preparation of the manuscript. I must finally mention my
friends Pat Stansell and Betsy Smith for their editorial comments,
and my husband, Allan, and children Stephen and Ewan for enduring
the process.

Library of Congress Cataloging in Publication Data
Main entry under title:

Pioneer efforts in rural social welfare.

   1. Social service, Rural--United States--History--
Addresses, essays, lectures. I. Martinez-Brawley,
Emilia E., 1939-
HV91.P66   361'.973   79-5142
ISBN 0-271-00233-6 cloth
ISBN 0-271-00245-X paper

Contents

Foreword

Leon H. Ginsberg

This collection of articles on rural social work ought to provide
further evidence of something many students of social work and social
welfare have observed for a long time—that there is too little
emphasis on historical materials in the field. The neglect of history in social work education, which is a fact in all but a few
undergraduate and graduate programs, is part of a general problem in
the field. That general problem is an over-reliance on the social
and behavioral sciences and an under-use of concepts and materials
from the humanities, of which history is a part.

Social welfare problems do, of course, respond to solutions that
are informed by the social and behavioral sciences. Understanding
human problems, engineering solutions to them, and evaluating the
results are closely akin to the scientific methods employed by such
fields as psychology and sociology. However, the crucial issues in
social welfare are not only matters of quantitative information.
Neither are there always specific, scientific answers to specific,
rationally defined issues. Instead, the problems of poverty and disadvantage, family relations and child care, crime and corrections,
social planning and human organization are, in equal proportions,
problems of values and problems of morality. In our efforts to render rational and scientific the analysis and alleviation of social
problems—efforts which all of us should applaud—we may have forgotten the questions that are better addressed by the humanities,
the questions of morals and values.

We discover a number of things by reading the papers that Emilia
E. Martinez-Brawley has so effectively collected and organized. We
learn first that the issues in organizing and delivering social services to people in rural communities are not very new. They existed
in similar ways and the solutions offered were similar to those that
are offered now by writers on social work in small communities. I
discovered, for example, years after I had written about social work

in rural communities, that others had said substantially the same things, decades before. The details may have been different and the specifics may have differed markedly from those of the 1970s, but the general issues are very much the same.

But that does not mean we study history in order to learn about the successes and the failures of the past—although such learning can be helpful to some professionals in some ways, at some time. In addition, we learn about human values and attitudes toward programs of social welfare which are, in many ways, more significant than the specific ideas, problems, and programs themselves. How the public feels about social welfare programs and the problems of those who face them is often more significant than we have imagined. History is one of the best ways to learn about them because attitudes and values are more likely to be cyclical than linear. For example, we have not moved from very conservative attitudes of the past to more liberal attitudes of today—on any subject. Instead, we can find eras in which attitudes as liberal as those we have now were the norms of the day and times when attitudes toward social welfare were as negative as they are in the most negative belief systems we encounter now.

Attitudes and values about social welfare are affected by the times as much as anything else. History provides us important—unique, really—insights into the contexts in which such attitudes and values develop.

So this volume has merit for students of rural social work. It provides the best collection of information ever gathered together in one place on approaches through the years to the problems of American small towns and rural areas. It also offers a useful model for and new evidence of the utility of teaching historical materials to social work students. Learning how we came to be what we are is both interesting and enjoyable. It also helps us do our jobs more adequately. Perhaps this well-organized and exciting volume is only one example of what we can and will learn from the humanities for other special areas of social work practice.

Leon H. Ginsberg
Commissioner
West Virginia Department of Welfare

Preface

Many of the issues which are now being discussed by rural social
workers have had their counterpart in years past. The problems presently affecting service delivery and training of practitioners for
rural communities are not without precedent. Yet it is apparent
that few are aware of the long and rich history of struggle with
similar notions which is available and waiting to be tapped by those
who wish to examine practice and education from a historical perspective. It is the purpose of this volume to render accessible to
the contemporary rural practitioner, educator, or student some of
the wisdom of the past. It is also the purpose of this collection
to pay tribute to the early pioneers of social welfare in rural communities.

It must be stated at the outset that in most cases it is more
appropriate to speak of the broader arena of social welfare efforts
in the rural field than of the narrower scope of social work intervention. The reasons for this statement will become apparent to the
reader through the interdisciplinary writings of this volume. For
the purposes of this anthology, the term social work must be understood broadly rather than strictly methodologically. It must be
understood to include a varied group of people committed to the welfare of rural areas.

The birth of rural social work can be traced to the Country Life
Commission of 1908 appointed by President Theodore Roosevelt and the
National Conference of Charities and Corrections of the same year.
The budding efforts and struggles of developing youth can be recognized in the services of the American Red Cross during and following
World War I. The maturing and broadening of rural social work or
of the practice of social work in rural communities was a Depression
and New Deal phenomenon. These periods in the development of rural
social work have served as central topics for each of the three
sections of this anthology. Within each period, however, it is

possible to identify subtopics which preoccupied particular segments of rural practitioners. These subthemes, generally subordinate to the basic thrust of the periods, have been utilized as heading for individual chapters.

The 19th century idyllic vision of the country began to dwindle in the first decade of the 20th century. Between 1908 and 1917, some prominent rural social work spokesmen spent a great deal of their time attempting to focus public awareness on the social problems of the country. The first two chapters of Part I of this anthology include a sampling of such efforts. Although calling attention to the problems of the country was probably the main thrust of the period 1908-1917, other country lifers continued to stress community building and education as the means to achieve rural social progress. Their thoughts and activities are reflected in the contents of Chapters 3 and 4.

Between 1917 and 1927, social work practitioners struggled to bring forth to the country the advancement and methods of social work which had proven successful in urban areas, particularly through the efforts of the American Red Cross, the YMCA's, and the Family Welfare Association—later Family Service Association of America. Basically, this appears to have been a period of expansion of a city-conceived and nurtured practice rather than one which confirmed the identity of a distinct rural approach. The monopoly of psychiatrically oriented casework was being experienced by the rural areas during this period and many community developers who had remained true to the Country Life themes regretted and criticized the nature of professional social work intervention. This was also a period of organization of the country into units, generally larger than single villages, for which social services could be best planned and in which they could be most efficiently delivered. Part II is devoted to World War I and postwar activities and developments. Chapter 4 includes articles illustrative of the activities of the Home Service. Chapter 5 is devoted to the group work movement as it affected the country during and after the war. Chapter 6 deals with the topic of country-level organization and Chapter 7 is devoted to methodological suggestions and critique of the rural practice of the period.

Part III of this volume covers 1928 to 1939, the Depression and the New Deal. During the Depression years, which in the rural areas preceded the crash of the stock market, and until the passage of the Federal Emergency Relief Administration Act, social workers and country spokesmen struggled with the lack of organized relief efforts in the rural counties. Many events of the 1920s prepared the nation to receive the progressive New Deal measures. The articles in Chapter 8 pivot around these important pre-Depression occurrences.

Chapter 9 is devoted to the discussion of the legislative proposals of the New Deal and their effect on rural areas. Between 1933 and the beginning of World War II, social workers, who were now engaged in relief activities in the remotest corners of the nation, focused their attention upon the identity of their practice. Was rural social work different from the urban variety? How should rural workers be trained? What were their special problems? Chapters 10 and 11 deal respectively with each of these questions by presenting selections written during that fruitful period of identity development of rural social work.

Some words of caution must be inserted at this point. First, the term rural social work has been used throughout this volume to mean social work practice in rural communities. This anthology is not intended to settle the controversy that began in the early days of rural social work and has continued to the present: whether the social work method remains, in essence, the same when applied to rural communities or whether the modifications are so extensive that the method becomes an essentially different discipline or practice.

Second, the chronologic periods utilized in the organization of the material in this book must not be viewed as neat compartments which clearly determine beginnings and endpoints at which discussions of certain topics occurred in the literature. The periods identified have been used as tools for better understanding of the thrust of social work practice in rural communities during those particular years. Discussions and debates, however, like ideologic trends or even fashions, tend to overlap and intellectual themes as well as particular modalities of practice tend to emerge and re-emerge throughout the years in unpredictable ways.

Third, it must be recognized that pioneer Social Welfare leaders were not exclusively identified with any one profession. Rural sociologists as well as rural social workers will discover that their ancestries are embodied in many common figures. Clear-cut and zealous professional identities did not appear in the social sciences until the prosperous decade of World War II. In remembering the early contributors to the rural social welfare field it was therefore imperative to transcend the parameters of any single modern field and to acknowledge the efforts of many disciplines and professions.

A Comment on Sources

Although many journals and books were searched for sources, the reader will notice that the *Survey* constituted a particularly fruitful resource. Since the *Survey* is no longer in existence, it deserves some explanatory statements. This journal was published in

New York between 1897 and 1952. Its original title was *Charities: A Weekly Review of Local and General Philanthropy*. In 1901 it absorbed *Charities Review*; in 1905, *Commons* (also known as *Chicago Commons*), whose full title had been *Commons: For Industrial Justice, Efficient Philanthropy, Educational Freedom and the People's Control of Public Utilities*—an astonishingly progressive title and journal which survived from 1896 to 1905. In March 1906 it absorbed *Jewish Charity*. Between 1905 and 1909, the periodical was known as *Charities and The Commons*. It finally took the title *Survey* in 1909.

Between October 1921 and May 1922, the *Survey* published one weekly illustrated issue which provided pages for the dissemination of the newly discovered art of social photography. This issue was called the "graphic number." Between 1933 and 1948, the journal was published as two separate periodicals, the *Survey Graphic* and the *Survey Midmonthly*. These two separate versions combined once again in 1949, continuing the volume numbering of *Survey Midmonthly*. Naturally, the periodical changed hands and editors many times. Its tone was often reflective of these changes, although it always translated the social mood and philanthropic viewpoint of each period. For example, the issues for the years 1913 and 1914 are reflective of a deep religious and moralizing perspective; the 1922 and 1923 issues are more social reformist in tone. What is important for the purpose of this volume is that throughout its different early owners and moods, the magazine provided a forum for the dissemination not only of urban but also of rural perspectives. For the sake of clarity, all references throughout the text have been made to the *Survey*.

Another record of pioneer social work efforts, including the rural view, was provided by the *Proceedings of the National Conference of Social Work*. The "National Conference of Social Work," now "National Conference of Social Welfare," existed from 1871. In 1871 and between 1880 and 1881, it was known as "Conference on Charities and Corrections." From 1875 until 1879 it was "Conference on Charities." Between 1882 and 1916 its title was "National Conference of Charities and Corrections," changing to "National Conference of Social Work" in 1917, and to "National Conference of Social Welfare" in 1956.

The "National Conference" published the *Conference Bulletin* and the *Proceedings*. The *Proceedings* were published under varying titles at different times, the most prevalent being *Proceedings, Selected Papers of the Annual Meeting*, and *Social Welfare Forum, Official Proceedings of the Annual Forum*. The *Proceedings* were published in cities across the nation, which varied generally from year to year; during the years of World War II, the *Proceedings* reflected the fact that the conference met regionally.

Several other journals provided material for this volume.

Rural America, which was the publication of the Country Life Association between March 1923 and May 1941. In 1923 and 1924 this periodical was also known as *Country Life Bulletin.*

Social Forces, whose complete title is *Social Forces: A Scientific Medium of Social Study and Interpretation.* This periodical began publication in 1922 as the *Journal of Social Forces* by the University of North Carolina Press and is still in existence.

Family, probably known to most social workers as *Social Casework,* began publication in New York in 1920, and was known throughout the years as *Family* (March 1920 to February 1940), *Family: Journal of Social Casework, Journal of Social Casework,* and finally *Social Casework.* Of all the journals used, it was *Family* which was the most methodological in nature and the only one solely or primarily intended for an exclusively social work audience.

Other periodicals published articles on social services in rural communities but with less regularity. Worth mentioning as sources of study are *Sociology and Social Research* (which began in 1934) and *Rural Sociology* (which began in 1936). Both are still in existence.

On the issue of selection of articles, the choice was often arbitrary and thus reflects the biases and interests of the editor. While selecting material for the first section was relatively simple due to the paucity of publications, the process grew increasingly complicated as the more fertile years, such as those of the Depression and the New Deal, were approached.

Efforts were made to include controversial or dissenting points of view. While such attempts were relatively successful for the late periods, when debates permeated the literature, they were difficult and often unsuccessful during the earlier years, when the periodical literature seemed to reflect what was accepted as the prevalent view of the day. In many ways, selections had already been made for the author by the editors of those early journals who published then, as they often do today, the most politically viable perspectives.

Many of the dreams and hopes about which the early rural social work pioneers wrote never materialized. It is the purpose of this anthology to credit their efforts as the profession presently struggles with similar concepts and problems.

I
Rural Welfare, 1908-1916

1

The Country Life Movement

The 19th-century idyllic vision of the country as a problem-free environment dwindled during the first decade of the 20th century. The social workers of this decade were men and women of elevated social consciousness who came from all walks of life. The members of the Country Life Commission established by President Theodore Roosevelt were among those instrumental in developing public awareness of the needs of the rural communities. No real understanding of this period can be reached without some knowledge of the Country Life movement. "Country-lifers" are also considered the forebearers of rural sociology, and in that sense, rural social workers and rural sociologists claim a common ancestry.

Four excerpts have been included in this chapter. The first, by Merwin Swanson, succinctly summarizes the role of the Commission in the history of American rural social welfare and requires little preface. It traces the life of the movement from its inception in 1908 to its demise in the 1940s.

The second excerpt is the Special Message to Congress sent by President Theodore Roosevelt on February 9, 1909, on the occasion of the transmittal of the report of the Country Life Commission. Roosevelt's commitment to the ideas of the Country Life movement was obvious. "The welfare of the farmer is of vital consequence to the welfare of the whole community," he said to the nation, and he recommended that the Department of Agriculture should become the Department of Country Life, "fitted to deal not only with crops but also with all the larger aspects of life in the open country." And although the change never took place, the Department of Agriculture did become involved in country matters beyond the raising of crops.

The third document included is the summary of the actual report of the Commission on Country Life. This report was still being read widely in 1929, as evidenced by the fact that *Rural America* reprinted it in that year—the Senate document and the private publishers' editions being by then out of print. The Commission's report emphasized the need for developing a highly organized rural society, able to rise to the challenge of the cities, a society where the farmer would be kept in his land through the enhancement of all rural resources.

The paper by Liberty Hyde Bailey, a prominent leader of the Country Life movement, was presented to the 1908 National Conference of Charities and Corrections (later the National Conference on Social Work). This paper not only highlights the nature of the human problems of the country but also suggests, as did the Commission's Report, "remedies" or courses of action. A novel call for the reevaluation and redirection of country institutions within their existing indigenous framework is issued by Bailey. Such a timeless call would not be inappropriate if sounded today.

In January 1913 the *Survey* published an article by George Frederick Wells, chairman of the Country Church Commission of the Methodist Federation of Social Service. This article was entitled "Is an Organized Country Life Movement Possible?" Although the article has not been included in this anthology, it merits special attention. Besides discussing the need for organization of Country Life efforts, Wells first expressed a theme that was to become prevalent in the twenties, that is, the use of "scientific" surveys in the assessment of country problems.

Science began to exert a fascinating influence on all areas of activity at the beginning of the 20th century. Surveys, measurements, and predictions were seen as means for the solution of all kinds of problems. This was the period of Edward L. Thorndike's influence in education, Frederick W. Taylor's efficiency movement in industry, and scientific agriculture. Other aspects of rural life were not to be exempted from this national mood.

The field of social welfare is now once again undergoing a period of fascination with scientific measurement, exactitude, and prediction, even in the rural field. Let us humbly recognize that the theme is not altogether new.

THE COUNTRY LIFE MOVEMENT: AN INTRODUCTION

Merwin Swanson

Between 1900 and 1940 a group of men and women in the United States supported a country life movement. The movement was a broad effort to improve the quality of rural life in an increasingly urban world. Few of those individuals have names that are now familiar, even to historians. They were presidents of A & M colleges, directors of rural projects for national religious groups, personnel with character building organizations such as the YMCA, rural sociologists, and rural educators; their professional contemporaries honored them but they are now forgotten.

In the first decade of the twentieth century these people began to argue that something was seriously amiss with rural life, something more subtle than economic injustice. They believed that the superior standard of living that urban Americans enjoyed was luring away the most talented of the rural young people, thus debilitating rural communities. Further, the growing numerical and cultural dominance of urban America drew national attention away from this rural degeneration. Without remedial measures the rural world that many Americans idealized as a major source of their nation's strength would disappear. The "Report" of Theodore Roosevelt's Country Life Commission in 1909 broadcast this concern and kindled much discussion about how rural schools, churches, community clubs, social work programs, youth groups, and eventually even missionaries could make rural community life as attractive as life in the city. The people who responded to the Commission's "Report" shared a loyalty to the superior virtues of rural living with nearly all American agrarian movements, but the application of science to the improvement of agricultural production and the techniques of farm management also had impressed them. The participants in the country life movement hoped that a parallel scientific approach could provide techniques for community organization that would make rural living as attractive as urban. The individuals in the country life movement combined a loyalty to science with an attraction to the myth of the superiority of rural life.

This conscious loyalty to the idea of creating a better life in rural communities and an informal network of personal contacts

The American Country Life Movement, 1900-1940. Unpublished doctoral dissertation in history, University of Minnesota, 1972 (revised). Merwin Swanson is Associate Professor of History at Idaho State University in Pocatello. He has written about rural reform in the 20th century, concentrating on measures of the New Deal years.

formed the basis of the country life movement between 1910 and the
end of World War I. In that decade the movement enjoyed more public
attention than during any other period in its history. The founding
of the American Country Life Association in 1919 culminated attempts
to give the movement formal structure. A few facets of the country
life movement such as education did flourish, but the burst of enthusiasm for the country life movement that the founders anticipated
did not occur. The movement did not wither but neither did it mature;
the movement stagnated because it did not claim the primary loyalty
of any of the professional specialties that composed it. When enthusiasm waned, however, those same leaders became YMCA secretaries
with rural Y programs or Presbyterian ministers serving just their
congregations instead of integrating themselves into a broader program of community development. The country life movement encouraged
the growth of rural sociology, but that discipline's initial interest in the definition and identification of rural communities as the
first step in community reform slowly gave way to an emphasis among
rural sociologists on studies of society in a rural environment; the
founding of the Rural Sociological Society in 1937 symbolically
climaxed this process. The country life movement slowly fractured
and a variety of specific rural interests replaced it.

The inability of the participants in the country life movement to
cite persuasive examples of their program in action also contributed
to the movement's decline. In the years immediately following the
Country Life Commission, they could attribute this lack of success
to insufficient time, but by the early twenties the dearth of rural
communities that had successfully organized themselves along the
lines of the country life movement gave a hollow sound to the exhor-
tations and claims of the movement's leaders. Finally, the economic
trauma of the Depression undercut a major premise of the country
life movement because the movement had always minimized the importance of economic solutions to rural problems. A few of the people
connected with the movement did take posts in the Farm Security
Administration during the New Deal, but the projects to build communities that involved those in the country life movement emphasized
the very poor in the South instead of focusing upon the middle class
farm areas of the Northeast, the Midwest, and the Great Plains that
had originally interested the country life movement. By World War
II the country life movement that its early leaders had envisioned
in the early twentieth century was dead.

The leaders of the country life movement believed that the United
States had to improve drastically the rural social opportunities and
rural standards of living to keep the most talented rural citizens
from migrating to the cities. Rural improvement, in turn, depended

upon the vitality of rural community life. Establishing or improving rural churches, schools, youth and adult clubs, community centers, roads, and telephones were important details in the program, but the more amorphous process of building strong rural communities was the core of the country life movement. Proponents assumed that rural communities existed naturally, but that these required cultivation because of the persistence of an individual tradition in rural America. Ideally, the men and women in the country life movement hoped that a rural community would spontaneously organize some kind of a representative council to guide its improvement program; in practice, however, the country lifers believed that an outside stimulus and supervisor in the form of an extension agent, a progressive minister or teacher, or some other local leader was prerequisite to the success of the program for community development. The movement did not prevail and rural America did not attempt the kind of community development that the country life movement had envisioned.

REPORT OF THE COUNTRY LIFE COMMISSION SPECIAL MESSAGE
FROM THEODORE ROOSEVELT

I transmit herewith the report of the Commission on Country Life. At the outset I desire to point out that not a dollar of the public money has been paid to any commissioner for his work on the Commission.

The report shows the general condition of farming life in the open country, and points out its larger problems; it indicates ways in which the government, national and state, may show the people how to solve some of these problems; and it suggests a continuance of the work which the Commission began.

Judging by thirty public hearings, to which farmers and farmers' wives from forty states and territories came, and from 120,000 answers to printed questions sent out by the Department of Agriculture,

Senate Document No. 705, 60th Congress, 1909. This document was reprinted at readers' request in *Rural America*, January 1929.

the Commission finds that the general level of country life is high
compared with any preceding time or with any other land. If it has
in recent years slipped down in some places, it has risen in more
places. Its progress has been general, if not uniform.

Yet farming does not yield either the profit or the satisfaction
that it ought to yield and may be made to yield. There is discontent
in the country and in places discouragement. Farmers as a class do
not magnify their calling, and the movement to the towns, though, I
am happy to say, less than formerly, is still strong.

Under our system, it is helpful to promote discussion of ways in
which the people can help themselves. There are three main directions in which the farmers can help themselves; namely, better farming, better business, and better living on the farm. The National
Department of Agriculture, which has rendered services equalled by
no other similar department in any other time and place, the state
departments of agriculture; the state colleges of agriculture and
the mechanic arts, especially through their extension work; the
state agricultural experiment stations; the Farmers' Union; the
Grange; the agricultural press, and other similar agencies; have all
combined to place within the reach of the American farmer an amount
and quality of agricultural information which, if applied, would
enable him, over large areas, to double the production of the farm.

The object of the Commission on Country Life therefore is not to
help the farmer raise better crops, but to call his attention to the
opportunities for better business and better living on the farm. If
country life is to become what it should be, and what I believe it
ultimately will be—one of the most dignified, desirable, and sought-
after ways of earning a living—the farmer must take advantage not
only of the agricultural knowledge which is at his disposal, but of
the methods which have raised and continues to raise the standards
of living and of intelligence in other callings.

Those engaged in all other industrial and commercial callings have
found it necessary, under modern economic conditions, to organize
themselves for mutual advantage and for the protection of their own
particular interests in relation to other interests. The farmers of
every progressive European country have realized this essential fact
and have found in the cooperative system exactly the form of business
combination they need.

Now, whatever the state may do toward improving the practice of
agriculture, it is not within the sphere of any government to reorganize the farmers' business or reconstruct the social life of
farming communities. It is, however, quite within its power to use
its influence and the machinery of publicity which it can control
for calling public attention to the needs and the facts. For example,

it is the obvious duty of the government to call the attention of farmers to the growing monopolization of water power. The farmers above all should have that power, on reasonable terms, for cheap transportation, for lighting their homes, and for innumerable uses in daily tasks on the farm.

It would be idle to assert that life on the farm occupies as good a position in dignity, desirability, and business results as the farmers might easily give it if they chose. One of the chief difficulties is the failure of country life, as it exists at present, to satisfy the higher social and intellectual aspirations of country people. Whether the constant draining away of so much of the best elements in the rural population into the towns is due chiefly to this cause or to the superior business opportunities of city life may be open to question. But no one at all familiar with farm life throughout the United States can fail to recognize the necessity for building up the life of the farm upon its social as well as upon its productive side.

It is true that country life has improved greatly in attractiveness, health, and comfort, and that the farmer's earnings are higher than they were. But city life is advancing even more rapidly, because of the greater attention which is being given by the citizens of the towns to their own betterment. For just this reason the introduction of effective agricultural cooperation throughout the United States is of the first importance. Where farmers are organized cooperatively they not only avail themselves much more readily of business opportunities and improved methods, but it is found that the organizations which bring them together in the work of their lives are used also for social and intellectual advancement.

The cooperative plan is the best plan of organization wherever men have the right spirit to carry it out. Under this plan any business undertaking is managed by a committee; every man has one vote and only one vote; and everyone gets profits according to what he sells or buys or supplies. It develops individual responsibility and has a moral as well as a financial value over any other plan.

I desire only to take counsel with the farmers as fellow-citizens. It is not the problem of the farmers alone that I am discussing with them, but a problem which affects every city as well as every farm in the country. It is a problem which the working farmers will have to solve for themselves; but it is a problem which also affects in only less degree all the rest of us, and therefore if we can render only help toward its solution, it is not only our duty but our interest to do so.

The foregoing will, I hope, make it clear why I appointed a commission to consider problems of farm life which have hitherto had far too little attention, and the neglect of which has not only held back life in the country, but also lowered the efficiency of the whole nation. The welfare of the farmer is of vital consequence to the welfare of the whole community. The strengthening of country life, therefore, is the strengthening of the whole nation.

The Commission has tried to help the farmers to see clearly their own problem and to see it as a whole; to distinguish clearly between what the Government can do and what the farmers must do for themselves; and it wishes to bring not only the farmers but the nation as a whole to realize that the growing of crops, though an essential part, is only a part of country life. Crop growing is the essential foundation; but it is no less essential that the farmer shall get an adequate return for what he grows; and it is no less essential—indeed it is literally vital—that he and his wife and children shall lead the right kind of life.

For this reason, it is of the first importance that the United States Department of Agriculture, through which as prime agent the ideas of the Commission stands for must reach the people, should become without delay in fact a Department of Country Life, fitted to deal not only with crops, but also with all the larger aspects of life in the open country.

From all that has been done and learned three great general and immediate needs of country life stand out:

First, effective cooperation among farmers, to put them on a level with the organized interests with which they do business.

Second, a new kind of schools in the country, which shall teach the children as much outdoors as indoors and perhaps more, so that they will prepare for country life, and not as at present, mainly for life in town.

Third, better means of communication, including good roads and a parcels post, which the country people are everywhere, and rightly, unanimous in demanding.

To these may be added better sanitation; for easy preventable diseases hold several million country people in the slavery of continuous ill health.

The Commission points out, and I concur in the conclusion, that the most important help that the government, whether national or state, can give is to show the people how to go about these tasks of organization, education, and communication with the best and quickest results. This can be done by the collection and spread of information. One community can thus be informed of what other communities have done, and one country of what other countries have done. Such help by the people's government would lead to a comprehensive plan of organization, education and communication, and make the farming country better to live in, for intellectual and social reasons as well as for purely agricultural reasons.

The government through the Department of Agriculture does not cultivate any man's farm for him. But it does put at his service useful knowledge that he would not otherwise get. In the same way the national and state governments might put into the people's hand the new and right knowledge of school work. The task of maintaining and developing the schools would remain, as now, with the people themselves.

The only recommendation I submit is that an appropriation of $25,000 be provided, to enable the Commission to digest the material it has collected, and to collect and to digest much more that is within its reach, and thus complete its work. This would enable the Commission to gather in the harvest of suggestion which is resulting from the discussion it has stirred up. The Commissioners have served without compensation, and I do not recommend any appropriation for their services, but only for the expenses that will be required to finish the task that they have begun.

To improve our system of agriculture seems to me the most urgent of the tasks which lie before us. But it can not, in my judgment, be effected by measures which touch only the material and technical side of the subject; the whole business and life of the farmer must also be taken into account. Such considerations led me to appoint the Commission on Country Life. Our object should be to help develop in the country community the great ideals of community life as well as of personal character. One of the most important adjuncts to this end must be the country church, and I invite your attention to what the Commission says of the country church and of the need of an extension of such work as that of the Young Men's Christian Association in country communities. Let me lay special emphasis upon what the Commission says at the very end of its report on personal ideals and local leadership. Everything resolves itself in the end into the question of personality. Neither society nor government can do much for country life unless there is voluntary response in the personal ideals of the men and women who live in the country. In the development of character, the home should be more important than the school, or than society at large. When once the basic material needs have been met, high ideals may be quite independent of income; but they can not be realized without sufficient income to provide adequate foundation; and where the community at large is not financially prosperous it is impossible to develop a high average personal and community ideal. In short, the fundamental facts of human nature apply to men and women who live in the country just as they apply to men and women who live in the towns. Given a sufficient foundation of material well being, the influence of the farmers and farmers' wives on their children becomes the factor of first importance in determining the attitude of the next generation toward farm life. The farmer should realize that the person who most needs consideration on the farm is his wife. I do not in the least mean that she should purchase ease at the expense of duty. Neither man or woman is really happy or really useful save on conditions of doing his or her duty. If the woman shirks her duty as housewife, as home keeper, as the mother whose prime function it is to bear and rear a sufficient number of healthy children, then she is not entitled to our regard. But if she does her duty she is more entitled to our regard even than the man who does his duty; and the man should show special consideration for her needs.

I warn my countrymen that the great recent progress made in city life is not a full measure of our civilization; for our civilization rests at bottom on the wholesomeness, the attractiveness, and the completeness, as well as the prosperity, of life in the country. The men and women on the farms stand for what is fundamentally best and most needed in our American life. Upon the development of country life rests ultimately our ability, by methods of farming requiring the highest intelligence, to continue to feed and clothe the hungry nations; to supply the city with fresh blood, clean bodies, and clear brains that can endure the terrific strain of modern life; we need the development of men in the open country, who will be in the future as in the past, the stay and strength of the nation in time of war, and its guiding and controlling spirit in time of peace.

THEODORE ROOSEVELT.

The White House, February 9, 1909.

REPORT OF COMMISSION ON COUNTRY LIFE

Introductory Review or Summary

The Commission finds that agriculture in the United States, taken altogether, is prosperous commercially, when measured by the conditions that have obtained in previous years, although there are some regions in which this is only partially true. The country people are producing vast quantities of supplies for food, shelter, clothing, and for use in the arts. The country homes are improving in comfort, attractiveness and healthfulness. Not only in the material wealth that they produce, but in the supply of independent and strong citizenship, the agricultural people constitute the very foundation of our national efficiency. As agriculture is the immediate basis of country life, so it follows that the general affairs of the open country, speaking broadly, are in a condition of improvement.

Many institutions, organizations, and movements are actively contributing to the increasing welfare of the open country. The most important of these are the United States Department of Agriculture, the colleges of agriculture and the experiment stations in the states, and the national farmers' organizations. These institutions and organizations are now properly assuming leadership in country-life affairs, and consequently in many of the public questions of national bearing. With these agencies must be mentioned state departments of agriculture, agricultural societies, and organizations of very many kinds, teachers in schools, workers in church and other religious associations, traveling libraries, and many other groups, all working with commendable zeal to further the welfare of the people of the open country.

The Most Prominent Deficiencies
Yet it is true, notwithstanding all this progress as measured by historical standards, that agriculture is not commercially as profitable as it is entitled to be for the labor and energy that the farmer expends and the risks that he assumes, and that the social conditions in the open country are far short of their possibilities. We must measure our agricultural efficiency by its possibilities rather than by comparison with previous conditions. The farmer is almost necessarily handicapped in the development of his business, because his capital is small and the volume of his transactions limited; and

Senate Document No. 705, 60th Congress, 1909. Also reprinted at readers' request in *Rural America*, January 1929.

he usually stands practically alone against organized interests. In
the general readjustment of modern life due to the great changes in
manufacturers and commerce inequalities and discriminations have
arisen, and naturally the separate man suffers most. The unattached
man has problems that government should understand.

The reasons for the lack of a highly organized rural society are
very many, as the full report explains. The leading specific causes
are:

A lack of knowledge on the part of farmers of the exact agricultural conditions and possibilities of their regions;

Lack of good training for country life in the schools;

The disadvantage or handicap of the farmer as against the established business systems and interests, preventing him from securing
adequate returns for his products, depriving him of the benefits
that would result from unmonopolized rivers and the conservation of
forests, and depriving the community, in many cases, of the good
that would come from the use of great tracts of agricultural land
that are now held for speculative purposes;

Lack of good highway facilities;

The widespread continuing depletion of soils, with the injurious
effect on rural life;

A general need of new and active leadership.

Other causes contributing to the general result are: Lack of any
adequate system of agricultural credit, whereby the farmer may readily secure loans on fair terms; the shortage of labor, a condition
that is often complicated by intemperance among workmen; lack of
institutions and incentives that tie the laboring man to the soil;
the burden and the narrow life of farm women; lack of adequate
supervision of public health.

The Nature of the Remedies

Some of the remedies lie with the national government, some of them
with the states and communities in their corporate capacities, some
with voluntary organizations, and some with individuals acting alone.
From the great number of suggestions that have been made, covering
every phase of country life, the commission now enumerates those
that seem to be most fundamental or most needed at the present time.

Congress can remove some of the handicaps of the farmer, and it
can also set some kinds of work in motion, such as:

The encouragement of a system of thoroughgoing surveys of all
agricultural regions in order to take stock and to collect local
fact, with the idea of providing a basis on which to develop a
scientifically and economically sound country life;

The encouragement of a system of extension work of rural communities through all the land-grant colleges with the people at their homes and on their farms;

A thoroughgoing investigation by experts of the middleman system of handling farm products, coupled with a general inquiry into the farmer's disadvantages in respect to taxation, transportation rates, cooperative organizations and credit, and the general business system;

An inquiry into the control and use of the streams of the United States with the object of protecting the people in their ownership and of saving to agricultural uses such benefits as should be reserved for these purposes;

The establishing of a highway engineering service, or equivalent organization, to be at the call of the states in working out effective and economical highway systems;

The establishing of a system of parcels posts and postal savings banks;

And providing some means or agency for the guidance of public opinion toward the development of a real rural society that shall rest directly on the land.

Other remedies recommended for consideration by Congress are:

The enlargement of the United States Bureau of Education, to enable it to stimulate and coordinate the educational work to the nation;

Careful attention to the farmers' interests in legislation on the tariff, on regulation of railroads, control or regulation of corporations and of speculation, legislation in respect to rivers, forests, and the utilization of swamp lands;

Increasing the powers of the federal government in respect to the supervision and control of the public health;

Providing such regulations as will enable the states that do not permit the sale of liquors to protect themselves from traffic from adjoining states.

In setting all these forces in motion, the cooperation of the states will be necessary; and in many cases definite state laws may greatly aid the work.

Remedies of a more general nature are: A broad campaign of publicity, that must be undertaken until all the people are informed on the whole subject of rural life, and until there is an awakened appreciation of the necessity of giving this phase of our national development as much attention as has been given to other phases or interests; a quickened sense of responsibility in all country people, to the community and to the state, in the conserving of soil fertility, and in the necessity for diversifying farming in order to con-

serve this fertility and to develop a better rural society, and also
in the better safeguarding of the strength and happiness of the farm
women; a more widespread conviction of the necessity for organization, not only for economic but for social purposes, this organization to be more or less cooperative, so that all the people may share
equally in the benefit and have voice in the essential affairs of
the community; a realization on the part of the farmer that he has a
distinct natural responsibility toward the laborer in providing him
with good living facilities and in helping him in every way to be a
man among men; and a realization on the part of all the people of
the obligation to protect and develop the natural scenery and attractiveness of the open country.

Certain remedies lie with voluntary organizations and institutions.
All organized forces, both in town and country, should understand
that there are country phases as well as city phases of our civilization, and that one phase needs help as much as the other. All these
agencies should recognize their responsibility to society. Many
existing organizations and institutions might become practically co-
operative or mutual in spirit, as, for example, all agricultural
societies, libraries, Young Men's Christian Associations and churches.
All the organizations standing for rural progress should be federated, in states and nation.

The Underlying Problem of Country Life

The mere enumeration of the foregoing deficiencies and remedies indicates that the problem of country life is one of reconstruction,
and that temporary measures and defense work alone will not solve it.
The underlying problem is to develop and maintain on our farms a
civilization in full harmony with the best American ideals. To build
up and retain this civilization means, first of all, that the business of agriculture must be made to yield a reasonable return to
those who follow it intelligently; and life on the farm must be made
permanently satisfying to intelligent, progressive people. The work
before us, therefore, is nothing more or less than the gradual rebuilding of a new agriculture and new rural life. We regard it as
absolutely essential that this great general work should be understood by all the people. Separate difficulties, important as they
are, must be studied and worked out in the light of the greater
fundamental problem.

The commission has pointed out a number of remedies that are extremely important; but running through all of these remedies are
several great forces, or principles, which must be utilized in the
endeavor to solve the problems of country life. All the people
should recognize what those fundamental forces and agencies are.

Knowledge.—To improve any situation, the underlying facts must be understood. The farmer must have exact knowledge of his business and of the particular condition under which he works. The United States Department of Agriculture and the experiment stations and colleges are rapidly acquiring and distributing this knowledge; but the farmer may not be able to apply it to the best of advantage because of lack of knowledge of his own soils, climate, animal and plant diseases, markets, and other local facts. The farmer is entitled to know what are the advantages and disadvantages of his conditions and environment. A thoroughgoing system of surveys in detail of the exact conditions underlying farming in every locality is now an indispensable need to complete and apply the work of the great agricultural institutions. As an occupation, agriculture is a means of developing our internal resources; we cannot develop these resources until we know exactly what they are.

Education.—There must be not only a fuller scheme of public education, but a new kind of education adapted to the real needs of the farming people. The country schools are to be so redirected that they shall educate their pupils in terms of the daily life. Opportunities for training toward agricultural callings are to be multiplied and made broadly effective. Every person on the land, old or young, in school or out of school, educated or illiterate, must have a chance to receive the information necessary for a successful business, and for a healthful, comfortable, resourceful life, both in home and neighborhood. This means redoubled efforts for better country schools, and a vastly increased interest in the welfare of country boys and girls on the part of those who pay the school taxes. Education by means of agriculture is to be a part of our regular public school work. Agricultural schools are to be organized. There is to be a well-developed plan of extension teaching conducted by the agricultural colleges, by means of the printed page, face-to-face talks, and demonstration or object lessons, designed to reach every farmer and his family, at or near their homes, with knowledge and stimulus in every department of country life.

Organization.—There must be a vast enlargement of voluntary organized effort among farmers themselves. It is indispensable that farmers shall work together for their common interests and for the national welfare. If they do not do this, no governmental activity, no legislation, not even better schools, will greatly avail. Much has been done. There is a multitude of clubs and associations for social, educational, and business purposes; and great national organizations are effective. But the farmers are nevertheless relatively unorganized. We have only begun to develop business cooper-

ation in America. Farmers do not influence legislation as they
should. They need a more fully organized social and recreative life.
 Spiritual Forces.—The forces and institutions that make for morality and spiritual ideals among rural people must be energized. We
miss the heart of the problem if we neglect to foster personal character and neighborhood righteousness. The best way to preserve
ideals for private conduct and public life is to build up the institutions of religion. The church has great power of leadership. The
whole people should understand that it is vitally important to stand
behind the rural church and to help it to become a great power in
developing concrete country life ideals. It is especially important
that the country church recognize that it has a social responsibility
to the entire community as well as a religious responsibility to its
own group of people.

Recommendations of the Commission
The Commission recommends all the correctives that have been mentioned under the head of "The nature of the remedies." It does not
wish to discriminate between important measures of relief for existing conditions. It has purposely avoided indorsing any particular
bill now before Congress, no matter what its value or object.

There are, however, in the opinion of the Commission two or three
great movements of the utmost consequence that should be set under
way at the earliest possible time, because they are fundamental to
the whole problem of ultimate permanent reconstruction; these call
for special explanation.

1. Taking Stock of Country Life.—There should be organized, as
explained in the main report, under government leadership, a comprehensive plan for an exhaustive study or survey of all the conditions
that surround the business of farming and the people who live in the
country, in order to take stock of our resources and to supply the
farmer with local knowledge. Federal and state governments, agricultural colleges and other educational agencies, organizations of
various types, and individual students of the problem should be
brought into cooperation for this great work of investigating with
minute care all agricultural and country life conditions.

2. Nationalized Extension Work.—Each state college of agriculture should be empowered to organize as soon as practicable a complete department of college extension, so managed as to reach every
person on the land in its state, with both information and inspiration. The work should include such forms of extension teaching as
lectures, bulletins, reading courses, correspondence courses, demonstration, and other means of reaching the people at home and on
their farms. It should be designed to forward not only the business

18

of agriculture, but sanitation, education, home making, and all interests of country life.

3. A Campaign for Rural Progress.—We urge the holding of local, state, and even national conferences on rural progress, designed to unite the interests of education, organization, and religion into one forward movement for the rebuilding of country life. Rural teachers, librarians, clergymen, editors, physicians, and others may well unite with farmers in studying and discussing the rural question in all its aspects. We must in some way unite all institutions, all organizations, all individuals having any interest in country life into one great campaign for rural progress.

The Call for Leadership

We must picture to ourselves a new rural social structure, developed from the strong resident forces of the open country; and then we must set at work all the agencies that will tend to bring this about. The entire people need to be roused to this avenue of usefulness. Most of the new leaders must be farmers who can find not only a satisfying business career on the farm, but who will throw themselves into the service of upbuilding the community. A new race of teachers is also to appear in the country. A new rural clergy is to be trained. These leaders will see the great underlying problem of country life, and together they will work, each in his own field, for the one goal of a new and permanent rural civilization. Upon the development of this distinctively rural civilization rests ultimately our ability, by methods of farming requiring the highest intelligence, to continue to feed and clothe the hungry nations; to supply the city and metropolis with fresh blood, clean bodies, and clear brains that can endure the strain of modern urban life; and to preserve a race of men in the open country that, in the future as in the past, will be the stay and strength of the nation in time of war and its guiding and controlling spirit in time of peace.

It is to be hoped that many young men and women, fresh from our schools and institutions of learning, and quick with ambition and trained intelligence, will feel a new and strong call to service.

> L. H. Bailey
> Henry Wallace
> Kenyon L. Butterfield
> Walter H. Page
> Gifford Pinchot
> C. S. Barrett
> W. A. Beard

Note:

Liberty Hyde Bailey was chairman of the Commission and Director (Dean) of the New York State College of Agriculture at Cornell University; Henry Wallace, born in Pennsylvania, was founder and editor of *Wallace's Farmer*, an Iowa paper, and the forefather of a three-generation dynasty of agricultural journalists; Kenyon L. Butterfield was President of the Massachusetts State College; Walter H. Page was editor of the progressive journal *World's Work*; Gifford Pinchot, later two-term governor of Pennsylvania, was then a notable conservationist, chief of the U.S. Forest Service and founder of Yale University's School of Forestry; Charles S. Barrett was President of the National Farmers Union, and William A. Beard was editor of *Great Western Magazine*. Sir Horace Plunkett, a renowned Irish agriculturist, leader of the Irish cooperation movement, and a good friend of Roosevelt, was recognized as an inspirer and made a member of the Commission. [E.M-B.]

RURAL DEVELOPMENT IN RELATION TO SOCIAL WELFARE

L. H. Bailey

We need to give as much attention to the social and economic welfare of the rural country as to similar questions of urban regions. Our studies of social questions have been confined very largely to congested populations, but these questions are just as important in communities of scattered homes as in cities and towns. Even the question of congestion of population is not a city problem alone. Part of the city population comes from the country and this movement may distress the country from under-populating it at the same time that it distresses the city from over-populating it. But even if city congestion were to come wholly from the city itself, it nevertheless would still affect the country, not only because some of the surplus might find its way into the country, but because all populations are inter-relating and inter-acting. While it is customary to divide human beings into city people and country people, all great human problems are fundamentally the same, differing chiefly in their phases and symptoms. There is a city phase and a country phase of every great question. The city phase has been studied with much care and, therefore, we have come to think that social problems

Proceedings, National Conference of Charities and Corrections, 1908.
Liberty Hyde Bailey was chairman of the Commission on Country Life and Director of New York State College of Agriculture at Cornell University.

are city problems. But whatever vitally affects the city likewise in some degree affects the open country. One of the great needs of the time in social studies is that we discover the rural country. There is a city phase or application and rural application to all questions of education, truancy, public health, pauperism, immigration, charities, correction, civic relations, labor, density of population, moral standards. We have made the serious mistake in treating some of these questions as separate problems for the city and the rural districts, largely, however, by disregarding the one. We are at this moment making the great mistake of considering agricultural education as a thing apart, whereas it is only a phase of education in general and cannot be isolated without leading us into serious error. The so-called rural question is not a new or a separate question, but only an overlooked or neglected question.

Economic and social questions are by no means problems of centralized communities. Every person, however isolated, is a fact; and he is a member of society even if he associates with no one but himself, even as every stone in a field is a fact although it may never be placed in a building. We are just beginning to realize that there is such a thing as rural economics. Until very recently, the writings in this field have been for the most part, in this country, a treatment of the subject from the old theoretical point of view, illustrated here and there with agricultural examples.

If these statements are sound, it follows that the country should not be exploited in the interest of the city. The country must be developed for itself and out of itself. There must be a country social order, as there is a city social order. One might think, from many current discussions, that the country exists for the convenience and benefit of the city, providing occupation for those who have failed to attach themselves in cities and an asylum for the undesirables. To some persons, the country question seems to be only a congeries of isolated problems of needy families and of vicious communities; but these are not country questions more than city questions. In either case, they are but symptoms. Want must be relieved and vice must be controlled. No small amount of the vice of the country districts is that which is forced out from the cities. Questionable road-houses and other resorts are mostly the result of the reprehensible policy of compelling this class of persons to "move on" rather than to meet the issue squarely within the city limits and solving it there. The open country has problems enough of its own without being obliged to receive the dump from the cities.

What I have in mind is far more than the mere relief of symptoms here and there. I want to see the development of a virile and effective rural society; and I know that such a society can come only as the result of forces arising directly out of the country, as a natural expression of the country itself, not as a reflection or transplanting of city institutions. My city friends, for example, are proposing ways whereby country people may have entertainment, but they make the fundamental error of fashioning their schemes on city ways. The real countryman does not think of theaters and recitals and receptions and functions in the way that the city man does, and it is not at all necessary that he should. On the contrary, it is very important that he should not. The countryman needs more social life; but his entertainment and contentment must come largely out of his occupation and his contact with nature, not from mere extraneous attractions. Herein lies the root of my concern in nature-study and nature-sympathy; the countryman must be able to interest himself spiritually in his native environment as his chief resource of power and happiness.

Rural Needs

Before we can intelligently discuss the remedies for the social ills of the open country, we must inventory the needs. These needs seem to fall chiefly into five great groups, which I will briefly state.

1. The need of greater technical knowledge of agriculture. This knowledge of discovery and teaching is being rapidly supplied by the experiment stations and colleges of agriculture. The knowledge that we already have is far in excess of the practice of it; this is necessarily true in any branch of human activity, but this does not argue against the necessity of still more knowledge. As much as we have learned, all the great fundamental problems of rational agriculture are yet unsolved and many of them are not even explored. Great as our lack is in these directions, it is still greater in the social and co-operative lines; the great country problems are now human rather than technically agricultural.

2. Lack of governmental protection, whereby the disabilities that are not a part of his business may be removed from the farmer. Governmental protection and control are least applicable and least effective in the farming country, and the farmer has more burdens to carry than those pertaining to the rearing of crops and animals and to the contest with climate and weather; some of these handicaps will be removed or their effects minimized in the future.

Corollary to this is the lack of any kind of organized supervision over country living. For example, there is no continuing oversight of public health in the farming country, except a more or less effective effort when communicable diseases break out.

The lack of attention to health regulations is little less than appalling in its consequences. The physicians in the farming country are general practitioners, commonly out of close touch with specialists and experts. Public health information is likely to be meagre. It is pitiable that so many of the good country population are lost from neglect, and antiquated treatment of disease. I have no means of knowing whether the country suffers more than the city in this particular regard; but well enforced sanitary regulations are powerful educators, and the country does not have the benefit of them to the same extent that the city has.

3. Lack of the co-operative spirit in business. The development of our rural country has proceeded on the basis of isolated occupancy of land, with the marked individualism that goes with it. Definite co-operation was not at first necessary; and what has once become an established order soon becomes tradition. It is not strange that farmers do not co-operate, but it is none the less important that they should do so. Any business co-operation brings about far-reaching social changes. This kind of co-operation will be forced in the near future, with the great changes that are arising in commercial affairs, but it needs to be started and fostered by some definite agency.

4. Absence of centers of interest in the localities, due to the rapid growth of towns and the direction of attention townward.

5. Lack of real personal initiative and enthusiasm; of gumption; of enterprise that gets things done. This is due to lack of contact with fellows, to the arrested development that results from individualism, and to the sterilization of rural institutions consequent on the removal of centers of interest to the towns. In the last analysis it is conditioned on the low earning power of the average farm.

Remedies

Only the most general suggestions can be given as to the remedies for the social shortcomings of the open country, but I think that it is fairly possible to indicate some useful points of view.

Of course, the fundamental corrective of it all is education, but we should indicate what the nature of this education should be. We much need to know how to use our increasing technical knowledge and to systematize it into practical ideals of personal living.

It is fundamentally important that we start with the proposition that farming people be kept on the land. The centers of interest should be established or re-established in the open country itself, not further concentrated in the town or city. It is easy to see how interest converges in the city or town. Markets are there; roads lead there; trolleys and telephones lead there; the best churches, schools and entertainments are there. Farming is a local business; it rests on a particular piece of land; if the farmer is to be

effective he must be content in his locality. The development of
living local interest is the real root of the rural social question.
I will mention four groups of efforts that should operate toward
this end.

(1) By developing local fact. A thorough-going survey of the
exact agricultural status of every state should now be made, and it
should be made by the state itself. Such an inquiry made carefully
and without haste by men who are thoroughly well prepared, and continuing over a series of years, would give us the data for all
future work with local problems. We must have the geographical
facts. We are now lacking them. We talk largely at random. We must
discover the factors that determine the production of crops and
animals in the localities, and the conditions that underlie and control the farm life. One part of this inquiry should consider the
soil conditions. A study of these conditions involves a knowledge
of the kinds, classification and distribution of the soils of the
state and the relation of place and altitude to production of crops
and live-stock; determination of the best drainage practices on
various soil types; a study of the cultural experience and manurial
needs as adapted to the types; and other questions in furtherance
of surveys and investigations now generally under way. Such a survey of the state should be broad and general enough to consider the
status of all the agricultural industries in the state, and it
should also take cognizance of educational and social conditions.

(2) By developing the rural institutions. The great constructive
movements of the time have passed these institutions by.

While there is no real decline or decadence in the occupation of
agriculture, it is nevertheless true that the country institutions
and affairs need radical redirection. The work may be done very
largely through existing agencies or organizations. A new meaning
must be given to societies. No society should be maintained merely
for the purpose of entertainment, but it should have vital relation
to the real affairs of the communities in which it is.

Every kind of organization that now exists in the open country,
or which can be readily extended to the open country, may be made
the means of carrying the gospel of co-operation, companionship and
better farm life to the persons who live on the land. The number of
such organizations and associations is surprisingly large, even not
counting the technical agricultural societies and groups (which are
really the most effective of all). It is not so necessary to organize new groups as it is to fertilize and redirect the old ones.
Rural institutions ought to be effective because they are for the
most part natural expressions of indigenous needs, the outcome of

the community's work. Many of the city institutions are creations of some person's philosophy or the expression of some fad or fashion.

Let me enumerate some of the group-associations that might easily aid in the regeneration of country life if they were not so closely tied to their customs and traditions: the school; the church; fraternal societies of all kinds; christian associations for men and women and for both; all singing schools, and musical clubs; reading clubs and library associations; women's clubs; historical societies; athletic organizations, and all groups that might develop the play spirit and revive the native games; local political organizations, that might give as much attention to developing or promoting the community as to putting some one in office; the good roads interest is now easy of organization and direction; banks might have relation to the welfare of the community as well as to themselves, as is shown by various European experience; chambers of commerce and business men's organizations in the smaller cities might extend their efforts beyond the corporation lines, associating the country merchants and traders with them; civic societies; improvement and art societies. In the way of economic group associations, the co-operative creamery may be cited as a representative example. In a dairy country, such an institution not only works an improvement in farm practice, but develops a market and meeting place in the neighborhood and thereby affords a most useful center of local interest.

(3) By developing applicable education. The older education, which even yet dominates in the open country, has little relation to living or to locality. We have begun with the remote, and often we have never reached the real environment of the pupil. The pupil's mind can be trained by means of the things that naturally condition his existence, at the same time that the work puts him into sympathy with his surroundings and enables him to understand them. If the affairs of life should be made the means of beginning and directing the training of the pupil, then it follows that nature-study and agriculture should dominate the rural school. The country life pursuits will never appeal to the farm youth as really worth the while until they are taught in schools and are thereby given the same dignity and importance as other subjects.

(4) By developing particular persons for special kinds of work. The failure of our fairest and most perfect plans traces itself to lack of good local leaders. In small towns and the open country there are club houses vacant or of no account because there is no one person to organize and energize.

In cities, great things are accomplished by settlements of one kind and another, something of the kind can be done in the country, but it will need to be in the nature of better examples of actual farming as a base, with the farmer taking a new kind of enthusiastic interest in all the public and organized affairs of his community. The greatest aid will probably come by means of individual effort rather than by large settlement organization. The farming people are characterized by individualism and they must be reached through individualism rather than through institutionalism. (The speaker suggested ways and means by which educated men and women might establish themselves as farmers, and while making a living from the land could conduct a kind of social effort such as is quite unknown in this country today.) There is great opportunity for young persons to fit themselves for this kind of work, developing leadership and serving their fellows without the handicap of over-organization, which is likely to be a serious drawback in the highly specialized work of the cities. Nowhere will the individuality of personal leadership count for so much as in the country.

It is important that the country work be founded on occupation (that is, on agriculture), since all country interests rest on occupation. That is to say, the good social worker should be a farmer, rather than a missionary, charity organizer, officer of correction, or philanthropist. It is not a question of slumming. The rural people are not lost; they need opportunity and leadership. So far as possible, the work should be established in real rural regions, outside the towns. The worker must be resident the year round, not migratory, and above all he should not be of the summer boarder class.

Inasmuch as personal leadership in country work must rest on a good foundation of agricultural knowledge, it follows that the best training place for this class of workers is the agricultural school and college. Heretofore, these institutions have devoted their attention chiefly to technical agricultural instruction, but they are now rapidly taking up the social and the larger economic phases of country life. From some of the colleges the young men and women go back to the country thoroughly alive to the necessity of organizing the social forces there. The time cannot be far distant when there will be some kind of a voluntary association between the students of all agricultural colleges, looking to the elevation of agricultural communities as well as to the elevation of individual farmers.

Recommendations to this Conference
I shall mention no specific things to be done, but indicate points of view to be established.

    1. Extend your customary efforts to all people irrespective of

where they live, and let them apply equally everywhere. Recognize the fact that your work is broadly human.

2. Aim to create a public sentiment that shall aid in removing the disabilities under which the farmer works and that shall allow him his share of the benefits of the progress of the race.

3. Advise the organization of good public health supervision for both the people and their domestic animals. You should be cautioned, however, that this supervision should have due regard to existing rural conditions and not be imposed as a piece of theoretical legislation.

4. Endeavor to interest good countrymen in the work that you are doing, bringing them into your organizations, making them in effect your local agents and representatives; this is very much better than to attempt to reach the problem by merely sending persons into the country.

2

Social Problems of the Country

Between 1908 and 1917, rural social work spokesmen focused public attention on the social problems of the country. The following three articles illustrate the efforts of those pioneer rural voices. The similarity of many of the early themes to those which are still affecting social welfare in rural areas is striking.

In 1909 John C. Campbell of Demorest, Georgia, presented to the National Conference of Charities and Corrections a paper entitled "Social Betterment in the Southern Mountains." Campbell highlighted the problems of Southern Appalachia and suggested the adaptation of the remedies and panaceas of the time to the reality of local conditions.

In "The Cost of the Cranberry Sauce" Charles L. Chute discussed the problem of migrant farm workers in New Jersey, and although the tone of the article might strike the contemporary reader as melodramatic, many rural workers presently involved with migrant laborers might suggest that in the half-century gone by, conditions have not improved radically. In a recent publication Leon Ginsberg stated that "migrant workers constitute what might be called another ethnic group in rural areas"[1] and that there are all sorts of problems migrants face because the crops they work are not price-supported.

Neglected child welfare services is the theme of "Children in Rural Districts," by J. J. Kelso, formerly General Superintendent of Neglected and Dependent Children for the government of Ontario, Canada. The international dimensions of rural social work, particularly the Canadian perspective, were obvious from the incipient stages of the practice.

[1]Leon Ginsberg, "Social Work in Rural Areas," in Ronald K. Green and Stephen A. Webster, ed., *Social Work in Rural Areas: Preparation and Practice* (Knoxville: University of Tennessee, 1977), p. 8.

Housing in small towns and villages enraged Katherine Piatt Bottorf in "Tragedies of Village Slums." Once again, the housing theme is an ever present one for rural areas. Richard J. Margolis, former Chairman of Rural America, Inc., remarked at the National Conference on Social Welfare in May 1977, "Sixty percent of all the nation's bad housing is out there in rural areas, yet less than ten percent of HUD's housing subsidies go to rural people."[2] The relevancy of the past grows constantly apparent.

[2] Richard J. Margolis, "Rural Health and the Politics of Neglect" in *Human Services in the Rural Environment* (Madison, Wisconsin: University of Wisconsin-Extension, 1977), Vol. 2, No. 8, August 1977, p. 5.

SOCIAL BETTERMENT IN THE SOUTHERN MOUNTAINS

John C. Campbell

My subject is one that presents difficulties at the outset. Conditions in the Southern Appalachian region are little known, and the people have suffered much from unqualified generalization. Those who are interested in them and are laboring zealously for them, speaking necessarily from a limited or local viewpoint, and under the stress of money raising to carry on special work, have unconsciously added to the misinformation and misunderstanding regarding this people. Many of us, interested in our own work, plead so earnestly for the needs of our own fields that we leave the impression upon the minds of our auditors that the conditions which we depict are general conditions.

Not only has the mountaineer been injured by his friends, but he has also been misrepresented by some writers of fiction, and, consequently, he is to many people merely a picturesque type in litera-

Proceedings, National Conference of Charities and Corrections, 1909. John C. Campbell was with the Russell Sage Foundation at Demorest, Georgia.

ture and a desperate character of newspaper headlines, who spends
his days in feudal strife and his nights in illicit distilling of
whisky. Those who do not regard him as a pathetic object of missionary appeal, or a fire eating desperado, call him "the mountain
white," a term synonymous in their minds with "poor white trash";
and certain of the low-landers of the South join in spirit with
these Northern detractors when they apply to him the half humorous
and half contemptuous term of "hill billy."

We cannot generalize. The mountain region of the Southern Appalachians includes in places wide and fertile valleys and other long
trough-like valleys, occupied by people able to supply their own
needs. There are also in the more remote sections, little villages
and groups well able to take care of themselves; and in some sections
there are people who have had advantages equal to those who live in
more urban sections. Often these groups are close together in neighborhoods.

With this foreword, and remembering that mountain conditions are
constantly changing for the better or for the worse, we may speak,
realizing that we may be misunderstood by some of our auditors, who
may fail to keep in mind that we are speaking of the needy groups
and of their environment.

We speak, then, of the needy groups, and there are many such.
Imagine an intensified rural section, with poor roads, poor schools,
with teachers to match (excepting, of course, many of the church
schools and some of the public schools), with comparatively few
well-trained physicians and ministers—a people developed to the
highest point of individualism, with practically no community spirit,
with forests disappearing; land being washed away in consequence,
and unwise methods of farming; with little, if any, farm stock of
high grade; with large families; with homes lacking much that seems
to be essential. What can be done?

You and I decided some years ago that education was the "cure-all,"
and we recall with what joy and elation we left the railroad, as co-
workers, and traveled far up into the mountains to do this people
good.

It was early May. The distant hills were clothed in purple. In
the foreground were the rich green of cedar and of pine, interspersed
with the variant green of the oaks. The iris and the violet contended in friendly rivalry for possession of the roadside. The bees
hummed busily among the azalea, and from the topmost branch of the
blossoming dogwood a mocking-bird was singing. Here and there a
thrush or cat-bird sought to outdo him in melody, and in the lapses
of their song were borne to our ears the woodland sounds of running
brooks and whispering leaves.

Surely we had come into a goodly land! How we were thrilled with
its beauty and with the self-satisfaction of a worthy mission! But
we recall now how we were rudely awakened from the spell that the
mountains had cast upon us by the plaintive voice of a woman, who
had slipped to the side of our carriage to ask our driver to exchange
the few eggs that she brought for coffee and snuff. She was dressed
in clinging calico, which served but to accentuate her angular figure. Her face, beneath the shadow of her sun-bonnet, was sallow and
worn, and her eyes were tired. We drove on and Nature failed to reassert her charms, for there was ever before our vision that lone
figure by the roadside, so out of keeping with the beauty of the
scene.

But education would surely correct all the needs that are thus
suggested to us, and we open our school with enthusiasm. As the
weeks go by, we find we have won the confidence of the community,
and our advice is followed. We have proved to the fathers and
mothers that a knowledge of grammar is of use to their boys, and
that arithmetic and physiology will at least do no harm to their
girls, and for the first year we take a certain satisfaction in the
number who spell correctly and who can read with some expression.
Later our satisfaction becomes profound when we have successfully
carried through the elementary and high school grades a few of the
most promising. And here at last are two who go to their state university, and there one who has entered Harvard, and another who
supported himself at Yale.

We have noted, however, that our girls were irregular in their
attendance—"Mammy" is a little ill and "Sis" must stay at home, or
corn needs to be planted or the fodder pulled. It is the boy of the
family who has the chance, if the teacher has had success in keeping
alive the educational consciousness in the father.

One day that troublesome little question which we try to hold down
by the weight of our satisfaction demands an answer, as Amanda,
voicing the doubt of many of her sisters in the mountains, comes to
our desk and says, with tears in her eyes: "I am going to leave
school. What is the use of educating me—I am only a girl, one of
many in the family? We live in a one-room cabin. You have taken
me and lifted me above the level of my family. You have given me a
glimpse of better things—things that cannot be realized in my surroundings. The best boys of the community who have accepted what
you have taught them have gone elsewhere, and I am left to become a
burden on my parents, dissatisfied with my home, or to marry a boy
above whom you have lifted me. You would have done better to have
left me in my ignorance."

Were we doing what needed to be done—creating discontent, without

a training which could work the cure within the community? How much
had we lightened the darkness of this community by stealing from it
the few lights that were needed and setting them where they were not
needed, and leaving in the community a few tapers to burn themselves
out? Under the impelling logic of this girl's plaint, we persuade
those in charge that something more ought to be done to prepare for
the life that must be lived in the community, and we perhaps secure
a domestic science teacher, who instructs our girls that "Pillsbury's
best brand of wheat flour and fresh compressed yeast every day are
absolutely necessary for successful housekeeping," and she distri-
butes to the women in the community who cannot read, a pretty magazine, "The Kitchen Queen," to teach them how to make macaroons and
Charlotte Russe.

There are many efforts such as ours, for we have all been caught
in a system inherited from other times and other sections somewhat
different. But if the test of education is in its adaptation to
life, it is the "cure-all," not only for intensified rural conditions
but for intensified urban conditions. With this truth before us,
made operative by men and women of largeness of vision, with hearts
filled with the essence of religion—social love—men and women
willing to spend and be spent, who come to learn as well as to teach,
there is great promise of betterment.

The life that the mountaineer must live is a rural life, and his
education should be adapted to meet the needs of that rural life. A
number will always seek the larger centers, but our rural schools in
the mountains and elsewhere must teach the youth to develop the resources of their own environment, and to find within that environment the proper response to legitimate needs and desires.

The question naturally arises at this point as to whether there
are enough material resources in the mountain section to supply the
necessities of living for an increasing population, if these resources are properly developed? So far, speaking generally, the
resources of the mountains have been exploited by those from other
sections, and the mountain people have had little return.

This question as to the resources of the mountains is one that
cannot be answered offhand. A careful inquiry, directed to government and state experts, warrants the statement that there are large
sections in the mountains where life could be made more livable by
development of what is there and what may be raised there. The
finding out of what is in the neighborhood and its proper development
is a part of the scheme of education that is needed.

Another great need is a vigorous campaign for better health conditions. Tuberculosis is a rival of typhoid, and in certain large

sections claims more yearly victims than typhoid, which is commonly regarded as the mountain scourge.

Intimately connected with the question of health is that of dietetics. The common foods of the mountains, lacking perhaps in some of the elements regarded as necessary in a normal diet, do not produce the full effect that might be expected from the food values they contain. Even where the food values are not affected by the preparation, the method of cooking is such as to produce in the individuals an enfeebled condition which prohibits a complete assimilation of the food.

Social life, as it is generally understood, is, from one cause and another, lacking almost entirely.

We have no cut and dried method for betterment, but it would seem wise to avail ourselves of the forces already working for betterment; to test them to the full by adjustment, adaptation and co-operation. As has been stated before, the schools have been the strongest influence for betterment, and when we say schools, we mean the church and independent schools. The question that presents itself now is as to whether the time has not come for withdrawing these schools and leaving education to the public schools. There is a difference of opinion here, but it seems to us that those who really understand the mountain field will be loth to say that the day of the church and independent school is over. They should, however, be preparing the way for the public school, and this would seem to us to be done best through an adaptation of their activities for development of material resources, and, socially, for the development of a community spirit, so that eventually the needs which called them into existence may disappear through communities aroused to their social obligations, and enabled, through increased property holdings, to maintain, on the basis of local taxation, the public schools which they have come to feel are needed. This process, of course, will mean that eventually many of the church schools will lose their lives by having gained the object which called them into existence.

We have no fixed educational method as a panacea for the material health and social needs of the mountains. A purpose in the minds and hearts of trained men and women co-operating with one another, and with betterment forces without the mountain field, will develop the method.

As a beginning, we suggest the following: An initial, and perhaps a continuous co-operative effort from without, to place in the best managed and most broad spirited of these schools, and in the good public schools, men trained for the development of rural life and who love rural life; who should be the friends of the neighborhood perhaps more than teachers in the school; who should study the needs

of the neighborhood; be scientific enough to know what can best be
raised and how to raise it; ready also to organize the farmers and
co-operate with them in finding the best market. We would have,
also, instruction in common carpentry, planning of homes, etc., but
all on such a level as to create hope rather than discouragement.
We would have boys trained to make the best of the material that
could be found in the environment in which they are to live and with
the tools that they themselves are able to own. We would have
courses in domestic science and household economy adapted to the
existing conditions. We would have home nursing, by nurses trained
to make the best of whatever comes to hand.

Nurses of this stamp, such domestic science teachers and preachers
and teachers of rural life, will do much for betterment. If the
best thing under normal conditions cannot be done, they will be willing to teach the best under abnormal conditions. A number of schools
with such teachers linked together for a common effort, and with
some means to bring to them the experience of other groups, and to
connect them with outside forces, would eventually meet many of the
crying needs.

It may seem to some that the greatest thing of all—the spiritual
need—has been disregarded. The means that have been suggested, in
their development, will tend to produce that social love which is
the essence of all true religion.

It will be found, we are sure, that the churches in the mountains
will co-operate, when it is seen that these efforts are, in fact,
practical, modern ways of the Great Teacher, who commanded His dis-
ciples to heal the sick, feed the hungry, clothe the naked, and to
open the eyes of the blind.

The training that we advocate will, we believe, dignify labor and
spiritualize it. The system we have followed so long in the past
has caused young men to feel that a lawyer, a minister, a physician,
a teacher—professional men—are higher types of manhood than he
whose brain directs his hand in the common tasks of life. It is
little wonder that so many seek urban life, when all our training
tends to send them there by embellishing urban life and disregarding
the beauties of rural life.

Let us ask once more, has the time not come for us to assert that
the true test of education is adaptation to life? Man cannot live
by bread alone, but He who uttered those words taught us, by example,
to feed the multitude as well as to preach to them. We do not plead
for mere utilitarian training, nor do we seek to minimize the benefit
of cultural training; but may we not, in this intensified rural
section, in which our best schools have been so inadequate, try the
experiment that may be too costly to begin elsewhere, because of the

grip of custom—the experiment of schools adapted to the needs of their environment, and to prove that there are cultural and spiritual values in finding what one's environment can best produce, and in producing it, gain not only subsistence but life itself?

Let one who has been a worker for many years in the mountain section of the South bespeak your sympathetic imagination, as you endeavor to get some view of the great task of social betterment in this highland region. May he go further, and not be misunderstood in so doing, to ask your sympathetic imagination as you view all southern questions? We of the North have been wont to regard the South as provincial, unmindful of the fact that there is a western provincialism and an eastern provincialism as well. There are real questions to be solved in the South, questions that are national in their bearing, and need to be looked at in the large.

This question of the mountain dwellers is a national question. You have it in your New England hills, with less hope of solution it is sometimes felt, and although it is a larger question in the South, it is, after all, only a question of intensified rural conditions. If you cannot altogether understand the South, may we not hope for your patience and for your sympathy? Perhaps it is easy for you to respond in sympathy for the mountaineer; easy, too, for many of you to feel sympathy for the negro; but may we ask that you be not lacking in sympathy for the intelligent South, mistaken as she may be at times? Bound though she be, on one hand by the ignorant white, and on the other hand by the ignorant black, she nevertheless is heroically breaking from the charm of a romantic past and struggling to the light of a new and brighter day.

She needs you and you need her, if our national life, in its entirety, is to be strong.

THE COST OF THE CRANBERRY SAUCE

Charles L. Chute

In agriculture the seasonal character of the work is an ever-recur-
ring problem. At certain times in the year, particularly during the
harvesting season, there arises an urgent demand for labor—a demand
hard to satisfy. This problem confronts the grower of all small
fruits. In harvesting the cranberry crop in our eastern states the
problem of meeting the great temporary demand for labor was for many
years an acute one, and many a cranberry crop was sacrificed to early
frosts because of a lack of hands to gather the scattered harvest.
In recent years, however, this problem has been solved from the
standpoint of the growers by recourse to the crowded immigrant col-
onies in our large cities. Most of the cranberries which are in so
great demand all over the country this year were picked by Italian
and Portuguese men, women, and children—no small proportion by the
children.

After the publication in *The Survey* [7 January 1911] of the results of an investigation made last year for the National Child Labor
Committee into the work and living conditions of Italian cranberry
pickers in New Jersey, indignant protests were made by certain prominent growers in that state. A leading newspaper took up the cud-
gels for the growers. New Jersey has been libeled; evils had been
exaggerated; conditions were misrepresented. However, the quarrel
was not so much over the facts found as over their general application and the varying interpretations put upon those facts.

Upon the return of the brief cranberry picking season this year,
bringing the usual migration of great numbers of families from the
cities to the bogs, a new and more thorough investigation was undertaken by the organization which began it last year. This has just
been completed. Agents visited cranberry growing sections of Massachusetts and covered most of the larger plantations in the four
cranberry producing counties in New Jersey. In general, it may be
said that all the essential facts of unrestricted child employment,
loss of several weeks' schooling to thousands of children, an un-
American system of labor under a padrone, and the crowded and unsanitary camps reported last year were this year again found to be
the rule rather than the exception. Young children were found work-

Survey, 2 December 1911. Charles L. Chute was a member of the
National Child Labor Committee.

ing long hours under a padrone, in Massachusetts as in New Jersey, and families were crowded into unsanitary shacks. However, as a much greater proportion of the harvesting in Massachusetts is done by means of "scoops" operated largely by Portuguese men, the evils of family migration and child and woman labor were found to be not as extensive as in New Jersey, where nearly all the picking is done by hand. This year, in the latter state, there was somewhat less crowding, slightly shorter hours, and less Sunday work, due to a smaller crop. Otherwise the situation has not improved except in the housing conditions on one bog.

In New Jersey the picking is done almost entirely by large gangs of Italians. These gangs are largely recruited in Philadelphia by padrones employed by the growers. These padrones take advantage of their ignorant countrymen if they can, charging them varying amounts for the privilege of a job and obtaining a "rake-off" on transportation rates. In seven cases padrones were paid a commission on each bushel of berries picked; on the other bogs they were paid wages.

When picking begins the entire family may be seen on the bog. Babies are left to amuse themselves as best they may, while all the children who are old enough work. Upon seventeen of the bogs visited where a careful count was made, 32 per cent of the pickers were found to be under fourteen, 18 per cent were under ten years of age, and on twelve bogs some children under five were found working. These children are encouraged, when they are not compelled, by both the padrone and the parents to keep at work throughout the long day.

The work is in the open and undoubtedly has its healthful features; but among the conditions which make it unsuitable for young children are the prevailing wetness of the ground and the swarms of mosquitoes from which the workers suffer constantly. Many of the padrones are rough in dealing with the children. Heavy boxes must be carried to and from and the boxes vary in size, although the price paid per measure remains the same. All these conditions are of constant recurrence.

The worst evils are in the camps, where the children live from five to seven weeks. The surroundings are often unspeakable. The congestion out-slums the city. Families of five, six and even eight were found living in one room measuring six by eight feet, without any sanitary provisions whatever. They are not even provided with screens against the swarming mosquitoes. Barracks measuring eighteen by thirty feet were found housing sixty to seventy-five people. Refuse and filth of all kinds pervade these dwellings and are scattered about the doors and windows. Yet certain growers claim that the children return to their city homes after a life under such condi-

tions in better health than when they came out. Their condition
when seen in the camps does not justify the claim.

Much might be done by the growers under the pressure of public
opinion to improve these conditions. Four suggestions have already
been made to one of their number, as follows:

1) That children of tender years be excluded from regular labor.

2) That temporary schools be established on the larger plantations
which children of school age shall attend for part of each day.

3) That the hours of work for children under fourteen be shortened.

4) That reasonable supervision be given to housing conditions, so
that the quarters provided shall be adequate, decent, and sanitary.

But, apart from voluntary action on the part of progressive growers, there is in the New Jersey situation a problem for the school
authorities of two states which perhaps can be solved only through
legislation. Many hundreds of children from Philadelphia lose at
least six weeks' school attendance at the beginning of the school
year. Some of these lose much more through failure to return to
school promptly after the picking season is over. The compulsory
school laws of Pennsylvania and New Jersey should not be set aside
for the benefit of the cranberry growers whose profits are already
large, however willing the parents may be to profit by the labor of
the children. These children need their full schooling. If they
cannot be reached by Pennsylvania laws while outside that state, is
not New Jersey responsible? Why should not her child labor law
regulate such agricultural employment as well as other forms of work?

The evils of this annual migration could in such ways be minimized
and the children to a degree protected; but should we not go further?
Is not this sporadic family labor inherently bad? The employment of
children in this industry, as in all others, means depressed wages
and a low standard of living.

The system itself is intolerable. The wholesale removal of these
families is not for an outing in the New Jersey pines, as one of
their employers naively expresses it, but to labor for the support
of their families in a region where there are no restrictions as to
age or sex, hours and conditions of labor, nor regulated living conditions.

On the plantation referred to, the largest in New Jersey, housing
conditions are much superior to those in the other camps. This was
found to be the case last year. This year conditions have become
better, by the addition of several houses, so that the occupants of
six and one half by eight foot rooms average but a small fraction
more than three persons to a room. On this bog also sanitary outdoor toilets with cement base have been erected this year. These

38

conditions were not found on any other of the twenty three plantations visited in New Jersey.

CHILDREN IN RURAL DISTRICTS

J. J. Kelso

In past years the great bulk of philanthropic effort has been confined to cities. There organization is much simpler and financial
support is more readily obtained. Social conditions are evident to
all, and where there is distress or poverty, relief is promptly extended. If there is vice or wrong-doing the public eye is equally
certain to discover it. In the country, where people are scattered,
there is little public opinion and little effective organization to
relieve the individual complainant from personal responsibility.
Then, too, the generously disposed usually send their gifts to
popular city charities.

This means that an important social work is left undone, and too
often vice flourishes and degenerate children grow up to be a burden
and a menace to the community. Few people realize how serious this
problem is, or what an expensive and vexatious addition this means
to the dependent and criminal population.

I once made the statement in a public meeting of social workers
that many tramps, vagrants, and other undesirable characters are
born in the country and afterwards gravitate to the city. This did
not accord with the general view, as the majority believed that
nearly all criminals and vicious persons are the products of the
city slum; but I still believe that a large share of unfortunate
characters come from the Ishmaelite class in the country. When the
neglected child of the rural district reaches the age of fourteen
or fifteen he almost invariably commits some offence that brings him
under the censure of the law, and then he either voluntarily or by

Survey, 21 October 1911. J. J. Kelso was General Superintendent of
Neglected and Dependent Children for the Government of Ontario,
Canada.

compulsion disappears from the neighborhood, drifting to larger cities, or tramping about from place to place without home or occupation. Few people realize how many cases, both of boys and of girls, there are of this kind, because so little attention has been paid to the subject.

Without doubt the worst cases of immorality, incest, cruelty, and neglect of children in my experience have been found in the country. In the cities and large towns there is a strong Christian sentiment and greater social activity. People are better educated in right living, and any serious lapses from the right path are quickly reported and the necessary corrective measures applied. In the rural districts there is little public sentiment of that sort, no united social activity; but, on the other hand, there is the toleration that is often inspired by fear of personal harm. Undesirable characters in the neighborhood are sometimes well known throughout a large area, but no one can be found to lay an information for fear of injury to his person, stock, or property.

The school attendance law is rarely enforced in rural districts. Not only is there lack of effort to get children to attend, but many cases occur where neglected children have been encouraged by the school teacher to stay away. Such cases have come within my experience. Children from a neglected home, if they should happen to turn up at the school untidy and verminous, do not receive a welcome. Other children taunt them, and the teacher, for the sake of the better class of children, tells them to stay at home until they are cleaned up, which practically means banishment. Neglected children frequently use bad language and so are a menace to respectable children. For these conditions the children themselves are not responsible; and yet, unfortunately, they bear all the reproach, and any incentive they might have to a better life is crushed out by the treatment they receive.

In the country it is rare that any definite steps are taken to lift them out of their evil environment. In most rural districts there is great ignorance of the law, and the village or rural constable is usually a man-of-all work who has taken on this extra duty to add a little to his income. Clergymen and church-workers have never had opportunity to study social reform work, and are sometimes as innocent as babes as to the real evils that exist in the world. A rural clergyman, long engaged in the ministry, wrote me concerning a notoriously bad woman in his neighborhood, bad because she was feeble-minded, saying: "I am afraid Miss—is not very respectable, for she has had four or five children, although she has never been married." Others have approached grave social dangers and moral pests in the community with the same timid and hesitating method of introduction.

On another occasion a clergyman wrote me that there was a vile resort in his district, and that all the respectable farmers would drive a mile or two out of their way to avoid seeing and hearing the evil-doing that went on there on Sundays, when the wild youth of the neighborhood would gather to carouse.

"Instead of allowing the farmers to drive around this place," I remarked, "why not call a meeting of a few of your influential men and insist on their driving through it?"

"But what can we do?" he asked in astonishment.

When it was explained that the parties could be arrested for disorderly conduct and for keeping an improper resort, etc., he eagerly agreed to have action taken; and as a result of a conference and legal advice, the place was raided, several inmates sent to public institutions or to friends in other districts, and the hovel pulled down so that it could not be used for wrong purposes again.

Among the children growing up in poor families in rural districts there are often physical defects in infants and young people that remain unattended to, and the children grow up with imperfections that could easily have been prevented had there been proper medical and surgical care. Feeble-minded children also are found in these families, and when no steps are taken to place them under custodial care they are led astray at an early age, often marry some worthless degenerate, and perpetuate an undesirable class.

All these things point to the strong necessity for better organization, greater vigilance, and more practical measures in eliminating from our rural districts the ignorance, crime, and degeneracy that now exist. Many of these families need sympathetic encouragement. They have been given a bad name, are shunned by the rest of the community, the children grow up recognizing that every man's hand is against them, and so naturally develop all the badness that is expected from them.

The establishment of travelling social secretaries, who could organize social work in towns and villages, create the right kind of public sentiment, and deal radically with extreme cases, would be a step in the right direction. I have often thought that if instead of appointing constables for purely detective and punitive work we could have social up-building and preventive work as their main duty the results would be much more satisfactory. Above all, more attention should be given to education in rural districts; for if children can be kept steadily under the beneficial influence of the school-room during the formative period of their lives, their prospects for future usefulness and happiness are materially increased.

There is a great lack of rational amusement and recreation in the country. Every small town or village should have a social center

building and a good playground. These features, with a competent
director, and with club rooms and hall for concerts, dances, etc.,
would exercise a healthy, pleasure-giving influence that would offset to some extent the deplorable exodus to the cities. If municipal
councils and philanthropists would take up this project they would
be doing the highest kind of service for the community.

Wealthy and influential city charities should exercise some oversight over the nearby rural districts. Some charities actually draw
a line around the city and refuse to touch any case, no matter how
urgent, that happens to be outside that line. This is a narrow and
short-sighted policy, as it is really the duty and privilege of all
charities receiving money from the public to take cognizance of the
needs of the surrounding territory. One often hears the excuse,
"We have received our funds from the city, and what right have we to
spend any of them in the country?" It is doubtless true that county
and town councils have been extremely parsimonious in making grants
for social or charitable work; but at least there should be constant
educational work carried on until the necessary funds are secured to
cover the much-needed rural work.

It would be a mistake to say that we have found the solution to
these problems in Ontario, for there are many districts where much
remains to be done; but it is at least true that some effort has been
made to cope with the need. Our Children's Aid system, which covers
the entire province, and is a uniform and co-operative plan, is in
itself unique. Outside of many individual workers and correspondents
there are between sixty and seventy Children's Aid Societies actively engaged in work for the protection of children, with all the
social uplift that such work implies. Further, this united work
centers in a head office in the Government Building at Toronto to
which the people everywhere in the province are not only invited,
but urged, to report any cases of child neglect, so that proper
steps may be taken to bring about improvement. In addition to the
many societies and committees and correspondents, there are, in
various sections of the province, inspectors of Children's Aid Societies who, as representatives of the central office, are prepared
at any time to go anywhere when instructed to make these special
investigations. In addition to this there is a special officer,
attached to the head office, who is constantly on the road enquiring
into the cases that are reported to the superintendent. In this way
many families are warned and encouraged to put themselves in the way
of timely assistance; immoral and vicious conditions are done away
with; children are removed to a new environment, when that is obviously the best thing to do; and at all places touched the agent or
inspector endeavors to interest influential residents in child-

protection work.   Literature and letters requesting cooperation in
the great work of lifting the social status of the people are sent
out daily from the central office, and every possible effort is made
to create new conditions of moral wholesomeness and material prosperity where there was formerly degradation, poverty, and despair.

TRAGEDIES OF VILLAGE SLUMS

Katherine Piatt Bottorff

Scattered all over our country are small towns and villages that to
the casual observer seem to be the embodiment of peace and plenty.
The vine-covered porches and streets where elms and maples arch
across the way look restful and quiet to the traveller, hurrying
from city to city.   The man of business, weary of his ceaseless
struggle for a fortune, thinks, wistfully, that if he could only
end his days in the quiet of one of these lovely villages, he might
forget the rush and hurry of the city, and have time to be a better
man.   He fancies himself in a pleasant home, with honest neighbors,
and nothing to do but to watch the procession of sweet country days
pass by to fill a changing year.   But alas!   how little he realizes
that down those broad streets and under those green trees are found
conditions that are harder to deal with than the problems of the
city slums.
    Let me show you the homes of the poor in one beautiful Indiana
town.   Let me lead you from cabin to hovel and show you the close
relation existing between physical and moral degradation; let me
point out how much the environment means to a family of children,
who reflect, inevitably, in conduct and character, every phase of
the descent in social and moral scale.   I want you to cry "Enough!
These conditions must be remedied by legislation, and it must be
immediate and thorough."

Survey, 21 September 1912.

Just where our main street becomes a country road, a little red cabin of two rooms stands back in an open lot. The ground around the house is a village dump, and is littered with tin cans and broken crockery. No attempt is ever made to cultivate it, although the renters that live here have needed, sorely, the potatoes and cabbages that might have been raised. There is no water supply except from a hole in the ground near the front door, where perhaps in ordinary weather two buckets of water may be secured in a day. When it rains the hole overflows with muddy seepage, and in the long hot summers it is baked and hard. A poor washer-woman with a family of thirteen, ten children and three adults, lives here. She gives two days work every week to pay the rent for this apology for a home, and cheerfully tries to feed and clothe all of this flock with the money earned on the other five days.

At one time the oldest daughter lay in the front room with an illegitimate baby on her lap. Out in the lean-to shed the oldest boy was hiding from the marshal because he had stolen a suit of clothes from a village merchant, and the majesty of the law had been set in motion. During the heat of summer after a dry spring this poor woman would call all of her children to help her carry water for the next day's washing from a spring half a mile away. I can see this little procession now as they plodded along the dusty road, carrying their precious load, which would enable their mother to earn fifty cents the next day. One child stumbles, and gasps with dismay as a part of her bucketful splashes out. Another is crying softly, because she is so tired, and even the two year old baby, clinging with one hand to her mother's skirt, carries a tiny bucket made of a tomato can. And perhaps at this moment, the owner of the house was sitting on her vine-covered veranda, swaying back and forth in her chair in the coolness, chatting with some neighbor about the unsatisfactory work that home laundresses do.

How could this mother keep her ten children clean? How could she be expected even to know their moral tendencies? In fact she did not, for she has wept bitterly over four illegitimate children that have come to her daughters. Personal cleanliness is more closely connected with moral uprightness than this superficial critic would think, and before we condemn these girls for their lapses in morals, we must try to fill the empty water pail.

A little further up the street is a four-room house set flat on the ground in a lot that is overflowed annually by a small river branch which dries up in summer. It is owned by a man who boasts that he has a clear title to one hundred pieces of property in two adjoining counties. There is no water supply here when the branch is dry except one rain spout and a series of barrels, each lower than the other, to catch the overflow from its neighbor. Dogs, babies and chickens drink from the one nearest the ground. This family carries water for cooking from a well on the premises of a Negro family near by, but it is a rare thing for a bucket of water to be secured without a battle. All of the little Olcotts accompany the one deputized to draw the water, and all the little Swans come to repel the invaders. Sometimes the air is filled with profanity, sometimes they hurl tin cans and rocks at one another, but every bucket of water used by the Olcott family represents one step lower in the ladder of decency, down which those children are descending. Time and again has the town marshal interfered in these fights, and once arrested an Olcott boy for cutting a small girl of the other family with a piece of tin. The child was sent to Plainfield, and is still there, but the conditions of the two families have not been remedied.

Morals do not thrive in such surroundings—neither does physical health. When such a disease as tuberculosis occurs in a home of this sort, it is inevitably contracted by other members of the family. These poor little thin houses, flat on the ground with walls reeking with dampness, leaking roofs, rotting sills, and the foul moisture from dish water and slops thrown around the door, are breeding places for those bacilli that thrive in the filth. An epidemic disease such as scarlet fever or diphtheria is terrible in such a home. There can be no such thing as isolation of the patient. Every child in the family is liable to be a victim, showing symptoms one by one, till the family suffers severely from a protracted quarantine. More than this, disinfection cannot be thorough in a home of rags and tatters, torn wall paper and broken furniture. When the children go back to school, each becomes an agent for the further dissemination of disease.

Still, I would rather my children would sit beside a child with the scales from scarlet fever only half washed out of his clothing, than to listen to the tales that these slum children tell. Poor little untaught waifs! Who can blame them if they try to win friends and companions in school by telling the tragic happenings of their daily lives. The drunken fight, the vile dance held in some vacant house, the time "pa" was arrested, the cold day when we were put out of our house for not paying the rent, the time the baby came—these are the tales your child and mine hear from their little classmates in the public school.

These village slums do not present the problem of the ill-nourished city poor. These neighbors of mine all have enough to eat. The problem is one of neglect and abandonment. The necessities for decency are not provided and they are too poor to supply them.

Last summer a baby was born in a hovel in one of our side streets; a dear, blue-eyed little fellow of whom any mother might be proud. This mother lay upon a mattress so filthy that the dirt came off in flakes, and vermin crawled under the pillow and in the seams. There was no closet, and the three other children did not, and really could not, use the commonest decency in their toilet. Flies swarmed over the food, the baby, the mother, the soiled clothes, the filth in the yard, and back again to food and baby. When the baby was two days old, this mother began carrying water from the spring three squares away, two bucketsful at a time, for cooking and washing. Do you blame her for not using any more water than was absolutely necessary?

I have heard persons say that there is no excuse for the very poor being so dirty, but I tell you, there is. Suppose your children's underwear was made of worn out knit goods that someone had thrown away and that their stockings had been refooted until they had lost all semblance of stockings. Suppose that there was not a nightgown in the collection of clothing and that for warmth the children slept in their clothes, four in a bed. When you wake at dawn you must hurry to the spring for a bucket of water for breakfast and toilet purposes—then another bucket must be procured before the dishes can be washed. More water must be carried to get dinner and wash dinner dishes, and still more brought for supper. If any washing is done, that water too must be carried from the spring or neighbor's well. How long would one of these critics of the poor endure this servitude to selfish landlords, who, to save a few dollars build these poor cabins without cisterns or outbuildings, and then rent them for 200 per cent more than decent houses bring?

When I think of a water bucket it obscures my vision. I want to hold it up so closely before the eye of the public that nothing can be seen but this perpetually empty vessel. I want hearts to ache with pity for the poor who see their little children converted into criminals just through lack of the common decencies of life. Sad as it is to see a child die it is sadder to see one live in such homes as these.

When my washerwoman's son was sent home from Plainfield dying with tuberculosis, the little town roused itself out of its self-complacency and murmured that the state should have provided care and medicines for the boy, instead of sending him home for his widowed mother to nurse. The child had been sent to Plainfield for some trivial offense—before the day of the juvenile court (he found a pocketbook with a little money in it and didn't try to find the owner, but spent twenty cents of the money before the pocketbook was missed). His mother had a younger boy and when she went away from home she tied the little one to ꞁe table and left him in the room with Ferdie, who was dying of tuberculosis. The last week of Ferd's life the mother worked away from home every day. The baby would follow her to the door and say "Ferdie will take care of me, mamma—don't cry." Then he would climb up in Ferd's arm and sit quietly listening to the strange stories the dying boy would whisper to him. The last day he came to the door when his mother returned from work, and said, "Ferdie's asleep, mamma, but he saw angels with white wings in the room all afternoon, and talked to them—he told them he was so tired, mamma—and so am I." It was only a few months before this baby too was found lulled asleep forever by the angels with white wings. Truly, the child of the slums is blest when he dies. These conditions of disease, vice, immorality, and crime could be swept away. If our legislature would give us a housing law that would cover every piece of rental property used for habitations, from the big tenement house swarming with human beings, down to the one-roomed cabin in the country town, their knell would be sounded.

3

Building and Strengthening
the Rural Community: The Country Church

In spite of the fact that between 1908 and 1917 many country lifers
hoped to accelerate social progress by concentrating on the problems
which affected rural areas, just as many worked for the enhancement
of the quality of life in the small villages and the open country
in other productive ways. Community development and education continued to characterize the efforts of members of the Country Life
movement until the United States entered World War II. Local
strength and cooperation in rural endeavors, from medicine to church
work and recreation, were themes stressed.

In 1913, Charles Otis Gill, a Congregational clergyman, and his
more famous cousin, Gifford Pinchot, published *The Country Church:
Decline of Influence and Remedy*. This intensive social study of the
rural church in one Vermont and one New York county focused attention on the factors associated with the decline of rural church
membership, and set up quite a trend among leaders of the period.

The building and strengthening of community resources through
church work was the dominant theme of the articles appearing in *The
Survey* in 1913 and 1914. The expanding of the role of the country
church was a subject of constant discussion. "Recreation and the
Country Church," and "Farmer Smith and the Country Church," both by
Fred Eastman, and "The Institutional Church for the Rural Community"
by Harry Deiman illustrate the notion which most religious leaders
seemed to have shared that the rural church should be a provider of
needed social services. This notion is still a particularly significant one in rural communities. For example, a recent publication
of the Southern Regional Education Board states that "religion

exerts greater influence on the lives of rural residents than it does on the lives of urban dwellers."[1]

"The Rural Church," a poem by Liberty Hyde Bailey, presents his rather utopian perspective of the country church as a vital center of life and work. Finally, "Rural Advance," written by Kenyon Butterfield as a greeting to the year 1914, summarizes far beyond that single year the major thrust of the country life campaign.

The year 1919 witnessed the foundation of a nationwide, privately supported agency concerned with the study and resolution of the socioreligious problems of the country: the Interchurch World Movement. This organization and its successor, the Institute for Social and Religious Research, introduced to the field of social welfare many other prominent people whose names would endure the test of time and the vicissitudes associated with the short-lived Interchurch World Movement. Of those tribulations, suffice it to say that early attempts at ecumenism among Protestant denominations and intervention in the American labor movement when it received little public sympathy sealed the fate of the organization. During its brief existence, the Interchurch World Movement was estimated to have involved in its program "one-third of the Protestant ministers and church leaders in the country."[2]

The Interchurch World Movement had carried out many significant surveys and studies of church-community relations. The Institute for Social and Religious Research, under the leadership of Edmund de S. Brunner (see Chapter 11), carried out this fine tradition of practical research well into the 1930s.

[1]SREB, "Summary of the Symposium on Rural Social Work held in New Orleans, LA, October 30, 1971," in *Educating Social Workers for Practice in Rural Settings: Perspectives and Programs* (Atlanta: Southern Regional Education Board, July 1974), p. 4.

[2]Lowry Nelson, *Rural Sociology: Its Origin and Growth in the United States* (Minneapolis: University of Minnesota Press, 1969), p. 47.

RECREATION AND THE COUNTRY CHURCH

Fred Eastman

For a long time the attitude of the church toward recreation has been
much like that of the good Puritan father who had tasted his first
spoonful of ice cream. Pushing the dish away from him he said, "Anything that tastes as good as that must be of the Devil."

But the church is getting a broader vision; it is coming to see
that whatever makes a man a better man is a holy thing and a possible
instrument for its use. It is coming to see too that recreation is
a universal need, physical and moral. All work and no play makes
Jack a dull boy, and it makes him hate farming.

Now the economic changes of the last few years have played havoc
with old-time recreations. The quilting and husking bees, the log-
rollings and the barn-raisings—these have passed with the passing
of the settled population and now new forms of play have taken their
place. The recreations of the average young person in the country
today consist in an occasional baseball game, often played on Sunday,
two or three dances a year, an oyster supper, a strawberry festival,
and the picnic. The first two are offered for money. In fact, they
are offered more for the sake of filling the church's pockets than
for meeting the need of the people. It is hard to tell where the
church would be today if it were not for the oyster and the strawberry. They have saved many a church from the financial scrap heap.

"What," says Old Moses Breeze, "would you think of a bank that had
to give an oyster supper once a month to pay its cashier?" From a
business standpoint, let us not condemn the supper until we can offer
something better. From 50 to 60 per cent of rural churches now make
ends meet in this way.

Some churches, however, have made decided advances over the commercialized forms of recreation. The famous country church near Plainfield, Ill., has a singing school, baseball team, lecture courses,
and community holidays.   The pastor of the village church at Caze-
novia, N.Y., organized a Sunday school during a barn dance, with the
good will of all the people. "And because," he says, "on Tuesday I
had taken the people where I found them, they found me where I
preached on Sunday." This man has introduced into his church the
celebration of holidays for agricultural exhibits and field sports
for the young.

Survey, 18 October 1913. Fred Eastman was associated with the Matine-
cock Neighborhood Association of Locust Valley, New York.

Eighty miles from Pittsburgh, among the Slavs and Bohemians who labor in the coal mines and around the coke ovens, a country pastor who has a circuit of four churches has built near one of them a Neighborhood House, a two-story frame structure 42 by 72 feet. The lower floor has a gymnasium, bath rooms, dressing rooms, and steam heating apparatus; the upper floor is the auditorium. The pastor calls it his "melting pot." It is where Slavs and Bohemians and Americans are being melted together in Christian citizenship. Four miles from this Neighborhood House the same pastor has just finished a similar building. Toward its construction the Friel Coal Company has given $1,200 in materials and labor, not as charity, but "because," it says, "such work makes for a stable and industrious population."

In Wisconsin a country pastor, who was once half-back on the Wisconsin team, until recently had a football team among his young men, and no one rooted louder on game days than he, in spite of the earnest prayers of some of his elders that "their pastor be a more spiritual man." In the village of Redwood Falls, Minn., a church has three boys' clubs which are Sunday school classes on Sunday and baseball, hockey and skeeing teams through the week. One of these clubs numbers twenty-four and is led by the proprietor of the motion picture show of the village. These classes have monthly socials and weekly club meetings. They are recreation organizations where the boys are learning the principles of co-operation, fair play, and sportsmanship.

It is the unanimous testimony of these churches that are trying to furnish uncommercialized recreation to their communities that the results have been gratifying to the communities and the churches. It enlivens the people, and a live church was never built among a sluggish people. It makes a point of contact with the outsider, the tenant farmer, and the stranger. It gets the people into the habit of coming to church for something besides funerals, preaching services, and temperance orations. Best of all, it meets a need of the people.

FARMER SMITH AND THE COUNTRY CHURCH

Fred Eastman

Farmer Smith needs help. He needs it here and now. He is trying to
keep his family supplied with food and clothes. He is struggling to
give his children an education and at the same time to pay off the
mortgage on the farm and to save enough to keep his wife and himself
from want in their old age. All around him are those who are waging
the same battle, but they give him little help. Each one fights
alone, as his father did before him.

Twelve years ago Farmer Smith had a $5,000 farm. It yielded him
an income of about $500. That was a return of ten per cent. Today,
because of the general rise in land values, that farm is worth
$10,000. It yields him about $700. It is now only a 7 per cent investment. His profits have decreased. Moreover, his land is poorer
than it was twelve years ago. Smith never learned how to farm in-
tensively. He knows only the crude methods used by his father in
the days of virgin soil. The years ahead give him no promise that
he will be able to make even as much from his farm as he is making
now. The economic pinch has left its marks upon his social life.
Many of his old neighbors have sold their farms in the hands of tenants who are robbing the land of its fertility. Community spirit
has vanished. The old forms of recreation have lapsed with the
passing of the settled population. No new forms have taken their
place except in the towns, and these are usually of a character that
would not be tolerated in the country. Smith's boy is waiting his
first opportunity to get off the farm. His has been a life of all
work and no play, and while it has not exactly made him a dull boy,
it has made him hate farming. Smith's wife is leading the life of
a drudge, and she swears her daughters are not going to live on the
farm if she can help it. With the stagnation in social life has
come stagnation in moral and religious life, for morals do not flourish in a stagnant community.

Yes, Smith needs help. He needs to know how to farm more scientifically. He needs a better income. He needs to know how to organize
with his fellow farmers to protect themselves against the inroads
of the middlemen and the tenants. He needs better markets for
his crops and better transportation facilities to those markets.
He needs a school for his children that will give them as good an
education as they would get in any city school, a school that will

Survey, 17 May 1913.

instill in them a love of the country, a knowledge of farming and an appreciation of its economic significance. He needs more recreation facilities for the whole family. He needs a handier kitchen for his wife and daughter and many more opportunities for them to broaden their lives and enrich their minds in literary and social activities.

The question is, Should the church give it? Should it go to Farmer Smith and say:

"Smith, I am a bit ashamed of myself: I have not been doing for you what I ought. I have been preaching about Elysian fields and allowing the riches of bluegrass, corn, and wheat fields to be squandered with prodigal hand; I have been trying to pave your road to glory land, but I have paid no attention to your road to the nearest market; I have talked about mansions in the skies and cared little about the buildings in which you and your family must spend your lives here and now; I have been teaching your children God's word in the Bible, but I have left his word in the rivers and the hills, in the grass and the trees, without prophet, witness, or defender.

"Forgive me, Smith; I am not going to do it anymore. I am going to take an interest in your every day affairs—your crops, your stock, your markets, your school, your lodge and your recreations. I am going to see if I can help you in your effort to get your boy started on a farm of his own. I've preached a long time against Sunday baseball; now I'm going to try to give your children so much recreation through the week that they won't care for it on Sunday. I am going to take as one of the articles of my creed, 'I believe in better roads for Smith, and I propose to have them.' I am going to try to save you and your family not only for Paradise, but for America and American farms."

Should the country church take its place shoulder to shoulder with Smith in the line in which he is battling for existence? Should it take up the task of encouraging agricultural organizations that will work for more scientific farming, better roads and better markets? Should it throw open its doors, not three hours a week but three hours a day to Smith's sons and daughters that they may have a place to meet and to play and to mingle with each other in literary, athletic and social activities? Should the church forget all about itself and its creedal and polemic differences? Should it forget its own salvation in its effort to save Smith? Should it lose itself in his service, even if some churches have to die in the attempt, as long ago their Master died? Should it?

THE RURAL CHURCH

In some great day
    The Country Church
    Will find its voice
And it will say:

    "I stand in the fields
    Where the wide earth yields
        Her bounties of fruit and grain;
    Where the furrows turn
    Till the plowshares burn
        As they come round and round again;
    Where the workers pray
    With their tools all day
        In sunshine and shadow and rain.

    "And I bid them tell
    Of the crops they sell
        And speak of the work they have done;
    I speed every man
    In his hope and plan
        And follow his day with the sun;
    And grasses and trees,
    The birds and the bees
        I know and feel ev'ry one.

    "And out of it all
    As the seasons fall
        I build my great temple alway;
    I point to the skies,
    But my footstone lies
        In commonplace work of the day;
    For I preach the worth
    Of the native earth—
        To love and to work is to pray."

        Liberty H. Bailey in *Rural Manhood*.

THE INSTITUTIONAL CHURCH FOR THE RURAL COMMUNITY

Harry Deiman

For years the city has boasted of its "institutional" church. At first it met the criticism of other Christian organizations. This criticism was due to ignorance of the fine nature of this new type of church work, or the incapacity to sense the varying needs of a densely populated community. Institutional churches, nevertheless, did much good and helped adjust the religious world to new situations brought on by the expansion of commerce, the new industrial order and the congestion of population in manufacturing and business centers.

The necessity that called them forth, however, was soon met increasingly by other agencies. The spirit of community service spread and the local government has been led to assume many of these social functions undertaken by private or religious organizations. The institutional church differed from others not so much in spirit or in any change of theological interpretation, but rather by extending and adjusting its work more completely to the concrete needs of the people. In so doing it only gave expression of Christ-like love in terms of practical service. It applied Christianity practically to personal and community needs.

We are confronted in the country at present with needs that are just as urgent as were ever faced by a city, and the rural church organizations, as they at present exist, are often as inadequate as the older type of city church organization often proved to be. We need in the country a church organization that shall at once take cognizance of the actual state of affairs and be willing to perform many tasks to which it has heretofore been totally unaccustomed. The church of the country must not be satisfied with a gospel of personal salvation, but must be filled with the passion of vitalizing the life of the entire country-side with ideals that do justice to our social Christianity. It must be willing to inspire men and institutions with a zeal to make such adjustments of policy and aim as shall make them factors for the betterment of the community. The church must so energize rural life that it may keep pace with our advancing civilization. It is the purpose of this article to suggest the character of the rural institutional church and the specific steps to accomplish its social mission.

Survey, 24 May 1913. Harry Deiman was a fellow in Rural Sociology at the Chicago Theological Seminary.

We have become aware of a situation in many of our rural districts startling to many who have rested under the assumption that the country districts were inhabited by sturdy Christian men and women without problems and somehow absolved from making adjustments in a civilization that is constantly undergoing change. The country-side, as surely as the great cities, has undergone radical transformations. While the growth of large cities, the shifting of population and the changes in the industrial and educational requirements of our life were setting in, our country people for the most part held to their conservatism, cherished their old institutions and looked with pride upon their customs and traditions. Many of the most capable men and women were drawn from the country to the cities by the enchanting calls of industry and commerce. Advancing educational ideals, quickening religious interests and the adoption of scientific methods of business left the country comparatively untouched. Failing to keep pace with the advance of the nation as a whole, and in some respects deteriorating, we do not wonder that it now presents a problem.

Frederick C. Howe says that a rural civilization which has been in the process of formation since the fall of the Roman Empire has been destroyed by the industrial development and preponderant growth of the cities. George A. Russell takes a slightly different attitude, but comes to the same conclusion. At the annual general meeting of the Irish Agricultural Organization Society held in December, 1909, he delivered an address entitled The Building of a Rural Civilization. We quote from the address:

> Outside the cities there have always been the same country-sides of little homes, the same neglect of culture, the same want of education, the lack of organized intellectual, political and economic power which set up a barrier between the country man and his access to the finer things of life.
>
> We hear the cry "back to the land" continually, but for one who goes back a thousand go away. The miracle to be wrought is the creation of a rural civilization. Civilization implies some measure of comfort and luxury. It can only be attained when the community is organized and has strength to retain some surplus of wealth beyond what is required for the bare necessities of life. The organized industries and the organized communities are always wresting any surplus from the unorganized. The business mind of the country must be organized to counter the business mind of the town.

So the task that faces the country church is no less a task than the rebuilding of an entirely new rural civilization able to promote its own interests and properly support its own burden in an expanding national life.

The most pressing need of this new church for the country is a minister who understands the situation to which his predecessors have

been blind. He must be a man who has vision to see the immediate
needs and is capable of relating these needs to the progressive movements of the nation. Not only must he have consecration, devotion
and religious fervor, but an inclusive objective view which will enable him to determine the exact status of his people in relation to
life as a whole.

We would never consider the captain of a sea-going vessel competent
if he knew only his ship thoroughly. The captain must be able to
determine longitude and latitude, his position at any moment of the
day or night, the dangers that may possibly be encountered and the
destination of the ship. In addition, he must be able to inspire
those under him with confidence, to secure their obedience, and direct
the vessel as he desires. So our country minister must have not only
knowledge of the immediate local situation, but also must be a man
of nation-wide vision, in order to be able in some degree to determine the position of his people, politically, economically and socially. Thus only can he have such a command of facts as to be able to
give his people confidence that he can lead them to more worthy attainments in harmony with the best tendencies of the time.

The greatest need which is now facing the country is for the development of a social morality. The farmer is mentally constituted to
be a thorough-going individualist. From the first settlement of the
soil it has been necessary for him to survive and succeed through
his own initiative and by his own strength. His dwelling has been a
comparatively isolated farmhouse. Only occasionally does he see
much of other people. Those who cannot endure such a life retreat
to the cities. Others retire within themselves and their family
circle. So social morality developed in the city. There people are
forced to consider one another because they are dependent upon each
other. But this consideration is shown least and last toward the
rural people, upon whom the city dwellers do not hesitate to prey.

Many inventions, however, have promoted the social spirit in the
country. People have been brought more closely together by the rail,
the telephone and rural delivery. Specialized and scientific farming encourages and almost compels the farmer to meet and confer with
other men. Thus the social spirit is more and more becoming the
atmosphere of rural life and labor.

Although the farmer is thus ripening for this change in his mental
attitude, he is nevertheless conservative and clings tenaciously to
the past. He needs education and guidance along social lines, in
order to do his duty and achieve his legitimate success.

Religion is surcharged with social impulses and motives. The
Christian religion was founded upon a fellowship of plain men with
the Son of Man. It grew to supersede all other forms of faith in

the Roman Empire because of its founder's ideals of brotherhood and
of a saved society. It has of late received a new birth. The church
of the social ideal in the country is in a position to work miracles
in the transformation of the rural mind.

The social regeneration of the country is the opportunity of the
church. Its minister must preach and teach a social morality. He
must make the farmer sensitive to the interests of those whom he does
not see, as well as those of his neighbor. One farmer is reported
to have refused to sell milk to his neighbors because he was suspicious of its quality, but disposed of it to city consumers without
any qualms of conscience over the sickness and death it might produce.
The kind-hearted farmer must have his natural sympathy tinged with
an imagination unusual to him. He must have a spiritual basis to
enable him to co-operate with his fellow men for industrial and political progress. Never before have so many people been dependent upon
the farmer for their daily bread. The farmer must produce more and
get better distribution for his products. Our schools of agriculture
are teaching him to produce more, but only when the farmers attain
the spirit of co-operation among each other and cease to distrust
their fellow men in the cities will any solution be found for the
waste in distribution due to inadequate business organization.

Farmers must learn to co-operate politically. The prejudices of
intense partisanship and personal antagonism are paralyzing forces.
There must be a class interest among farmers, however, in order to
take concerted action for the protection and advancement of their
legitimate interests. But this involves the advance of the whole
farming community. The stronger farmers have too little concern for
those who are unsuccessful. The spirit of sacrificial service must
be born into the life of the strong. The strong must share with the
weak the vision of a regenerated country life, and the realization
of that ideal should be the religious passion of every country-side.

The institutional church should supply a place for the discussion
of public questions. The country store has been a valuable forum.
President Wilson has attributed the debating powers of western public
men to the interest in politics and the practice in discussion promoted by the country store debates. But a better forum is needed,
which shall be conducted at stated intervals and shall be guided by
parliamentary procedure. The discipline and stimulus furnished by
participation in deliberative assemblies can not be overestimated.

Prof. Edward A. Ross maintains that the success of parliamentary
government in Anglo-Saxon countries, over that of other European
lands, is due to parliamentary procedure. It does away with personalities. It lessens friction. It gives time for fair discussion
and for arriving at judicial decisions. Those taking part in debate

under such regulative restraints learn to be cool headed, to respect their opponents, to detach themselves from personal fears and address themselves to the question at hand. The farmer needs this discipline. Our farmer legislators rarely demonstrate their strength and usefulness because they lack this training. If our rural life is to be regenerated it must be a redemption from within.

The country church can furnish the means and opportunity for this self-development. Its minister should be foremost in prompting it. He should be familiar with rural issues both in his own locality and throughout the whole country. He should know how the issues of state and nation will affect his people and their interests. Commercial associations in the cities are alive to every influence which legislation and public policy exert upon their constituents. Our farmers are too often dependent upon politicians who, to retrieve their waning fortunes, champion those who have found no other voice through which to appeal. If the church is to become an agency for the formation of vigorous opinions upon pressing issues it must bring them to bear upon local needs. Interest in public policies and social movements elsewhere often becomes indifference and hostility when application is made to local interests and surroundings.

The rural church must find young men capable of being inspired with the opportunities for leadership in the country. Such leaders can do much to retain in rural communities those temperamentally fitted for life and labor. The country pastor, moreover, should promote efficiency among the young people of his community. The country church should also give the country a fair hearing for its own youth. Something more than scientific farming must be shown to be necessary. The country youth should be made to see that social and political efficiency is as necessary to the welfare of the community as scientific farming. We need country social workers, editors, lawyers, ministers and most of all teachers to lead the way from bondage to freedom. Leaders who spring from the soil can best raise the standards of country life.

To help determine the normal standard of living for a rural community is another great mission of the country church. To assume that country life is exceptionally healthful and sanitary is a most mischievous assumption. Country dwellings are generally poorly ventilated, insufficiently heated and badly lighted. Country food is generally wholesome, but the cultivation of the garden and orchard for variety of diet is often neglected. Contagious or infectious diseases are frequently considered natural or unavoidable and are allowed to pass unchallenged. If the same percentage of deaths occurred in the city, inquiry into the cause of it would be demanded and those responsible would be held to account. Rest, recreation and the hours of work are ignored or forbidden topics. Children are assigned to tasks too heavy and prolonged for their welfare.

More accurate information on these vital human interests needs to be acquired and disseminated among country people. Local pride should be stimulated and careful plans made for the direction of all activities of country life. The church should be the prime mover in this stimulation and planning. It should broaden its function and method to meet these needs. It should be a pioneer in attempting these new tasks and in grappling with these old problems. It should co-operate with all existing organizations, giving its strength and support to those needing its help and getting help from those who can give it. The "institutional" church in the country is really the church whose functions and methods are defined by the manifest needs of the country community.

RURAL ADVANCE

Kenyon L. Butterfield

The new rural awakening is upon us. New plans are developing. There are new visions of a revivified community life in our rural neighbor-hoods. There is a keen eagerness in all rural welfare work. The forces of the countryside are gathering for a great forward-looking movement. What shall the New Year bring us in our country-life campaign? What shall be the chief notes of our rural campaign slo-gan for 1914?

It is to be remembered that the fundamental task of the rural ad-vance is local rural community building—the gradual erection of stronger community units, founded on better farm practice, securing a fair profit through better farm business, and growing mightily

Survey, 27 December 1913. Kenyon Leech Butterfield was President of the Massachusetts Agricultural College (1906-1924) and of Michi-gan State College (1924-1928). He was also associated with the International Missionary Council.

ambitious for a better farm life. How can this fundamental rural
task best be forwarded in 1914?

First, organize local community campaigns in as many neighborhoods
as possible. Seek the formation of a community council or federation,
made up of representatives of all the organizations in the neighborhood that have any interest in the common good—church, grange,
women's club, farmers' club, civic improvement society, etc.

But do not make the mistake of coming together merely for the pleasure of it. Seek to discover the needs of the neighborhood that
perchance may be met by the organized forces of the neighborhood itself. Endeavor to make an intelligent plan of operations for improving the community in all needful respects.

Second, seek to develop the collective or co-operative method of
doing the business of the farm. Farmers can save money by cooperative buying of supplies needed on the farm. It is possible that they
can make a larger profit by selling their products in the same co-
operative manner. The cooperative plan is spreading. It should not
be entered upon hastily, but it promises to render more help to the
farmer than does perhaps any other one thing.

Third, push the idea of an agricultural high school or an agricultural department in the public high school. Farming demands educated
men and women. The agricultural colleges, neither in the class room
nor in their extension services, can meet the full need. Every boy
or girl desiring the equivalent of a good high school education in
and for agriculture should have the opportunity of acquiring that
training.

Fourth, join in the demand for the passage by Congress of the Lever
bill appropriating federal money to the several agricultural colleges
for extension work in agriculture and home economics. This means
the democratizing of agricultural education the nation over. It
means that the best knowledge gained in agricultural research will be
placed at the disposal of the humblest farmer; that a great educational campaign for better farming in all its aspects will be carried
into every farming community.

This bill, if enacted into law, promises not only a distinct advance in the agricultural educational field, but indeed a national
intellectual uplift of great proportions and significance.

Fifth, strive for at least preliminary steps to bring together on
a national basis the various agencies that are seeking rural welfare.
This is merely the nationalizing of the plan for local rural community building. The many activities and institutions engaged in promoting agriculture should be correlated. The country life movement
should be integrated. We should look upon the rural problem as a

unit. We should try to solve it on large lines and with solidified
endeavor.

Sixth, above all perhaps, try to stir religious forces to new
effort in the rural field. The country church faces a crisis. Rural
advance is leaving the church behind. But the rural movement must
not become materialistic. It can easily be spiritualized. It needs
the leadership of that institution that stands supremely for the
great ideals of love and brotherhood and service. The rural Sunday
school, the rural YMCA and YWCA should be encouraged and strengthened
everywhere. We need their point of view and above all we need their
ideals of character building and of community building.

So may the New Year set a new standard in all rural life endeavor.

II

World War I, the Postwar Years,
and the Regionalization of
Rural Services, 1917-1927

4

The Home Service of
the American Red Cross

In 1917, the United States entered World War I. The war became a
central national concern and rural welfare activities were affected
by wartime organization. The Home Service of the American Red Cross,
which had been created to serve soldiers' families, was a significant force in developing a regional approach to social service delivery in the interior of the country. Even during the war years,
the Home Service had extended its scope to cover civilian families.
After the war, those extended services became their main function.
Many of the names associated with the Home Service of the Red Cross
—Jesse Steiner, Henrietta Lund, Josephine Brown—continued to be
leading national figures in rural social work for many years.

The articles included in this chapter are illustrative of Home
Service activities. "Home Service in One Rural County" by W. Frank
Persons discusses the development of Home Service outreach. In
"Home Service and Civilian Charities," Anna King asks whether the
Home Service would be useful for peace as well as war and in so doing introduces, much ahead of their time, two important notions for
the reader's consideration: relief as an entitlement of servicemen
and civilians; and the shortcomings of the popular family casework
agency.

"Training for Home Service" is a brief news report which suggests
the idea of utilizing the agricultural colleges as "natural resources
for training rural workers," a concept which recurred frequently
enough in later years. The diagram entitled "Extension of Home
Service" shows the broad geographical areas to which its influence
had extended during the war. It also shows the beginning efforts
toward expansion after the war years.

The news report by Neva R. Deardoff, "Red Cross Home Service:
1919," illustrates the efforts to adjust programs so that they might
meet local community needs, and "A Morning of Home Service" exempli-

fies the locality-specific flavor of services in a remote Louisiana parish of the Gulf Division.

Finally, the Southern mood is captured in "The Red Cross Volunteer," a profile which was included in a special "Feature Story on the South and the New Citizenship," published by the *Survey* in anticipation of the 1929 National Conference on Social Work held in New Orleans.

HOME SERVICE IN ONE RURAL COUNTY

W. Frank Persons

What a group of untrained volunteers did in developing Home Service for the Red Cross in a territory innocent of social agencies is told in the following report from the secretary of a Home Service section in the northeastern part of the United States. Although this report is unusual in some respects, it illustrates the way in which people in smaller cities and towns all over the country are arising to the new responsibilities that Home Service puts upon them:

The Y———county chapter of the American Red Cross has jurisdiction over the entire county of 2,880 square miles (half the size of Connecticut), having a population of 90,000. This territory is made up of one city of 14,000 inhabitants, four villages of from 3,000 to 5,000, numerous smaller villages, much open country, woods and mountains. The county is mainly a dairy county, the chief industries including butter and cheese making and milk condensing. There is some lumbering also, with its accompanying pulp and paper mills, as well as furniture manufacturing. The one large exotic industry is a manufacturing plant employing 3,000 men, representing fifty-one nationalities. There is in the population an element of French-Canadians, but the majority are of Yankee stock. The winters are

Survey, 29 June 1918. W. Frank Persons was Director General of Civilian Relief of the American Red Cross.

long and severe. From Thanksgiving to April the ground is covered
with snow. Train accommodations last winter were very bad, the snow
drifting so that often even mail did not reach outside communities
for two or three days.

The Red Cross chapter has an executive committee chosen from the
county at large. At the time of organization a branch was formed in
the city and in each of the four larger towns. The territory of the
entire county was divided among these five branches. They have at
present forty-five auxiliaries. The chapter retains from the membership fees only a small percentage for administrative expenses, and
the balance goes back to the branches and their auxiliaries. The
branch does its own buying, shipping and financing. All the workers
are volunteers. There is not even a paid stenographer. The workers
are not even people of leisure but are professional and business men,
business women and housewives, who give of their spare time simply
because they think they ought.

The Home Service section consists at present of a chairman and myself, both appointed by the executive committee of the chapter. The
chairman can not give me a regular day or time for conferences so I
handle all the business and call upon him for advice when necessary.
He takes care of general newspaper notices, form letters, policies,
and whatever I wish to refer to him for decision. The fact that he
is both a lawyer and a good business man has helped our work. I
carry on the correspondence with the branches, take care of systems
and reports, and try to keep all the branches informed about such
work as must be done immediately. We are now holding monthly meetings with the chairmen of the branches, but this was impossible during the season when automobiles could not be used, as our branches
are from fifteen to thirty miles from the most centrally located
town, and train accommodations are very bad. It is possible for the
secretary or chairman to get to the branch occasionally. Aside from
that we carry on all business by correspondence and telephone.

Each branch has a Home Service section composed of a chairman,
secretary, and two or more visitors. It has charge of all the Home
Service work in the territory assigned to the branch, and receives
a fund from the branch treasury. The entire responsibility for
handling cases rests with the branch, except in the cases forwarded
from outside sources such as the Canadian Patriotic Fund.

To get in touch with the families of the eight hundred or more men
already enlisted from the county is a difficult task. The chapter
chairman published in nine county papers a letter calling attention
to the allowances due relatives under the war risk insurance law and
offering the help of the Red Cross in explaining the law and making
out application papers. The addresses of the Home Service secre-

taries of the branches were in this article. To supplement this
general advertising the chapter printed circular letters giving the
same information. These were sent to the families as fast as they
were located.

The Home Service secretaries of the branches cooperated with me in
preparing the lists of men. The secretaries living in the towns
where the exemption boards are located procured complete lists of
the drafted men and the villages from which they came. Lists of
those who enlisted at the regular recruiting stations in the county
were obtained in the same way. These names I divided according to
branches, sending a list to each branch with a request that it add
the names of other volunteers. Three branches are completing the
lists by having a village paper publish a Town Roll. The addresses
of the men are obtained in any way possible. Some the exemption
boards supplied. In one branch, at a weekly section meeting, the
members filled in all the addresses they knew and divided the rest
of the names among themselves to be hunted up—not an impossible
task in a village of 3,000.

Actual work for Home Service has so far been concerned mainly with
problems arising under the war risk insurance law. While few families are actually suffering for money, many are being greatly in-
convenienced and want to know why their allowances do not come. Some
allowances, of course, have come, and the Red Cross has helped to
get some of these cashed. Assistance has been rendered, also, to
wives who are worried in making applications in the proper way. In a
village, where a branch worker can oversee the securing of affidavits, the preparing of an application is an afternoon's task; and we
have found that when the wife lives in the country and the work has
to be done by correspondence with an auxiliary, ten days is often
required to obtain a correctly prepared application. Our chairman
prepared two sample affidavits. Each application goes out accompanied by these, ready to be filled in and sworn to before a notary.
We have asked that each application be sent to the county chairman
of Home Service for forwarding to Washington. In this way we try
to prevent loss of time and unnecessary annoyance at Washington.

Many mothers getting allotments from sons wish to know if they are
entitled to government allowances in addition. For our work with
them Judge Mack's explanation of the law (Bulletin 3, Treasury Department) has proved invaluable. Those now receiving more from the
allotment than the son ever gave them before are satisfied when told
that they are entitled to no more under the law; they simply want
to be sure that they are getting their due. When it is difficult
to tell whether the mother is entitled to more than she is getting
—and this is the most frequent case, for the boys live at home and

give the mother an irregular amount each month, covering their share
of food and lodging--we explain the con[tribution scheme carefully
and . . . ed.] we advise her to urge her son to get advice from his
captain before asking for an allowance for her.

In only one instance has a case under this law been referred to us
from outside. The State Council of Defense notified the Red Cross
that the governor had received a letter from a mother who said that
the government had taken her three sons and left her to starve and
freeze; she had received not a penny since they left, she said. On
investigation the branch found that the woman knew about the Red
Cross but preferred to tell her anger to the governor. She was a
working-woman whose husband was an invalid, and although she was not
suffering for necessaries, the loss of the financial support of all
three sons had, of course, made it very hard for her. By the time
her letter reached the governor, allotments from two sons and an
allowance from one had arrived and she was willing to accept the cooperation of the Red Cross.

The attitude of this woman toward Home Service is unusual. Generally the mother is willing to take an allotment from her son only if
she is assured that he has left enough for his own needs. Dealing
with mothers is one of the most pleasant parts of Home Service work
because of their pride in their sons, their unselfishness and courage.

The following cases illustrate rural difficulties:

1. We were requested by the Canadian Patriotic Fund to investigate the welfare of two children of a private in the English army.
The father had left the children in the care of a sister-in-law when
he enlisted, and had written back to make sure that they were getting all the allowance they were entitled to. The M_____ Branch
found a doctor who knew the family with which the children were
living. The children's aunt (their mother was dead) lived with her
husband on a farm four or five miles from the branch. At the time
the letter came automobiles could not be used. The aunt and her
husband were tenants; the doctor knew the partner of their landlord;
he telephoned this partner and from him learned that the man had
the house, garden, firewood, and $35 in cash. (The woman and her
husband were already receiving $35 a month for the care of the
children--$20 separation allowance and $15 assigned pay.) The request, it was clear, had come from the father and not from the
children's aunt and uncle. The committee therefore recommended
that since the children added nothing to the expenses of the uncle
and aunt for rent, light and fuel, since the only cost of educating
them was school text-books, since the uncle as a farm hand received

his food at a very low price, the thirty-five dollars was sufficient and the patriotic fund should not be asked for more.

2. A grandmother thought that she was to receive five dollars a month board for the two grandchildren she took into her home when the father was drafted. At the end of three months she traveled thirty miles to see a lawyer about collecting it. The lawyer referred her to the Home Service section. She went home and wrote a letter to the secretary. In this she explained that she had been promised five dollars a month for board for each of her grandchildren when her son broke up his home to go to camp; that she had taken care of them and of the mother, when the mother was out of work, and she wanted her pay. Unless she got it she would take care of them no more.

We tried to find out what the woman meant by the promise of $5 a month for board. I suppose she had seen our advertisement about five dollars a month government allowance for each additional child and our purpose to see if mothers were getting their proper allowances from the government. The mother was entitled to $47.50. I sent her an application blank and two affidavits ready to be filled in and signed before an attorney, if she wished to make application. Her husband had never supported her entirely. The next day the woman both wrote and telephoned that she had the day before received a first check for $47.50 from the government. The secretary reported that she thought the mother would now pay the grandmother for caring for the children.

3. A woman appeared at my door with a much worn allotment paper. She wanted to know if I paid the allotments. She had been waiting a long time, she said, and needed the money. Her son, she said, gave her an allotment of $15 and the government an allowance of $10. This had come only once, however. The husband worked and the oldest of the five children left at home worked. A still older child, her sixth, had enlisted and they had been able to get along without his help until this week. Now the boy who worked had been injured in the paper mill. They had depended upon his pay to meet the overdue rent. I asked about compensation. It was not time for that. Moreover, she feared she would get none as the boy was working on a machine which the child labor law forbade his using at sixteen. Also, the boy was not getting well. The leg had been splintered and an X-ray must be taken before the leg could be set. This was the fifth day and the X-ray had not been taken. The company doctor was to have seen to the matter the day before but had been called into the country on another case. The nearest hospital is thirty miles away and only when a case is too severe for the operating room of the local surgeon is it sent to the hospital. The doctor had been angry

because she had gone to his office the day before with complaints that the bone had not been set. The neighbors were urging her to sue the company for putting her son on a prohibited machine, but "what chance had a poor woman against a rich company?"

The two immediate needs seemed to be to satisfy the landlord who threatened to eject them, and to see that the boy had immediate medical treatment. I advised her to see the owner of the house (she had been dealing with the husband who acted as collector), show her the allotment paper and tell her that the Red Cross had told her it might be twenty-four hours and it might be a month before she received her next instalment of pay. I knew the owner; she is born stingy and hardhearted; moreover, she is very ignorant. But I thought a message from the Red Cross that the seventy-five dollars due from her tenant would come some time might influence her to wait a while longer. I assured the woman that the Red Cross would interview her landlord if she failed to get more time. She was to notify me if the woman refused to wait for the rent, or if the doctor did not set the boy's leg before night. She promised to let the Red Cross try to settle the case with the corporation responsible for her boy's injury, rather than put it in the hands of a lawyer. It is too soon to hear from her yet on the legal matter and I have not seen the visitor to whom the case was assigned by the branch, but the relief of the woman at learning that the Red Cross would help her through her difficulties showed how much just having somebody to consult means to many of the families of soldiers who can manage all right for themselves until something out of the ordinary happens.

The sectional Home Service conference was for me a turning point in my attitude. At the conference I obtained not only a vast amount of new information and many warnings of mistakes not to make, but for the first time an understanding of the *spirit* of the work. I saw also others who were as uncertain as I, and I came home with more courage to go ahead. The opportunity to meet and talk to the director from division headquarters was also a decided benefit. It is always easier to understand instructions if you are acquainted with the writer. I took notes on the fifty-one questions that were the basis of discussion and sent a copy of the questions and my notes to each branch, on my return. Several branches have already developed ideas suggested there. So often since my return has something at the convention influenced my decision that I am beginning to feel that I preface my remarks by, "At the convention," like the woman who has been to Europe once on a three-months' tour and always begins, "When I was abroad."

HOME SERVICE AND CIVILIAN CHARITIES

Anna King

Not many years before the war began, case-work had begun to realize
the strength of a new ally in giving constructive service and in
broadening the public understanding of its principles—medical social
work. The medical social worker has a happy introduction to the
home and can learn incidentally of the broken family ties or economic
tangles which more frequently form the less welcome introduction of
the charity organization worker. This new form of case-work, often
reaching out to the whole family, had already before the war shown
the great ease with which it could recruit volunteers, and had thrown
into stronger relief the frequent shrinking from the "relief approach"
or the "family rehabilitation approach" to social service. Yet medical work is a specialized form of social service, because when the
health problem is met, if a relief problem also is involved the
family must be transferred to another agency.

With the war came Red Cross Home Service, whose "approach"—conserving the homes of the men who are in service—is as appealing as
healing the sick; whose opportunity for service is as extensive as
that of the charity organization society; whose clientele, because
of the draft, is more broadly representative than that ever known to
a social agency before. Home Service has also the great advantage
over every other agency of being in the position to discharge an
obligation incurred instead of placing its client in the position of
a debtor. It has been happily said that "Every man who enters the
service has paid his family membership dues in the Red Cross Home
Service Section." In the window of almost every home where the
Home Service visitor calls there is the Red Cross sign which the
family translates to mean, "Not Charity (word of hapless fate in
spite of such noble ancestry!) but Humanity." Home Service has the
opportunity to give every service that the civilian agencies have
sought to give, and Home Service is trusted by the public because
the Red Cross is financed by money raised from the general public
and because it has on its various committees representatives of the
various groups of public interests.

And now, just as our Home Service teams are beginning to play
steadily, the war seems to be over, and we ask, Is Home Service use-

Survey, 26 April 1919. Anna King was Executive Secretary, Home Service Section of the Boston Metropolitan Chapter of the American Red
Cross.

ful for peace as well as for war, or shall it be discharged from public service like the Students Army Training Corps, to be called out only if there is another war? The answer we hear is that there is to be a Red Cross Home Service program for the future, that it is to be based on "self-determination," and that the chances are good that Home Service may continue and expand in cities and towns having no family social agencies, while in places where there are other agencies, Home Service will continue only long enough to "finish the war job."

But what does finishing the war job mean? What of the sensitive young woman who was slow to give her confidence to the Red Cross visitor, and who now confides that "W___ used to do this before he went to war, but I hoped he'd be better when he got back; but here he's gone again, and I can't work now as I used to—with the baby coming." Is this a part of finishing the war task, or should this girl now have the additional burden of feeling she must turn to another society—just as eager to serve truly, but to the girl's mind labelling her as belonging among the unfortunate? Isn't there danger of jeopardizing the civilian agencies' chances for usefulness if such unwilling applicants are thrust upon them?

How long will the sentiment demanding special treatment for the ex-soldier and sailor last? The Red Cross Home Service is recognized by the affiliated war organizations as the suitable agent to serve soldiers' and sailors' families. The regimental auxiliaries have cooperated with the Red Cross. Recently various leagues of veterans are being formed. Can all these war organizations, which apparently plan to continue and perhaps expand, be expected to refer a soldier or his wife or mother to a civilian charity?

What of the town where one group of charities does not care to register in a social service exchange run by a society whose board of directors represents chiefly one element in the community, but where both organizations come to the Red Cross Home Service visitor to consult regarding their respective families? Will this situation be helped by demobilizing the Red Cross? Is there not a permanent service of coordinating the social agencies of this community? Are not cities with this or some similar problem more numerous than we supposed in the pre-war days? Such a situation as this suggests that social workers had idealized what had been achieved by the family case-work agency; that often such an agency was supported only by a prominent few and was therefore not recognized or regarded with local pride by the representative many who felt they had no voice in its control, no responsibility toward raising its funds, and who consequently distrusted the use to which its power might be put.

Of course there is the danger of also idealizing Home Service. Some question whether Home Service has realized its opportunity even in war time, and none of us can tell how much of this great emotional support the Red Cross Home Service can win in peace times. Some question whether the Red Cross can continue to secure funds for Home Service. But others affirm the Red Cross can always get money— and at any rate the best way to win public support is not by curtailing activities and hoarding, but by using the money entrusted to us thoughtfully and constructively so that the results can justify our appeal when the funds run low. How backhanded it would be to try to transfer this support to a civilian agency, and how impossible of achievement those of us can imagine who have gone to families first as a "charity visitor" and later as a Red Cross worker. The name of the Red Cross insures a welcome, and no one objects when our services include analysis of budgets and consultation with teachers, as well as medical care and immediate aid, for it is recognized that we are bound not only to serve the family, but to give just account of the way we expend the funds that our clients and their neighbors have given to the Red Cross.

If, however, we suppose that the question of finishing the war job can be settled, why should the social program for the future in relation to Red Cross Home Service make a geographical rather than a functional division of service? If the civilian agencies' scheme of organization is sounder than that of the Home Service, why should not their organization be extended into the communities where they do not now exist? If, on the other hand, Red Cross Home Service has a more strategic introduction to service in a community than the other organizations and it is right that it should give service in that community, why should it not give service also in cities where there are already established family agencies?

Why must the two—Red Cross and civilian family agencies—remain absolutely unrelated? It is conceivable that somehow the good that each has to give can be pooled for all—small town and large city— and that the civilian agency's skill in organizing community service, its trained staff, its interest in local initiative, can be combined with the public goodwill, the democratic method of raising money, the broad representation and the felicitous name of the Red Cross Home Service. Where there are already established social agencies, the Red Cross might maintain certain centralized social service functions, such as the Volunteer Service Bureau and perhaps the Confidential Exchange, and serve to coordinate the activities of the various civilian case-work agencies which should themselves have representation on the Red Cross Home Service Committee, the committee confining itself to deciding broad questions of case-work policies and mutual responsibility, and leaving to the local organizations questions of detailed administration. Under this scheme a subcommittee on soldiers' and sailors' families might work out in cooperation with the other family agencies the question of continued service to the ex-soldiers' and sailors' families. The national and public character of the Red Cross makes it more nearly free from becoming the tool of narrow partisan interests than any other organization; its appeal is to all citizens, not to groups, and its local representation can be made strong enough so that it will not hamper local initiative.

Most of us have accepted in some form the idea that a league of nations is wise for the world. Should not we in social work, who are supposed to be thinking of the social future of our communities, see in this league of nations an idea to be worked out in other phases of social organization? The Red Cross is in some ways in a position analogous to that of the United States in the European council. Can it not be the leader in working out a league of social agencies?

Perhaps this is too idealistic; perhaps we are not yet ready. Perhaps the world must have more wars before the league can even be formed; perhaps the idea which Home Service has conceived—of the community joined in serving the community—must die and be born again before it can become serviceable for less emotional days than wartime. But surely it is yet too soon to decide this.

We in the Home Service are urging the returning men not to let their government insurance lapse. We agree with them that perhaps they will not be able to keep it all when it has to be converted into one of the more expensive peace-time government policies, but we explain to them that they do not have to convert for five years and that before the end of that time they will see their future plans more clearly and will be able to make a wise decision, and that if, meantime, they have let the insurance lapse or have reduced it, they can never recover what they have lost.

My plea is this: Let us do the same in our social organization. We are too near the war to make binding decisions for the future, but let us not lose our chance to decide wisely later when we shall see the facts clearly on which to base a decision. Let us not allow this venture in social service, this "war social insurance," to lapse until we are sure that civilian agencies have a community insurance as far-reaching, as widely understood and as universally subscribed to as is Red Cross Home Service.

TRAINING FOR HOME SERVICE

The question of Home Service institutes has become of special importance since the Red Cross has decided that Home Service sections
may, under certain circumstances, widen their clientele to include
any civilian family which stands in need of such service. During
the war the course had, of necessity, to be brief. Soldiers' and
sailors' families had to be served, and there was a dearth of trained
workers. For the quick training of new workers the institutes were
organized and for the same reason are now being temporarily continued.

These facts have not undermined the theories of the Red Cross as
to what constitutes good training for carrying out a peace-time
program. The general educational program of Home Service—institutes,
chapter courses, conferences, field visits—has succeeded beyond the
hopes of the most optimistic, but it has not satisfied the Red Cross
with a six weeks' training course for social workers. The training
policy is now undergoing its readjustment. From the beginning the
Red Cross has looked upon this work as a cooperative enterprise in
which appropriate educational institutions were persuaded to help
prepare people to do home service. Schools for social work lent
their aid, even at a considerable sacrifice sometimes to their regular work. Many colleges and universities gave the use of their
plants and some of the time of the members of their sociology facul-
ties. The Red Cross supplemented the teaching, procured field-work
opportunities—in which the social agencies assisted willingly—
carried the overhead expense, and recruited the students. It is now
expected to develop this cooperation with educational institutions
and in time to get it taken over entirely by them.

The six schools for social work will naturally be the first institutions asked to assume responsibility. Next come the state universities and state agricultural colleges, which are the natural resources for training rural workers, for whom there is now great
demand. It is thought that the experimental work necessary for the
development of laboratories of rural sociology in these schools is
a proper responsibility for the Red Cross and should be its contribution in the cooperative arrangement. It is expected to loan competent members of the Red Cross personnel to assist in the teaching
and to supervise the field work training. Cooperative agreements
of this nature have already been made with the following universities: Cornell, Berea College, Western Reserve, Tulane, Emory, the

Survey, 10 May 1919.

University of Cincinnati, and the state universities of Alabama, Minnesota, Kentucky, Ohio, Wisconsin, Louisiana, Kansas, Colorado, Oregon, Washington, Idaho, and Utah.

Already the training courses are being lengthened. Plans are now under way to have the minimum course cover twelve weeks with additional advanced courses covering a period of one year or more. The workers who have had only the short courses will, in peace-time, be rated accordingly. The war emergency past, higher professional standards will be set up and Home Service workers will be required to meet them.

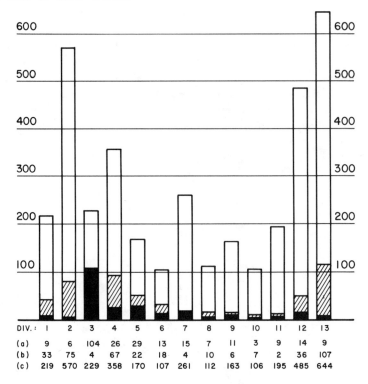

EXTENSION OF HOME SERVICE

This diagram represents for each Division of the American Red
Cross the progress which has been made in the extension of Home Service up to November 1, 1919, according to figures published in the
Red Cross Bulletin for December 1. The entire column represents the
total number of Home Service sections in the Division as they existed
last spring when the program of extension into the peace-time field
was announced. The solid black portion of the column at the bottom
shows the number of sections in which extension of activities had
been authorized up to November 1; the shaded portion just above shows
the number of additional applications for extension which were under
consideration on that date. Figures (1-13) are used under the
columns to indicate the Divisions, and the key to these figures, together with the states included in each Division, is given in the
following list. The statistics on which the diagram is based are
given below the diagram; (a) extension authorized, corresponding to
the black part of the column; (b) applications for extension under

Survey, 3 January 1920.

consideration November 1, 1919; (c) total Home Service Sections in
the Division.

1. Atlantic Division: New York, New Jersey, Connecticut.
2. Central Division: Illinois, Michigan, Wisconsin, Iowa,
Nebraska.
3. Gulf Division: Alabama, Mississippi, Louisiana.
4. Lake Division: Ohio, Indiana, Kentucky.
5. Mountain Division: Colorado, New Mexico, Wyoming, Utah.
6. New England Division: Maine, New Hampshire, Vermont, Massachusetts, Rhode Island.
7. Northern Division: Minnesota, North Dakota, South Dakota,
Montana.
8. Northwestern Division: Oregon, Washington, Idaho, Alaska.
9. Pacific Division: California, Arizona, Nevada.
10. Pennsylvania-Delaware Division: Pennsylvania, Delaware.
11. Potomac Division: Maryland, District of Columbia, Virginia,
West Virginia.
12. Southern Division: Georgia, Florida, Tennessee.
13. Southwestern Division: Missouri, Kansas, Oklahoma, Texas,
Arkansas.

RED CROSS HOME SERVICE: 1919

Neva R. Deardorff

The resignation of J. Byron Deacon on January 17, after a year's
service as director-general of the Department of Civilian Relief,
American Red Cross, to enter the field of industrial relations,
points off an interesting period. It was a year with two quite separate phases. Though in many departments of the Red Cross work could

Survey, 24 January 1920. Neva Deardorff was assistant to the general
manager of the American Red Cross during World War I; she later became Secretary of the Pennsylvania Children's Commission, President
of the Child Welfare League of America, Director of Research of the
Welfare Council of New York, and Associate Professor of Social Economy
at Bryn Mawr College. Dr. Deardorff was a recognized social welfare
statistician and member of the executive committee of the National
Conference of Social Work.

be rapidly closed out early in the year, in Home Service the obligations mounted higher as the months passed by. For January, 1919, 54 per cent of the Home Service sections reported nearly 300,000 families dealt with. In March 60 per cent of the sections reported nearly 100,000 families. In August there were 360,000 families—over twice the number that were dealt with in August, 1918, when the war was in full swing. During the remainder of the year the diminution in numbers was very gradual, reaching a figure at the end which was but slightly less than it had been in the beginning.

The experience of the Home Service sections seems to indicate that it is in the period immediately following the discharge of the man from service that the greatest number of family problems present themselves. It is thought at national headquarters that six months is a liberal allowance of time for the service man and his family to accomplish a return to civilian life. As demobilization was practically completed by the end of 1919, it is assumed that, with a few exceptions, Home Service will have fulfilled its obligations to the able-bodied man by the middle of 1920. In the case of the disabled man, doubtless more time will be required in a considerable group of cases. Likewise the Home Service carried on in the forty-five hospitals of the United States Public Health Service will doubtless be required for many months to come. The year 1919 saw, however, the great bulk of Home Service work accomplished.

The second phase of the year's work was in the sturdy growth of certain aspects of the peace program. The fact that Civilian Relief continued actively at work for a year after the end of the war served to focus attention upon the service which it was performing and to give opportunity to show its peace time applications. Two hundred and fifty-nine chapters have already extended Home Service to civilian families and some four hundred more have applied for permission to extend. (See the *Survey* for January 3.)

The war-time organization of the Red Cross, which was really a congery of departments operating in widely separated fields, was not adapted to the promotion of a well-balanced peace program in the United States. No part of the Red Cross was more aware of this than the Department of Civilian Relief. At a meeting of the division directors of civilian relief held in connection with the Conference of Social Work in Atlantic City last spring, proposals were drafted and submitted to the general management which looked toward a unification of the whole Red Cross—Health Service, Home Service, Nursing and Junior—and the concentration of its forces upon the development of "Red Cross Service." This was interpreted to mean that in any given town or county the Red Cross in a concerted effort would undertake to promote and stimulate such activities as would best serve that particular community. All that national and division headquarters had to offer in the way of help to the local community should come through one channel rather than from several loosely connected departmental sources.

A MORNING OF HOME SERVICE

One "dark, damp, cold, gloomy, dripping day" the Red Cross Home Service secretary in a Louisiana parish was ill and her sister, Bessie Sanders, volunteered to go to the office and attend to anything that needed to be done. Evidently the offer was due to a sense of duty, or a sisterly desire to set the mind of the invalid at rest, for Miss Sanders set forth looking forward to "a long, cheerless, uninteresting day." How it turned out she has told in the Gulf Division Bulletin:

Hardly had I reached the office when an alert, blue-eyed soldier came rushing in. He was so tired waiting and anxious to start his vocational training, but could do nothing unless he located his discharge paper. This he had lost some months before, and had been trying so long to recover, Could I help him? Of course I could. I was all interested and eager to fill out papers, write to different departments, etc., and the boy went out so happy.

Soon I looked up to see a timid young colored man twirling his hat. Could I, "please ma'am," tell him when he would get the allotment and allowance he had made to his wife and paid out each month while in service? Uncle Sam had overlooked his name on the long list and the wife had never received a dollar. Finding out that it was being carefully looked into he silently stole away.

I heard a brisk military step and there was a dashing, handsome soldier, "just home from the hospital"—had to come tell they had all been "dandy" to him down there and he was feeling fine. Looking at him there I began to picture him as he was a few months ago—so

Survey, 20 March 1920.

weak, miserable and dispirited. But, "Yes, ma'am, I'm well, going to get a job quick and be married." I thought of the lovely young girl from a nearby town, who had been at his bedside one day when I called. "Vocational training? No, Ma'am, a job and a job quick." When he left an hour later, he held my hand for a moment, "I'm going to think and think hard about that fitting myself for a real trade and a permanent employment for life. If Uncle Sam will do all that for me. That $115 per month, if I marry while taking vocational training, sounds good—thank you."

I looked out to see if the rain had stopped, when I heard a heavy tread and a fat old negro mammy came panting in. "For de Lawd, I done got all dat money and want to show it to you." A long-delayed allotment and allowance of $274.62 looked like a million to the delighted old woman, who went away promising not to spend it on "food eats," but to pay the note owed on her tiny home.

Hardly had her ample person gotten through the door, when a slender young chap, with a sad face, came in to tell me he was again in trouble. His mother and father had died while he was in service and now death had claimed another. With so much sickness and death he had to ask the Home Service to lend him something to help bury his tiny babe.

While fitting out the requested check, three prosperous men from a neighboring town filed in and seated themselves. Theirs was a most unusual story. One of their number had lost both parents in Italy and now a young sister there should be brought over to enjoy her brother's offered support and protection, but the Italian government said that first there must be a certificate showing that the brother here had assisted his adopted country during the late war. The military offices having been closed for a year or more, the American Red Cross was called upon to assist in this dilemma. Having heard the sad young father's thanks for the assistance in laying away his baby, two of the men said they wanted to give a donation to the Red Cross, which I accepted.

In quick succession there was a telephone message about a sick man from the lower end of the parish going to the Charity Hospital, and a man from the next town came hurriedly in to find a way to bring home a brother who, six months ago, had volunteered in the United States Marines and had been sent to the West Indies. The old father had had a stroke and wanted to see his youngest boy before the end, which the doctor said was imminent. After a rush message for a cable to be sent immediately was off hand, I looked up, saw it was time to be home for dinner and thought—not such an uninteresting, unprofitable morning's work after all.

THE RED CROSS VOLUNTEER

Joseph C. Logan

> Trust the South to lend glamor to good works—however much they
> may be cast in modern form. The G.A.M. and the D.A.S. do not
> stand for those jaw-breaking eleemosynary titles that have been
> coined so laboriously in the cities of the North; but for the
> "Good Angel of the Mountains," as the hill people of an Arkansas
> district call a nurse who "sticks" when she could so readily
> "go outside"; and for the "Darling Attribute of the South"—as
> old Mammy Rachel calls one new Red Cross secretary.

She is a Red Cross institute graduate, twenty-two years old, pretty,
bright, perhaps a little spoiled and stubborn, but the "Darling
Attribute of the South" says old Mammy Rachel. Since early in 1918
she has been secretary of a chapter in a mountain county of North
Georgia, a county from which a goodly number of people annually
attend grand opera in Atlanta, and a smaller number the enclosure
at the same place for the compulsory entertainment of illicit dis-
tillers. The county's politics are turbulent—it has gone Republi-
can—and the most famous lynching in the history of America occurred
within its bounds. Government is rather incipient. The suppression
of the social instinct is comparable only to its violence when
aroused.

She first volunteered her services. Nobody recognized the need
for any social work, even for soldiers' families. When the division
supervisor who preceded her started to work, the chairman of the
chapter felt so sorry for her idle and isolated position that he
paid a little Negro boy a quarter to find a couple of Negro women
whose allotments had not been received to give her something to do.
In a month our secretary had seventy-nine active cases under her
care. She found one of them suffering from typhoid fever in a
neighborhood where it had thrived for years. She told her committee
of it and brought about the inoculation of the entire neighborhood
and the eradication of the source of infection. Not many months had
passed before she persuaded the chapter to pay her a salary, not
primarily for her remuneration but for "discipline and stability."
Next, she raised the funds independently of the chapter treasury for
the salary of a nurse. Then the two of them lobbied the state
health law through the Grand Jury and secured a $5,000 appropriation

Survey, 3 April 1920. Joseph Logan was Assistant Manager of the
Southern Division of the American Red Cross. "The Red Cross Volunteer" was part of a feature story which included profiles of the
rural teacher, the factory inspector, and the social worker. The
motto following the title preceded the presentation of the feature.

from the county commissioners for the first year's work. The nurse is now on the public payroll and "stabilized."

Then she got herself appointed attendance officer under the state law. She receives $3 a day when engaged in that work, and credits it on her salary. She has made good as attendance officer. Opposition to the law was centered in one conspicuous instance of a father who threatened to shoot anybody who "messed in his private affairs." When she drove up to the village store in the neighborhood where he lived, a group of citizens excitedly heard her mission, and refused for her own safety to direct her where he lived. But she found him, and the would-be murderer, after fiercely looking her over, burst out laughing: "Wal," he exclaimed, "I've said the President of the United States caint make me send my chilluns to school; the United States army nor the mayor nor the sheriff caint make me do nothing and I don't care if I do send 'em." Two days later he appeared at the office of the secretary and without assistance purchased shoes and clothing and books for the prospective students.

Now that more children are to attend school, she has inspired the women to inaugurate organized recreation, and has secured the services of an expert playground director to make a month's demonstration to the community. Rachel who calls her the "Darling Attribute of the South," is an old Negro woman whom she recently coaxed to nurse a family of ten who were all down with the flu. Rachel didn't want to do it, and when told it would be a meritorious action replied, "Yes'm, but I'se already done so many good deeds." "I feel like that myself sometimes," says our subject—but there is no end to well-doing.

5

War and Postwar Rural Group Work Organizations

During the first decade of the twentieth century, the cities witnessed the emergence of group work as a popular form of social intervention. The settlement house movement, spearheaded by Jane Addams, established the groundwork upon which later social group work practice grew. Social participation, association and interaction of peers, democratic processes, and impact upon surrounding environmental conditions were key principles which survived the decline of settlement houses.

The rural areas of this country did not remain immune to group work influences. Although the progressive and reform-oriented efforts of the settlement house movement were not felt in the country, the recreation programs which became important in the cities after the war years were the major thrust of group work organizations in the country during and after the war.

The Country Life Commission had emphasized church-based service and recreation programs for rural areas. The war efforts provided the backbone of governmental resources to organizations like the United States Boys' Working Reserve, which was discussed by Helen Dwight Fisher in "The Boy, the War, and the Harrow" (*Survey*, 30 March 1918). This article, although not included here, is suggested to those readers who are particularly interested in the idea of utilizing a juvenile work force in rural projects

No agricultural-recreational organization has endured the test of time as has the U.S.D.A. Extension-sponsored 4-H Club. Although the clubs had been in operation before the war, the war-strengthened communal spirit gave them a boost. 4-H Clubs thrived throughout the 1920s. "Rural Clubs for Boys and Girls," by Ross B. Johnston, a West Virginia agent, describes the purposes and activities of this group work organization.

The work of the Y's cannot be by-passed in any discussion of recreational organizations in the country. The development of local leadership was perhaps the prevalent theme of the YM and YW leaders of the first and second decades of this century. In "The Rural Work of the Young Men's Christian Association," presented by D. C. Drew at the 1922 meeting of the National Conference on Social Work in Providence, Rhode Island, the author illustrates the work of the association in rural areas. The article documents, far beyond expectations, the existence of a theoretical basis on the functioning of small groups which present-day professionals tended to attribute to the encounter group movement of the 1960s.

An early international perspective on rural social welfare is illustrated by "Think Together, Work Together, Play Together: Community Clubs in Manitoba," by Fred C. Middleton, Community Secretary of the Social Service Council of Manitoba. This article, presented at the 1919 National Conference of Social Welfare, refers to Canadian attempts to perpetuate, beyond the war years, the cohesive community spirit which had developed as a result of that crisis. Although prohibitionist in tone, the article exemplifies the efforts of pioneer social welfare and recreation leaders to rechannel the natural gregariousness of the barroom into more constructive organizations.

RURAL CLUBS FOR BOYS AND GIRLS

Ross B. Johnston

There are more than half a million boys and girls in the United States who are members of government agricultural clubs in their respective states. The clubs are so organized that individual work on the part of the members is their keynote. The club itself is merely a framework. A definite plan of work must be mapped out by each member. Each boy and each girl must compete for honors in

Survey, 24 January 1920. Ross B. Johnston was an extension agent at West Virginia University.

raising the best corn or potatoes, the best sheep or chickens, the best wheat or cotton, or in some other way must prove his or her ability in the things that make up everyday life. The club projects are elastic so that they will fit into the agricultural life of different sections of the country.

Through such practical home work as gardening, canning, poultry-raising, and corn-growing, boys and girls learn to appreciate the privileges and responsibilities of ownership. To manage a home project gives them a real sense of membership that is fundamental in all training for good citizenship. The partnership which may be developed between boys and girls and their parents through club work is another factor of great importance in good citizenship. They may be partners in the maintenance of the farm and the home. Parents who encourage their children to take over the management of home projects, such as canning or care of poultry, find that they become genuinely interested in the farm and the home. The cooperation of the parents is, however, necessary to make the partnership real. The "boy's calf and the father's cow" type of partnership will not accomplish the desired results.

The clubs have many parties. The annual county camps are good-time gatherings as much as anything else. The state fair winner's courses are as much social as educational. Instruction in organized play and games is furnished.

The club work always focuses on the four-fold life development, the Head, Hand, Heart and Health of the boy and girl. The emblem of the club is a four-leaved clover. Each leaf of the clover stands for an H and these Hs are conferred for hard work on the part of the club members. They are distinct from the honor of doing the best work in any of the club projects or contests, although they are all found to fit into the work of these special activities.

To earn the head H the boy or girl must prove that he has brains and can use them. "What's in your head? What do you know?" The test chart scores 1,000 points. An individual must make 700 points in order to win his H—the "coup" for knowledge, just as the Indian, by a brave deed, won the "coup" that gave him another eagle plume. Into the determination of his fitness for such honor goes schooling, the carefulness of his work in helping to prepare a club project, health education, sex education, home reading, observation, and short courses.

Next steps up a boy or girl who would earn an H under the hand chart. "What can you do with your hands? How strong are you? What skill have you?" Touch, steadiness and endurance are equally important, with dexterity, skill with tools, handiness about the farm or home and things actually made as the factors that compose the rest of the scoring points.

The third H is the most difficult to win. It judges the bigness of the heart of the boy or girl and his unselfishness. Service to others, club cooperation, daily devotion come first, but Sunday school or church activity, four-fold ideals, practical Christianity and love of nature also figure largely. Creed or denomination have no influence, and the boy who has no church near at hand may score just as high as others who have.

The fourth H is one that appeals most to the boys and girls, for into it enters the play side of life. This H is health. Carriage and general physical condition, including breathing, sight, hearing and teeth, cover almost half the points, but team games, swimming, running, jumping and throwing are big factors.

Of the clubs in West Virginia, William H. Kendrick, state agent says:

> Any boys' leader should take into consideration all the facts known about the management of boys. A club leader should never undertake the organization of the country young folks without first investigating all other club work, especially that of the Boy Scouts, Knights of King Arthur, Boys' Brigade, Y.M. or Y.W. C.A., the organized Sunday school class, or other similar groups. In West Virginia, when we say a boys' and girls' agricultural club, we mean a group of five to fifteen boys or girls who have elected a president, vice-president, secretary and treasurer, who meet at regularly stated times, and who keep a record of these meetings. In most instances, the meetings are purely young folks' meetings. Seldom are the community folk invited.
>
> We should always keep in mind this one point, which is the key to work in West Virginia: The rule of a boy's life is loyalty to the gang. We all well know that no one boy can be loyal to two gangs at once, but that he can shift his loyalty from one group to another pretty quickly. In our agricultural club work we may think that, because our country boys do not have an opportunity to hang around some street corner, smoke cigarettes, and swear, they do not have this gang instinct. The greatest need in the development of the life of our country boys today is real, good, wholesome social opportunity, and partly upon this basis we have made our work in West Virginia.
>
> We find from a recent survey made by the department of vocational education that we are holding boys in West Virginia to a greater age than thirteen of the other southern states. Here in West Virginia we have endeavored to have a strictly boys' and girls' organization. Our club members feel somewhat responsible for the whole movement in the state and while it is headed and operated by the extension office, we have made it a young folks' movement and that is one of the things that has given it health and strength.

The agricultural clubs have now been tried out long enough to prove their practicability and stability. They have a real work to do. They are meeting a plainly defined need. In addition they offer the complete machinery by which various other organizations can most readily reach the young people of the rural communities—

the 'Teen-Age Department of the International Sunday School Association, the Boy Scouts, the United States Bureau of Education, state
health departments, and so on—no organization for social work among
boys and girls, whether it be for educational development, health
improvement or anything else, is superseded by these clubs. Instead,
all can function together through the machinery here offered. Efficiency in rural juvenile work necessarily means the fullest cooperation of all units that are active among country boys and girls.

It is not surprising, therefore, that the demand for an association
of boys' and girls' agricultural clubs is growing stronger and
stronger every day. Indications now point to some definite steps
being taken very soon to bring about a conference of club leaders
from the various states to consider in detail the matter of this
national union of the clubs. The plan of procedure would be exceedingly simple. While the various state clubs are not working as a
national unit, the work is strikingly similar everywhere and the
organizations themselves are much alike. Their programs are similar.
The clubs are financed in the same way. The county agents are the
big factors in the club work in all cases. These are the only clubs
of their kind that have a paid leadership. In most states, the clubs
in the various counties send the prize winners in various club projects or contests to a state prize winners' course for further instruction. Most of the states have strong organizations of these
clubs, which are showing vigorous growth.

As most of the states have their state meetings of the various
club leaders, it would merely be necessary to elect delegates at
each state meeting to a national camp conference. This camp might
be called a national older boys' and girls' camp conference and conducted in accordance with the four-fold life program.

A few years ago the annual national conference of the agents of
state boys' and girls' agricultural clubs in Washington discussed
the question of a national meeting of "'teen-age" agricultural clubs.
The idea was not ripe at that time and nothing came of the discussion. Since then, however, the growth of the various state clubs
has been so rapid, that there is now no doubt that the time for a
national meeting of such clubs has arrived. The advantages seem
obvious. Great impetus would be given the club everywhere. The
young delegates would bring back to their home communities helpful
impressions of the work in other districts.

THE RURAL WORK OF THE YOUNG MEN'S CHRISTIAN ASSOCIATION

D. C. Drew

In order to gain an accurate impression of the Young Men's Christian
Association as it operates in rural areas, one must first eliminate
from his thinking the city institutions with dormitories, gymnasium,
baths, and other equipment for the service of young men and think
rather of the origin of this movement. Young Williams, its founder,
and a group of his fellow-workers from his store met in a room loaned
for this purpose with the distinct aim of lifting the ideals of those
working in the establishment under the inspiration of the religious
motive. It was the methods of its founder rather than the institutional development of later years that gave hope to the leaders of
the Association movement that there might be an opportunity through
the process of volunteer leadership using meager equipment to constructively influence groups of boys and men in rural areas.

The natural and primary social groups of men, young men, and boys,
therefore, have formed the social environment for the development of
the rural Association program in its recreational and service aspects.
The constant changes and uncertainties of these primary groups in
rural localities have necessitated constant expert leadership called
supervision.

The county, through a process of experimentation, has been found
to be the best unit of administration. A county committee is organized and a county secretary expert in matters of group organization
and religious leadership selected. The rural movement of the Association is thus called County Work, which has been defined as the
method "by which the program of the Young Men's Christian Association
is adapted to the needs of towns and country communities: using the
county as the unit of supervision, with an employed secretary working through local leadership in each community and placing emphasis
upon personality rather than upon equipment." Although in its present development the County Work plan has included various community-
wide and county-wide aspects which we will later consider, let us
first give our thought to the methods in rural communities. An
illustration will indicate the process.

A crowd of young fellows in a New Hampshire village, some at work
and some at school, but all members of the same gang, organized a

Proceedings, National Conference of Social Work, 1922. D. C. Drew
was National Secretary of County Work of the Young Men's Christian
Association of New York.

social and recreational club. Their equipment consisted of a fourth-rate pool table, a few chairs, two tables, and decks of cards. They were not bad fellows nor hoodlums. Soon the parents of the boys were concerned with some of the things that went on. The county secretary, at the invitation of a local business man, looked into the situation. A board of directors comprising fifteen men from the various churches was organized, talked the matter over with some of the leading young men, provided a suitable meeting place where a recreative and social program could be provided. The young fellows organized themselves into a Community Club. They appealed to an outstanding young man to be their leader. They accepted the Y.M.C.A. program. Their first efforts were crude but with right motive. It was the same old gang but with a different objective, supported now by the leading business men. Individuals within this group accepted the higher standards of personal conduct and gradually the whole group was socially converted.

What are the principles upon which this group enterprise is conducted? First, the Association utilizes a natural group, not a select body but a street corner gang, farmers, a high-school crowd, ranchmen, or any other industrial group which logically belongs together. Admitting the theory that groups have a cycle of life, a genesis, a period of growth, expanding life, decline, and death, adaptations are made to meet the change which each year or season imposes.

The second principle is group leadership. There is some person in every locality who is the one man whom a group of young men and boys most admire and most desire to be their counselor or leader. Such a one must be enlisted to assume responsibility of meeting with this group at least once a week.

The third principle is self-government. Under the limitations of working in harmony with the ideals of the Association these groups are self-governing, electing their officers, appointing committees and controlling affairs according to their best judgment: an experience in democracy within the community process.

The fourth principle is a program developed and accepted by the group. As an outgrowth of the Association ideal of the rational development of one's recreational, religious, educational, and service life, a program termed by Association leaders as "Four-Fold" becomes in many cases the concrete expression of the group's life and experience. It has been discovered that this ideal of personal development becomes a natural ambition of a normal young man and boy. This does not imply an equal development of the different phases of personality nor a standardized program of personal growth.

The fifth principle is the co-operation of interested business and professional men which gives stability to this community enterprise.

Sixth, the group becomes a force to be utilized by community and county welfare rather than a club merely for self-improvement and self-satisfaction.

The organization of vital interest groups along the ideals of the Association has been thus a basic method in the approach of the Y.M.C.A. to rural areas. Reports from 1,923 such groups were made to our national yearbook committee.

The religious energies of young men cannot be pent up. They must find expression within the area of their immediate influence. Group action for only those social units which render a real service to society, therefore, is the next logical step. How this works is illustrated by a group of high-school students under the name of Hi-Y Club up in Maine. Some of its members had been at the State Boys' Conference, and were determined to eliminate smoking both from the high and grammar schools where it was known that many had contracted the habit. Entirely of their own initiative, the Hi-Y Club posted notices in the school buildings that all boys caught smoking would be ducked in the town watering tub. Up to the time of this notice, the fellows went into the horse sheds behind the church, and the church officials were considering whether or not they should put doors on each shed to prevent the boys from entering. The Hi-Y Club informed the church officials that they had taken action on the matter and it would not be necessary to go to that expense. This method of group action may not be approved but it is evident that this determination to stop a known physical peril among boys was the result of group ideals and individual conviction.

Under the stimulation of the county secretary these local groups and the local committees which give them backing and guidance put on for the community a large variety of tremendously valuable community-wide events, the most notable of which is the annual Father and Son Banquet. On this occasion all the boys and men of a locality are brought together to face up to their mutual responsibilities and opportunities of fellowship. The relationship between the farm boy and the farmer is frankly faced with the result that a new comrade-ship between the dads and lads have developed and have given a new incentive for sticking by the home farm.

High-school groups often invite students from a neighboring college and entertain them in their homes for a three-day period. The students have personal interviews with the boys, set them right upon life's ideals, and show them how the keenest athlete takes his religion into every contest. The "Keep Fit" campaign has been brought to a locality as a result of the desire of the groups to bring the message of clean thinking and clean living to all the boys of the locality. Sunday afternoon forums, community Christmas celebrations, have been put on by the boys and their adult advisors. In fact every group actuated by the religious principle must be dynamic. As soon as it thinks only of its own good times, it is dead. Unwholesome conditions in the community have been removed by the action of the young men themselves without waiting for public officials. Gambling machines have been thrown out and disorderly houses closed up by young men who have resolved to make their community clean.

Little has been said thus far of the county secretary. It is he after all who discovered these natural groups, found their leaders, set them going with a program, and has brought about these notable results. This he does through the local forces. He does not seek to build a kingdom of his own but to stimulate the self-expression of the men and boys of each locality. His is a sacrificial life. One who understands rural life will quickly appreciate the self-sacrifices and Christ-like spirit involved in discovering and developing leaders in those areas from which leadership has been constantly going for many years.

Besides the stimulation of local groups in their service program for the locality, the county secretary undertakes through the county committee a service of co-operation. In many cases he is the only paid social worker in the county. One of the most fruitful opportunities is with the rural school. Inasmuch as many secretaries have been thoroughly trained in recreation, the school superintendent is glad to have him make the rounds of the rural schools in the county, taking charge of the children, teaching them schoolyard games, or demonstrating indoor recess games. The way is open in teachers' institutes to train and inspire in rural recreation. Play picnics of school children and their parents, sometimes reaching the entire county, have been developed. The county athletic meets on a simplified, informal basis are most successful.

Co-operation with the rural church has also been a productive field of helpfulness. The formation of a county ministers' association, if none exists, assisting in church picnics and socials, helping in Sunday schools and in young people's societies by calling conferences, providing speakers, all offer such opportunities.

Co-operation with the Farm Bureau is usually welcome in boys' and girls' contests. In some cases the groups organized for Y.M.C.A. work undertake some definite agricultural project under the supervision of the farm agent. Agricultural exhibits have been held in certain places where the Farm Bureau was not equipped to handle such an event.

Besides these services rendered to other agencies, there are certain county-wide responsibilities of the county Association. The County Young Men's Conference held annually is an outstanding religious event. It brings young men in their teens and above to face the great decisions of life. Delegates are urged to take some forward step. They are challenged with advance in their character and achievement. Cases could be enumerated where they have gone back to their locality and through the group to which they belong or through the Sunday school of which they are a member, made their impress upon the lives of other fellows. Such conferences last year were attended by 9,060.

The impressions gained at such a gathering are thus focused into action through local organization. The county camp exerts a similar influence where boys for a week or more in each locality are brought with the leaders of the county and the county secretary in recreation of body and refreshment of spirit and are sent back to their localities with a new determination of service.

Back of each individual county there are the state and international committees ready to assist in organization and guidance. Two schools of rural leadership have been established, one at Chicago and the other at Springfield, Massachusetts, both offering four-year courses preparing young men for the county secretaryship and other forms of religious service. In addition to this there are six summer schools giving courses of two weeks to which the secretaries come each year as a continuation school in which methods and inspiration are brought by competent leaders. They have done much in upholding the morale of this important group of pioneers.

This, then, in summary is the process; a group is organized about the ideals of self-expression, self-control, and a normal personal development. The natural outgo of this group is service to the community, participation in the larger events, county-wide or state wide, stimulation of individual idealism, and a better community spirit. The result of this process is the development of initiative, self-reliance, and leadership among boys and young men.

I believe that the outstanding contribution of this movement is in producing rural leadership. Starting in many counties in an extremely limited way, it has been noted that over a period of years, genuine leadership has been developed through these processes. In one county twenty-two out of twenty-seven local "Y" leaders were once members of a local group. Teachers for Sunday-school classes and those now leading the movements for better schools, better roads, and better community life, it has been observed, were former members of a "Y" group. From one small group operating ten years ago, there is now one man who is an agricultural leader for an entire state, another is giving his life to the Christian ministry, and the third is in Association secretaryship, but more have stayed in the home town, to help the local institutions. Here, then, is a means of producing practical, homegrown, and for the most part, home-utilized leaders.

Are there no difficulties or limitations? Yes, indeed! The two big difficulties have been first to find men with leadership qualities and undiscouragable spirit to serve as county secretaries and second to finance them out of the resources within each county. There is no state or national subsidy available and each county must pay for its own Association. Failure of a county committee to function with genuine financial and administrative responsibility has too often broken the spirit of a young man willing and able to serve as a secretary. These difficulties can be best overcome when a state Y.M.C.A. committee places on its staff a man to give his entire energies to the organization, supervision, and guidance of the county committee and secretaries of a given state.

City Associations lend their friendly resources especially to the county in which they are located. The whole Association movement has pledged its support to this little band of less than 200 men who are out in the villages and open country like miners digging out precious ore of Christian leadership. It is with a consciousness that their task is of vital importance to the making of a new and better social order that they ridicule the difficulties and are daily producing mighty results.

THINK TOGETHER, WORK TOGETHER, PLAY TOGETHER:
COMMUNITY CLUBS IN MANITOBA

Fred C. Middleton

To usher in the day of the new democracy; to make actual in the life
of every community the principles for which the war was fought; to
secure liberty, equality and fraternity among all citizens; to so
apply these principles of human brotherhood in our relationships

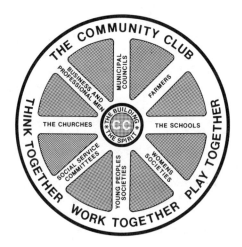

each with the other that our own community will be a better place
in which to live—this is the task that faces us today.

Shall we be equal to this task? Not unless the "get together"
spirit, so much in evidence during the years of war, continues to
be manifested during the years of peace.

Canada developed a fine community spirit during the great war.
For almost five years, in common with the rest of the empire and
her allies, private interests were subordinated to those of the
public good. Men and women learned to think in broader terms; and
co-operative service, born of a common danger and a common need,
was noticeable everywhere. Gifts of men and money, red cross
supplies, comforts for the soldier boys (including clothes, food,
and dainties) all these were supplied with a lavishness and good
will that will always stand to our credit.

Proceedings, National Conference of Social Work, 1919.
Fred C. Middleton was Community Secretary of the Social Service
Council of Manitoba, Winnipeg, Canada.

Now the war is over. The Prussian military machine has been broken beyond repair, the spirit of militarism has been everywhere dethroned and the world has been made safe for democracy. Without detracting one bit from the credit due the armies at the front, we can say that in great measure, this victory was made possible by the unity of aim of those who remained at home. The question is: Shall we go back to the selfish individualism of the past, or move forward in the spirit of co-operative service which we have developed during the war?

We dare not go back! Already we are finding the problems of peace are as great, if not greater, than the problems of war, and we shall not solve the problems of peace unless we face them as we did the problems of war—in the spirit of altruism, sympathetic co-operation and unselfish service.

All over Canada there are evidences that this wartime community spirit will be carried forward into the reconstruction period. The present industrial unrest is not evidence to the contrary. The revolutionary labor leaders, it is true, are refusing settlement of their disputes by conciliation, but the bulk of Canadian labor wants to see the change in our industrial system come by constitutional means. A third factor in the fight is the great middle class, who belong to neither organized labor, nor organized capital. They are workers, indeed, and form the majority of our citizenship, but until now they have been unorganized and inarticulate. They are taking a hand in affairs now, however, and if the movement grows, this stable centre of society will be the medium of conciliation between the two extremes and one of the most important factors in the ushering in of the new democracy.

In Manitoba the Community Club Movement promises to be of great assistance in the organization of this great middle-class citizenship, especially outside the cities. It is under the direction of the Social Service Council, which is a federation, non-partisan in politics and religion, whose purposes are the study of social welfare ideas and the encouragement of all forms of social service. There are twenty-four provincial bodies represented in this federation, including the various religious denominations, the Grain Growers' Association, Educational Association, Retail Merchants' Association, and the Union of Municipalities.

For some years past the activities of the council have been mainly directed to the securing of legislation prohibiting the manufacture, importation and sale of intoxicating liquor for beverage purposes. We have had all along a general program of social welfare, but until the menace of the licensed liquor traffic was removed, we had little time or opportunity for this general program. Now, however, we are attempting to carry out a constructive program. Prominent in this program is the question of community organization. We feel that we must put something in the place of the bad social centre that was taken away when we banished the bar-rooms. The Community Club, of course, aims to do more than merely replace the social centre provided by the hotel keepers in the past. It seeks to provide an organization through which the people of our rural sections can learn to live together in the spirit of the Second Commandment and the Golden Rule, and to put on a program of community activities through which life in the country may be more wholesome, more attractive, and more complete. The organization takes in the whole community, the basis of membership being citizenship. There are usually many other organizations in the town and district but they are all sectional. The board of trade takes in the retail merchants and other business men, but excludes any one else. The Grain Growers' Association takes in farmers only; the Home Economics Society takes in women only; the lodges recognize only initiated members who have taken the degrees and whose dues are paid up; the churches appeal to those only who are members or adherents of their particular denomination. And so it goes—every one of these organizations is, from its very nature, sectional, and indeed, consciously or unconsciously, each acts as a divisive element.

We seek to overcome this defect, and a glance at the picture of the community wheel will illustrate how we propose to do it. There are eight spokes in this wheel, representing eight factors in the average community. Hitherto these organizations have worked along parallel lines, each seeking to carry on their own work without much thought of their relation each to the other, or to the community as a whole. The Community Club movement seeks to have them move along concentric lines, all working towards a common centre, the good of the community. It seeks to remind the farmer, the school teacher, the merchant, the preacher, that while they may have a special work to do through their own organization, they are a part of the whole community and must share in the community tasks.

The organization locates in the villages and towns, but ministers to the life of the whole community surrounding these centres. The activities of the club are grouped under five standing committees whose duties are outlined as follows:

1. Public Forum Committee—

(a) To arrange for local debates and secure speakers from time to time who shall deal with public issues and matters of social welfare generally.

(b) To co-operate with the Extension Department of the Agricultural College and the University.

(c) To encourage the formation, use and upkeep of a community library, using the school as headquarters wherever feasible.

(d) To arrange for an annual address from the local Member of Parliament, preferably before the opening of the legislature.

Note—It is distinctly understood that, while contentious public issues may be discussed on their merits, the community club will not allow its forum to be used for the purpose of party propaganda.

2. Better Business Committee—

This committee shall be composed of farmers and business men, and shall take under review the following:

(a) Local marketing conditions and possible improvements; good roads campaign; Hotel accommodation.

(b) The wisdom of establishing a flour mill, a creamery, a market garden, or any other local enterprise.

(c) Better methods of buying and selling by the local merchants.

(d) Better methods of fire protection.

(e) Sympathetic co-operation between the farmers and merchants of the community.

(f) Better credit facilities for farmers by local banks.

(g) Helping men on rented farms to become owners.

3. Young People's Committee—

This committee shall be composed of those interested in young people's work:

(a) To co-operate with the churches in undertaking a definite program of activities through the Provincial Boy Scouts, the Manitoba Sunday Schools Association, the Rural Y.M.C.A. or the Rural Y.W.C.A.

(b) To co-operate with the School Board, in introducing manual training and domestic science classes in the public schools.

(c) To initiate where necessary action looking toward the organization of a consolidated school.

(d) To arrange, if necessary, separate meetings for the young people, especially 'teen-age boys and girls.

4. Public Health Committee—

It shall be the duty of this committee

(a) To work in co-operation with the local health officer in encouraging the use of garbage barrels and regular removal of refuse.

(b) To see that the streets, lanes, and vacant lots in the town are kept free from litter and rubbish.

(c) To encourage the use of a sewerage system for both towns and country homes.

(d) To secure where necessary an improved water supply.

(e) To arrange for holding of lectures and exhibits, and the distribution of literature on child welfare and the care of the mentally defective, and to take action in any local cases needing attention.

(f) To initiate where necessary action looking toward the building of a municipal hospital, the employment of a district nurse, and the regular medical inspection of the schools within the community.

(g) To boost the "Clean Up Week" each spring.

5. Recreation Committee—

This committee shall have the general supervision of the play life of the community as follows:

(a) Making provision for skating and curling in winter, if possible, securing a municipal rink.

(b) Providing baseball and basketball grounds, tennis courts and swimming pool for summer.

(c) Arranging for local presentation of dramatic plays and choral programs.

(d) Providing regular moving picture programs for the fall and winter months, in co-operation with the Community Department of the Social Service Council.

(e) Arranging for Soldiers' Memorial.

(f) Arranging for an annual community picnic in June.

Special Committees shall be appointed for any special tasks that may present themselves.

It might be well to say that these committees do not necessarily carry out all or any of these suggestions themselves. Sometimes all that is necessary is to suggest certain lines of action to the organizations affiliated with the club. For instance, much of this program could be carried out through the agency of the local Board of Trade, the Municipal Council, the School Board, and so on. It is a fine thing, however, to have a vehicle through which the whole community can have its desires brought before these affiliated bodies. Of course, in many cases, the work would have to be done by the committees of the club, especially where no board of trade exists, or where the village is one of several centers within the municipality.

A glance at the reproduction of the community wheel will give a good idea of how the club is organized. Any public-spirited man or woman may take the initiative in the matter. A public meeting should be called, care being taken that the ministers of the town and the officers of the various organizations be interviewed; representatives from the various churches, Grain Growers' Association, Board of Trade and other organizations noted on the community wheel should be present at the meeting. An address by a visitor from a nearby club or by the provincial community secretary could be given, and if thought wise, the organization proceeded with.

An executive of seven should be elected as follows:

President, who shall be convener of the Public Forum Committee; 1st vice-president (convener of Better Business Committee); 2nd vice-president (convener of Young People's Committee); 3rd vice-president (convener of Public Health Committee); 4th vice-president (convener of Recreation Committee); secretary; treasurer.

Care should be taken that these officers are elected from the various elements of the community life, town and country being equally represented.

In addition to the executive a general committee should be appointed of one or more representatives of the various organizations represented in the club.

Results

Since the Social Service Council established this department twelve months ago, work has been done in thirty-two places, twenty-six of which have organized clubs. From the very commencement of our work we have been asked to quote results. "How is the scheme working out?" has been an oft repeated question. Such a query is perfectly fair; the community movement must submit to the acid test of "results." Until recently, however, we have had to reply that it was too soon to ask for results, and the best we could do was to quote from clubs in the United States. Even now it is a little early to ask the question. Five years would not be too long a period in which the test might be carried out, yet most of our clubs have not been going five months. Still, results are noticeable and these might be grouped under three headings:

The Community Forum

It has been clearly demonstrated that through this forum any person
with a community message can be assured of a community audience. The
people are learning to "think together" and when we have two hundred
such forums scattered over Manitoba (as we shall have) they will be
one of the greatest factors in the preparation of the public mind
for the coming of the new democracy. It may also become, especially
in the rural centres, the medium through which the great stable centre of society, the general public, may become organized and articu-
late.

The Community Task

The second phase of club work has very encouraging results. One
secretary writes: "There have been so many questions of interest
and importance coming up for the club's attention that we have had
little time for special programs." The activities have been many
and various and include the following:

Better transportation facilities; encouragement of technical education in the public school; hospital accommodation, and the employment of a district nurse; action looking toward the building of consolidated schools and community churches; law enforcement re gambling
and the sale of cigarettes and malt liquors to minors; the revival of
the town newspaper; the setting up in business of returned soldiers
who have taken a post war business course; the securing of a weekly
half holiday for local store employees, a spring clean-up campaign
for May, and community picnics for June.

It will be evident to even the casual observer that the results
here quoted could not have been secured without co-operative effort
on the part of the various factors in each community. A glance at
the personnel of the executive committee of the local clubs will
show how real the desire is to get together. In fourteen out of the
twenty-six clubs for which I have the data, the following representation appears on the executive:

Farmers, 18; merchants, 15; preachers, 8; bankers, 8; school
teachers, 6; editors, 3. The lady members of these fourteen executives are represented as follows: Farmers' wives, 1; merchants'
wives, 2; preachers' wives, 2; editors' wives, 1; doctors' wives, 1.

It will be seen from this summary that the club is providing a
medium through which local farmers and merchants can get together
for the mutual advantages of each. The fact that altogether too
little of the community business flows through local channels has
been apparent for years past and the small towns have stood still or

gone back in consequence. Winnipeg, in the meantime, has continued
to grow so that this year 50 per cent of the population of our so-
called rural province is located in the city. If we are to save the
small towns from further depletion, if not from practical extinction,
a much higher percentage of the retail business of the community must
be done at home, and this will be brought about not by the cry of
"home loyalty," but by the business men adopting better business
methods and rendering better service, together with a more sympathic
attitude on the part of the farmer toward the merchant. These two
are team-mates, pulling on either end of the whiffletree for community progress—and they are learning now to pull together.

Recreational Features

The entertainment and recreational features of community life in
learning to play together is one of the tasks set before each community, and progress can be reported in this connection. In some centres extra play equipment will be installed on the school grounds.
In others steps are being taken to build a municipal skating rink.
Moving pictures have also been introduced and the fact demonstrated
that good films can be secured. In some places the support of the
"good people" to this class of picture has not been as hearty as it
should have been, but as a rule the audiences have been large and
appreciative.

One club has done good work along amateur dramatic lines presenting
a three-act play, "The Private Secretary." There are great possibilities in this direction, and also for choral programs. Community
singing will be featured among the clubs next fall and it is likely
that a community song book will be published in the near future to
be used at a "sing song" at the opening of each public meeting of
the local clubs. Such a book would contain the old favorites, the
latest popular choruses and national hymns and songs.

The matter of the building of community halls has been brought up
frequently, but so far action has only been taken in one or two
cases. Such buildings are not essential to the success of the movement and clubs can function without them. Where there is no decent
auditorium, however, the need for such a hall is very great and it
is likely that a number will be built in such places. The cost will
vary from $6,000 to $20,000.

In closing I would emphasize the fundamental importance of our
community work in the country by quoting from an address delivered
in 1909 by the late ex-President Roosevelt, in which he says: "I
warn my countrymen that the great progress made in city life is not

a full measure of our civilization, for our civilization rests at bottom on the wholesomeness, the attractiveness and the completeness of life in the country."

The same warning needs to be issued to the people of Manitoba, especially the leaders. Only as we make life in the country more wholesome, more attractive, and more complete can we preserve the local community, which is after all the ultimate unit of democracy.

6

County Level Organization
of Rural Social Welfare

Perhaps the most important idea discussed by rural practitioners of
the 1920s was the organization or regionalization of rural social
welfare services into units larger than individual villages or small
communities.

As already noted in Chapter 5, the Home Service of the Red Cross
spearheaded this notion during the war years. After 1919, rural
leaders began to refer to it with increased frequency. Discussions
of the county, the region, or even the state as alternative units
for the organization of the interior of the country became common-
place at meetings and in the literature. Although the dialogue
basically had to do with administrative organization of services,
regionalization and standardization were also themes noted in specialized fields such as the codification of child welfare legislation
(see, for example, "Child Welfare Studied in Oklahoma").

From 1917 to 1927 social work was characterized by the introduction
of systematic surveys of social conditions. These surveys were
utilized, in both city and country, to bring about legislative
changes and reform. The efforts at standardization and regionalization of rural social services utilized data rendered by these systematic social studies of the country.

The establishment of the most appropriate unit for rural community
development was one of the central problems surveyed. Defining the
rural community and establishing a "workable social unit with its
boundaries" were themes which concerned students of rural life.

There was one other piece of legislation which also brought about
extensive reorganization of social services in the country. In 1899,
Illinois had enacted the first juvenile court law, "An Act to Regulate the Treatment and Control of Dependent, Neglected, and Delinquent Children." By 1919, all of the states but Connecticut, Maine,
and Wyoming had enacted juvenile court laws. In the rural districts,

the juvenile court operated on county, bi-county, and even tri-county bases. In many cases, the existing court of record functioned dually as the juvenile court.

The articles selected for this chapter are primarily illustrative of the broad organization theme. The need and benefits of standardization of child welfare services through codification are discussed, as already mentioned, in the report "Child Welfare Studied in Oklahoma." The use of surveys and adequate definitions in the establishment of the most appropriate unit for rural organization is the subject of Hermann N. Morse's "The Underlying Factors of Rural Community Development." The significance of appropriately defining the scope and functions of the juvenile court are the subject of Wiley H. Swift's paper, "A Redefining of the Scope and Functions of the Juvenile Court, in Terms of the Rural Community."

It is important to note that during and after World War I, North Carolina established a broadly acclaimed statewide social welfare system. By legislative mandate, every county had to set up a welfare board with jurisdiction over various services. The North Carolina plan was in many ways a precursor of obligatory county-based social welfare programs established by FERA during the New Deal. Because the North Carolina plan was used as a model of county-level organization by many other states, two more papers which discussed the scheme are included. They are E. C. Branson's "The North Carolina Scheme of Rural Development," and Howard W. Odum's "The County Unit as a Basis of Social Work and Public Welfare in North Carolina."

Branson's article includes a very profound and stirring statement on the need for cooperative organization which is worth special attention:

> Our ills are not mainly those of congested population centers where, in Rousseau's phrase, the breathe of man is fatal to his fellows. . . . Our ills are mainly the social consequences of (1) farming as an occupation (2) in sparsely settled areas —the ills of solitariness, remoteness, and aloofness. We are far removed from socialism, in any sense, good or bad. On the other hand, we have always been a hair's-breadth away from individualism, raw, raucous, and unorganizable. . . .

The interesting article by Margaret Reeves entitled "The Indirect Responsibility of a State Department for Children" has been included on the theme of organization of social welfare services to illustrate a seminal perspective on governmental responsibility for services in rural states. From the perspective of New Mexico, which she felt was applicable to "other western states of large rural areas," Reeves wrote that on matters of public welfare "the value of private undertakings is recognized but it is felt that the state must have ultimate responsibility." Reeves also discusses the problems of operationalizing county or local level organization, although she does this trying to get across a strong bias in favor of "professional" social work delivery of local services.

The final excerpt of this chapter, Louise Cottrell's "Organization Needed to Support and Free the Local Worker for Undifferentiated Case Work" deals with practical suggestions on the subject of county level organization. It also introduces both the term and the notion of "undifferentiated" social work, an idea which was to permeate the proposals of most rural workers during the Depression, the New Deal, and the present day under the rubric of "generalist approach."

CHILD WELFARE STUDIED IN OKLAHOMA

Just now when agriculture is assuming such importance in its relation to national defense it is disheartening to learn that of all the farms in one of our large rural states over one-half are worked by tenants. The renters of this state "own nothing but what they can put into a wagon and drive off with." Much has been written about the poverty of people living in cities, but "little is known of the poverty in many of these rural tenant homes. The country has been pictured as a beautiful place to live, where all human wants are supplied—a picture that never reveals the suffering and privation these tenants endure in order to live the barrenest kind of life."

These sentences, quoted from a report on child welfare in Oklahoma, published by the National Child Labor Committee, tell only part of the story contained in that report. The report seeks a basis for action in knowledge of the whole gamut of conditions surrounding child life. Up to the present four states have taken action to codify their child laws—Ohio, Minnesota, Missouri and New Hampshire. With the exception of Missouri the method in the four states was practically the same: first, to appoint a commission to study the

Survey, 30 March 1918.

laws, then, on the recommendations of that commission, to take legislative action. The result has not been all that it should be. In Ohio, there was no preliminary state-wide survey of conditions, and the social workers of the state did not awaken to the importance of the code until it had been submitted to the legislature. Consequently there was controversy among the different groups, resulting in many changes in the code and partial mutilation. A previous general study would have enabled social workers to get together on a program. In Missouri social organizations did attempt a joint effort for cooperation.

The social workers of Oklahoma felt that any effort to codify its laws would be futile unless such action were preceded by a state-wide survey of conditions. The advantage of this method is that after a broad view or picture is obtained it is possible to determine whether the picture requires action, and if so, in what direction. The authority of an official commission may then be sought to codify the laws and to bring them up to standards recognized as fitting. It was on this basis that the committee was asked to make a survey of the state for the University of Oklahoma, the investigation being conducted under the direction of Edward N. Clopper, of the Committee's staff.

Social workers and others who have worked for the protection of children have long appreciated that there should be some coordination of the different standards, functions and activities, not only in the interest of effective administration by state and local authorities, but of the children themselves. For example, in the field of poor relief, the problem of mothers' pensions hinges directly upon that of compulsory school attendance and the restriction of employment of children. But in some states, as in Oklahoma, the measure of relief afforded to mothers under the law is entirely inadequate, granting the observance of the school and child employment laws. Yet this is exactly the sort of thing that results when legislation proceeds along unrelated lines. Bring all the laws affecting children together under one code, proceed from the point of view of the child's welfare, and you will produce effective instead of haphazard and piecemeal results.

The report covers the fields of public health, recreation, education, child labor, agriculture, juvenile courts and probation, the institutional care of children, together with home finding and poor relief. The closing chapter knits all these together and makes recommendations looking toward the coordination of the various functions and activities. In comparison with other proposed codes, a unique addition here is the setting forth of the questions relating to the parentage and property rights of the child, both the present

laws and desirable changes. Perhaps the most striking finding is in
the discussion of the land tenure problem. In the August 1917, *Child
and Labor Bulletin* a report was made on the causes of absence from
rural schools in Oklahoma; the present report goes into the basic
conditions responsible for these causes. It shows that "farmwork,"
"illness," etc., while the immediate causes of non-attendance, are
not the real causes; these are to be found in the economic system to
which the tenants and small landowners are obliged to submit.

Discrepancies in the laws themselves are pointed out. For example,
the juvenile court, having committed a delinquent child to an institution, may order the release of that child although the superintendent of the institution would not be willing even to grant him parole.
The power on the part of the court to retain jurisdiction over the
inmates thus interferes with the very important parole work done in
the institutions. The conflict is a direct result of the lack of
standardization.

The report is evidence of the growing interest in the codification
of child welfare laws, and the realization that a knowledge of conditions governing the care, education, recreation and work of young
children must precede legislative action. In this respect the problems of Oklahoma are of national importance, for they are the problems that every state faces in greater or less degree.

THE UNDERLYING FACTORS OF RURAL COMMUNITY DEVELOPMENT

Hermann N. Morse

As I see it, the distinctly rural elements in the problem of community development go back to a few simple propositions. These need
not be argued here, but may be stated arbitrarily. They are the
efficiency and economy, under average American conditions, of a one-

Proceedings, National Conference of Social Work, 1919. Hermann N.
Morse was associated with the Presbyterian Board of Home Missions,
New York. This Board, under the leadership of the clergyman and
educator Warren H. Wilson, was one of the precursors of the Interchurch World Movement.

family farm as a unit of production; that each farm family should
own the land it tills and live on the land it owns; the inability of
the average farmer to individually cope with modern business conditions and of the average family acting alone to satisfy the complex
social needs of modern life; and lastly, the increasing specialization in the business of agriculture which makes necessary the cooperation of the tiller of the land with all those others concerned
in the business, as the merchant, the banker, the carrier and others.
Since, as Professor Branson has shown in his address, we have in the
country no workable social unit with its boundaries and its status
fixed by civil law, there must be developed a unit of action which
shall be sanctioned by the social law, fixed by custom and articulated in organization, to satisfy all the needs of the situation.

Rural Life Surveys, Made or Projected
There are many signs that we are making hopeful progress in this
matter. The experience of the war helped us. The rough urgency
shook many a rural community together and provided it temporarily,
at least, with some machinery for getting things done. The rural
studies carried on for a number of years past by certain church
boards and also by state colleges of agriculture, have thrown light
on the problem. The recent action of the Department of Agriculture
in enlarging the function of the office of farm management and securing Professor C. J. Galpin of the University of Wisconsin to
direct the making of farm life studies, should have significant results. There is another practical proposal just now taking definite
shape which I wish to discuss.

There has recently been formed an organization representing practically all Protestant denominations known as the Interchurch World
Movement of North America. This is definitely a movement of missionary and benevolent agencies of Protestant churches. In order that
the constituent bodies might proceed with the development of their
work on sound lines, not only of comity but of policy, the Interchurch Movement is preparing to carry through an exhaustive and
country-wide study of existing conditions confronting religious organizations. As one part of this study a thorough survey will be
made of every habitable rural county in the United States, some
3,000 in number. The organization for this is now being assembled
and the work has actually been begun. No such prodigious piece of
survey work has ever been undertaken before and there are many difficulties in the way of its accomplishment, but that substantially
this result will be obtained in due season we have no doubt. The
method of this survey will be to utilize local forces and local men
for the study of all local problems in accordance with uniform

methods. The results will be not only concrete programs for the development of local communities, but also the assembling of a vast array of data out of which can be built the underlying policies of social and religious development.

What Is a Community?

The elements in the problem of such a survey are the elements in the problem of community organization and development. The first of them is in the definition of the word community. Professor Morgan's remarks on the baffling character of the word make it appear foolhardy to attempt a definition. Last year at the meeting of this conference there was a certain amount of discussion as to the unit on which the social organization of the country should proceed. The proposal of the Council of National Defense for the utilization of the school district as the unit occasioned much comment, pro and con. The whole topic now seems exceedingly remote. Surely we have learned that no one unit arbitrarily selected can be made the unit of community organization. The question, it seems very clearly now, is not what unit we would like to use, but what the unit actually is; that is, the unit of territory and population within which people actually do work together. I will do the fool-hardy thing and suggest a tentative definition of a community as the unit of territory and population characterized by common economic and social experiences and interests. That, at least, is the definition which our survey assumes.

The problem here is basic. It is comparatively easy to make a catalogue of those things which need to be done, which can best be done by the united action of the community. It is also comparatively easy to set forth the measures by which we may cure our social and economic ills. The real difficulty is to determine the unit which should actually be concerned in any action required, then to secure within that unit workable organizations. This raises many other problems. If in the country you take the whole of an average group having practically identical economic and social interests and activities, you have probably included some kind of a town or village with a certain amount of open country; not necessarily, but probably. We know far less than we ought to know of the relations of the small town to the open country, but the thing we do know is that whereas they ought to work together in close harmony since they are one in interest, they commonly pull apart and are separated by many real or imaginary grievances. The average small town, while setting its own face toward the city, is apt to assume that the surrounding country owes it a living. Every country merchant takes it as a personal affront if, after he has invested his money in a business,

a farmer refuses to patronize him and instead undertakes some form
of co-operative purchase or sale. To hear many such men talk, you
would think that the farmer had no right to do anything but patronize
the village merchant, irrespective of the quality of service rendered
or the toll exacted for it. The small town learns slowly that if it
would survive in the estimation of the country, it must produce;
that is, render real service at a reasonable rate. The farmer, on
the other hand, is rather prone to pity himself as being exploited.
This is the popular key note to strike in a farmers' meeting. Point
out the way in which the retailer, the jobber, the carrier, the
wholesaler, the banker, the manufacturer and even the consumer all
milk the farmer's cow, and you are sure of a sympathetic hearing.
Of course the farmer needs to realize on his part that only one
stage in the business of agriculture is the stage of the tilling of
the land, and the man who gives time and place value to the farmer's
product makes a real economic contribution.

This cannot be discussed in detail here, but obviously there is a
big task involved to discover these units of community interest and
activity, to propagate and popularize the idea of that unit as mark-
ing the boundaries of the actual commonwealth and then to build a
program of social action on that basis.

Dependence of Social Institutions upon Economic Life
The second element in the problem, once the community is discovered,
has to do with the economic foundations of its life. So far as this
problem is a technical one, it need not concern this conference,
though problems of economic justice, of land tenure, of business cooperation and the more primary problems of the methods of production
have very great social significance. Let it suffice to say that
social, educational and religious institutions are slowly learning
the lesson that progress in their particular fields depends upon the
creation of an economic margin and its retention within the community
for the support of its institutions and social life. We in church
boards, for instance, have long since discovered that if we could
indicate on a map all the areas in the country which are characterized by thin soil and an unprofitable agriculture, we would be showing at the same time the areas characterized by "thin soil" churches.
There are such churches which take root in thin soil and will thrive
in no other, which accept a low standard of living and make their
appeal on that basis. Institutions which demand a high standard of
living can only thrive in such areas as they set in operation movements designed to make such a standard of living possible.

The third element in the problem has to do with social character and attitudes. No social or religious work can get far and no task of community organization can get far which does not take into account the question of the social characteristics of the people. Professor Giddings, in his suggestive paper on "Social Self-control," instances certain actions taken by the town meeting of Dorchester, Massachusetts, in the early days of its settlement. Two are in point to the effect that no one who was a member of the meeting could sell his property to any outsider whom the community "might dislike of." The other was that any one elected to an office must perform the duties of that office irrespective of his own inclinations. As Professor Giddings points out, this meeting was aware that it was attempting team work and that in order to do something *for* itself effectively, it must do something *to* itself. The ability of a community to work together was determined largely by its social character. I have been told a story of a certain community which in the early days was in a territory under dispute between Lord Baltimore and William Penn. I have later been informed that it was in some respects apocryphal, but venture it for its homiletic value. William Penn with Quaker shrewdness hurried men into the territory to survey it. Then fearing that his Quakers hadn't the qualities of pugnacity essential in a buffer state, settled the community in question with a colony of Scotch-Irish Presbyterians. I was informed, though I do not vouch for the veracity of the statement, that it was on record in the Philadelphia meeting that the only instance in which the Quakers actually engaged in serious combat was with these same Scotch-Irish Presbyterians planted there to protect them from the inroads of Lord Baltimore's minions. However that may be, the community is still there and has a remarkable degree of cohesion, secured, I think very largely because there has always been among these people a high degree of social like-mindedness. Now it seems to me that the ability or willingness of a given group to achieve a real community consciousness determines its possibility of progress, and a community consciousness I define simply as a dominating social point of view, an active recognition of our essential community relationships, that no one can or should play the lone game who lives among neighbors but that each must share a community of interest and activity. It is simply a controlling community motive. It requires some means of constant social expression, formal and informal, some definite channels of common activities, some form of common pressure which will secure a social leverage on all. It is obvious that there are in every community things which need to be done which everybody knows need to be done, which everybody indeed would like to see done, but which never get done. I remember fording a creek with some little discomfort in northern Alabama, not an unusual necessity in many parts of the south, but made annoying by the fact there was across that creek a splendid bridge, concrete abutments, iron superstructure, complete in everything but one particular. No one could get on it, or having gotten on it, could get off. On inquiry I learned that an agreement had been made between the community and the county that the county would build the bridge if the community would build the approaches. The bridge had stood there for two years. The gravel was in the bottom of the creek that ran under the bridge. I found absolute unanimity of opinion as to the desirability and necessity of providing the approaches, but it hadn't been done. That is an extreme instance of a very common thing.

Elements in the Problem of Social Progress
Now if I were to attempt to chart the way through such problems, I would do it in this fashion. Community progress, as Professor Morgan so clearly indicated to us, has come to be a question of social action. We are definitely emerging from the time when it is possible for the action of philanthropically-minded individuals to solve our community problems. Social action, however, depends on social feeling. We cannot work together without common bonds of sympathy and understanding. Social feeling, I suspect, depends largely on social discipline, a thing which the farmer has largely been without and which he has resented. So every farmer the world over has resented efforts to make him conform to certain standards of production, efforts to make him co-operate with his neighbors for the elimination of some common menace like the cattle tick or the boll weevil. He has resented it in religion. He has insisted on multiplying sects in the country, that he might satisfy his own preferences rather than seek the community's good. Social discipline is expressed through the social order which we must learn how to create in the country. A social order is simply the sum total of our generally accepted disciplinary standards. It is the quintessence of what is being done. We create social standards on the level of our greatest common denominator; so the laggards in the procession tend to set our standards. George Russell, in his brilliant essay on "Co-operation and Nationality," gives a sparkling picture of the way in which the Irish farmer, although persistently resisting attempts to make him sink his own preferences in common standards, nevertheless actually does do pretty much what the social order makes him do. He cites an instance of a friend of his who went down the street in Dublin and in some sixty stores sampled the butter and in all but

one instance found it adulterated, the moral of course being that what one did the rest did.

Now, the social order comes back fundamentally to our social philosophy. Do not make the mistake of under-estimating the value of the spiritual side of our rural problem. It is fundamentally a human question and a spiritual question, one which concerns the spirit and temper of the people. There is plenty of knowledge believed by all to solve all of our rural problems, but we do not appropriate it. It is a question of application and that is a question of the spirit.

Lastly, if I have not more than used up my time, I might speak of the part played by community institutions. I only want to mention two things. The place of any given institution in community development is going to be marked, first, by whether it has a community-wide outlook and a constituency at least potentially community-wide. A church which aspires to community influence must be ready and willing to serve the whole community. The second thing is whether the institution has a genuine community program, that is, whether it has set before it concretely every aspect of the community's life, or whether it limits itself to some small detail, merely a phase of existence.

These are the elements as I see it in the problem of community development, the underlying factors which must be taken into account if we are to make progress at the job of so organizing the country side that every farmer will live within a group large enough to serve all his major interests and yet small enough to let him stand out as an individual in it.

A REDEFINING OF THE SCOPE AND FUNCTIONS OF THE JUVENILE COURT,
IN TERMS OF THE RURAL COMMUNITY

Wiley H. Swift

It is only a few years ago that the people of a mountain community
gathered on a Sunday morning around a woman of about forty-six or
seven years as she lay pale and almost speechless on a bed on a
little front porch of a tiny home. They had gathered by request.

The preacher was there in their midst and made a little talk to
the effect that the sister who lay upon the little bed before them
had, up to about a year before, lived a strong life and hadn't had
scarcely a pain or an ache; but that here of late she'd been a-
havin' her troubles, that she had drunk all sorts of teas, taken
all kinds of medicine sold at the store, and had had two doctors
a-tendin' on her regular without gettin' any better whatsomever.
He said that the doctors had done the best they could, but had finally give it up, that they didn't know what wa a-aildin' of her
unless there was something the matter with her innards, and that
they had decided to take her to the hospital and have her cut open
to see what was the matter and if anything could be done. The
preacher, continuing, said that the sister, realizing the uncertainty of life, especially when one goes to the hospital to be cut
open, desired that all the people gather about her bedside and sing,
"God, Be With You Till We Meet Again." They gathered and sang as
requested, and then they lifted the sister on her little bed into
the hack to be jolted down the rocky road ten miles to the train to
be carried on it thirty miles to the nearest hospital. They brought
the sister back, not on the little bed, but, utterly speechless, in
a coffin. The jolt of the hack, the ride on the train, and the
operation had been too much for her.

A gruesome tale, and told simply to say that the sister was quite
as near to a good hospital as the child of much of the rural country
with which I am familiar is to a well-organized and efficient juvenile court, or any other organized social agency public or private.

There are children in these rural counties, thousands of them.
Some are abused, some are neglected, some are dependent, some are
just poor, and some are going wild. Unfortunately, there are no
private agencies, such as you have in the city, to cover the field.

Proceedings, National Conference of Social Work, 1921. Wiley H.
Swift was Special Agent of the National Child Labor Committee in
Greensboro, North Carolina.

The church does a little, oh, so little, but about all that is done. The Red Cross, hard as it may be trying, is touching only the high places. I see no prospect of any very great improvement in this respect, and therefore, feel not only free but forced by observation to say that whatever is to be done in strictly rural communities for the care of children, unfortunate for any reason, will have to be done by someone employed to do it and paid for his work out of public funds. Rural social work will have to be paid for just as school teaching is paid for—a thing well recognized in well-organized cities, a thing that must come to be recognized everywhere.

Every child should be under the geographical jurisdiction of an efficient juvenile court. The rural child is entitled to have his interests cared for and promoted by the best juvenile law that can be evolved for the care of urban children, but you cannot expect the same type of full-time juvenile judge as in large cities. There cannot be a full-time juvenile judge for every county. The expense would be burdensome, and besides there would not be enough work to keep him content. Some other plan must be thought out.

The best we can do, perhaps, is to make some already established court of record a juvenile court. Where by reason of rotation the judge is absent from the county much of the time, someone must be provided to sit in his place. If nothing better can be had, a referee under an already established court of record would serve, but I think that not much difficulty will be met in finding an officer for the place. In North Carolina we took the clerk of the Superior Court. In Tennessee the clerk and master in chancery seemed to be the proper officers. After all, almost any honest person of good common sense and with good probation service would make a fair juvenile judge. The rules of practice are simple, and the probation officers are, or should be, there to tell the judge what to do. It would be a great mistake to undertake to press full-time juvenile judges upon rural communities. Any attempt to compel small rural counties to support a special full-time juvenile judge will fail, as it ought to fail, being altogether impractical.

The rural juvenile court, just as the city juvenile court, should be a court of record and on a level with circuit, district, superior, or criminal courts and should have exclusive original jurisdiction of all children under eighteen years of age. It may be necessary to give the juvenile judge the right, in his discretion, to remand children over fourteen years of age to criminal courts for trial in certain extreme cases. I am not at all sure that any child under eighteen years of age should ever be tried in a criminal court; but if he is to be tried there it should be always by the permission of the juvenile judge. The juvenile and not the criminal court should

be named as the court of hearing in the first instance; first, because if this right is not distinctly placed in the juvenile court
it will be exercised by the criminal court; and second, because I am
seeking to avoid any excuse for trial by jury in juvenile courts.

It is now admitted by all that a juvenile court should be a chancery court. I am thoroughly convinced that no rural juvenile court
should ever proceed by jury trial. Jury trials mean delay and a
lack of well-considered treatment of the case. On the other hand,
no person should ever be convicted of any crime without the right of
trial by jury. In fact, he cannot be legally convicted of a crime
without this right. To say that the right of appeal protects this
right means nothing except delay, a possible hearing by criminal
court, and that your juvenile court is made a second to the criminal
court whereas it should be on a level with it.

No person should ever be tried in a rural juvenile court for the
commission of a crime. So far as children are concerned the very
prime purpose of a juvenile court is to deal with the child as a
child and not as a criminal. As for adults, the court should proceed
by orders leaving the matter of conviction for crime and punishment
to the criminal courts. The court having jurisdiction of the child
should make orders with reference to it reaching adults, and all such
orders should be enforced by contempt proceedings.

At present, I am of the opinion that the juvenile court for rural
counties should have exclusive original jurisdiction of all delinquent, neglected, and dependent children. If there is to be a
mothers' pension it should be administered by this court.

There is no question as to delinquency and it seems to be generally
admitted that the juvenile court should handle cases of neglect, as
well as cases of dependency, when the guardianship of the child is
to be transferred. The time may come when simple cases of dependency and mothers' pensions, if there are to be mothers' pensions,
will be handled without juvenile court action, but that cannot possibly be until well-articulated state and county child-caring agencies
are established. In some parts of the country they do not now exist.
The juvenile court idea is coming to be understood by rural people.
A county board to expend public funds for the relief of dependent
children is not so well understood, except as a function of county
courts or boards of county commissioners, and they are what I fear
most.

Whenever state and county child-caring boards are created with good
county workers much of the work for the relief of dependent children
can be carried on without hearings in the juvenile court, but even
then it will have to be done in very close co-operation with that
court, and I am inclined to the belief that orders for the expendi-

ture of public funds for relief should be issued by that court. In my opinion it will be a most serious mistake to attempt to build up state and county agencies to care for dependent children apart from the juvenile court and at the expense of preventing the extension of its probation system. It must never be forgotten that it is no easy matter to get even one full-time public social worker in most counties. In many, many counties there is not one, and no great assurance that there will be even one soon. For me the juvenile court is the first hope. It would be a great mistake to allow anything to come in to interfere with its development in rural counties or to attempt to withdraw a part of the children from its jurisdiction.

I doubt the wisdom of a mothers' pension law as it is now understood. A comprehensive system for the relief of all children in need would be much better. But if we are to have mothers' pensions the administration in rural communities should lie in the juvenile court. So far as I can see it is the only rural agency that is likely to have competent investigators and supervisors until state and county child-caring boards are developed and when they are developed they will have to work with the juvenile court. And besides, if the juvenile court is to have the right, after investigation, to order a parent to make payments for the support of his child, why should not that court order payments for children in need out of public funds? For the time being, therefore, I am of the opinion that in the rural sections of those states about which I know something, the juvenile court should have jurisdiction of all delinquent, neglected, and dependent children. In saying this I seek not so much to preserve the jurisdiction of the court as to insure at least one competent social agent for every county. There is no hope of getting two soon; there is no great assurance of getting even one in the rural counties of some states.

Probation service or, since I am thinking of dependents as well as delinquents, competent investigation and constructive social work is the key to the whole situation. This worker, investigator, supervisor, and probation officer must be had in every county. There are almost no private agencies; but, even if there were, there would be need for probation officers and official workers, as has been found in urban work. It is no part of the business of a judge to go nosing around, and there is no assurance that his nose will be in good working order. It all rocks back to the social worker. He must be had or else rural children will fail to get that care which should be theirs by right.

That is what you have in the cities with all your private agencies. That is what we must have in the rural sections where there are no organized agencies of any sort. He should be the very heart and brain not only of the juvenile court but of all public social effort. I'd put all, except strictly judicial functions, into his hands and, in order to get the best, most of the money now available into his pocket. His employment in every county is an absolute necessity. Rural children by scores, by hundreds, by thousands will go on being neglected until the government, state, or county, sets an eye to see and a head to decide what needs to be done, and to insist that it is done promptly, continuously, and effectively.

Just how to get this worker in the rural counties of every state is not now entirely clear to me. He should, of course, be selected in a manner that does no violence to existing institutions or legal inheritances, which means that the manner will be somewhat different in different states. In my own state (North Carolina) he is a general welfare agent. He is employed by the Board of County Commissioners and the Board of Education sitting jointly. He must be approved by the State Department of Welfare. His salary is fixed by the two boards sitting jointly to elect him. He has to his aid a county board consisting of three members appointed by the state department. The plan seems to work very well, but it is no part of my business to urge any other state to take over the North Carolina plan. In fact, no other state could take it over outright and make it work. Good systems cannot be imported, they must be developed at home, grown out of all the inheritances and experiences of the people.

There is, however, this to be said: North Carolina through its juvenile court, a part of the superior court, its state board of public welfare, its county boards of public welfare, and its county superintendents of public welfare, who are the chief probation officers of the juvenile courts, is trying to keep a constant oversight of children and of agencies undertaking to care for them. It means something that we do have an actual juvenile court in every county and a legal agent charged by law and paid to look out for children both before they come into this court and after. We do have our court with its probation officer, we do have our county social worker, not the best perhaps, and we do have state supervision of child care outside the juvenile court. These are the elements of a system, however poorly we may be making application of them.

THE NORTH CAROLINA SCHEME OF RURAL DEVELOPMENT

E. C. Branson

I am not meaning to be impertinent when I say to the Local Community
Section of the National Social Work Conference that the welfare problems of forty-four million people in the United States are not industrial and urban, but agricultural and rural. The multitudes that
dwell in the vast open spaces of America beyond our city gates have
not yet had their day in court. These country multitudes have problems that are of pressing national importance, and they must be fully
considered at some early day if we are to keep our town and country
civilizations in sane, safe balance. There is no more important
problem than that in any land or country. It may not be amiss,
therefore, to fix the attention of this conference for a little while
upon the country end of our national life.

Our Countryside Social Problems
I have been asked to present to you the North Carolina scheme of
rural development. The phrasing of my subject is not my own, which
gives you a chance to acquit me, if you will, of what a Cracker
friend at home calls "toploftical assumacy."

North Carolina is a rural state, like all the rest in the cotton
and tobacco belts of the South. Our industrial bread-winners are a
larger portion of the entire population, than in any other Southern
state, but in 1910 they were only 133,000 all told, or less than
one-seventh of the total number of persons engaged in gainful occupations, and more than half of these live under rural conditions in
mill villages of fewer than 2,500 inhabitants. Our welfare problems
are, therefore, mainly rural. Which means that for two and a half
centuries we have been unaware of social ills and unconcerned about
them; or so until our present governor, Thomas W. Bickett, in epoch-
making fashion, focused public thought upon their superlative importance.

Nearly exactly four of every five people in North Carolina are

Proceedings, National Conference of Social Work, 1919.
Eugene Cunningham Branson was Kenan Professor of Rural Social Science
and founder of the Department of Rural Social Economics at the University of North Carolina. His background had been rural education,
first in country schools and then as President of Georgia State
Normal School. He was a member of the North Carolina Commission on
Farm Tenancy and a great advocate of those "who own not an inch of
the soil they cultivate nor a single shingle in the roofs over their
heads."

dwellers in the open country, outside towns and villages of any sort
or size whatsoever, only eight families to the square mile the state
over, both races counted. And they dwell not in farm groups or communities as in the old world countries, but in solitary, widely
scattered farm homes, fewer than four families per square mile in ten
counties, and fewer than seventeen per square mile in our most populous country county. Our country civilization is analyzable in terms
of individual farmsteads, settlements, and neighborhoods. Compactly
settled country communities conscious of common necessities and organized to secure common advantages are few and rare. County community is a term that means something in the Middle West, the North and
East; it means little as yet anywhere in the South. We have such
communities here and there, but they are infrequent, sad to say.

Our ills are not mainly those of congested population centers where,
in Rousseau's phrase, the breath of man is fatal to his fellows. We
know little of the bewildering, baffling city problems of progress
and poverty, magnificence and misery side by side. Our ills are
mainly the social consequences of (1) farming as an occupation
(2) in sparsely settled areas—the ills of solitariness, remoteness
and aloofness. We are far removed from socialism in any sense, good
or bad. On the other hand, we have always been but a hair's-breadth
away from individualism, raw, raucous and unorganizable. Both the
best and the worst of my home state lies in the fact that too long
it has been excessively rural and intensely individualistic—in
business enterprise, in legislation and civic rule, and, worst of
all, in religious consciousness. Our fundamental ill is social in-
sulation and our fundamental task is local organization for economic
and social advantage, for local self-expression and self-regulation
in community affairs, and for generous, active civic interest in
commonwealth concerns.

Such, in brief, are our problems, and they are the problems of
some forty-odd millions of people in countryside America.

A Common Social Menace
In passing, let me call your attention to a social ill of fundamental
sort that increasingly menaces our town and country populations
alike, namely, the steady decrease in the number of people who live
in their own homes and till their own farms, the steady increase of
landless, homeless multitudes in both our town and country regions.
These homeless people shift from pillar to post under the pressure
of necessity or the lure of opportunity. They abide in no place
long enough to become identified with community life, to acquire a
proprietary interest in schools and churches, and to develop a robust

sense of civic and social responsibility. Instable, irresponsible citizenship is a seed bed—a hot bed, if you please—for every sort of irrational impulse.

Already three-fifths of all dwellings in the United States are occupied by tenants and renters; in Boston the ratio rises to 80 per cent and in Greater New York to 89 per cent. Fifty-five million people in these United States spend their days and nights, like poor Dante, going up and down somebody else's stairs. In general, the fatal law of our civilization seems to be that the more populous and prosperous an area becomes, the fewer are the people who live in their own homes and dwell unmolested and unafraid under their own vines and fig trees. I have yet to hear in this conference the discussion of any social ill that is not sequentially related directly or indirectly to home-ownership by the few and land orphanage for the many. I shall hope to hear this foundational problem threshed out at length at some early day in the National Social Work Conference. It concerns both our city and country civilizations in fundamental sort.

Social Activities in North Carolina

I was drafted into the service, I presume, to give you a modest account—if such a thing is possible—of North Carolina's brave attack upon the social problems of a rural people during the last four years. The story is full of detail, but, briefly, it covers a common-school fund nearly doubled during the war and a fifty per cent salary increase for public school teachers as a legal requirement; an illiteracy commission with a support fund of $25,000 a year; a compulsory school attendance law, together with a standard child-labor law; three and a half millions of bond money for enlarging and equipping our public institutions of learning and benevolence; nearly $250,000 a year for public health work, for the medical and dental inspection of schools and the free treatment of indigent school children, and for the defense of our homes against the ravages of social disease; around a million two hundred thousand dollars a year of local, state and federal funds for agricultural education and promotion; a law sanctioning co-operative enterprise in general, and in particular the best co-operative credit-union law in the United States, as a result of which we have more farm credit-unions than all the rest of the states combined; a state-wide cotton warehouse system based on the best law in the South; a public welfare law establishing a state welfare board with ample authority and support, and calling now for county welfare boards and superintendents, not optionally, as in Indiana, Kansas, Minnesota and other states, but mandatorily; a juvenile court and probation officer in every county, and in every city with 10,000 inhabitants or more; a rural township incorporation

law and a state commission charged with rural organization and recreation; a state-wide social service organization, and public welfare courses at the state university.

And so on and on. Thirty-five laws of economic and social import
have gone on our statute books in four years, all of them directly
or indirectly related to rural social welfare. It is a new kind of
legislative activity in North Carolina and we have had more of such
legislation during Governor Bickett's administration than can be
found in any hundred years of our history heretofore. It has been
epoch-making legislation and it ushers in a great new era in North
Carolina. The valley of humiliation located between two mountains
of conceit, as a Tarheel is accustomed to describe his state to
Virginians and South Carolinians, has suddenly become the Valley of
Decision that the prophet Joel saw in his dreams.

The Rural Township Incorporation Law

So many experiments are recently under way in North Carolina, that I
have been at a loss to guess just which one of them the chairman of
this section had in mind when phrasing my theme for me.

I have, however, a vague suspicion that she meant for me to discuss
in particular our Rural Township Incorporation Law—a law that makes
it possible for the people of our country neighborhoods to create by
popular vote the civic machinery necessary to self-expression and
self-rule. It is the familiar town meeting of New England. It was
indigenous to the democracy of a people compactly settled in communities in limited areas.

The idea has been slow to develop in the South because of our vast
spaces, and the settlement of our people in early times and at the
present day in individual farmsteads. Our counties are large as a
rule, many of them larger than the state of Rhode Island. Our townships are large. They are geographical divisions and administrative
units in the political scheme of things. They are nowhere economic
or social groups.

The net result has been a feeble sense of civic and an almost utter
lack of social responsibility in our country counties. A perfectly
natural result has been honest but inefficient and wasteful county
government in the South, or so as a rule. The remedy for this sad
state of affairs, as Thomas Jefferson clearly saw a hundred years ago,
lies in organized community life and local discipline in righteous
self-rule. It is essential to the perpetuity of American democracy
and the lack of it threatens our entire civic structure, said he.
Our rural township incorporation law is a tardy recognition of Thomas
Jefferson's wisdom.

124

The law is two years old and, because it rests upon our ancient rights of local option in static farm areas, township organization under this law is slow—so slow that only six communities in the state are so far organized even on paper. It is a hopeful experiment of the right sort, and in time it will head-up into great results.

Legislation and Local Social Welfare

Lest you think we a Bourbon and not a democrat in political philosophy, let me hurry to say that I think of legislation as related to social aspiration and effort about as I think of the steel tubing in a Hudson River tunnel.

The tube of steel is indispensable to permanency. So are law and civic machinery necessary to give form and permanency to social activity. Of course, I believe that true democracy is the outward evidence of inner grace and worth; that it must be developed from within and cannot be imposed from without. But ours is a represented democracy. Our own representatives make our laws and, if they are unfit, sooner or later we freely elect new representatives and repeal obnoxious laws.

Such reform legislation as I have discussed is not dropped down from above like manna; it is grown out of the social soil under the hand of our chosen civic servants.

This I know—a vast deal of the gospel of co-operation, say, has gone to waste in America, because it has lacked fit legal sanction in state legislation. Co-operative credit unions, for instance, are rapidly developing in North Carolina because we have what other states lack—an effective co-operative enterprise law.

Our local welfare problems are being directly attacked by county juvenile courts, county public welfare boards, county probation, parole, and school attendance officers, and county factory inspectors charged with enforcing our new child labor law. There is nothing new to you in these forms of social activity, except perhaps the fact that these county boards and officials have come into existence in North Carolina under state-wide compulsion and not by community choice as in other states.

It is highly significant that a rural individualistic people has at last been willing to lay aside the sacred rights of local option and to choose instead the sacred rights of childhood as an imperious commonwealth concern. A full four-fifths of our children are country children and they have long suffered from the social inactivity of remote rural counties; not more nor worse in North Carolina than in similar counties in other states—say in Clinton and Franklin counties in New York state, or in Fayette county, Pennsylvania, or in Windham county, Connecticut, or in Aroostook county, Maine, or in the delta region of South Illinois.

But at last the great common heart of North Carolina has heard the cry of her children, and as a state she has sounded a call to the colors for a grand army attack upon the enemies of childhood—upon poor schools in rural areas, upon bad health conditions, upon the be-numbing drudgery and unrelieved loneliness of life in solitary farm homes. Nothing less than this will avail to explain the ground swell of legislative reform in North Carolina. When one stops to think it through, it becomes plainer than a pikestaff that our radical legis-lative reforms are sourced in a newly awakened, immense concern about the children of North Carolina.

The simple fact is that every really worth while economic and social activity is related to the supreme purpose of making "this dirty little spot in space that men call earth," a safer and happier place for children to be born into and to grow up in. This is the very essence of the mind and message and meaning of Miss Lathrop to this generation of men and women the world around. May God multiply her kind ten thousand times over in every land and country.

Note: The writer is referring, of course, to Julia Clifford Lathrop (1858-1932), co-founder of the Chicago School of Civics and Philan-thropy, first Chief of the United States Children's Bureau (1911-1921), and advisor to the Child Welfare Committee of the League of Nations (1925-1931). [E.M.-B.]

THE COUNTY UNIT AS A BASIS OF SOCIAL WORK AND
PUBLIC WELFARE IN NORTH CAROLINA

Howard W. Odum

This paper will be a clear-cut disappointment to all if it is expected to set forth the story of a system of county unit work which
has made good in anything like an adequate coordination of social
work agencies and resources. Our purpose is to discuss a concrete
situation in order to approach a very important general problem. The
paper, therefore, will present briefly a simple analysis of the
situation, with its promise, its problems, and its limitations. The
keynote, however, is one of considerable hopefulness. The North
Carolina plan appears to offer one of the most hopeful experiments,
both for the reason that those who work in North Carolina are fully
aware that the experiment has only begun, and has yielded little of
definite final value, and because it is an admirable system, well
adapted to rural areas. The experiment is most promising, further,
because it approaches the problem of governmental social work with a
concrete plan, and because in the initial years there is ample evidence that a good beginning has been made.

We may discuss the topics briefly under four general headings.
The first will include a brief statement of what the North Carolina
county plan involves, or may involve, in terms of actual organization.
The second will present a brief statement of some of the underlying
principles and problems involved in social work as public welfare in
rural areas. A third will raise the question as to how well North
Carolina is measuring up to its opportunities, including favor and
disfavor with general social work organizations. A fourth important
aspect will include consideration of important study, research, and
experiments which must be made before the system can be fairly
tested by a necessary technique yet to be evolved. Growing out of
these it is possible that we may find stimulating challenge and object lessons for the whole field of social work and public welfare.

Perhaps the first point of emphasis should be that the North
Carolina plan provides pre-eminent emphasis in rural social work.
No one, I believe, will challenge adequately the statement that rural
social work has never yet been done successfully. Whether a county
unit plan such as North Carolina has provided in connection with its

Proceedings, National Conference of Social Work, 1926.
Howard W. Odum was Chairman of the Department of Sociology at the
University of North Carolina. At North Carolina, Odum directed the
School of Social Work and the Institute for Research in the Social
Sciences.

governmental public welfare can become the basis for utilizing all resources, coordinating efforts, finding personnel, and adapting itself to the much needed tasks will depend upon a number of factors, some of which will be enumerated subsequently. North Carolina has one hundred counties. Each county with a population of 32,000 or more is required to employ a county superintendent of public welfare. He is elected jointly by the county commissioners and the county board of education. As an advisory group there is a county board of public welfare, of three, in each county. A state-wide juvenile court act creates a juvenile court in each county, with the clerk of the superior court as judge. In the counties having a population of less than 32,000, the superintendent of schools may serve in the capacity of superintendent of public welfare where no full-time superintendent of public welfare is elected. The county unit system is a part of the state-wide plan of the State Board of Charities and Public Welfare which performs its work through a commissioner of public welfare and bureaus of county organization, child welfare, institutions, mental health and hygiene, Negro work, promotion, and publicity. In turn, there is a similar general division of activities of the county superintendents, including county administration and cooperation with the state board, general child welfare work, charities and corrections, probation and juvenile court work, school attendance work, community organization, and recreation. The large problem of school attendance work, while limiting the activities of the superintendent of public welfare toward community organization and coordination, may, nevertheless, become an admirable basis for cooperative efforts in child welfare and family case work.

Difficult problems which the North Carolina plan faces are many. In addition to the usual problems involved in rural situations with sparsely settled areas, isolation, bad roads, undeveloped attitudes toward social work, limited personnel, limited resources, and uninformed leadership, there are other problems to be faced. How coordinate other social work agencies and voluntary groups in the county? How effect cordial cooperation between town and country? How bring about both intelligently planned and executed work and cooperation on the part of social worker and farm and home demonstration agent? Public health nurse? County physician? Schools and teachers? Churches and social service? National social work organizations? How bring about effective social work and public welfare among Negroes? How interpret public welfare as the social work part of government? How overcome the elements of limited training and political habits? How, in fine, make social work and public welfare the great process of discovery, interpretation, adaptation, and leadership so essential in rural communities? Can the county be a county unit, or will it be only an approximate substitute for a unit? Will there be parallel systems and efforts in town and country? Will each of the separate workers in public welfare, voluntary social work, home and farm demonstration, public health, as technician, perform badly only a part of the work?

The basis of the present North Carolina plan of public welfare is found in the legislation of 1919 with minor amendments in 1921. To what extent has North Carolina succeeded during these seven years, first in terms of actual numerical efforts, and second in terms of the larger beginnings? The last report of the Commissioner of Public Welfare shows that although only twenty-nine counties are required by law there were, nevertheless, fifty-five counties which had appointed superintendents of public welfare. Numerically, therefore, the showing is very creditable. There has been also a steady growth in the amount of work done, and a constant improvement in its quality. There has developed, too, a steady professional spirit among the county superintendents of public welfare, and continuous improvement in their qualifications and methods. They now have a state-wide organization which meets annually with the institutes of public welfare held at the University of North Carolina under the auspices of the Commissioner of Public Welfare and the University School of Public Welfare. For six years now these institutes have been held each summer, with increasing effectiveness and with an average attendance of more than fifty. During the last two years Mrs. Johnson has provided regular lecture courses and examinations and has given certificates to superintendents completing the work. The superintendents themselves have joined in suggesting that standards of certification be set and that ideals be set continuously higher and higher. For this summer Mrs. Johnson has provided not only for the regular institutes, but also for a reading course to extend throughout the year as a follow-up to the main divisions of study at the institutes, and for work in the state and county departments. The University will provide the outlines and questions, and Mrs. Johnson and her staff will take care of the rating and classification. The main divisions of the institute work this year and of the manual of study will include modern social problems and trends, industrial social relationships, social and mental hygiene, child welfare, and family case work, together with organization and administration. Other specific discussions will include certain concrete problems relating to North Carolina.

The fact that the number of counties employing superintendents of public welfare has been continuously on the increase, and that such variations and fluctuations as have occurred have not affected the general progress of public welfare, is an acknowledged asset. An important factor in the development of public opinion both in the state at large and in certain counties has been the enthusiasm and influence of the state Federation of Women's Clubs, the League of Women Voters, and other women's organizations. A large number of concrete attainments might be cited as evidence that the North Carolina plan has achieved substantial and successful beginnings.

Nevertheless, it must be admitted that up to the present time there has been no county organized successfully on anything like a complete or satisfactory basis. There has been no county organization which has ample personnel and resources. There has been no county in which the work of town and rural areas has been adequately correlated. There has been no county with a satisfactory permanently going county council. There has been no county in which the work of the superintendent of public welfare has met the wishes and standards of all other social work agencies. There has been no county in which the county board of public welfare has functioned with complete satisfaction to all concerned. There has been no county in which the home demonstration community clubs, the work of the farm demonstration agent, the public health nurse, and the school folk have been satisfactorily correlated. There is no county in which rural case work can be satisfactorily demonstrated. There is no county which the School of Public Welfare can use as a satisfactory type of field work. In other words, for the purposes of demonstrating a type of county unit of all social work such as would illustrate community organization, community councils, community chests, and other technical and theoretical aspects of the work, there is no North Carolina county which can be cited even as a reasonable example of success.

It must not be understood, however, from this that there are not outstanding examples of excellent work, or that there are not now many nuclei around which may be built in the near future more successful organizations. The very statement of limitations and of the partial achievements are but added to make of the county unit plan a more exemplary form of organization upon which to build rural social work of the future. Wake County has this year, through the cooperation of the State Board of Charities and Public Welfare and the Four-County Demonstration work in public welfare, made remarkable strides. A new superintendent of public welfare has been elected, a new probation officer (a man on full time, graduate of the University) has been appointed, a supervisor of case work and a regular case worker have been utilized, a full-time Negro social worker has been employed, and the assistance of the head of the Bureau of Negro Work has been utilized continuously. In addition to this, a teacher-social worker has been employed by the Superintendent of Schools, and she has experimented with truancy cases and other cases alongside the work of the Superintendent of Public Welfare. She is a trained worker with the Master's degree from the University of North Carolina. There have been also meetings in the city in which county-wide invitations were extended; there have been efforts to establish a detention home, and in many ways beginnings have been made to interpret public welfare to the county.

In Cherokee County, a typical mountain community, there has been developed one of the most successful demonstrations of public welfare possibilities in recent years. This plan was initiated from the cooperative efforts of the local folks and the Commissioner of Public Welfare. The first steps were the preliminary weeks of residence and organization by Miss Lily Mitchell, supervisor from the State Board of Charities and Public Welfare, and Miss Ruth Medcalf and Miss Elizabeth Smith, from the School of Public Welfare. Following the preliminary months, Miss Smith was elected superintendent of public welfare, and has since developed an admirable illustration of what can be done in a limited and practical way. She has had the cooperation of the state board and has exemplified to some extent the possibilities of the general utility social work leader in a county community which has not hitherto been acquainted with professional social work.

If, then, the county unit plan in North Carolina has in no sense demonstrated successful coordination of social work, and if at the same time, paradoxically, it is set up as an experiment of great promise, what are the considerations through which these conflicting judgments may be reconciled? Aside from the time element, and assuming the constants and variables which have been ever present in all new movements for social work and education, what are some of the principles and tasks which must occupy the attention and efforts of social work for the next decade? And, assuming the normal growth and progress along present and traditional lines, what are added features which must be worked out?

The first task is manifestly one of study and research, although in many cases problems of research must go hand in hand with problems of experiment, which is the second large task ahead.

First, there is perhaps no greater need now than that of finding out a proper technique of approach to adult population of rural areas in matters of social work and in subjects and problems involving different standards and social conflict. Recently I was much interested to hear the most experienced specialist in rural work among the churches for the United States complain bitterly of the failure of ministers and social workers in all rural areas within his church domain. I have found unanimous agreement with this sentiment among social workers in mountain areas and extremely rural regions. But

is the fault all the fault of the country folk? Our specialists admit that the major trend of the times is for the more energetic and
better educated folk of the rural areas to move on to cities. There
are left, then, the other groups of folk who have manifestly limited
leadership, while the technique of all of our own leadership is aimed
at the city, or more highly educated folk who have left the country.
Added to this is the almost universal missionary emphasis, which
ought never to be substituted for the scientific or social work keynote which is always essential to ultimate success. Some new studies
proposed in the field of teaching adults matters related to social
concern, therefore, ought to yield results in time.

Other important studies to be made are numerous. Taking a county,
for instance, there are the following fields in which something more
must be known before any final conclusions can be reached: genetic
studies of marginal families, with all the varied possibilities and
significance to social work programs and possibilities; comprehensive
studies of the general topography and areas, with suitable maps of
roads, communities, and resources; the plotting of centers of leadership and other community areas in these maps, with adequate studies
of leadership resources; intensive and concrete studies of special
communities within the county; concrete and special studies of school
attendance and school delinquency; special studies and mental tests
of groups of children; special studies of health and dietary conditions and practices; special studies of pre-school children in the
country, and their family relationships; special inquiries concerning
home, school, and vocational adaptations and opportunities in the
rural places; special studies of attitudes toward social work and
cooperation, and of organizations available for social work; special
inquiries into resources for voluntary social work and leadership;
special case work studies of rural families compared and contrasted
with other standard case studies; special inquiries into matters of
cooperation between superintendents of schools and superintendents
of public welfare; special inquiries into matters of cooperation
between superintendents of public welfare and county boards of public welfare, county public health agencies, and the voluntary agencies; special historical studies of all matters of public welfare in
the county, to discover traditional or other handicaps; special
studies of all social work agencies in all counties.

It is clear, however, that this is a long-time task, and that all
such inquiries should be made gradually, with common sense and sympathetic study, and, wherever possible, in such way as to render
actual service and promote the cause of social work and public welfare. The studies, therefore, will often require an experimental
basis of social work alongside schedules of inquiry. Among the

experiments which ought to be inaugurated will be: special efforts
to make contact with particular leaders, and special programs and
methods of stimulating sentiment for social work and public welfare;
special experiments in which the visiting teacher or the social work
teacher, as assistant to the county superintendent of public welfare,
may bring about closer coordination between the two departments;
special experiments in which the public health nurse may become a
general social worker; special experiments for coordinating the work
of home and farm demonstration agents with the county-wide program
of social work; special experiments in which county-wide organizations of parent-teacher associations may center efforts upon the pre-
school child, utilizing agencies of public welfare, health, home
demonstration; special experiments in child welfare to determine
something of the relation between undernourishment, school work, and
conduct; special experiments with farm and home demonstration agents
and school teachers in vocational guidance and direction, in connection with juvenile delinquency; experiments in county-wide community
organization, with special provisions for the small community; more
thorough experiments in case work, case supervision, and record keeping; special experiments in several counties for obtaining more
effective and intelligent work on the part of the county board of
public welfare; a series of experiments for interpreting public welfare to county-wide groups, and especially to county commissioners
and members of boards of education; special experiments in Negro
public welfare; special experiments in the coordination of county
public welfare and industrial social work; a demonstration county in
the mountain areas; a demonstration county in the east Carolina sand-
hills; a statewide plan of cooperation between the State Superintendent of Schools and the Commissioner of Public Welfare for coordinating community education, adult teaching, and school attendance work;
a state-wide demonstration for more effective state cooperation and
supervision of many aspects of public welfare work.

Growing out of the results of these studies and experiments would
come, of course, certain larger conclusions, questions, recommendations, and the basis upon which the whole field of public welfare
might be interpreted to the public. Along with these studies and
experiments would be provided, of course, field work and observation
for students in training for social work. This is, of course, a major
difficulty, and a major problem second to none in the list, but
omitted from the primary problems of study and experiment in order
to give it a special emphasis in the whole problem and to separate
it from local tasks. It seems clear, therefore, that if the studies
and experiments needed are to be worked out in a simple, slow, but
continuous way, the resources for training social workers must not

only be utilized to a large extent in cooperation with the State
Board of Charities and Public Welfare, but that this important objective should not be lost sight of in planning methods and resources.
In this way the results of studies and experiments may be brought together and made usable, not only to many counties and communities in
the state, but for social work in general.

THE INDIRECT RESPONSIBILITY OF A STATE DEPARTMENT FOR CHILDREN:
STIMULATING LOCAL ORGANIZATION

Margaret Reeves

Probably everyone engaged in rural social work will agree with Professor Steiner of North Carolina that "vast differences in rural
conditions may require various methods of approach in dealing with
rural social problems." The small truck farms of the New England
states, the extensive grain producing areas of the middle-west, and
the vast stock raising ranches of the Rocky Mountain states present
problems which differ from one another almost as greatly as do those
of urban centers, contrasted with rural districts, in general.

The point of view of this paper will be largely that of a Rocky
Mountain state of huge distances, spare population, and a few organized social resources, because it is in New Mexico that I am engaged
in developing rural social work. A few weeks ago a field representative of our State Bureau of Child Welfare found it necessary to drive
her car four hundred miles over the weekend in working on one case.
Another worker recently drove forty miles on mountain roads in going
from one community to the next town without passing a house, an automobile or without seeing a person. In New Mexico, there are 120,000
square miles with a population of less than 400,000.

Social work is now a pioneer undertaking. There is no family

The Family, July 1927. Margaret Reeves was Director of the State
Bureau of Child Welfare in New Mexico.

welfare agency which is a member of the American Association for
Organizing Family Social Work, no mother's aid fund, no private child
placing agency of any standards, no psychiatrist in the entire state,
no child guidance clinic, no Big Brother or Big Sister organization,
no protective agency or women police. Until two years ago there was
no paid, trained probation officer in the state; funds for a state
institution for the feebleminded were secured from the last Legislature but the buildings have not yet been erected. Without facilities either in the local communities or in the state for handling
many types of social problems, the case workers on the staff of the
New Mexico Bureau of Child Welfare must try to "make bricks without
straw." The ends desired are the same as those of a city case work
agency but the means employed must necessarily be adapted to meet
actual conditions of our state. A worker must not only diagnose her
case but often she must try to create the means of treatment rather
than to make use of existing facilities. This lack of organized resources should constitute not a reason for discouragement but a
challenge to one's inventive powers and to the worker's ability to
bring things to pass.

Prior to taking the first steps in program-making for a modern,
progressive, constructive plan of public welfare for any state, we
as social workers need to study very carefully certain important
factors. We should give careful consideration to governmental questions, matters of taxation, existing legislation in the state and
its administration, and facilities available for treating and preventing social disorders. Of even more importance, however, than
the study of these questions is a definite effort to understand the
point of view of the majority of the citizens of that state toward
their government and toward public welfare in general.

In New Mexico, for example, our people sincerely believe in state-
supported, state-controlled enterprises. It is an accepted principle
of government with us that final responsibility for public education
and public health rests with the state. The value of private undertakings is recognized but it is felt that the state must have ultimate responsibility in these matters. We are using the word "state"
here as meaning the public, the government as versus private undertakings; these activities may be financed by the state, county, or
municipal governments. The task of the New Mexico Bureau of Child
Welfare is to foster the growing conviction that the state has as
much responsibility in positive child welfare and social work in
general as it has shown for some years in the fields of education
and public health. This view of state responsibility is accepted in
New Mexico first of all as a principle of government but it also has
gained many adherents because state supported enterprises seem ex-

pedient. In this pioneer territory there are too few people and too
limited financial resources to support many private undertakings,
which would maintain accepted standards, whether in the field of education, public health, or social work. We find here a reason for
the emphasis on our State University and other state supported institutions of higher learning, on the State Bureau of Public Health,
and on the State Bureau of Child Welfare. The latter is the only
division of state government in New Mexico with any type of social
service program.

The people in our part of the country believe not only in giving
the state final responsibility in these matters, but they also approve granting their state departments and state officals broad,
general responsibilities and powers; then holding them accountable
for the results obtained. For example, in New Mexico the rules and
regulations formulated by the State Board of Public Welfare, under
which the State Bureau of Public Health operates, have the effect of
law without specific legislative action. The statute under which
the State Bureau of Child Welfare operates makes it legal for us to
do almost anything which is "for the betterment of the children,"
unless these activities have been specifically assigned to another
division of government. It is extremely unlikely that an older,
eastern state would consider giving such broad powers to a state department. We feel in New Mexico at the present time that there are
advantages in such general legislation which permits us from time to
time to initiate activities as we feel they are needed and can be
accomplished, yet does not require us to do those things for which
we are not equipped, or which it may be unwise to undertake at this
time.

In New Mexico, the State Bureau of Child Welfare is trying to serve
dependent children; this is largely an indirect responsibility, hence
the topic assigned me for discussion. Our responsibility for dependent children is indirect in the sense that no children are committed
to the Bureau by the courts, no children are made our "wards." Recent legislation, however, has given us direct responsibility in a
few, particular types of cases. No adoption of a minor child may be
consummated in New Mexico without an investigation by a social worker
on the staff of the Bureau of Child Welfare, with subsequent report
and recommendation to the district court. A report from our office
is jurisdictional before an adoption may be consummated, though, of
course, the district judge need not accept our recommendation. In
actual practice we have not to date had the experience of a district
judge acting contrary to our recommendation in an adoption case. The
New Mexico Bureau of Child Welfare also has direct responsibility
in cases of violation of the state child labor law as our office is

the central, state administrative agency named in the law. We are
engaged in other types of children's case work but only until further
local organization may be effected. Often the community, the district court, the public schools or a church society is actually the
"case" as much as the child involved. The case work of the Bureau
of Child Welfare is part of a broad, state-wide educational program.
Sometimes a field representative from our office remains in a given
county a month, or even two months, to show what would be done by a
full-time, resident social worker for the court, public schools, or
county commissioners. I am not sure that we are "stimulating" local
organization as the topic assigned me would indicate; we are definitely encouraging a normal, natural development of local units of
social work in our state, with the hope that there may be permanency
for the project.

There are numerous important factors in developing local organization for social work on a state-wide basis. We can here consider
briefly only three essentials: a carefully prepared state-wide plan;
trained personnel for social case work; a definite relationship between the local units and a state department or bureau.

The state-wide plan should emanate from a central office, whether
a state office, as in New Mexico, or a private organization such as
the State Charities Aid Association of New York. It is very important, however, that this plan should be elastic so as to meet the
needs of each individual community and county. The carefully worked
out plan is necessary if there is to be consistent rather than haphazard growth but in New Mexico we do not want legislation providing
a uniform pattern for all local units of social work. We have thirty-
one counties which are divided into nine judicial districts. The
district judge serves as juvenile judge and for these special duties
receives additional compensation. In New Mexico all the district
judges are members of the bar and in fact generally leading attorneys.
In the past two years the Bureau of Child Welfare has developed, with
the cooperation of the district judges, the first two units of social
work in our state. The first unit, established in March, 1926,
covers the Sixth Judicial District, or three counties. This worker
is paid entirely from court funds though she does all types of children's case work in her territory. The second local unit, secured
in March, 1927, is co-extensive with the Ninth Judicial District,
four counties. This worker is paid jointly by the juvenile court and
the public schools. She also undertakes various types of children's
case work, though emphasis is being given to a preventive program for
the public schools. The third unit, now pending, will probably be
limited to one county with the worker paid jointly by the county
commissioners and the district court.

For the two local units now functioning in New Mexico, which together serve seven of our thirty-one counties, trained social case
workers have been brought in from outside the state. They have been
employed, and are now working, prior to the securing of any specific
law in New Mexico on the subject of local units of public welfare or
child welfare. These first local workers were secured under existing
statutes. In New Mexico the county commissioners and the governing
board of any incorporated city, town, or village are "authorized and
empowered to make such provision as they may deem proper for the relief of deserving indigent persons who are objects of charity, re-
siding within their respective limits;" juvenile courts may have
probation officers; public schools may employ attendance officers.
With this existing legislation it is possible to work out various
combinations for paying the salary of a local social worker.

So often legislative action has come before conditions are actually
known and before social workers are in a position to ascertain the
particular type of legislation most beneficial. In New Mexico we do
not desire a law regarding local units of social work until these
first units have functioned at least a couple of years. At the end
of that period we should know the type of legislation best fitted to
our needs. We already know, however, from our experience that we do
not desire a law prescribing a non-elastic, uniform pattern for this
local organization. We want to be free to continue to vary the type
of these units of social work according to the different situations
found. For example, there may be district, county, and city units
within one state; they may be financed from different sources in
different localities. We do not want a law in our state making it
obligatory to have a county superintendent of welfare in every
county.

The second essential in developing local organization for social
work can scarcely be overemphasized; trained personnel for case work
is vital for the greatest success of the project. While sincerely
believing in the participation of lay people in the development of
the program we do not want to secure local units of social case work
in New Mexico where the community is not yet ready to receive and
does not actively desire a trained worker. With us these local units
must do actual case work which we do not desire to entrust to lay
people without the guidance of a resident, trained case worker. We
realize that on this point there is great difference of opinion and
variety of experiences. In some states stress is given the large
number of county boards of welfare established. Upon inquiry regarding the number of trained workers employed we learn that many do not
have such service. Where there are other social agencies with trained
workers operating in the community, or on a state-wide basis, it

may not be so important to secure trained social workers with the establishment of each local unit of public welfare. We feel in New Mexico, however, that the workers in these units will set the standards in case work in their communities for years to come as there are no other agencies and standards are as yet unformulated. In our first two units, the workers secured have each had approximately five years of social case work experience, with some previous special training for this task. So far we have been considering professional training but, of course, certain personal factors are of equal or even greater importance. We try to find workers of attractive personality, with ability to work through local groups and to utilize the assistance of volunteers and with genuine liking for the life and work of a pioneer community. No doubt it is easier for us to find these workers for New Mexico than it would be to find rural workers for some parts of the country which do not offer the same stimulation to the imagination.

We very much want advisory groups to assist and guide these local workers but such organization has not yet been effected in New Mexico. In securing additional units it may be that these groups will be organized prior to the coming of the trained worker. The sequence will be determined in each case by actual conditions. If the local group is organized before the securing of a trained worker it will not be expected that this group will engage in social case work.

The third essential in this program is very important but it may well be developed after the actual work of several local units is under way. There should ultimately be some definite relationship prescribed by law between these local units of social work and a central office. In New Mexico there is as yet only an informal relationship on a friendly, cooperative basis between these local workers and the State Bureau of Child Welfare. In establishing the first units, the judges and city school superintendents have asked us to find for them trained workers. These workers voluntarily render reports to the Bureau of Child Welfare and our field representatives visit them, endeavoring to help them with their problems. By the time our State Legislature meets again, we shall probably be ready to introduce a law to legalize this relationship. It should ultimately be provided by statute that the State Bureau is to concur in the appointments of local social workers in order that standards of personnel may be maintained even though district judges and school superintendents change. This legislation should also outline the responsibility and power of the State Bureau in reference to supervision of these units.

While we agree that "lack of uniformity in rural conditions makes

generalization concerning rural social work very unsatisfactory"[1]
the few principles here indicated seem to apply in New Mexico and
probably to other western states of large rural areas where social
work is still in a pioneer stage of development.

[1]Howard W. Odum: *An Approach to Public Welfare and Social Work*,
p. 21.

ORGANIZATION NEEDED TO SUPPORT AND FREE THE LOCAL WORKER FOR
UNDIFFERENTIATED CASE WORK

Louise Cottrell

The facts regarding social needs in rural communities have been so
vividly presented by the preceding speakers that general opinion to
the contrary, this audience will grant, first, that social problems
identical with those in cities exist in villages and in the country;
and, second, that they exist in sufficient numbers to warrant organization for their study and treatment.

The minimum organization for adequate work in dealing with these
problems must include a strong state agency, a countywide program of
undifferentiated case work indorsed by the local county officials
charged with the administration of public relief, a governing board
representative of the county with county jurisdiction, local advisory
committees, and the organized help of township officials and volunteers.

The state agency may be under private or public auspices. It may
be entirely without formal authority. But to be of real service it
must be equipped to offer able help to the counties of the state in
the following ways: first, through educational methods to convince
local people of the existence of serious social problems in their

Proceedings, National Conference of Social Work, 1927. Louise
Cottrell was initially a social worker and then Extension Director
with the University of Iowa, Iowa City.

own communities, of the damaging results of these, and of the value of skilled service in dealing with them; second, through familiarity with problems and resources in state and county so to guide the organization of the local county work that the program planned will meet the primary needs of the county concerned; third, to help in finding a worker whose qualifications are especially suited to the program and the personality of the county; fourth, to keep in sufficiently close contact with worker and board that both not only welcome advice and help but seek it, not alone in time of crisis but whenever broader experience would give needed enlightenment. When the relationship between state and county agencies is sufficiently close and sympathetic, then the county agency will recognize new policies and facilities needed throughout the state and will supply the wider understanding and support needed to bring them about.

Before undertaking a local program of undifferentiated case work, it is necessary to win the understanding and support of county officials charged by statute with the administration of public relief. We feel that the opposition of these officials can so neutralize the value of the work that effort is better invested in winning the understanding of opposing officials than in trying to carry on against their opposition. If, as is seldom the case, their minds are so closed on the subject that reason has no appeal, then the wiser course lies in educating the public to demand either a change of attitude in the officials or a change of officials before the program is undertaken. A convinced official becomes a veritable rock of Gibralter.

The county is the logical and the simplest unit for work in states largely rural because it is the governmental unit. Taxation is levied by counties, and in rural work tax funds usually support a substantial share of the financial cost of the work. Furthermore, it is unjust to tax an entire county to support work limited to incorporated places. Unless the county unit system is adopted, it is difficult to devise a system which will eventually include all of the territory of the state in a program of social work. We have already noted that social problems exist in rural places. These would probably be excluded from treatment if incorporated places became the units for work. Finally it is difficult to ignore county boundaries. Combining parts of two counties into one jurisdiction makes it necessary for the worker to deal with two sets of officials instead of one.

The county governing board may, and in most cases should, include public officials charged by statute with the control of public relief expenditures and resident judges. But it must include a group of private citizens so convinced of the local need for the work that they have reached that "white heat of determination," made famous by Mr. McLean to launch and maintain the work "in sickness and in health until death do them part." After having thus assumed definite responsibility for the organization of the local work, this board shares its burden with the staff continuously. It meets in regular session at least monthly. It serves in an advisory way to the executive in formulating policies and it helps interpret the work to the community and the community to the worker. The county organization should encourage definite program planning among the local agencies. This means frequent meetings of county case worker, public health nurse, farm bureau workers, county superintendent of schools, and local representatives of national agencies. The county board's clear realization of the tremendous demands on the local worker with the resulting physical fatigue and nervous strain places it in a position to counter-balance this strain to a marked degree. This realization on the board's part should lead to consideration for the worker expressed by effort to lift from her all of the burden of the work possible for the board and its individual members to assume. This will include entire responsibility for budget raising, considerable public speaking, provision for increase of staff when the work makes that necessary, arrangements for adequate vacation periods, attendance at state and national conferences, and opportunity for some recreation. The habit which some board members have adopted of dropping in at the office occasionally for personal interviews with the worker, if they are opportunely timed, affords an encouragement to the worker little realized by those board members themselves.

Local committees in certain population centers throughout the county are extremely valuable. The organization of these had best be postponed until the first local worker has had long enough experience in the county to know prospective committee members personally, to predict with some accuracy what contribution each would make as a committee member, and to learn to what degree his or her leadership is accepted in the local community. Local committees assume leadership for the work locally and function at small subboards. Through regular meetings and continuous work they become an informed group and an educational force. They give thought and study to local problems involving determination of policy and offer recommendations to the county board but do not act independently of it. Local committees should be represented on the county board in order that a common understanding of common problems may be maintained.

A program of undifferentiated case work integrates case work services of all varieties into one program instead of limiting itself to one specialized field as do most city agencies. It employs one staff which in a rural county usually consists of a case worker and a stenographer. Schools, courts, churches, physicians, hospitals, public officials, private agencies, and individuals all use this one organization in their work with people in trouble. Local agencies outside the county as well as state and national agencies call on the county organization for help in service to people from the local county in trouble elsewhere or to relatives of local residents under treatment by those agencies. The duties of the social worker are as varied as her organization's program.

It is humanly impossible for one person alone to carry this variety and volume of work. The worker's salvation and that of her work lies not in her doing it all herself but in her seeing that it gets done. In the country volunteer help is a necessity, and under skilled leadership it accomplishes much. I have seen a board member, long a devoted volunteer, in a rural county, assume temporarily an acting secretaryship and carry on a piece of constructive case work of which any trained worker might well be proud. Outside of a wealth of individual volunteers, the rural county supplies a few local agencies usually pressed into service in a case work program. The way in which these agencies stretch the letter of their law in order to maintain the spirit of it furnishes outstanding cheer for the future of county organizations for undifferentiated case work. The superintendent of a small hospital received as a patient a perfectly well delinquent girl, then hid her clothing to prevent escape in order to keep the child from spending a night in jail awaiting the train that was to take her to the institution to which she had been committed. A Young Men's Christian Association secretary served as chauffeur for the local county worker in order that she might make a necessary night visit fourteen miles distant over bad roads, thus adding to his own strenuous day's work. A busy neighbor drove into the country at a cost of half a day to attend a sale where for seventy-five cents she equipped a kitchen in a motherless home of very limited means. An overworked nurse appeared as witness on a court case on which the county case worker was collecting evidence. But in spite of the finest possible organization of volunteer help within the county, the local worker is largely dependent on resources outside the limits of her county. Here again her ingenuity in the use of resources is taxed to the limit. Not alone must she know the usual state agencies equipped to serve local people and the correct procedure for securing their service, but she must call on some for unusual service. One clever county worker called on the state insurance commissioner for help in forcing the collection of insurance benefits due a local family. On behalf of the local worker, state workers visiting a particular community outside the county concerned have given volunteer service in taking an interview with a reference located there.

Cleverly directed volunteer service multiplies the skill of the worker many times; in fact it is an essential without which rural work cannot carry on.

This entire Conference emphasizes an increasing realization of the need for the extension of organization for social work to include rural as well as city territory. As a result various national agencies are fostering county programs. This new interest in the rural situation, unless wisely guided, is accompanied by grave dangers that may retard social progress in small communities and in the country instead of fostering it. The logical agency for guiding the extension of work into the rural communities is the state agency already outlined above in terms of organization and function. National agencies are prone to interpret the interest in rural work as a call for local organization of their specialized services. When this results in even three or four such trying to organize in a local county independent of each other, only chaos can follow. The very forces that should unite and direct social thinking create cliques and separations. Local social forces which need to be cemented for the common good are driven farther apart through the efforts of various local cliques trying each to outstrip the other in winning public support. And unfortunately it is not infrequent that these local divisions are each following the voice of leadership of national agencies which should have conferred together in advance of entering the county but did not. Local people at first interested and responsive become confused and either withdraw their participation or realizing the waste of time, effort, and money, condemn future efforts to provide adequate organization for effective work. Consultation with the state agency by the national agency concerning local organization parallels the use of the confidential exchange by city agencies, because the county agency already knows the local agencies and the local units of the national agencies which are at work in the county concerned. The state agency is also apt to be acquainted with prominent local leaders. By this more intimate knowledge than is possible to most national agencies, the state agency can serve the national agencies at the same time that it helps the county build a program to meet primary local needs. In Iowa we have counties in which the public poor department, the Red Cross, the Salvation Army, a statewide children's agency and the extension division of the state university are all working simultaneously. Some of these agencies have integrated their programs, but the fact that any two began functioning locally without consulting the other is eloquent of the absence of the spirit of teamwork which constitutes the danger already mentioned. Before the most effective program for undifferentiated case work in the rural communities can be attained, national, state, and local agencies must drop organization loyalties and unite in real teamwork to study the county as a whole and then build a program to meet the county's primary social needs in the most direct and effective way possible.

My subject includes no mention of the qualifications of the county social worker, but since they determine so largely the success or failure of the local program, this paper would be incomplete without some mention of them. The county worker must have case work skill and capacity for executive work. But the one qualification more important than any other is her sympathy with country people which comes from an understanding of rural life. Without these three, plus health, resourcefulness, and a quick sense of humor, the worker in the country cannot carry on: and no county organization, no matter how strongly built, or how strongly backed by state and national agencies, can long survive under the leadership of a worker who does not possess both adequate professional training and a personality which especially qualifies her for work in the country.

7

Awakening Rural Social Workers to Practice Dilemmas

During the 1920s, because of the movement toward professionalization, social workers began to feel, more acutely than ever, the pull between professional standards of practice taught in schools of social work and local community values and ideas. Nowhere were these dilemmas more evident than in the rural areas, where workers were but few voices amidst crowds of laymen serving on county welfare boards. This pull of forces often earned social workers the enmity of local leaders. It also made broader the distance between community-oriented sociologists, extension workers, and adjustment-oriented social workers.

All subjects began to be discussed from this new perspective of professionalism, and voices rose in favor of the trend as well as against it. Social workers, by now being called "case workers" to denote both their training and ameliorative method orientation, were indicted for their new detachment from community ideals. This was the theme of the opening excerpt by Walter Burr entitled "The Philosophy of Community Organization: The Rural Community Ideal."

Some of the names which were to become household words among rural workers in later years initiated discussion of practice issues. Josephine Brown, later author of *Social Casework and the Rural Community* (1933), discussed at the 1922 National Conference on Social Work in Chicago the utilization of volunteers in "The Use of Volunteers in Rural Social Work." In that paper, Brown attempted to bridge the gap between theoretical training and community mores by advocating the intelligent utilization and cooptation of local volunteers by flexible "case workers" who would be ready "to abandon in emergencies [their] most precious theories."

Another problem of which rural social workers became cognizant during this period of incipient professionalization was that of continued personal and professional development. In the cities, where the supervisory system had taken strong hold, workers were to grow from the wisdom of the more experienced as well as from exposure to colleagues. But in the rural areas, the isolation of trained workers made for a very different situation. The worry became not only to train rural workers adequately, through the inclusion of appropriate content in allied subjects, such as rural sociology, but to maintain their interest in their own development once they were practicing in isolated regions.

Jesse Frederick Steiner addressed the issue of appropriate content to be included in the training of rural social workers in a paper entitled "Rural Sociology—Indispensable or Merely Desirable?" presented at the *Professional Standards and Education Section* of the 1927 "Conference on Social Work" in Des Moines. This article by Steiner touched upon a spot which was to remain tender for many decades, and which, in the minds of many, still represents a delicate matter of balance: the relationship between sociology and social work, and most particularly, rural sociology and rural social work. Steiner's article could have been written as an arbitrating document for many a contemporary university department which includes both disciplines.

Harold J. Matthews addressed the problem of the continuing development of rural workers in an article appearing in *Social Forces*, September 1927, entitled "Special Problems of Rural Social Work." Matthews exhorted lonely rural workers to attend State Conferences, to subscribe to the professional journals, and even to constantly "read and refer to *Social Diagnosis* and other reliable books on case work."

Although the Matthews article was a prime example of the exaggerated concern with professionalism during the period—a concern quite unrealistic in the rural areas—it goes beyond that topic to provide a summary of the "state of the art" and a listing of practical suggestions and answers to the dilemmas of rural practice. And, as the reader will quickly realize, many of the problems and solutions suggested by Matthews in 1927 are still quite timely.

THE PHILOSOPHY OF COMMUNITY ORGANIZATION:
THE RURAL COMMUNITY IDEAL

Walter Burr

If considered at all in an absolute sense as equivalent to the ideal
rural community, the subject assigned me is quite meaningless. One
may not correctly speak of "the" ideal community or of community
ideal. There are as many concepts of the community ideal as there
are persons who enjoy dreaming in terms of community life.

Dreamers of this sort, whether in the guise of those seeking for
themselves some holy grail of blissful happiness, or professional
social workers who carry the halo of divine election to save a world
that really doesn't seem to care to be saved by the various nostrums
suggested—these dreamers have worked a great deal of damage to
themselves (if they tried their own medicine) and to others who became their victims.

All society is in the process of social evolution. There is nothing fixed, nothing nailed down. Social life is a process, from
lower to higher, and not a fixed entity now or at any time past or
to come. There might be agreed upon certain ideal or desirable factors in the process of any given time or place, but immediately the
time is changed, and often the place, and the factors are related to
each other in a different way, some of them disappear and others
enter to take their places.

This process may be studied, especially in rural society, because
of the less complex nature of that society.

We have witnessed, during the past few years, the emphasis upon
the rural demonstration idea. In the work of agricultural agents on
Smith Lever funds, as well as of women agents, certain theories of
agriculture and home-making have been demonstrated. Chemical sub-
stances in the soils and their relation to time elements and to air
and moisture nature and content are facts to be counted on.

Even in this well-understood field, where nearly all the factors
are material things that can be moved about at will and controlled—
where the soil and the seed and the insect pests and the machinery
have no powers of thought nor volition to cause them to upset the
program of work through which the ideal is to be reached—even here
there is grave danger in assuming that an ideal can be safely fixed
and attained.

Proceedings, National Conference of Social Work, 1925. Walter Burr
was Professor of Sociology at Kansas State Agricultural College in
Lawrence. He was the author of an early text in rural sociology,
Rural Organization, published in 1921.

How much more so, then, in the field of human social action! Here you have not only all the physical factors that have any bearing upon community life, but plus that you have the annoying fact—annoying from the standpoint of the one who persists in saving the world or the community to his particular ideal—that here are humans to deal with, who have a way of springing new ideas, adopting new loyalties, making new discoveries, and even moving away from the field of action suddenly and entirely.

It is not our business to build communities after a preconceived ideal. It is our business to come in upon the life of a community as it actually is now, help to release resident forces for expression, study the process by which they continue to operate, and proceed from lower to higher. Anything other than this partakes of despotism, however benevolent the intention may be.

The status of the community at any given time is the result, up to that time, of certain living moving factors peculiar to that community. The social worker is likely to have fixed his ideal as the result of experiences and observation of other social phenomena in entirely different communities. The fact that one rural community is not like another or a group of others does not tell anything about that community being ideal or not being ideal. For it, it may be better off for not being like the others. Because a cooperative cheese factory makes an ideal basis for economic and social success in certain communities in Wisconsin, a Wisconsin worker comes down to certain live-stock or wheat sections of Kansas, and assumes that the cooperative cheese factory would make the economic basis for community success there also. This entirely without consideration of the fact that the atmospheric and climatic conditions are different, and that beef-cattle farmers and wheat farmers do not ordinarily make good milkers of cows.

In social organization the illustration holds good. Sister Kennicott may import from the outside all sorts of ideal programs which should take the place of Main Street activities. But they are not of Main Street, and have no place there. Neither is Main Street to be blamed; it has as much right to be itself in its own way as has Broadway or Lake Shore Drive.

One who desires to see efficient community life will wish above all else to have resident forces released for free and progressive action. This awakening to action may come from the outside. As to what the action shall be, will be determined entirely by those same resident forces. The awakening may be through the business life of the community, and will probably be brought about naturally by the desire of business men in the town to profit more by the increased demands which such an awakening will bring for the goods which they have to sell. Chambers of commerce are getting more and more alive to such new opportunities. Since business is becoming more of a recognized unit, business organizations, from the United States Chamber of Commerce down through the states to the counties and into the communities, may be depended upon to bring this type of awakening through what may be termed the legitimately selfish interest of business success.

Politicians also play their part in bringing about such an awakening and release of resident forces. Of course their claim is a desire to save the "deer peepul," but that is only a part of the political program for personal and party success. It is good for this community awakening to have in a state a fairly equally divided force as between parties, so that the campaigns may be hotly contested. No one needs to work this up. The outside forces, for their own interests, will search out local leaders and put them into action.

Religionists play their part in awakening the local community and releasing local forces. The denominational leader wishes to make a better record for his church order this year, and word goes out all along the line to whip up the sleepy ones. We must have this year so much more money, so many more converts, and certain other concrete evidences of advance. This all has its effect to awaken the sleeping and almost dead in the rural community. Sometimes, of course, the denominational leaders wish they had not wakened the sleeping lion—for the awakening sometimes results in a rebellion against the denomination and the starting of a community church.

The school forces are inseparably connected with state headquarters, and the state leaders are always heckling the legislature for increased requirements for teachers and equipment, etc. This makes for awakening the local community to its need.

The point is that we need have no worry about the awakening of resident forces and their release for action. When a rural community is awakened by business, or politics, or education, or religion, we find the tendency for social buzzards of various kinds to swarm in to see what they can get out of it for their organization. They have their various programs to impose upon the community. The rural community does not need them. It is made up of the same good American citizenship from which the self-elected saviors have come, and in many cases of purer American citizenship. If let alone at this point, local leadership will evolve plans and programs and projects native to the soil, that will be better than any that could be imported. When they seek sources of information there will be agencies ready with the information as to such sources. Our states are supporting liberally universities and colleges with amply maintained extension departments to serve exactly this purpose for all of our

communities, and the rural people are already paying taxes for the
support of these state agencies. There was never a time in history
when the people, through taxation, were supporting so many scientific
specialists and research men and women as they are supporting at the
present time. For the most part the people are doing this liberally
and willingly. None of this service is, or ought to be, forced upon
the rural community. It is there for the asking, and already paid
for by the people themselves. No one is justified in carrying it in
to the people until they want it and ask for it.

To enforce upon a community from the outside the ideal of any individual or organization is decidedly harmful. It is establishing
a benevolent tyranny. Social workers are usually the worst sort of
benevolent tyrants. Rural people have especially been tyrannized in
this regard by their well-meaning institutional friends. They are
continually being offered "the benevolent end of a despotism."

The rural community ideal, then, is to keep natural social forces
in politics, business, education, religion, alive and active and
operating within and without the community, arouse and awaken resident forces within the community, and then, as far as professional
social workers are concerned, give the community absent treatment.
The rural community ideal just now may be "self-determination for
the American rural community."

THE USE OF VOLUNTEERS IN RURAL SOCIAL WORK

Josephine Brown

Dakota County covers 600 square miles and lies directly south of St.
Paul, Minnesota. The cities of South and West St. Paul, so tiny
that they would probably pass as villages in the East, contain together 9,000 of the 29,000 persons in the county. The remaining

Proceedings, National Conference of Social Work, 1922. At the time
this article was written, Josephine Brown was General Secretary of
the Dakota County Welfare Association in Minnesota.

20,000 are divided among even smaller towns, villages of less than 500, and farms averaging 120 acres.

Outside of South St. Paul which has grown up around two enormous packing plants and which presents with its twenty-five or more different nationalities and its twin evils of moonshine and immorality the critical problems of a one-industry city, the county is a typical Middle Western community. Its population is composed of second and third generation Germans and Scandinavians. Farming is diversified and the towns and villages with their few factories and flour mills are largely trading centers for the farmer. In spite of a diversion of interest which comes from close proximity to St. Paul and Minneapolis, the county possesses a consciousness of its own which was recognized and used when the social forces in the community were organized on their present basis.

Prior to February, 1919, when the United Charities of St. Paul opened a district office in South St. Paul, social work in the county was limited to a Red Cross Public Health Nurse and an ineffective humane society which later died a natural death. The United Charities district office with one trained worker confined its activities to South St. Paul until June, 1920, when the Dakota County Child Welfare Board was organized by the Children's Bureau of the State Board of Control, and part of the time of the secretary was loaned to the new board. After that time the activities of the district office covered the county, a visitor and later a Ford car were added to the staff, and the number of cases grew in a year from 30 to 150 per month. Many of these were rural family cases which had come to the secretary's attention in the course of her work for the Child Welfare Board. This meant that the district office was already doing rural family work through the county when the time came in September, 1921, for a long anticipated reorganization which should place the South St. Paul office on an independent basis. It was therefore not surprising that the steering committee of the new association felt strongly their responsibility to the county as a whole and made their plans with this in view. In March, 1921, the American Red Cross had opened a health center in South St. Paul with the understanding that local people would take over its support at the end of a year. Assuming this responsibility also the new Dakota County Welfare Association was organized to do both family and health work on a county wide basis. This included responsibility for the county nurse and for the rural clinics of the Minnesota Public Health Association.

This picture would not be complete, in fact it never would have existed had it not been for the service given by volunteers. To them too much credit cannot be given for their patience, insight, and hard work. They have created the organization, it belongs to them,

on them depends its future, and it is from experience gained in working with these people that the following points regarding the use of
volunteers in rural social work are offered for discussion.

In an attempt to analyze the part volunteers have played so far in
this field, one is struck with what seems at first a startling difference between the rural situation and that in a large city.

The city worker today enters a field where case-work precedent is
already established. Her work is carefully defined and she follows
well-marked lines of procedure in selecting and putting to work
volunteers whether on committees or in more personal kinds of service. With varying degrees of success the volunteer fits into the
office of the case-working agency, given certain hours to the work
and receives a more or less definite course of instruction. The
trained worker who has been accustomed to working with volunteers
in this fashion will do well when she enters the rural field to dis-
possess her mind of all preconceived ideas on the subject. If she
does not know before she begins her county work she will soon learn
that her status here is quite different from that of the case worker
in town. There the volunteer while desirable was optional. In the
country the volunteer is a necessity. In town the volunteer is on
trial. In the country it is the social worker who is in that equivo-
cal position. The city volunteer usually works in a district far
from her own home and learns both method and facts regarding her
case from the trained worker and the case record, but in the country
the same trained worker may find that the volunteer has been a neighbor of her client for thirty years and knows more about his family
history and present situation than the average social worker could
unearth about a city family in a month. Often this information is
accompanied by a definite theory of treatment which the neighborhood
may have employed for years on that particular family, and at this
point the social worker needs an open mind, a degree of humility
heretofore unknown, and tact in abundance. She must realize that
the case by right of long acquaintance and treatment belongs to the
volunteer, not to her. She is welcomed as an adviser, not as a
dictator, and it is her privilege to sift the salient points from
the mass of information, tactfully suggest other lines of investigation, and later direct the discussion of the case to the point where
the volunteer will herself make a reasonable diagnosis and possibly
plan the very treatment the social worker had in mind.

Such a volunteer may become either a great help or a decided hin-
drance, depending largely on the skill of the social worker in handling each situation as it arises. If she is a true apostle of the
family case-work method, she will be ready to apply this method to
the individual volunteer, to abandon in emergencies her most precious

theories, and to have great patience with the farmer's slowly moving mind, for she will see that the volunteer is bound to serve in the country as she should in the city, as the leaven of her community, and if carefully taught will prove the means by which a firm foundation for future work will be laid. One antagonized volunteer, however, can do untold damage, so closely knit is the rural population in business, in politics, and by intermarriage.

Valuable, however, as this education is to the volunteers themselves and to the community as a whole, the rural social worker soon realizes that the contribution made thereby to her own education is the most surprising part of the whole process. While she has probably come to her rural work with some understanding of life on a farm, with more or less definite information about crops, live stock, markets, the effects of weather on the farmer's income, and the political structure of a rural community, the more detailed information regarding local people and conditions which is so necessary to every step in rural community organization and case work alike must come to her from her volunteers.

The training of volunteers is necessarily of the most informal kind. A first call in the company of the social worker is useful as a demonstration, but she will be surprised to find that the volunteers will often outstrip her in understanding the situation. The most untechnical terms are necessary as is also deference to the volunteer's opinion whenever possible. By far the most important part of this informal training has been through personal interviews for the volunteers have largely been key people with social vision who would naturally be sought out in the course of a general educational campaign. They have included teachers, the county superintendent of schools, judges, members of federated clubs, church and sunshine societies, parent-teachers associations, welfare association board members, two county commissioners, bank cashiers, farmers, housewives, neighbors, and even relatives of clients, and nearly all of these are men and women of middle age.

Boards and committees have a very important place in rural work. As in the city the board charged with financial responsibility is inclined to put case work in second place, but it has been interesting to note that the more rural the community from which a board member comes, the more interest he shows in family work, and especially does he want to know how much of it is being done in his own locality.

One of the strongest arguments in favor of the individual approach to the rural volunteer is found in the situation created when several of them are somewhat artifically and entirely officially brought together as a case committee. A sense of official responsibility seems sufficiently oppressive to inhibit spontaneous participation with the result that when faced with a case problem the committee turns to the secretary and says in chorus "You know—do whatever *you* think best." Almost every effort made to put the members of a case conference to work on the cases which come before their conference and with which they have no close point of contact has been a flat failure. These same members, however, have done excellent and enthusiastic work on cases in which they have had some special interest, for example, because they were neighbors, employers, or teachers of those they are helping. And from this fact the alert social worker learns one more application of the case-work method to the volunteer, namely that when a real point of contact is found and a normal impulse stirred, the interest aroused invariably results in action and a far higher grade of work. As the committee members gain confidence in themselves and a better understanding of the ends toward which they are working, the feeling of inhibition in the committee meeting wears off and much difficulty of this kind may always be avoided if the members have been tried out on individual case work before they are put on the committee. Care has been taken not to add to the constraint existing in such a gathering by withholding names of clients. Confidences are closely kept and that bane of the rural community—gossip—has been scrupulously avoided.

Many times the person referring a case has been turned into a volunteer by the right kind of suggestion as to possible lines of investigation before the case is actually taken up by the social worker herself, especially where the suspicious attitude toward an outsider, so often encountered in rural communities, requires that the way of the social worker be paved by the volunteer. Or the possible antagonism of an entire community may be forestalled by the strategic use of a key person in such an investigation.

There is always the volunteer who is afraid to interfere or who for various reasons does not want the client "to know that she knows." Denominational jealousy, also, suddenly thrusts itself upon the innocent social worker's attention.

Volunteers have not yet been asked to make original investigations. A board member may telephone late in the afternoon from a town twenty miles away to report a new family who are destitute. He is asked to find out the number and ages of the members of the family, their immediate needs, and their religion, and to secure from the proper church society or from the county commissioner emergency relief until the social worker can get there. On the other hand such definite tasks as finding employment for the girl with delinquent tendencies, befriending her in a neighborly fashion, and placing children in temporary homes have been performed with great success, or an em-

ployer or other person of some standing in the community will often be
willing to use his influence, step in at the psychological moment
and admonish the neglectful father of a delinquent girl and encourage
a man who is trying to stop drinking moonshine.

Each volunteer will serve as a nucleus in his locality for committee work of whatever kind is needed. That keen interest has been
aroused seems certain and where interest is real and actual work has
been done by the volunteer, financial support ought to follow. It
is earnestly hoped that through this use of the volunteer in its
rural districts, Dakota County will learn the value and methods of
case work and come to regard its Welfare Association as chiefly concerned with those all important adjustments which have as their objects the welfare of both the individual and the community.

EDUCATION FOR SOCIAL WORK IN RURAL COMMUNITIES:
RURAL SOCIOLOGY—INDISPENSABLE OR MERELY DESIRABLE?

Jesse Frederick Steiner

The transition from the apprenticeship type of training for social
work to that offered by the professional school under university auspices has been marked by a great deal of confusion and uncertainty
concerning the role of the social sciences in this relatively new
field of professional education. In common with the other professions
during their early stages of development, social work has been characterized by a distrust of academic points of view and methods of work.
This has often found expression in the cynical comments of the social
worker upon the futility of armchair theory in dealing with practical
social problems. To a large degree this conflict between the social

Proceedings, National Conference of Social Work, 1927. Jesse Fred-
erick Steiner had been director of the training program for rural
Red Cross workers during World War I, and was Professor of Social
Technology at the University of North Carolina, Chapel Hill, from
1921 to 1927. Although his formal background had been in theology
and sociology, he was involved in social work throughout his career.
He was the author of *Education for Social Work* (1921) and *Community
Organization* (1925).

worker and the social scientist has centered about the field of
sociology, perhaps because this phase of social science seems most
closely related to the programs of the social worker. During the
past decade the relation between sociology and social work has been
a favorite topic for discussion at various meetings and conferences
without apparently leading to any generally accepted principles or
policies for the guidance of curriculum makers.

More recently, with the new emphasis upon the development of a
rural social work training program, there have arisen similar questions concerning the value of rural sociology as a part of the equipment of the rural social worker. Obviously the whole controversy
has grown out of misapprehensions of the precise nature of the interdependence of these two methods of approach to a common problem. Both
the sociologist and the social worker tend to pass judgment on each
other's methods and programs in terms of their own immediate interests, instead of emphasizing their larger aspects and relationships.
The social worker has no time to give to sociology if it does not
provide direct aid in solving the specific problems he faces. The
sociologist, in his turn, ignores the social worker because the
latter seems to be wrapped up entirely in the matter of securing practical results. Back of all this misunderstanding are two different
types of mind made divergent through the kind of training received
and inclined to be somewhat hostile because their very closely related interests make their fields at least potentially competitive.
The whole situation has been still further clouded by the too common
fallacy of basing conclusions upon worst instances and assuming the
continued existence of defects long since outgrown. The sociologist,
for example, too frequently retains his early and biased impressions
of social work as sentimental patchwork, while the social worker
thinks that the barren sociology with which he may have come in contact a decade ago is typical of its present status.

Fortunately the whole trend at the present time is in the direction
of a better integration of social science and social work. The old
misunderstandings and prejudices do not loom up as large as formerly,
and in some instances have almost entirely disappeared. In the
fields of rural sociology and rural social work, where as yet there
is no overcrowding of competitive workers and where the social situation as compared with that in cities is relatively simple, it ought
to be possible to bring together these two groups and find common
ground upon which they can stand. Perhaps a restatement of some of
the more fundamental problems faced by the rural social worker may
make clear the vital interrelationships of rural sociology and rural
social work and pave the way for a better coordination of their
forces.

In the first place the rural social work situation is beset by difficulties which the experience gained in urban social work has thus far not shown how to overcome. The great distances and the resulting difficulties of transportation, the scattered population often living in places not easily accessible, the lack of adequate economic resources, the small number of cooperating agencies, and the individualistic attitudes of the people are among the problems that account for the slow spread of social work in rural communities. Furthermore, some understanding must be reached concerning the proper unit of administration and the plan of organization before much headway can be made in building up efficient rural agencies. It is not merely a matter of arbitrarily enlarging the boundaries and budgets of existing city agencies so that the traditional forms of social work can be extended into the open country. Unless new policies are worked out in accord with the demands of the rural situation, the results of this more comprehensive social work program may prove to be disappointing.

In planning a program of rural social work it must be recognized that its problems are closely bound up with the vast changes now going on with such rapidity in the whole rural situation. The social problems of the open country cannot be understood apart from such phenomena as the drift to cities, the improved means of transportation, the raising of educational standards, the wider use of farm machinery, the hard struggle for adequate economic returns, the decline of the rural and small town population, and similar factors that are transforming the whole nature of rural life. Under these circumstances, to intrust the development of rural social work to persons whose training makes them primarily interested in extending to rural sections the particular technique of social work in which they are skilled is a policy not likely to lead to the best results. In this pioneer stage of development of social work in the open country, leaders are required who, through profound study as well as practical experience, are fitted to establish policies and adopt methods in accord with actual needs.

The preparation of rural social workers competent to do work of this nature is a difficult undertaking. Only a few of the professional schools give particular attention to the training of rural social workers, and these are not agreed concerning the subjects of study to be emphasized nor the type of work experience that would be most valuable. Certainly the well prepared rural worker should possess, in addition to social work technique, a keen insight into the characteristics of rural life and a well rounded knowledge of rural people. While many elements must enter into the acquirement of this thorough understanding of rural situations, the study of rural sociology would seem to be indispensable, for it represents that aspect of social science which during the past twenty-five years has attempted to organize in a systematic manner our constantly growing knowledge of the social forces at work in rural communities. Admittedly, this body of knowledge is not yet adequately organized, for rural sociology is one of the most recently developed phases of social science. Nevertheless, great progress has been made in this field, especially during the past decade, and the rural social worker can afford no longer to ignore the researches of this group of students who are throwing new light on rural social problems. Technical skill, to be effective in the long run, must go hand in hand with theory. Through careful study of the work of the rural sociologists, the social worker will become familiar with concepts useful in social analysis and will acquire a point of view and a method of approach of distinct value in formulating his social programs. While this may seem to bear more directly upon his intellectual equipment, out of this study may come profound modifications of his technique in handling actual situations. In order to make clear the precise nature of the help that should come through rural sociology, let us examine more closely some of the important factors that should enter into this intellectual equipment of the rural social worker.

In the first place there must be an understanding of the nature and significance of rural social attitudes. The farmer is commonly said to be individualistic and conservative. His reaction to proposed schemes of community improvement is likely to be unfavorable even though it seems clear that the changes would be in accord with his own best interests. New methods of farming, the building up of co-operative marketing, reforms in local government, the consolidation of schools, and in fact all matters that involve a distinct break with the past, are likely when first proposed to meet with his determined opposition. All this the social worker may be familiar with, but the first step in dealing with this problem of conservatism is a clear understanding of the way these attitudes have been developed and the role they play in the lives of the people. The social worker who is not familiar with what Galpin, Groves, Gillette, Hawthorn, and Williams have said about the nature and significance of the attitudes of rural people has closed an important door of knowledge which must have its effect upon the quality of his work. Without doubt, a part of the technique of rural social work must be concerned with the changing of attitudes, for unless this can be accomplished, social work programs cannot make much headway. Some means must be devised for building up new rural attitudes concerning relief work, juvenile delinquency, care of dependent children, and supervised

recreation. In the effort to bring this about all the resources of
the sociologists and social psychologists should be utilized, for
there we may find clues of real value in building up a more adequate
technique.

Of equal importance in this intellectual equipment of the rural
social worker is familiarity with sociological concepts that facili-
tate social analysis. Concepts are intellectual tools without which
constructive thinking is impossible. Every science builds up its
own concepts with very definite connotations and meanings that are
the outgrowth of study and experience. In sociology such concepts
as social contact, isolation, competition, conflict, accommodation,
assimilation, social forces, social control, and socialization have
become familiar to students in this field and are constantly being
used in the investigation and interpretation of concrete situations.
For the social worker to be unable to make adequate use of this means
of approach to a better understanding of social problems is to cut
himself off from a source of help that is becoming increasingly important. Rural sociology, it is true, has in its earlier development
been mainly a descriptive science in which emphasis has been placed
on the presentation of facts concerning the rural population, rural
institutions, and rural conditions. It is significant, however, that
the most recent book in this field, Hawthorn's *Sociology of Rural
Life*, is built up around the concept of socialization. In this book
the rural institutions and the various factors that enter into the
rural situations are set forth from the point of view of their bearing upon the social contacts of the people. Looked at in this way,
rural social problems take on a new meaning and clues are furnished
which open up more fruitful means of investigation and interpretation. The rural social worker who has become accustomed to think in
terms of the various sociological concepts possesses a more secure
foundation upon which to build constructive programs vitally related
to existing needs.

Again, in the planning of rural social work there should be full
knowledge of the recent studies of the nature and significance of
the community as a social unit. Among the rural sociologists, Galpin
was the first to make a searching analysis of the rural community in
order to determine its natural boundaries, the actual territory
served by its various institutions, and its interrelations with
neighboring towns and cities. More recently the urban sociologists
have directed attention to the ecological aspects of the city community and have pointed out the role of topography and other physical
characteristics in the development of natural communities, the significance of which has too often been ignored by those interested in
community organization. In these days of more rapid transportation

old neighborhood lines are breaking down and now forces are at work conditioning the natural organization of communities in the open country as well as in the city. All this has an important bearing upon the problem of the organization and administration of rural social work. In the selection of the most suitable administrative unit, due consideration must be given to the fact that our politically determined communities do not always coincide with natural and cultural communities. Before going far in the promotion of rural social work programs, there should be careful study of the inter-relations of city and country and of the nature of the enlarged community relationships made inevitable by existing conditions. Here is an important field of investigation which the rural sociologists have been cultivating during the past decade. While no reliable conclusions are as yet available, this bears so directly upon the success of practical programs that the rural social worker should keep himself informed as to the theories advanced and work hand in hand with the sociologists in further elucidation of the points at issue.

Another contribution which comes to the social worker through the study of rural sociology is the conception of the complex nature of rural social problems, and therefore the futility of remedying the situation by concentration upon any single program. From the point of view of sociology, the constellation of social forces in a community are constantly interacting upon all phases of community life. The breakdown of one institution is reflected in the status of other institutions. Poverty of tenant farmers may seem to grow out of low productivity of the soil, but is associated also with an incompetent class of people, low educational standards, poor living conditions, inadequacy of neighborhood institutions, and a bad system of farm management. A program adequate to deal with this problem of poverty would need to comprise more than the usual technique of an Associated Charities. This suggests that a social work program of a rural community should be simply one aspect of a comprehensive plan covering all the needs of the community. For rural social workers to proceed with the organization of social agencies without adequate steps being taken to improve the economic and educational situation may prove to be a shortsighted policy with no lasting good results. In the large city where the various civic interests are well organized, the social worker may with some justification confine his attention to the particular social problems with which he is concerned. Under such circumstances he may very well assume that adequate financial resources can be made available for his program and that properly equipped groups of people are taking an interest in other related and equally vital problems of civic improvement. But in the rural community every step in the development of a social work program must be considered in relation to other community interests. Will the proposed undertaking draw too heavily upon available economic resources? Will the leadership required in directing this new social agency divert leadership from other important community enterprises? Perhaps a more careful study of the whole rural situation may lead to the conclusion that the urban methods of organization to deal with social problems are unnecessary as well as inadvisable in the open country. At any rate students in the field of rural sociology are becoming more convinced of the wide reaching nature of the problems of our rural civilization and are skeptical of programs that seem to deal primarily with superficial conditions. Here again is needed the cooperation of the social worker in developing sound theory. Instead of standing aloof with little apparent appreciation of the efforts of the academic group to develop a social science upon which to base social programs, the social worker should continually evaluate the results of his practical experiments and endeavor to place his work on a more scientific basis.

In conclusion, it would seem that the closely related interests of rural sociology and rural social work would bring about general acceptance of the necessity of cooperation between the two fields. Since sociology is definitely interested in such topics of vital import to the social worker as the nature of rural attitudes, methods of social analysis, the community as a social unit, the complexity of social problems, and similar matters of mutual concern, it seems absurd to raise the question whether rural sociology is indispensable in the preparation for rural social work. Even granting that the present sociological discussions of these problems are disappointing from the point of view of the practical worker, the latter cannot afford to be ignorant of the current trends of academic thought concerning matters in which he has profound interest. During the past few years there has appeared evidence in some quarters that the wide gulf that has separated the social scientists and the social workers is being bridged to the mutual benefit of both groups. In a recent official statement by the psychiatric social workers published under the auspices of the American Association of Social Workers there is set forth in the following words their conception of the place of the social sciences in their training courses:

> Psychiatric social work requires such a specialized background of psychiatric and psychological knowledge, in addition to thorough training in sociology and the technique of social case work, that entrance into the field is practically limited to those who have had graduate training courses in psychiatric social work in a recognized school of social work. . . . An A.B. degree is usually required for admission to such schools, and

undergraduate majors in sociology and psychology and courses in biology, physiology, economics, and political science will be found helpful.

Unfortunately, this statement is offset by a still more recent pronouncement, issued under the same auspices, by the family social work group, who seem to find small place for the social sciences in training programs. The following quotation makes clear their position: "A well rounded college curriculum affording broad cultural education is regarded as the best training in family case work, rather than a course of studies too closely related to the social sciences." If this represents the point of view of the oldest and most influential group of social workers, then the outlook is discouraging for a closer alliance between social science and social work. Those whose business it is to deal with the problems of society are advised to avoid "a course of studies too closely related to the social sciences." This policy of indifference to the value of the social sciences is postponing the day when social work can successfully establish its professional status and make true its claims to scientific procedure. One of the next steps to be taken in the field of education for social work is a reorganization of the curricula of the professional schools so as to bring about a better integration of graduate courses in the social sciences with the usual technical courses of instruction.

SPECIAL PROBLEMS OF RURAL SOCIAL WORK

Harold J. Matthews

Case work in rural counties and small towns is comparatively new and we have not been able to tell just what difference there is in doing case work in a rural section and in an urban community. Can the same case work methods be employed in one as in the other? Could a

Social Forces, September 1927.

case worker who has always been on duty in a city come to a rural neighborhood and work without making very definite changes in her methods?

The object of family case work is the same everywhere, we will grant; i.e., to help people out of trouble. The general philosophy will probably be applicable in both sections; but methods may be different. The application of case work methods may be different, too. A rural case worker must have a knowledge of certain things which would not be expected of a city worker. It is not always necessary that a county worker be reared in the county if she has the ability to adapt herself and see these differences that probably exist.

The General Practitioner

A worker in a large city goes about her work more as a small part of a large social service machine. A county worker is usually the whole machine herself. The city worker does not have to worry so much about finances of the organization for which she works, for example; she has less contact with the officials of the city government, she may bother her mind little about the relationship of the city government and her organization or her case load. These things are done for her. Her chief makes most of these contacts and there is a special person or organization to attend to the financial problems. There are special agencies doing preventive work. The city worker, in other words, is more of a specialist, while the county worker is a general practitioner. She comes pretty near having to do everything. She must take her clients through all stages of their treatment. She must give attention to finances and preventive work. She must have daily conferences with the Mayor and the Chief of Police and the County Commissioners and the school people and doctors and lawyers and civic organizations and churches.

The Lone Worker

The average rural social worker is usually the only such person in her county. She may go for weeks without seeing another worker. This isolation makes it necessary that the worker be alert to keep from falling into a rut, to keep from lagging behind the general development of social work. She does not have the advantages of frequent conferences with social workers, she has no supervisor with more training and experience than herself to go to for help and counsel. She cannot compare notes with anyone easily. In order to overcome these obstacles the worker should at least take the *Family* and the *Survey* and buy one or borrow a couple of books a month and read, read, read. She should constantly read and refer to *Social*

Diagnosis and other reliable books on case work. She should visit
neighboring workers as much as possible. She should certainly attend
the State Conference on Social Work every year, and any other conferences when possible and take an active part in the discussions.
As often as possible she should invite or take advantage of the
visits of State or National workers and have her records and work reviewed. She has free use of the mails to write other workers on any
problem bothering her and ask for advice and suggestions.

A lone worker is liable to fall into the habit of not consulting
or properly using local assistance, or going to only one person who
is not so busy and talking things over a little. Nothing will make
a worker more stilted and will do more to make her "sour" on the job
and divorce her from the community, even though she may be doing
very good work with her clients. A lively "case committee" will do
a lot toward helping to make the work interesting and efficient and
help her to develop in the profession. It will do a great deal toward making her see her mistakes and stimulate new thoughts on old
problems. Besides a committee, there are always intelligent individuals one can consult and discuss matters, with surprisingly helpful
results.

A county welfare worker should take the time to stop and think
about her work, size it up in her own mind and wonder if she is getting anywhere. Look at the theory of her whole job, as well as individual cases, and see how it "stacks up." Is she on the right
track, generally speaking, or is she lost completely in minute details and only struggling with a maze of petty things, which get her
nowhere and cause nervous breakdowns? A worker who says she does
not have time to do this, does not have time to keep records, does
not have time to read, does not have time to go to conferences, does
not have time to be a county welfare worker, should get another job
or get married.

Knowing One's Community
"If it is a good thing for a city case worker to know her own community, I find it is essential for the rural worker," says Miss Josephine Brown of the American Association for Organizing Family Service,
who was very successful as a rural worker (*Family*, p. 187, viii,
no. 8). The rural worker must understand every working phase of her
county. She must know the political structure, she must know something of all the organizations and churches and occupations of the
people and markets. She must be acquainted with the social make-up,
the historical background of the county and even of its prominent
families. She must appreciate and have a sympathetic understanding
of farm life. The worker who is able to talk shop with the farmer

has a great deal to her advantage. She certainly should know the common problems of the farmer and his wife.

The Small Community

A small community or rural county is intensely personal in its make-up and attitudes. We have to be careful not to hurt its feelings in our efforts to better conditions and call its attention to bad conditions which it may have never known to exist before. Those who have always lived in rural sections usually adhere to this without realizing it; a case worker coming from the city may not realize that she must be slow, careful and tactful in these matters. The appeal must be made on the basis of pride with no apparent attempt to *make them* do anything. They have gotten along so far without you and they can possibly continue to do so, they think. The worker has to be careful not to impose her skill. She will have to wait for invitation here while she demonstrates her work there. She will have to learn how to make flexible her technique and work for a positive and common good with common people. She will have to respect the county's customs in social problems and not try to change them too soon. If the county has been handling its almshouse or its "pauper list" a certain way for fifty years, it has naturally come to think of that as being the accepted way and will look with interrogations on any sudden attempt of the new person to change it all. Such changes will have to be brought about by patient demonstration and friendly contacts.

Agency Relationships

If you are the only experienced and full-time worker in a county you will have to give some time, and a good deal of thought, to agency relationships. You will have to keep peace and harmony among volunteer agencies, the churches, the clubs, etc., who are all interested in social work. You will have to show them how you can help them in their "charity work," what they can do, what they should refer to you. You will have to operate a social exchange, without actually having a social exchange. It will have to be on a much more personal basis. One county worker told me of her troubles with the ministers of the town. Every minister wanted to help, but she had to constantly be on the alert not to pay too much attention to any one church, give one more to do than any other, hold more than one meeting in succession at one church, etc. This is an especially important point, for a rural case worker will be called on to do more than she can really take care of, so she must develop her volunteer workers to help her to do many important things, and the better she is able to make pleasant contacts and efficiently develop and educate her groups, the more successful she will be.

Discouraging Board Members
This brings us to another similar problem in connection with boards and committees. A certain problem will be brought up for discussion or you will seek advice from a lawyer, doctor, or business man and get this reaction: "Old Bill Jones, of course I know him! You're surely not going to try to do anything with him, are you? He's no account and never will be. You are wasting your time. All his kids are just like him. I gave him work one time and he wouldn't stick to it," or, "My wife gave the old lady some clean bed clothes one time and she sold them. I certainly would not waste my time with them." A committee with a new case will often work hard for a proper adjustment and let the easier case slide, as impossible of solution, just because they have known the people and do not consider them hopeful. It is more prevalent in rural districts because most people know each other.

Volunteer Services
For a single worker in a county, or where there are not sufficient workers to do the work they are called upon to do, an efficient system of volunteer service is necessary if the work is accomplished. A lone county worker cannot reach every community and neighborhood every time she is called there. It will likely, if she has developed her work properly, be impossible for her even to do all the casework she will be requested to do. A county worker has broad territory to cover, she must take advantage of getting people to help her.

One county welfare worker went to each community in the county and organized a "Welfare Committee" and outlined as their duties a few simple things to begin with; they were to make some follow-up reports on cases opened and make follow-up visits for the worker. In simple cases they were frequently given the entire responsibility. They usually took (or secured someone) the entire responsibility of looking after pension cases to see that the money was properly spent and watch after the person generally. If a case was getting along all right and the county worker let it alone for a while, she could detail the "Welfare Committee" to visit the family or person in question and report any "need" which might take place.

By the above means a host of details and worry is removed from the worker. If an emergency breaks in a distant community and needs the attention within an hour or so and the worker finds it impossible to get there the same day the "Welfare Committee" is there to call

over the telephone and ask to visit and give food or send for a
physician.

There are various ways in which a system of volunteer service can
be worked out. The need is apparent. A worker who sits down on the
job and says she can get no one to help in her work does not know
human nature. She has not comprehended how eager people are to do
those things and to realize they are a part of a real program for
public welfare. It can be done, not in a day to be sure, but it can
be done.

Resources in the Rural County

Lack of evident resources in a rural county is one of the apparent
differences in doing case work in a city. Many counties do not even
have a hospital where a worker can have clients treated or examined.
In some out-of-the-way sections of the county there will be no physician to visit families. She will sometimes have to see her client
put up with an untrained midwife with no physician's advice whatsoever. There will be many communities, or all of them, without any
organized or supervised recreation. This makes it all the more
necessary to work closely with the community and those who make
natural contacts with the families and to make a very careful study
of the client and his possibilities. To go deeply and intelligently
into a difficult case may reveal resources for solution never dreamed
of by a superficial study.

Finances

In the matter of finances we will say little: a county worker should
never have to actually raise money for her work. Her Board should
worry about such matters. It is the worker's duty to supply data and
general information to them to help them in an advisory capacity,
but to never actually do the work herself and there is something
wrong if she is giving her time to raising money.

Preventive Work

In the matter of preventive work or doing special community jobs
which lie outside of the realm of case work, the county worker has
many temptations. She will be called upon "to help get a Y.M.C.A.,"
or "to help clean up a certain part of the town," "to get a milk
ordinance passed," and many other similar matters of vital importance.
She is compelled to give some time and thought to these, much more
so than a city worker, but she will have to be constantly on her
guard not to give too much time away from her case work, which after
all is the real object of her job. She should not be expected to
help out in any such undertaking. The general community should take

the responsibility of such matters, because it is logically theirs
and because of the moral good it will do them. Furthermore, such
tasks are too frequently unsuccessful unless the larger group does
realize its responsibility. The more nearly that a community task
of this nature touches case work, the more, possibly, a worker
should give of her time; at any rate the more valuable she will be
to the group most interested. It is impossible and not at all right
for a county welfare worker to divorce herself from such community
or county-wide activities, but there are ways for her to give assistance without sacrificing her case work. It is certainly her task to
call to the attention of logical groups certain conditions which
must be looked into and cleared up.

Difference in Family Problems

The rural worker may find that she has many different family problems
which city workers do not have. There is the Negro tenant farmer,
the poor white tenant farmer, the anaemic, overworked, mentally
deficient woman with pellagra and too many children and too little
money to spend. The city worker will have cases like the latter but
her clients will not have the responsibility of all the chickens, a
couple of cows, some of the field work, etc., nor have to pick cotton
all the day and cook for her family after dark, as well as attend
to other chores. There are child marriages. There are families with
a long line of degenerate, feeble-minded, whiskey-making, chicken-
stealing, "crackers," with no desire whatsoever to attain a higher
standard of living. There are the common law marriages. There are
children living great distances from school. There is the problem
of the poor family feeding its children one article of food, day in
and day out for months, until the farm produces something else. The
rural worker must consider the boll-weevil, the Texas flea, the
tobacco worm, the droughts, the corn blast, etc., in her case work.

It is necessary that she consider and appreciate the religion,
the customs, the habits, the background, the prejudices of each and
every person and group she works with. I knew of one worker who
used a diseased man's belief in a fake "faith healer" to get him to
go to a specialist. Not once did she get irritated with him for his
superstition or distrust in a genuine doctor.

One rural worker drove me out to see some people and as we passed
a farm she told me of three women on that farm living in separate
houses, who worked for the owner, a broad-shouldered, hairy-faced
widower. Each woman had two or three children by this man and was
intimidated to the extent of protecting him and continually living
on the farm to work for him in abject poverty.

There is the problem of the aged Negro couple whose children have all gone to Detroit and cannot be located or made to realize their responsibility.

The Farmer

If we remember that the farmer, regardless of how poor or ignorant he may be, has a managerial psychology, we will get along with him much better. He is used to being his own "boss," managing his own affairs, and caring for his own family and problems. The writer while doing county work a few years ago had a man from the country who had moved to the county seat, to come in and ask for permission to put his boy to work rather than in school. After talking the matter over and looking into it a bit, it was clearly seen that he could easily keep his boy in school, so the permission was not granted. As he left the office he said: "Well I think I will go back to the country where I can manage my own children." Recently a volunteer worker told an interesting story of her attempt to help a needy family in the country. She gathered up some clothing, food and things and drove out to see them and tactfully presented her "charity." They received her cordially and accepted the things with thanks and promptly filled her buggy with canned fruit, vegetables, etc. She went away with more than she gave and with a rather strange and undefinable feeling. We will have to remember then that these people are used to doing things for themselves and let our attitude be as strongly as possible to help them help themselves. If ever the worker needs to take the role of a friend and not as a "professional" social worker, it is among the farmer class.

Getting Information

The rural people will possibly be more reluctant to give information about themselves or another family than a city family. The worker will have to do more to win confidence and show a genuine interest to get what she wants. To be able to talk shop helps wonderfully. To understand their attitudes toward life and outside interference also helps. One favorable thing is that a farmer can give more of his time than a wage earner in town. He does not have to punch a clock. He can stop his plow and talk for hours. Of course, no social worker should ever take notes while making a first interview, but matters of this kind are doubly serious in rural minds and nothing will arouse suspicion more.

Budgeting a Rural Family

The financial status of a rural family is more difficult to determine than a city family. Their income is often too helplessly intangible to put down in definite figures. The food and clothing does not come from one source, as in the city. Food from the garden, milk from their cows, eggs from their own hens, something is borrowed from a neighbor, a trade is made, quilts are made from scraps, a few things are bought. This makes it increasingly difficult to make out a budget for a family or determine its resources. We again see the necessity of close and patient studies of our clients.

Respecting Clients

The rural worker will have to be more careful not to expose her clients. Frequently people who have no legitimate interest in a case at all will know that the worker is helping an individual or family and will often think they have the liberty to stop and gossip about the matter. I believe a good many rural social workers are less careful about this than they may think. They do not realize how freely they discuss their clients with any and every one with whom they may chance to talk. This is a very common sin among many volunteer workers, who either do not see the bad ethics of such a practice or the novelty of working on an interesting case gets the better of their judgment. The open discussion of cases should be only with one's case committee, and they will have to be educated to the fact that it is all confidential. The information about these people is very personal and we cannot afford, nor do we have the right, to betray the confidences of our unfortunate clients who have faith in us that we can help them through a thorough knowledge of their lives and thoughts. If a rural worker merely mentions that she had to send a delinquent girl to a certain place, or that she had a peculiar case of mental trouble to handle, the person will likely know who these people are and manage more details from the worker. The rural worker must maintain absolute silence regarding her cases; which I know is harder to do than for a city worker, whose associates are not prone to be so inquisitive; a city is less personal.

If a county worker drives up to a county store where a group of hangers-on are and asks where the S--- family lives, those present will all but follow her to the place to see what is going to happen. In cases like this considerable tact will have to be used. I remember asking an old storekeeper where two aged spinsters lived. When I drove back by he hailed me, filled with curiosity, and wanted to know what I was going to do with the Browns. Such personal interest can often be used to advantage, but one has to be very careful. Another time I asked a school girl going down the road with her books where a certain old lady lived and she replied, "Yes, sir, she lives right over there. She's my Grandma and what do you want with her?"

The rural worker has to be careful what she says over the telephone in the country for the neighbors are likely listening in.

Conclusion: Opportunities

There are many other things one might mention, such as, the problem of travel, but which we will not take the time to go into now. There is plenty of room for an ambitious rural case worker to make a real reputation for herself, to say nothing of rendering a wonderful service to the profession by developing the technique of county welfare work. There has not even been a successful attempt at working out the problems of record keeping, etc. I might here add that one of the greatest sins of the rural case worker, which she is more guilty of than the city worker, is that she does not keep as good records. Too many times do we find them with only copies of letters and a few ragged notes, if anything at all. This is not fair to the profession and the development of the work in rural sections, to say nothing of being unfair to the client and the next case worker who comes along. It is bad business to say the least.

We must develop a loyalty among rural social workers if we do good work, keep records, study the job and not accept the first offer made by a city organization. The job of a county worker is a challenging one. She has more opportunities for real service, for personal development, for contributing something definite to the knowledge and literature of case work than a worker in a large city.

These few problems only go to show us how necessary it is for a county welfare worker to be alert, to be well trained, to be sincere, to be a hard worker, to be fitted for her job, to constantly read and study. We see that it is a real profession for a real person. Social work is one of the most comprehensive things a county does and it should be placed in the hands of a competent person.

III

The Depression and the New Deal

8

Moving toward the New Deal

Rural economic problems existed, with varying degrees of intensity, during the first two decades of the 20th century. The years of the Great War were an exception. American food production saved much of Europe from starvation, and consequently at least agriculture experienced a boom. But after the war, while urban dwellers were prospering during the frenetic twenties, rural areas were suffering and experiencing much economic turmoil. Robert Goldston wrote of those years:

> On the far side of Paradise during the golden decade lived the majority of American farmers and workers. Under the stimulus of war and post war demands for food, the American farmer had increased his yearly output by almost 15 percent. . . . But when European agriculture resumed production, the demand for American food products sharply declined. Farm income in the United States fell from $17.7 billion in 1919 to $10.5 billion in 1921. The farm price index fell, from 215 to 124 during the same period. And from this terrific slump American farmers did not recover.[1]

During this same period, miners were experiencing much strife in rural areas. Their efforts at unionization largely defeated, many were obliged to work for under subsistence wages.

As the twenties progressed, farm prices continued to fall but mortgages and taxes remained high. Furthermore, "adding social salt to the farmer's economic wounds was his feeling of being unaccountably 'left out' of American life. . . . And when farmers sought help from the national government through their senators, President

---

[1] Robert Goldston, *The Great Depression* (Greenwich, Conn.: Fawcett Publications, 1968), pp. 18-19.

Coolidge observed: 'Farmers have never made money. I don't believe we can do much about it.'"[2]

Clarke Chambers pointed out in *Seedtime of Reform* the "the 1920's were many things to many people." It was an era of contradiction, an era of normalcy but also an era of reaction, "an era in which old welfare programs persisted and were steadily expanded, while the exploration of new reforms and programs proceeded apace."[3]

It is in the context of these times that many spokesmen for the rural areas attempted to call national attention to their plight. Although the selections of the literature of the late twenties stressed the difficulties of farmers, during the same years, many other rural areas, particularly those which were rural industrial, were put on the map due to labor explosions. The textile mills of Gastonia and Marion, North Carolina, and Danville, Virginia, were scenes of terror and bloodshed.[4] The coal mining regions of Kentucky and West Virginia saw union disagreements which culminated in the disintegration of the United Mine Workers (UMW) in West Virginia in 1924. The situation grew increasingly worse until by early 1931, "Fred Croxton of the President's Emergency Committee called conditions so bad that they were almost unbelievable." During the first few months of the Roosevelt administration, "Louis Stark, after a swing through several coal areas, declared that the situation in West Virginia was the worst in the nation."[5]

After 1929, when the depression which had affected rural areas for years spread throughout the nation, rural communities across the country became more angry and vociferous about their problems. Angry Iowa farmers blockaded highways and refused "to bring food into Sioux City for thirty days or until the cost of production had been obtained." Farmers' Committees organized demonstrations protesting the foreclosure of mortgages. Frederick Lewis Allen writes of the farmers involved in the activities:

> They threatened judges in bankruptcy cases; in one case a mob dragged a judge from his courtroom, beat him, hanged him by the neck until he fainted—and all because he was carrying out the law.

[2]Goldston, p. 19.

[3]Clarke A. Chambers, *Seedtime of Reform: American Social Service Action, 1918-1933* (St. Paul: University of Minnesota Press, 1963), pp. 235, 236.

[4]Ibid., pp. 238-239.

[5]Irving Bernstein, *The Lean Years* (Cambridge, Mass.: Riverside Press, 1960), p. 382.

These farmers were not revolutionists. On the contrary, most of them were by habit conservative men. They were simply striking back in rage at the impersonal forces which had brought them to their present pass.[6]

The articles included in this chapter attempt to set the stage and convey the mood which brought about, shortly after the contradictory twenties, the widespread social proposals of the New Deal and their accompanying emphasis on social welfare activities. Chapter 10 provides examples and commentaries of the measures of the New Deal and their impact on rural areas.

The first paper, "Economic Problems of the Farm," was presented at the 1927 National Conference on Social Work in Des Moines. Written by Henry A. Wallace, editor of *Wallace's Farmer* and later Secretary of Agriculture during the New Deal, this paper describes and analyzes the roots of the economic problems of the farmers. Although many might have disagreed with the strong regulatory thrust of the suggestions offered for their economic betterment, all would assert, as did Grace Abbott at the Conference in 1927, that "unless we repudiate all our experience we must recognize the relation between economic conditions and social welfare." (It is important to note that the McNary-Haugen bills praised by Wallace were vetoed by Coolidge in 1927 and 1928. Their spirit, however, together with notions from other abortive remedies of the twenties, especially the M. L. Wilson "domestic allotment" plan, which restricted agricultural output, reappeared in the Agricultural Adjustment Act of 1933.)

The second paper was presented by Grace Abbott as Chief of the Children's Bureau at the same Conference in Des Moines. Although ostensibly the paper deals with standards of child welfare, it actually summarizes the economic and social conditions in which children found themselves in rural areas. Abbott condemns the lack of enforcement of much of the existing social legislation in the country and the disparity of standards from state to state across the nation.

The third article, "Our Newest South" by Florence Kelley, not only illustrates the nature and process followed by many of the labor disputes in rural industrial towns, but also introduces a strong call for legislative regulation of some of the emerging textile industries of the day. The article is not only pro-labor but strongly feminist in advocating the protection of women workers in remote rural areas.

[6]Frederick Lewis Allen, *Since Yesterday* (New York: Harper and Row, 1939, rpt. 1968), pp. 68, 69.

The next two articles, "Trends and Problems in Rural Social Work" by Dwight Sanderson and "A Preface to Rural Social Work" by W. W. Weaver, were published in *Rural America* in 1930 and 1932 respectively. Both emphasize the need for rural health and child welfare services and strongly advocate the establishment of county social service units across the nation, a situation which was to become a reality through the administration of the Federal Emergency Relief Act of 1933.

The article by Gifford Pinchot, an oldtime "country lifer" and two-term governor of Pennsylvania (1923-27 and 1931-35), is a call for a dramatic and influential piece of legislation, which was to drastically change the delivery pattern of services to rural areas. That was, of course, as already mentioned, the Federal Emergency Relief Act of 1933.

In February 1933, the *Survey* published a section devoted to summarizing "The Relief State-of-the Nation." Although this has not been included in this anthology, the reader is directed to it for an excellent review of urban and rural conditions (*Survey*, February 1933). Some of the rural contributors were Thomas Kennedy of the United Mine Workers (UMW) in Pennsylvania and Van A. Bittner of the UMW in West Virginia. Kennedy suggested that "the darkest places in the tragedy of unemployment which hangs over America are to be found in the coal mining regions." Helen Glenn Tyson, Assistant Deputy of Welfare of Pennsylvania, added that in a town of 2,000, 1,500 were on relief and yet starved. Those statements were, in fact, a synopsis of the painful conditions affecting the nation at the onset of the Roosevelt years.

ECONOMIC PROBLEMS OF THE FARM

Henry A. Wallace

For seven years the farm problem has been with us in an acute form.
Five years ago President Harding called a conference to examine it.
Congress appointed a joint committee of agricultural inquiry. Later
President Coolidge appointed an agricultural committee and more recently the National Industrial Conference Board published a book on
the agricultural situation. This past winter the United States
Chamber of Commerce empowered a committee to travel from point to
point over the United States taking evidence from people who were
supposed to know something about farming.

The trouble seems to be that farmers, comprising about 26 per cent
of the population, now get only about 10 per cent of the national
income, whereas, before the war they received about 20 per cent.
Some damage has also been done by the fall in land values, but this
is not nearly so serious as the drop in income. Land in 1919 was
about twice as high as it had been before the war and at that time
was really no higher relative to prewar than city real estate and
industrial stocks on the New York Stock Exchange are today. Even
during the land boom, however, most farmers were conservative and as
a result the decline in land values, which inevitably followed the
decline in farm income, forced out of business only about one farmer
in twenty. The farmers who stayed in business were hurt not by the
decline in land values but by the drop in farm income.

Pullman smoking compartment philosophers will tell you that farmers
are really better off today than they were thirty years ago and that
if they would only stop bellyaching and get down to work and use
modern efficiency methods there would be no farm problem. In all of
this there is an essence of truth together with a vast amount of
misunderstanding. Today nearly every farmer has an automobile and
perhaps a fourth of them have radios. In the Corn Belt most of them
use gang plows and riding cultivators. Perhaps a fifth of the houses
have the advantage of electric lights and furnaces. Undoubtedly it
is more pleasant to farm now than it was with grandfather in the
eighties and nineties.

Proceedings, National Conference of Social Work, 1927. Henry Agard
Wallace (1888-1965) was editor of *Wallace's Farmer*, a Des Moines
journal started by his grandfather,who had been one of the members
of the Country Life Commission under Theodore Roosevelt. Henry
Agard Wallace was Secretary of Agriculture and Vice President of the
United States during Franklin D. Roosevelt's administration.

The misunderstanding caused by the farm use of autos, radios, improved farm machinery, etc., traces to the fact that these things, even though they do cost a lot of money, are essential to efficient farming on most farms. It is because of these very things that most farmers now turn out about 20 per cent more per man than their fathers and grandfathers. Of course in some cases farmers abuse the auto and radio but generally speaking both are practical business assets on the farm. Prompt access to weather forecasts and market reports has enabled many a livestock farmer to pay for his radio in a few months. The auto is not a necessity for the town family but most farmers cannot get along without one.

The United States cannot expect to feed herself indefinitely by paying less than 10 per cent of the national income to her farmers, unless of course she is prepared to import large quantities of food from Argentina, Australia, and Canada. It is perfectly possible of course to continue to give farmers the short end of the stick for another ten or fifteen years. I do not mean to suggest that anyone has definite malicious intent to hold farm income down to the present point although I must admit that some of the administration statements sound that way to many farmers. But if there were a deliberate conspiracy on the part of the big industrial interest to buy food as cheaply as possible I feel quite certain that it could not be successful for more than fifteen years. As a matter of actual fact, of course, neither the industrial East nor the political East has any definite attitude on agricultural matters aside from a rather wearisome desire for those folks out west to stop making so much noise. Superficially eastern people seem more pleasant to meet than most farmers, whom some folks find to be a rather cross grained, cantankerous lot unless they know them well. I think most eastern people mean well toward their fellow men but I find some who have written most bitterly against the middle western point of view in the eastern press who say in private conversation, "The farmer has always had the worst of the deal and always will have. If you give him temporary prosperity he is sure to lose it in a land boom. The ultimate status of the farmer is peasantry and the quicker he can reach there without stirring up a political fuss or an economic disturbance the better it will be for all concerned." Fundamentally those people look on the farmer in the same way as the farmer looks on his milk cows.

It is astonishing how many people feel that the farmer is inefficient, that he has not kept abreast with the wonderful technical discoveries of the age. The *Saturday Evening Post*, for instance, last month had a cartoon of the industrial horse contentedly swigging down the dollars from the water trough of better methods but the agricultural horse stubbornly refusing to drink. Now it happens that hundreds of wealthy men have gone into farming in the spirit of this

cartoon only to find that there are not nearly as many dollars in
the trough of better methods as they had thought. Most farmers are
not ornery, ignorant fellows who are deliberately holding improved
methods out of use. On the contrary they are only too eager to use
every improved method which is at all likely to pay under their financial and soil situation. Every good farmer knows as a result of
sad experience that nine out of ten of the so called better methods
will not pay under his situation. It is true, however, that new
methods are having and will have a tremendous effect on agriculture.
The increased farm use of the automobile during the past fifteen
years has doubtless increased the agricultural output per farmer by
at least 5 per cent. Higher yielding strains of grain have increased
his efficiency by another 5 per cent. New methods of caring and
feeding for hogs now enable us to produce the same quantity of pork
as we did before the war with two hundred million bushels less corn.
The increased use of the tractor enables the farmer to get the same
amount of land taken care of with a hundred million bushels less
corn and oats. The new efficiency methods of agriculture, however,
are not as nearly clear gain as the new methods in industry. It
costs money to vaccinate hogs, to buy tankage, and to provide gaso-
line for a tractor. While thousands of farmers have found that the
new methods leave them a net profit, other thousands find that they
are unable to use some of the new methods profitably. They do not
like to be pictured as a stubborn horse deliberately refusing to
drink the dollars out of the trough of better methods. The *Saturday
Evening Post* cartoon makes thoughtful farmers angry because of a
situation which has been described as follows by Dr. E. G. Nourse,
of the Institute of Economics, in a paper read before the American
Farm Economic Association, last December:

> The outlook for American agriculture is far from bright, the
> industry being faced by portentous technological changes while
> its organization and institutions are such as to make extremely
> difficult, indeed in large part impossible, a prompt and suit-
> able adjustment to these circumstances. Stated as a paradox,
> the outlook for agricultural production is so good that the out-
> look for agricultural prosperity is distinctly bad.

The state and federal governments have spent hundreds of millions
of dollars during the past quarter of a century to make the farmers
more efficient. Before the war this may have been justified because
of the fact that food prices were rising faster than the prices of
other things and because there was a satisfactory European market
for any surplus. Today farmers are beginning to feel that a government which spends millions of dollars annually for increasing agri-

cultural production and is not willing at the same time to face the result of the surplus thereby produced is guilty of an almost criminal act.

Agriculture today is the victim of a combination of circumstances which will never hit it again in quite the same way. The immediate cause of the trouble is the post-war reversal in credit balances. Before the war we owed Europe several hundred million dollars every year because of the fact that we had borrowed during the seventies and eighties several billion dollars to build our railroads and start our industries on a large scale. It was perfectly natural when the railroads opened up the Middle West to pay our interest on this debt to Europe with our surplus wheat, pork, beef, and cotton. During the past fifteen years, however, we have loaned Europe on either government or private account about fifteen billion dollars, and now Europe owes us at least half a billion dollars every year instead of us owing Europe. Of course during the past eight years Europe has been able to borrow enough money from the United States to buy nearly twice as much food annually from us as they did before the war. However, the demand is no longer of the easy automatic type which results when trade balances are being settled by exports. The greatest trouble with our agriculture today is that domestic prices for farm products are being too largely set by the purchasing power of a poverty stricken Europe which has already borrowed from the United States more than she can ever pay back.

Industries which export to Europe, and notably corporations of the type of the United States Steel Corporation, do not suffer to the same extent as agriculture from the post-war reversal in credit balances. To illustrate with pig iron: we export several times as much pig iron as we import. The price for which it sells abroad, however, does not determine the price at home. Judge Gary says, for instance, concerning the 1926 export business of the United States Steel Corporation:

> Prices obtainable in the foreign market, and to some extent for domestic tonnage in markets bordering on the Atlantic, Gulf, and Pacific coasts of the United States, were, however, relatively low owing to the severe competition of European manufacturers.

In other words steel manufacturers follow the policy of dumping their surplus abroad at whatever price is necessary to meet foreign competition and they charge the cost of this dumping up to the interior points of the United States, specifically to the farmers and manufacturers of the Middle West.

If there were no tariff on pig iron or if pig iron were being produced by several million workmen freely competing pig iron would be as seriously affected by the post-war reversal in credit balances as any agricultural product. But pig iron has a tariff and is produced by a few large concerns which are able to take advantage of that tariff by intelligent dumping. Moreover the pig iron people have influence with the administration of the United States. For instance on January 29, 1927, Andrew W. Mellon, Secretary of the Treasury, announced in an official order:

> After due investigation I find that pig iron from Germany is being sold and is likely to be sold in the United States at less than its fair value, and that the industry of making pig iron in the United States has been and is likely to be injured by reason of the importation of pig iron into the United States from Germany.

The following month, the day before he vetoed the McNary-Haugen bill, President Coolidge increased the rate of duty on pig iron 50 per cent under the flexible provision of the Fordney-McCumber Tariff Act. In March pig iron prices advanced fifty cents to a dollar a ton and the price of United States Steel common stock soared above all previous records.

The problem of agriculture is to find the type of organization which will do for it what the corporate form of organization does for industry, and then to use the powers thus obtained in an intelligent way to overcome the handicaps of the post-war reversal in credit balances. Corporations are legal entities deriving their centralizing power from the government. It happens that the corporate form of organization does not fit agriculture. From the standpoint of the longtime welfare of those living in the cities as well as those on the farm it seems to be essential to find something which will give agriculture a centralized buying power more nearly equivalent to that enjoyed by industry and labor. This necessarily means legislation. Those who argue against legislation for the farmer should, in order to be consistent, also argue for doing away with all tariff laws and all laws having to do with union labor and all laws making possible the formation of corporations.

The outstanding effort on the part of the farmers to give them the moral and economic equivalent of the corporate powers enjoyed by industry, and at the same time meet the post-war reversal in credit balances as it affects our surplus crops, was found in the McNary-Haugen bill as vetoed by President Coolidge on February 25 of this year. This bill was doubtless imperfect in some respects, just as the Federal Reserve Act as passed in 1913 was imperfect. It may be open to many of the objections which can be urged against the tariff. Personally I am convinced that in spite of all its imperfections it would work and would give the farmer more nearly his fair share of the national income. I could have more sympathy with those who criticized the McNary-Haugen bill so strongly if they would make an honest effort to face the same problems as the McNary-Haugen bill attempted to solve. The farmers of the Middle West and South do not want to loot the national treasury and they know that the two hundred and fifty million dollars which Senator Fess and President Coolidge propose to loan to them will do them more harm than good unless they have centralized power for handling the export business as under the McNary-Haugen bill. In fact I cannot conceive of any way in which the proposed Fess bill can be of the slightest help to the corn and hog farmers of this section of the country.

There are alternatives for those who do not like the McNary-Haugen bill and who nevertheless are sincerely desirous of doing something to help the agricultural situation. One effective plan would be for the government to buy up and reforest or put down to grass ten million marginal acres of wheat land, ten million marginal acres of cotton land, and ten million acres of corn land. These marginal acres ought never to have been farmed and they are causing serious trouble to those who are farming the good land. The Reclamation Bureau of the Department of the Interior, instead of trying to bring more marginal land into use, ought to be turned into a bureau for reforesting and putting down to grass the marginal lands which already are in use. It would take several billion dollars to buy these marginal lands and put them into timber and grass. But from the standpoint of the longtime welfare of the United States the project would be well worth while. It is foolish to produce as much wheat, corn, pork, and cotton as we now do, and the government is certainly very largely responsible for that over production. From the standpoint of both immediate and longtime results the government might very well consider spending several billion dollars in buying up the marginal acres of our farm land.

In any event it would seem to be wise to cancel the debts owed our government by European nations. Annual payments to the United States by European governments now run over two hundred million dollars annually and will soon amount to more than three hundred million dollars. If these governments did not pay these huge sums annually into our treasury they would have more money available with which to buy our surplus food. Of course our government would have to raise a little more money by income taxes than is now the case but the net difference to any man with an income of ten thousand dollars a year or less would only be two or three dollars. I realize that the farmers of the Middle West have been strongly prejudiced against European debt cancellation because they feel that Europe got us into the war mess and that therefore European governments should suffer just as severely from debt payments as the farmers have suffered. It is perfectly natural for farmers to feel this way but those who have

been hard headed enough to think the matter through are gradually
beginning to realize that farmers producing exportable commodities
like wheat, pork, and cotton would stand to gain by cancellation of
the European debt.

A very logical scheme of meeting the post-war reversal in credit
balances, which should be advocated by all of those who believe in
less legislation, is to take the tariff off of all manufactured
goods which Europe can send into this country. In this way it might
be possible for Europe to accumulate enough of a credit balance in
the United States not only to pay the interest on her debt but also
to pay a somewhat higher price for the food and cotton which she
buys from this country. At the same time the price of manufactured
goods in the United States would fall. The chief trouble with a plan
of this sort is that the first effect is to throw a number of factory
workers out of employment and bring on a declining general price
level. During the period of temporary depression caused by a remedy
of this kind there is danger that the political situation will bring
the high tariff party back into power again. It is quite certain,
however, that after the period of adjustment is over a lower tariff
on manufactured products would increase the percentage of the national income going to the farmers producing cotton, corn, hogs, and
wheat.

The United States apparently has no more of an agricultural policy
today than did Rome two thousand years ago or England one hundred
years ago. There is some talk by folks in authority about loaning
money to cooperatives and reducing farm taxation, but farmers know
that talk of this sort does not mean anything. In reality our only
agricultural policy today is the same as that of England and Rome—
let things drift. Under this policy we have about four million fewer
people living on the farms of the United States today than we had
ten years ago. To date the people left on the farms have increased
their efficiency sufficiently so that the loss in population has had
no effect on agricultural output. Sooner or later, however, it is
to be expected that the policy of "let things drift" will result in
so many people living in town and so few on the land that the price
of farm products will again start advancing faster than the price of
other things. The differential advantage which has been enjoyed by
wage earners in the big industrial centers will then disappear. They
will again find it necessary to give about the same percentage of
their incomes for food as they did before the war. They will not
have as much left over to buy the products of city industry as is the
case today. No matter how long the present situation continues the
farmers will not do anything so very serious. They may elect some
Brookharts and do their best to beat Coolidge but they will never do

anything revolutionary. When the situation is reversed, however, and
labor finds itself getting a smaller percentage of the national income year after year there is danger of serious trouble. Laborers
are not conservative like farmers, and they are in position to cause
trouble that farmers cannot. If there are great disturbances in our
cities during the period extending from 1940 to 1960 they will trace
fundamentally to the injustices suffered by western and southern
farmers during the fifteen years following the World War.

Probably 40 per cent of our farmers today are making a fairly satisfactory living. From the longtime point of view national safety
demands that matters be reshaped sufficiently so that about 70 per
cent of our farmers can live well. This problem cannot be solved
merely by spreading efficiency methods to the poorer farmers.

The great industrial system is running away with us. Soon we shall
have four or five people living in the city to every one person living on the land. The immediate need is undoubtedly to drive more
folks from the farms into the cities so as to bring about a rise in
the price of farm products and a decline in the wages of labor. The
longtime need, however, may be the exact reverse. The statesmen and
historians of forty years hence may marvel at the blind folly of the
way in which the agricultural situation was handled during the fifteen years following the great war.

DEVELOPING STANDARDS OF RURAL CHILD WELFARE

Grace Abbott

The subject of the address which you have just heard was "Economic
Problems of the Farm." I have been asked to speak on rural social

Proceedings, National Conference of Social Work, 1927. Grace Abbott
(1878-1939) was a Nebraska-born social reformer. She was Chief of
the Children's Bureau (1921-1934), U.S. Representative to the League
of Nations Committee on Traffic in Women and Children (1923-1927),
and head of the U.S. Delegation to the Pan American Child Welfare
Conference in 1935. She was instrumental in the development of the
Social Security Act of 1935.

welfare, which includes more than social welfare of those living on
farms. But as to exactly what is meant by "rural" we are not always
agreed. In its statistics of population the population division of
the Census Bureau classifies residents in towns or villages of 2,500
or less as rural while the vital statistics division of the Census
Bureau classifies towns of 10,000 or under as rural.

There are disadvantages in these differences in definition. We are
not able to determine the infant or maternal mortality rate on farms,
which makes conclusions as to the progress that is being made in
health conditions in agricultural districts impossible. Census
statistics of illiteracy, etc., reflect not only farm but village
educational standards. But in considering the development of a general social welfare program there are advantages in consolidating
the farm with the village or small town. In a rural community the
small town serves and is dependent upon the surrounding farm life and
is part of the "rural" problem.

I do not need to point out to an audience like this that the great
cities have no monopoly of social problems. Poverty, disease, crime,
degeneracy, feeble-mindedness, ignorance, cruelty, neglect, and
emotional instability are found in the small town and in the country
as well as on the East Side of New York, or the Northwest Side of
Chicago. While it is correct to say that crowding people together
in a city, housing them layer upon layer in city tenements or apartment buildings, rearing children where there are no gardens or flowers or trees or play spaces, sending them early to work in factory
or workshop, are responsible for many of our city problems, it is
also true that extreme isolation, the dreary monotony of long hours
of work in the summer, of poor schools in the winter, of no group
recreation, and inadequate health and social resources of all kinds
are responsible for many of our rural problems. The same problems
have, however, different setting, different manifestations, different complications in the city and the country. Rural conditions vary
greatly in the different states and in different parts of the same
state, but certain fundamental needs are found in every place.

In discussing the subject which your president has assigned to me,
I am not going to try to piece together for you from the investigations made by the Children's Bureau and by other agencies and individuals a description of social conditions under which half the
people in the United States live. Neither time nor your patience
would permit. What I am going to attempt to do is to indicate in a
very general way the rural aspect of the most fundamental of our
common problems.

To my desk as Chief of the Children's Bureau come reports which
indicate that housing is a rural as well as an urban problem. For

example, in a study made by the Children's Bureau of a homesteading area in one of our western states small and crowded houses were found to be the rule rather than the exception.

Here are concretely some of the conditions found. A family of nine persons were living in two rooms. The main dwelling was a one room frame house covered with sod. Three of the children slept in a dugout about 25 yards away. In another instance eight persons lived in a one room house which was a combination of a tar paper shack and a dugout. The room is very large. At the back are four beds; in the middle, a small cook stove. A table, some chairs and boxes used as chairs, and a shelf of dishes make up the chief furnishings of the room. There is only one window, and so the back of the room is very dark. The outside of the house is picturesque, with a row of ears of red corn hanging across the front and some flowers in cans. Another family, consisting of five persons at the time the baby was born, lived in a small one room tar paper shack. They have now moved to a "fairly large" frame house, which consists of two rooms and a pantry. These conditions obtained in spite of the fact that the majority of the people themselves have high standards in regard to housing and sanitation. The scarcity of lumber and the difficulty of getting building materials, the dearth of masons and carpenters, the great distances from railroads and markets, the high cost of transportation, the lack of ready money, and the pioneer attitude that to "do without" things is a part of the homesteader's lot—these factors combine to explain the small house and the inevitable crowding.

In the studies of rural child labor, investigators found laborers' families in both Colorado and Michigan occupied any kind of shelter that was available for temporary use—abandoned farm houses, rude frame or tar paper shacks, and even tents and caravan wagons—though some of the sugar companies in Michigan had provided one or two room portable cottages for their laborers. The dwellings were in many cases in bad repair, dark, ill ventilated, and far from weatherproof. Overcrowding was extreme. In Colorado 77 per cent and in Michigan 40 per cent of the laborers' families lived with two or more persons per room. Sanitation was poor, and the water supply, especially in the irrigated districts of Colorado, was often neither plentiful nor protected against contamination. Most of the laborers occupied these "beet shacks" for five or six months a year.

The migratory laborers in the hop yards and orchards of the Pacific Coast were found by bureau investigators living in camps on the grower's premises, some of them real villages in themselves, housing several hundred persons. Nearly three-fifths of the families in the Willamette Valley district included in the study and nearly all in

the Yakima Valley district lived in tents; the others occupied one
room frame houses built in rows, each with one window. In both tents
and "bunk houses" extreme overcrowding was found; two-thirds of the
families in one district and almost all in the other had three or
more persons per tent or room, and the majority had five or more. A
regulation of the Washington State Board of Health called for a
specified amount of air space per person in frame houses in laborers'
camps, but the regulation did not extend to tents, as a similar one
in California does; and Oregon had no such regulation for either
houses or tents. The Washington regulation was not enforced in the
camps visited, although sanitary conditions in both Washington and
Oregon were better than in most farm labor camps visited by the
Children's Bureau in other sections.

In Anne Arundel County, near Baltimore, Maryland, individual truck
farmers maintained camps for the migratory workers they brought from
Philadelphia and Baltimore each summer. Most of them provided but
one building known as a shanty, which served as sleeping quarters
for all the workers. It was usually a weatherbeaten or unpainted
structure the windows of which usually lacked either glass or shutters or both. As a rule there was but one room on each floor, with
stairs on the outside leading into the upper room. On each side of
a narrow aisle down the center the floor was divided into sections
or pens by boards 10 or 12 inches in height, each being about 6 feet
long and from 4 to 6 feet wide and covered with straw for a mattress.
Each family was allotted one of these pens. At night men, women,
and children, partially clad, one family separated from the next by
the plank, lay side by side. One such shanty in one of the camps
housed ninety-five persons. More than one-half the families had no
toilet facilities.

These conditions are so serious but at the same time so concentrated in a few areas controlled and maintained by men engaged in
large scale truck farming that it should be easy for the state to
compel the correction of such conditions.

Much more difficult to cure are the conditions found in a study of
maternity and infant care in a southern state. Nearly three-fourths
of the families in the county under study were occupying small houses
of one, two, or three rooms, 14 per cent in houses of one room only.
The number of occupants in these houses ranged from two to ten persons, and in half of the single room houses there were five or more
persons. In two-fifths of the houses visited there was but one
sleeping room, and it was not unusual to see three or four beds in
the same room. This was a poor county with a high percentage of illiteracy in which relatively simple people live. Improvement in
housing in this area will come only with improved agriculture, better

education, and an interest in better living conditions not yet aroused in these people who belong to our old American stock.

In the provision for those groups of children in need of special care—the dependent, the delinquent, the neglected, the crippled, and the defective—who are found in rural areas considerable progress has been made in recent years. There is developing an appreciation of the needs of the whole state which is encouraging. In a few states a beginning has been made in the development of administrative methods which will make minimum state standards much easier of attainment.

We have as a nation been very proud of our size, without accepting the challenge which our size offers. Our greatest failures have been our failures to put into actual operation over a whole state a program which a state law makes universal in its application.

May I give a few illustrations? If you were traveling in Europe and were asked about whether the old system of criminal procedure against child offenders had been abandoned and the modern plan of scientific investigation and treatment had been adopted or was in process of being worked out by juvenile courts, you would, I think, hasten to say that this principal had found expression in our laws and judicial practices. You might even go on to explain that the idea originated in the United States and that we had developed it farther than any other country. As you spoke, you would visualize a specialized court with a large number of probation officers—many of them, to be sure, not very well trained for the work. You would, of course, patriotically refrain from mentioning that fact and would think of a psychiatric staff, good provision for detention, interested and cooperating private agencies, etc. You might even be led to say that owing to the progress we had made on this program our interest had shifted and that we were now concerned with other problems for which we would shortly offer a world solution. And yet what are the facts? A study made by the Children's Bureau a few years ago showed only three states in which juvenile courts which are functioning include within their jurisdiction from 75 to 100 per cent of the population; in ten states from 50 to 75 per cent of the population; in eleven states 25 to 50 per cent; in twenty states from 1 to 25 per cent. Thus in only thirteen states were 50 per cent or more of the population of the states served by juvenile courts, while in twenty states in which juvenile courts were organized, these courts served 25 per cent or less. These figures are taken from an inquiry made several years ago and there has been some progress made since that time, although it has been discouragingly small.

The story of mothers' pensions is a similar one. With statewide laws passed in some forty-two states, reports submitted to the

Children's Bureau indicated that the proportion of the population living in localities where aid is actually granted varied from 98 per cent of the population in one state to less than 5 per cent of the population of the state at the bottom of the list. In the new conception of the duties of state departments of public welfare there is great promise that real headway will be made in the improvement of such conditions as these. These departments are now concerned not only with custodial care or institutional training schools but with the prevention of social breakdown and the care in their homes of many for whom the only treatment in the past has been institutional isolation. For this new program, cooperation in a county program has been developed. In North Carolina, Minnesota, Virginia, and Alabama a broad program of public welfare or child welfare work according to a statewide plan is being put into operation. In California, Georgia, North Dakota, Pennsylvania, South Dakota, and West Virginia a program of social work promoted by the state department but not according to a uniform statewide plan is being developed. Iowa has an interesting plan for coordination of public and private relief promoted by the Extension Department of the state university. County care and supervision of dependent, neglected, delinquent, or defective children, with more or less close cooperation of the state department is under way in Arizona, Arkansas, Indiana, Michigan, New York, and Ohio. While the more populous communities find it possible and economical to provide their own specialists, the rural counties must look to the state for psychiatric help with problem children, for the necessary skill to care for crippled children, and for the expert in recreation and in social case work to assist in the handling of individual cases as well as in the development of a local service program.

In the past, with little or no knowledge of the facts, it has been assumed that rural child labor presented no problem. When the census returns showed hundreds of thousands of children ten to fifteen years of age engaged in agriculture there was little comment because it was supposed that this meant employment on the home farm during the vacation season—that it was healthful and educational. In order to learn the facts, the industrial division of the Children's Bureau has since 1920 made a series of studies of children engaged in agricultural work in typical farming areas in different sections of the country which it is believed give a fairly representative picture of the work of children on farms. By personal interviews detailed information was obtained regarding approximately 13,500 children under sixteen years of age engaged in full time, though usually seasonal, agricultural labor in fourteen states, including sugar beet-growing sections in Michigan and Colorado; cotton-growing counties in Texas;

truck and small-fruit areas in southern New Jersey, and in Maryland, Virginia, Illinois, Washington, and Oregon; wheat, potato raising, and grazing sections in North Dakota, a section in the Illinois Corn Belt; and tobacco-growing districts in Kentucky, South Carolina, Virginia, Massachusetts, and Connecticut.

There is a marked difference in the kinds of work children do and the ages at which they are employed on farms in the different states and even in those of different sections of the same state, and the extent to which their work is allowed to interfere with school attendance. The child workers on the truck farms of southern New Jersey, for example, included both the children of farmers, chiefly immigrants who had taken up small holdings in the farming districts and become permanent residents, and children who had come from the large cities as seasonal workers. In the Eastern Shore section of Maryland most of the children working on the truck farms lived on the farms the year round, whereas in Anne Arundel County, around Baltimore, about two-thirds of the child workers were found to be living on the farms or in small neighboring settlements, and one-third were migratory workers from Baltimore. In the Norfolk area of Virginia a very large proportion of the farm laborers did not live on the farms but came from nearby villages or from the city of Norfolk to work by the day. In the tobacco-growing districts of the south most of the children who worked on the plantations were farmers' children, whereas in the Connecticut Valley the children working on the tobacco farms were largely day workers from Hartford and Springfield. On the truck farms around Chicago also most of the hired workers came out from the city by the day, whereas on the great grain farms of the middle west and northwest the child workers were chiefly the farmers' own children.

Approximately 3,000 migratory child workers were included in the Children's Bureau studies, regarding as migratory workers those who were not living at home during the period in which they worked on the farms.

The most obvious evil resulting from the work of farm children is the loss of schooling. Largely as a result of their irregular school attendance, from 38 to 69 per cent of the white and from 71 to 84 per cent of the colored children included in the Bureau's surveys were from one to six years behind the grades which at their ages they should normally have reached. In all areas in which comparative material was available, the amount of retardation was much greater among working than among nonworking children attending the same schools. Where, you ask, are the school attendance laws? Some kind of compulsory school law is on the statute books in every state, but enforcement has frequently been effective in urban areas only.

Local officials unsupported by local public opinion have made little effort to enforce the law. For this reason there is much interest in the experiments being made with a larger unit of administration, in which the personal element does not play so large a part for the enforcement of compulsory school laws. At least ten states now have a county-unit form of school administration in which the county rather than the district school authorities are responsible for law enforcement. In this field also the cooperation of the state is being sought by the counties, and we have in Connecticut an excellent example of state cooperation in the local enforcement of the school attendance laws. But in most states practically the entire responsibility for the enforcement of the law is lodged in the local school board of each district. Especially in rural districts does the small unit of administration cause trouble. As between farm work and school, the farm work usually wins with the local enforcing official. An attendance officer in one of the districts included in one of our surveys kept in his pocket the notices which it was his duty to serve on parents, until the harvest was over and the children were no longer needed on the farms.

The schooling of migratory workers offers a particularly difficult problem, for responsibility for their school attendance is assumed neither by the community from which they come nor by that to which they go, even when their migration takes place wholly within one state. This problem is being attacked in a number of states. In Nebraska the courts have ruled that for residents of Lincoln to take their children to the beet fields of the western part of the state while school is in session is a violation of the compulsory school law, and under an agreement between the schools and the beet sugar companies the schools are requiring the children to remain in school until most of the school year has been completed. Pennsylvania has just enacted into law this principle so that it will be illegal to employ in Pennsylvania children from another state if they have not met the requirements of the school law in the state from which they come. Unfortunately New Jersey failed to pass the law which would have insured the children of Pennsylvania similar protection. The establishment in Colorado of summer schools for resident beet workers and in California of temporary schools for migratory workers are recent efforts, still in the experimental stage, to decrease the disturbing amount of nonattendance due to farm work. The question of direct regulation of rural child labor is also receiving some attention. In Kansas, Minnesota, and Wisconsin factory inspectors have made special investigations regarding children working

in the beet fields. In Wisconsin this inquiry has covered a number
of other types of commercialized agriculture and has resulted in the
introduction of a bill in the legislature which would give the industrial commission power to regulate the work of children in certain
kinds of agricultural work.

But although school attendance in relation to farm work is the most
obvious of the evils of rural child labor, it is not the only evil.
Of 2,457 children under fourteen years of age, included in four of
our surveys and reporting their hours of work, one-half had worked
more than eight hours a day at farm work, one-fifth had worked more
than ten hours a day, and some of them as much as fourteen hours.
Whatever the type of work, however short the season, however easy
and pleasant the work may seem, any task prolonged for these hours
is too much to exact of immature children. To guide a plow for a
few minutes as an experiment, Hamlin Garland has well said, is one
thing, but to continue it for hours at a stretch is a man's job.
Emergency employment of children is justified, but dependence upon
their labor from early spring until late fall is at great cost to
the child and to the community, and like child labor in the cities
perpetuates evils which seem to make the employment of the children
necessary.

Moreover this employment of young children as farm hands helps to
perpetuate the evils which the farm economist seeks to cure. It is
one of the explanations of farm poverty just as industrial child
labor is a factor in the vicious circle of low wages and inability
to educate his children which the industrial worker meets and, when
he turns to employment of his children as the way out, finds he is
perpetuating the system he would remedy. Mr. Wallace has just made
clear that the continued cultivation of farms which are on the margin or below the margin of profitable returns, in view of present demands, is responsible in part, at least, for the economic plight of
the farmers. It is the owners and tenants on such farms who find
themselves driven to employ the school time and play time of their
children because they cannot afford to employ adult labor. Obviously
it is no kindness to them as individuals or to farmers as a class
to encourage them to continue the cultivation of such farms.

Since it was first established the Children's Bureau has endeavored
to study the conditions and needs of all children. You will remember that the subject selected by Miss Lathrop for the Bureau's first
investigation was infant mortality. The first study was made in
Johnstown, Pennsylvania, but other studies were soon made in the
rural areas of the south, the middle west, and the far west as well
as in industrial towns and cities. As a result the evidence which
comes from a detailed study of some 23,000 babies was assembled.

It showed that there is great variation in the infant mortality rates, not only in different parts of the United States, but in different parts of the same state and same city, town, or rural district. These differences were found to be caused by different population elements, widely varying social and economic conditions, and differences in appreciation of good prenatal and infant care and the facilities available for such care.

While conditions were as a whole better in the rural than in the urban areas, the examples of greatest neglect were found in rural areas. Moreover, urban facilities were increasing so that rural communities were losing the advantages which they originally had.

At the time the Sheppard-Towner Maternity and Infancy Act was passed, the value of the child health and prenatal center as teaching centers for mothers had been demonstrated. That a prompt reduction of infant and maternal mortality followed their establishment had been shown in many places in this and other countries. But such services had been available to a relatively very small number of mothers, most of them mothers in the larger urban centers. Because what happens to babies is a matter of prime importance to the nation, and because it was believed that if the federal government cooperated with the state and local governments in the promotion of the welfare and hygiene of maternity and infancy, local interest and local facilities would be greatly increased, the well established principle of federal aid was invoked.

Forty-three states and Hawaii have been cooperating with the Children's Bureau in a maternity and infancy program, and the legislatures of two more—Maine and Kansas—have signified their intention of cooperating during the next two years. While the programs are initiated as well as administered by the states, all of them have had as their objective making service available to the mothers in the rural areas as well as in the cities. Since the act became operative, out of 2,827 counties in the forty-three cooperating states the work has been carried to 2,313 counties, and permanent county wide services have been established in many states. Many counties will need help for a long time if their children are to have a fair chance at health and vigorous happy childhood because of the present inadequate income and the greater unit cost of rural as compared with urban rates.

I have said that the states cooperating with the bureau have made a definite effort to reach the rural areas with the child health program, and it is a satisfaction to find that there has been a very encouraging reduction in the rural infant death rate as well as in the death rate for the whole birth registration area. In 1925 in thirteen of the thirty-three states in the birth registration area—

California, Connecticut, Delaware, Maryland, Massachusetts, New Jersey, North Dakota, Oregon, Pennsylvania, Utah, Vermont, Washington and Wyoming—the rural infant mortality rate was higher than the urban rate.

Why a federal subsidy was needed and justified is, I think, illustrated by two maps I want to show you. The first is a national market map known as Crowell's Market Map. It is based upon an analysis of certain items which it is thought may be considered reflectors of effective county incomes. These items include the number of income tax returns, the number of passenger cars, the total value of products, population, number of dwellings, and number of retail outlets. The method used in combining these items was not the same for all parts of the country, being adapted to meet the radically different conditions of the New England, South Atlantic, and mountain sections.

With this material, a map was made showing the counties of the United States which have the "best," "good," "fair," and "poor" incomes. It was prepared for use by advertisers and by large business organizations in working out a sales organization. County income means ability to buy. For our purposes such a map means ability or inability to buy good schools, or to buy health, to pay probation officers, mothers' allowances, and all the other items of a program which is necessary for social welfare. This map shows a concentration of the "best" counties in Massachusetts, Connecticut, Rhode Island, New York, New Jersey, Pennsylvania, Delaware, Maryland, Ohio, Indiana, and Illinois. The "poor" counties are in the states west of the Mississippi River and in the south.

It is not to be expected that the best counties in the matter of income will as a matter of course be the best counties in the provision that they make for children any more than one would say that the richest parents are the ones who are rearing their children most intelligently. As a matter of fact, excessive wealth means that the community is probably handicapped. It usually indicates industrial or mining communities in which there are great congestion of population and extremes of income. Moreover a rich community, like a rich individual, may be so interested in the wealth itself and its further accumulation that the real values in life are lost sight of. What a county, a state, or a nation does for its children depends on how much it cares and how intelligently it cares about what happens to its children; and the county with a fair income, like the individual parent in moderate circumstances, has perhaps a surer sense of values. But there is no such comfort to be found in the outlook for the poor counties. They are obviously unable to do all that they should do, no matter how great their efforts. This theory may be tested in part by the infant mortality rates. The Children's Bureau has prepared a map which shows the infant mortality rate by counties in the birth registration area for a five year period—1921-25 inclusive—when a much lower rate prevailed than for the period 1916-20. The best counties (marked red) had an infant mortality rate of below 55, the good counties (marked yellow) had a rate of 55-65, the fair counties (marked green) had a rate of 65-75, while the poor counties (marked blue) had a rate of 75 or above. It is sad to find only one red county in New England—that one is in Maine—and no red county —i.e., no county with an infant mortality rate of less than 55—in New York, New Jersey, Maryland, or Pennsylvania, the richest area in the United States of America. Although they had the greater means, these states have greater problems also and federal cooperation has resulted in an increased appreciation of those problems.

A great national endowment for education was provided in the school lands which were given to the states in this part of the country. Federal funds have been made available for agricultural education and agricultural experiment—for farm demonstration agents and home demonstration agents—and since 1921 through maternity and infancy funds for parental education also.

In seeking legislative help to meet city needs we have sometimes suffered defeat because county legislators did not understand and appreciate city needs. The development of an adequate rural program may be delayed or defeated because of the selfish indifference of the cities and industrial areas to rural needs. While there may from time to time be a lack of economic interest in the social welfare field we ought to be able to go forward together. The mutual interdependence of the urban and rural communities should be recognized. The temptations that beset the country boy and girl in the city are an old theme, and to-day city juvenile court judges see in the country—now so easily reached by the city boys and girls—the menace of unregulated commercialized recreation. It is the city children who do much of the farm work. Thousands of them go each summer to beet fields and truck gardens, and frequently live under conditions dangerous from a health and social standpoint.

What we need for both rural and urban communities is cooperation in the application of our developing social intelligence to our developing social needs. For both city and county the development of a well thought out program adapted to meet varying local needs is of fundamental importance. For both, efficient state departments of public welfare and public health are necessary.

I hope it is clear that I am not suggesting that there is any royal road to a rural social welfare program. At best, what we can look forward to is an opportunity for careful, thorough work both with groups and with individuals. Even this we shall not have without opposition. At the present time there are those who are seeking to undermine all social welfare activities, to label as communistic mothers' pensions, child labor legislation, or efforts to save the lives of mothers and babies. They would make opposition to all such measures a badge of patriotism. This would be very discouraging if we did not know something of the history of the social reform movement. Fifty years ago public schools were attacked as socialistic, while thirty-seven years ago (1890) compulsory school laws were so described. This quotation from a paper read by the State Superintendent of Education of Texas before the National Educational Association in 1890 has a familiar sound:

> The trend of the past two decades in this country has been indeed toward the Old World idea, and we have sought to extend the domain of law into new fields, which had before belonged to that of freedom. This movement, I am persuaded, is temporary and superficial, the result of a cross-current, in the deeper stream of our national life. Yet there are not wanting evidences of a drift toward the breakers of socialism sufficient to arouse concern in the mind of the patriot and the friend of liberty and humanity. To this drift is to be ascribed in large measure, I believe, the imperious demand which comes from many quarters that education shall be made compulsory, and that the compulsion be made effective. I hold that compulsory education is contrary to the dominant idea which has pervaded the development of American institutions, and further, that it is perilous to one of the most vital and essential of the institutions on which civilization rests—the family.

May I say in closing that I am grateful to the president of this Conference for giving the economic problems of the farmer an important place in our program tonight. Unless we repudiate all our experience we must recognize the relation between economic conditions and social welfare. We still believe that poverty can and must be abolished in both urban and rural areas, and we are encouraged to hold to our faith by the great progress that has been made in the last twenty-five years. We should lay the foundation for much greater progress during the next quarter century for the rural child and the rural community as well as for the urban child and the urban community.

OUR NEWEST SOUTH

Florence Kelley

From a little town in the Tennessee mountains there came to Washington in May, a slight, wiry, black-haired girl with high cheek-bones
suggesting some Indian great-grandfather, to tell the Senate Committee on Manufacture, of which Senator Robert M. LaFollette is chairman, and the twenty-fifth convention of the Women's Trade Union
League, her experience with our newest textile industry. She is
Margaret Bowen, leader of the five thousand strikers of the mills of
the Glanzstoff Corporation and the Bemberg Corporation in Elizabethton.

It was first-page news in the New York Times on May 15 that Colonel
Herbert H. Lehman, acting governor of New York (during Governor
Roosevelt's convalescence in Georgia), had resigned his position as
one of the directors of these corporations after the failure of his
efforts to persuade them to settle the strike by peaceable methods
on modern principles.

Far from doing so, they have induced Governor Horton to fill the
little town with soldiers and sheriffs. Why not? Elizabethton is a
typical southern industrial town. The corporations own not merely
the mills but the houses, the lights, and the water supply, which
latter they have been repairing after it was cut in the hope of diverting the mill supply, after the Glanzstoff Corporation had broken
its promises to raise wages made after a first struggle that began
in January. The corporations are new and their product, rayon—
artificial silk—is the newest of the textiles. But their dealings
with their employes, who are all 100 per cent native-born American
citizens dwelling in the mountains as their ancestors did long before
these corporations were heard of North or South, are as old as the
steel industry's ways in Pennsylvania in the early days of Andrew
Carnegie. Indeed, if we except the stockades (which are absent from
Tennessee) and substitute the huge proportion of young girls here
involved, there is everything to remind us of the bitter Homestead
strike in Pennsylvania over forty years ago.

The National Guard having been called into service in April, its

Survey, 15 June 1929. Florence Kelley (1859-1932) was a lifelong
champion of government regulation of child and women's labor. She
worked as an agent of the Bureau of Labor Statistics and as head of
the Factory Inspection Department in Illinois. Her name was associated with the settlement house and the U.S. Children's Bureau.
For 32 years she was head of the National Consumers League, which
had been organized to campaign against sweatshops.

accompaniments are evictions, the kidnapping of two responsible agents of the American Federation of Labor by a mob of well-dressed, well-known residents of the county, the mounting of machine-guns, the bombing of strikers' homes, wholesale arrests which filled the local highschool with prisoners, the jail being full to overflowing. Among other items is the presence in jail of a boy, fifteen years old, arrested for non-payment of rent because, during the strike conducted by his seniors, he can get no work.

The National Guard—sent by Governor Horton, in gradually increasing numbers of companies, at the request of the mill owners—have all along been friendly with the strikers. But as guardsmen they are compelled to patrol the streets from which they banish the citizens. Spread out along the lanes, they lie on their stomachs with bayoneted guns as though guarding the town from invasion by some foreign foe, though many of them are brothers and cousins of the striking youth and girls.

The population of Elizabethton when the strike began in January was in the neighborhood of 6,000 people, of whom something over 5,000 were employed directly and indirectly by the corporations. They were mountain people, accustomed to adding game to their diet by the habitual use of firearms. And they were non-union.

Indeed Margaret Bowen, their leader, was utterly ignorant of trade unions until she had gone out of the mill with the sixteen rayon workers for whose work she was overseer, in despair of ever getting the wage of $10.80 a week to demand which she had come by many short and painfully-achieved steps. Her "raises" had been spread out over many months and each had been ten cents or less a week.

The January strike had to do at first only with wages, but strikes in Tennessee corporation mills are new and this one brought to Elizabethton representatives of the rival textile unions. Weisbord of the Communists first, followed by McGrady and Hoffman of the United Textile Workers, affiliated with the American Federation of Labor. Today the demand for better wages is still vitally essential, for who can live, even in Elizabethton, and hold a position of responsibility in the mill on less than $10.80 a week, with other experienced workers getting even less? For wages will be only nominally won, as this year's experience has taught these thousands of country folk, unless there is a powerful union to back the demand.

Whatever the fate of this strike may be, the strike itself is of enormous national importance. For it is teaching the textile workers of Tennessee, men and women alike, their first lesson in trade unionism. And these are new women. They are voters. They welcome their experienced sisters from the North, bringing with them funds

and the results of a quarter-century of pioneer work in labor organizations.

Never again can a southern Chamber of Commerce advertise, in un-
suspecting ignorance of the truth, that southern mill hands are
"docile." Is it not a girl strike picket, Evelyn Heaton, who has
sued out a warrant, charging Adjutant-general U.C. Boyd with "aiding
and abetting an attempt to commit murder"? She had been seriously
injured when a bus charged a body of strikers who were blocking a
highway. The adjutant-general was released under bond. But "docile
labor" does not sue out warrants against adjutant-generals.

No publicity compares in importance with that of Congressional investigations. Senator Wheeler introduced the following resolution
in the Senate on April 29:

> Resolved, That the Committee on Manufactures . . . is hereby
> authorized and directed to investigate immediately the working
> conditions of employes in the textile industry of the States
> of North Carolina, South Carolina, and Tennessee, with a view
> to determining (1) whether the employes in the textile industry
> have been and are working for starvation wages despite the fact
> that the textile industry is the beneficiary of the highest
> tariff protection granted any industry in the United States,
> and is still appealing for more tariff protection; (2) whether
> men, women, and children are compelled to work as many as 60
> hours a week for wages insufficient to permit a human being to
> live in decency; (3) whether such employes have been and are
> the victims of oppression such as is prevalent in countries
> where peonage is the rule; (4) whether enormous dividends are
> being paid by the textile corporations that are made possible
> by the oppression of the wage earners in their employ; (5)
> whether the appeal of the textile interests of the South for
> higher tariff protection is justified; (6) whether United
> States citizens entering the textile districts to aid these
> underpaid and oppressed workers in their misfortunes have been
> kidnaped and deported into other States and threatened with
> death if they returned; and (7) whether union relief headquar-
> ters have been demolished by masked men and acts of violence
> committed against the workers that are making life unsafe. The
> committee shall report to the Senate, as soon as practicable,
> the results of its investigation, together with its recommenda-
> tions, if any, for necessary legislation. For the purposes of
> this resolution the committee . . . is authorized to hold hear-
> ings, to sit and act . . . during the sessions and recesses of
> the Senate until the final report is submitted. . . .

A startling prelude for Senator Wheeler's resolution is a legislative investigation in South Carolina of the State Department of Commerce, Agriculture and Industries under a resolution introduced on
March 13 last which reads:

> Creating a committee instructed to proceed at once and report
> its findings to the Attorney-General within thirty days after
> appointment. . . .

Among the findings are the following:

> The committee finds as a matter of fact that the Commissioner
> is quite indifferent to the industrial conditions in the state
> and frankly admits that he knows nothing of the methods adopted
> in the adjoining states. . . .
>
> The Commissioner frankly admits that about all he knew of
> mill people was what little he learned when he was a farm demon-
> strator in Lexington County and sometimes he would talk with
> them in reference to working little patches and gardens after
> their regular work hours.
>
> The Commissioner took no interest in the strike situations
> which recently occurred and are now in effect other than going
> to Greenville and spending a few hours in the vicinity of one
> of the mills where a strike existed and visiting several other
> strikes that same day.
>
> The Commissioner testified that he had no recommendation
> whatsoever to make in reference to the labor situations after
> having made a survey of the situations as he did on his hurried
> trip to the few areas. However, the committee finds that the
> Commissioner has been active and quite wakeful in one respect.
> That is, that he has been always ready to suppress and excuse
> practically every violation of the labor laws, to ignore all
> discrepancies as to weights and measures, to pass over all
> violations of the pure food law upon the mere collection of the
> inspection fee and to re-allot the salaries of those working in
> his department in utter disregard of the appropriation bill.

If anyone believes that the southern textile industry can be safely
left to state enforcement of state laws while Congress encourages
with tariff increases, the present manner of conducting these industries, that credulous optimist is strongly recommended to read
the whole of the South Carolina report of which the foregoing is a
condensed extract.

The element which Senator Wheeler and Representative Frear have
introduced during the present session is new and a long step forward.
Each proposes a committee to investigate from the human and social
point of view an active and powerful applicant for tariff increases.
In connection with a pending tariff bill, it is the human point of
view which is new.

Of the three applicants, sugar beets and cotton being old, have
undergone inquiries in the North, but rayon is new and not yet technically perfected. It is, however, already cotton's most threatening rival.

While rayon goes forward by leaps and bounds, both technically and
in the extent of investments in the industry (though by no means
socially), cotton in all three ways recedes. Women no longer wear
cotton underwear or hosiery; and it remains to be seen how far any
large-scale use of cotton dresses can be re-cultivated while silk,
both real and imitation, competes.

Cotton holds its own for sheeting, ticking and other bed coverings,
for automobile tires, mail bags, canvas awnings, worsteds, infant

wear and many minor articles formerly made of wool. But who would
dream today of entitling a volume Cotton is King! Yet such a book,
so entitled, stood thirty years upon my father's bookshelves.

The Wheeler resolution is of especial importance to women, who are
a large majority of the workers in both the rayon and the cotton industries, and of course, the worst paid. Since the Sutherland decision deprived all women wage-earners in April, 1923, of their only
statutory method of establishing a stable minimum in the lowest paid
occupations, the trade union with its clumsy and uncertain apparatus
of strikes is their only alternative, their sole effective safeguard
against the starvation standards of the southern mills.

As this issue of The Survey was in press, the strike was settled
through the offices of Anna Weinstock, a conciliator sent by the
U.S. Department of Labor, who was able to persuade both sides to re-
open negotiations and the strikers to return to work. A personnel
department has been set up under E. T. Willson, who was called to a
similar position in the Forstmann-Hoffman mill at Passaic, New Jersey, following the thirteen-months' strike in that market in 1926-27.
At best, the settlement is a patchwork of concessions local to Elizabethton. It emphasizes the need for a thoroughgoing congressional
investigation of textiles, North and South, and gives added point to
Senator Wheeler's resolution, which has passed in the Senate, and
has been endorsed by the Federal Council of Churches, President
William Green of the American Federation of Labor, and the National
Consumers' League.

TRENDS AND PROBLEMS IN RURAL SOCIAL WORK

Dwight Sanderson

To my mind the thing which is most fundamental for any permanent and
substantial growth of rural social and health work is to arouse a
sense of need for it on the part of rural people, to make them aware
of the amount of poverty and sickness in their own communities, and
that for their own interest as well as to assuage human suffering,
there should be an intelligent plan for its treatment and prevention.
Modern social and health work is the product of our large cities,
where it grew up out of necessity. In the open country the need for
child welfare and family case work and for the control and prevention
of disease has not been so apparent. The need is there, but the rank
and file are unaware of it. Before any program of rural social or
health work can secure permanent support, the better elements in the
community must be convinced that it is needed and practiced. Except
for the American Red Cross, there seems to be no one organization
which has sponsored such a movement throughout the country, and unfortunately it seems to have left the initiative largely to the local
chapters, and in many counties where such work is most needed local
vision and leadership are still lacking. However, in the field of
public health nursing the Red Cross has blazed the way and since the
World War there has been a remarkable growth of local public health
nurses with an increasing support for their work by public funds.

It would seem that if any general understanding of social and
health work is to be secured in rural counties, it must be promoted
by those organizations in which the rural people are already associated and whose objectives and interests involve the consideration
of such welfare movements. If the local farm and home bureaus, the
subordinate and Pomona granges, the local parent-teacher associations,
farmers' clubs, and similar organizations, can be interested to study
their own local situations and consider what might be done for their
improvement, a substantial basis for progress will be created. What
is needed is a definite and concrete study of local conditions. Is
the drinking water of the rural schools wholesome and safe? In our
own county an analysis of the drinking water of 15 rural schools,

Rural America, January 1930. Ezra Dwight Sanderson was one of the
founding fathers of the discipline of rural sociology. He was initially an entomologist. He was dean of the College of Agriculture
at West Virginia University (1910-1917) and became head of the Department of Rural Social Organization at Cornell in 1921. In Ithaca,
Sanderson was active in the Social Service League, the Family Society,
the Red Cross, and the Council of Social Agencies.

sampled at random, showed that in four cases the water was unfit for use. What of the medical inspection of our schools? Is it efficient, and if so why are more of the defects reported not corrected? What of defects in sight and teeth, which are handicapping rural children, the importance of which their parents do not always appreciate? How many cases of diptheria, typhoid, and malaria, are there in the community, and what is being done to eradicate these preventable diseases? These and similar questions might be investigated by any local organization, with the cooperation of local physicians and health officials, and would reveal the need for a more adequate service of public health nurses and better health supervision. To outline such local studies and to encourage the local organizations in making them and then following them up with a practical program of improvement is the opportunity of state and local leaders in all of these organizations which have close contact with the mass of rural folks. The greatest need of the specialized social welfare and health organizations of state and nation is to secure the cooperation of these organizations which are composed of rural people and to furnish them with suitable subject matter and methods for educational campaigns.

Recognizing such a process of self-education as prerequisite to any real progress, what are some of the essential features of a program of rural social and health work and what are the more outstanding problems? Let us consider health work first, for it seems to have a more immediate appeal, to be more concrete, and leads naturally to a need for better social work.

The First Step
The first step in a rural health program seems to be the employment of a public health nurse, much of whose time is usually given to work with the schools and to general health education. Wherever competent, public-spirited nurses have been employed long enough to demonstrate their value, they have won their way into the hearts of the people and have been the most potent means of creating new attitudes toward better health practices. Whether a nurse be employed by a local chapter of the Red Cross, by a township or county, by a school board, by a voluntary nursing association, or whatever organization may finance her support, the important thing is to secure one for a sufficient length of time for her to demonstrate the need of such service. With reasonable management the value of her work will soon be recognized and in due time should be supported from public funds.

An unsolved problem in many a rural community is how to keep a competent resident physician. Medical education is expensive, the

necessary medical equipment has increased and is more expensive, and
consequently young physicians are not going to rural communities as
formerly. Physicians in smaller cities do not seek rural practice
and their prices are necessarily too high for calling them except in
emergency. The farmer the farthest from the village, who often has
a poorer farm and therefore less cash, has to pay the highest fee
and therefore cannot afford adequate medical service. There is no
question that in many rural communities there is a real need for a
resident physician, but the possible income from fees on the usual
basis would be inadequate to give a reasonable living to a competent
man. Various experiments in the employment of a physician on salary
or by guaranteeing a minimum income, have been made, but in the
United States they do not seem to have been so permanently successful as to result in a growth of this method. A thorough study of
successes and failures of such efforts is much needed, as with other
features of the rural health program. There seems no reason why the
state should not subsidize the employment of a physician wherever
there is a sufficient local need. If it is good public policy to
subsidize the rural teacher so that country youth many have equality
of educational opportunity, why is it not as important to give country people an equal opportunity for medical care and health? This
does not mean "state medicine," but partial state support for a
physician employed by the locality.

The state of Iowa was a pioneer in legislation for county hospitals
and the movement has now spread throughout the country. There is
still, however, a real need for hospitals in many rural counties,
providing that they can be financially supported and competently
manned. An even more important question in connection with hospital-
ization is some better adjustment of rates through partial or complete support by taxation, so that middle class and poorer people
can afford to use them. Some rural municipalities in western Canada
have solved this problem by paying the whole cost of the hospital
from taxes and thus equalizing the cost to all. That hospitals are
being increasingly used for rural maternity cases is shown by recent
figures from Cattaraugus County, New York, in which the number of
non-resident births in the cities increased from 22 in 1916 to 194
in 1927.

The Health Officer
After the public health nurse the most important step in a rural
health program is a competent, full-time county health officer. Good
progress is being made in the organization of county health departments for whereas there were only three county health departments
in the United States in 1914, in 1929 there were 467, but the map

published by the U.S. Public Health Service showing their distribution is black in spots and white in other areas. Do not rural counties need the services of a full-time public health doctor as well as cities? That such an investment pays good returns on the taxes invested has been demonstrated again and again, but there is much opposition from the medical profession and a general apathy on the part of the laity. Here, again, we see the necessity of an educational campaign to arouse an understanding of the profit in reducing sickness and mortality by better health supervision. In New York State we have had an excellent permissive law for county health departments for some years, but only two counties have availed themselves of its provisions, although the state contributes half of the cost. Only this year has a systematic campaign been started for encouraging county health departments and the interest of local organizations in a study and discussion of the matter is being enlisted.

Inspection of School Children
A most important part of the rural health program is the medical inspection of school children. Although medical inspection is now compulsory in many states, it is far too often done in a more or less perfunctory manner and with little effort at follow-up, so as to ensure adequate treatment. The school nurse or the public health nurse is invaluable in securing a better follow-up and seems essential to make medical inspection really effective. In general it seems probable that a better examination would be made if one or two men in a county did all of this work rather than leaving it to the local physicians, and it would be desirable to associate this work with the county health department.

Health Education
Finally the health instruction in our rural schools should be made the means of ensuring a better appreciation and understanding of health in the coming generation. Too long have we taught anatomy and physiology which failed to function in the personal hygiene of the students. The recent work of the Child Health Committee of the Commonwealth Fund has demonstrated what can be done in the formation of health habits among school children, and the work of health teachers in demonstrations made by local chapters of the Red Cross has shown the practicability of such work. May we not look forward to the time when we shall have special health teachers in every county, for teaching both teachers and children?

The chief objection to all of these proposals is always the fear of a higher tax rate, and anyone who has had any contact with American agriculture during the past few years cannot but appreciate the

need of lowering local taxes. The best method of meeting this objection and inciting local interest is for the state to give a generous subsidy to all well-conceived programs of public health work,
and so equalize the cost throughout the state. In New York the state
now pays half the cost of any county health program which is approved
by the state department of health. Within the county much may be
done by scrutinizing the costs of county government and insisting
upon a reduction of unnecessary costs and larger expenditures for
health work. Finally, it can be shown that even an increase of tax
rates would be economy if smaller doctor's bills and less sickness
and mortality resulted. In many cases we get more value from taxes
wisely expended than from our own private expenditures.

A Social Work Program

As the public health nurse comes first in the health program, so the
child welfare worker is the pioneer agent for rural social work.
Everyone is interested in children and in every county there are
cases of neglected, dependent, and delinquent children who ought to
have the care and help of one who understands their needs and knows
how to meet them. Inevitably the child welfare agent meets many
problems of family adjustment and before long she is engaged in a
general program of social work. In due time she will educate her
constituency to see the need of a broad program of family welfare
work by both public and private agencies.

One of the difficulties of a child welfare worker in most rural
counties is that of securing satisfactory treatment of juveniles in
the ordinary local courts. Thus the next most important step in the
changed attitude of the judges toward juvenile delinquents and incompetent parents is most surprising. In very many cases these
judges are actively educating their constituencies in the need of
better social work and are more and more depending upon trained
social workers for investigation and supervision. As these courts
become more firmly established, it is becoming apparent that many of
their cases are due to bad domestic relations, and ultimately we
hope that their functions may be enlarged so that they may also become courts of domestic relations. Much of the practice of the
divorce lawyer might be obviated and many divorces might be averted
if the methods of juvenile court could be used in their adjustment.
In one New York county which has a very low divorce rate, it is the
boast of the child welfare agent that there have been no divorces in
several years among those couples which have come under her jurisdiction. There is a very real need of this sort of constructive
social work with disorganized families, which in many cases will

make unnecessary the placement of children in other homes or will ensure to them a better home environment.

As rural health administration requires a county health department,
so rural social work should be unified under a county board of public
welfare with a professionally trained executive officer. North Carolina and Missouri have led the way in this new field, and other
states are advancing in this direction by steps. Child welfare, poor
relief, the administration of mothers' pensions, and the care of the
neglected, defective, and delinquent, should all be centralized in
one organization which is competent to deal with the complex problems
involved. But before such a program can be successfully inaugurated,
the public must be educated to understand that these difficult problems of human relations cannot be adequately handled merely by the
furnishing of grocery orders and clothing, or medical attendance in
emergency, by one whose chief qualification is his or her loyalty to
the local political machine, but that they need the service of one
who has had the best possible professional training. We have come to
understand that we cannot entrust the supervision of public health
to anyone but a physician. It is equally important that the baffling
problems of adjusting human relationships be entrusted only to those
who by study and experience have qualified themselves for such a
responsibility.

General Principles

I have attempted to briefly sketch the essentials of a program of
rural social and health work. Out of the experience which has come
from these movements in various parts of the country, a few general
principles are becoming fairly clear.

The first is that there should be larger units of administration
so that there may be a sufficient volume of business to employ professionally trained executives. Throughout the northeastern states
we have inherited township health and poor officers from the days of
horses and mud roads. They served their day and generation as well
as possible under the conditions; but today we live in an age of
automobiles and rural people deserve as good care as they know is
given their city relatives. The county is now the most logical unit
for the efficient organization of both rural health and social work.
In some cases, however, where the population is sparse, or resources
are limited, even the county is too small a unit. So we see a general movement for cooperation between a group of counties in the
maintenance of a modern and efficient almhouse or in the erection
and support of a well-equipped and competently manned hospital. We
need to give careful study to the volume of business, the economic
basis for their support, and the natural social and economic areas

which may cooperate in such inter-county enterprises and so far as possible make these areas coincident. It is essential that we reconsider the units of rural government from a functional viewpoint and be not held in the grip of past tradition.

If the county is the best administrative unit, how shall its health and social work be organized? A most interesting pamphlet on COUNTY MANAGEMENT has recently been published by Professor Wylie Kilpatrick of the University of Virginia. In this he advocates the system of appointive county boards of health, education and public welfare to be selected from lists approved by corresponding state departments, who will appoint the executive officers of such boards. Experience seems to show that better officials for the determination of public policy in these fields can be secured by appointment than by election, and that those so appointed because of their interest in and knowledge of such work will be better qualified to select a competent professionally-trained executive to carry out the general policies which they establish. Attempts to make such systems of administration mandatory upon the counties by state legislation have not proven entirely successful, and it would seem wiser to pass permissive legislation with a proviso for as much state aid as may be possible for those counties adopting the new system. Although this procedure may be slow, it provides for the thorough discussion of the merits of the new plan and for the creation of a favorable public opinion before its adoption.

With such a general scheme of welfare work in view, the question arises as to whether there will still be a need for private agencies for rural health and social work, or whether the whole job may be adequately cared for by the public agencies. The answer to this seems to be at hand in the experience of our cities, in which private organizations for health and social work are as necessary as ever, and to which the people are increasingly generous through community chests, even where the public work is most efficiently administered. As parent-teacher association is desirable to bring about a better understanding between parents and the educational profession and boards of education, so private associations for health and social work will be necessary for creating and maintaining an intelligent and sympathetic public opinion to support the administration of health and social work and to carry on work which for one reason or another cannot, for the time at least, be satisfactorily handled by public agencies. Such organizations might well exercise a considerable influence on the appointment of well-qualified boards and competent executives. With mutual good-will and understanding, public and private agencies will find that they support each other and that only through carefully considered team-work can they best advance the general welfare.

Finally, may I call attention to what seems to be one of the greatest needs in a general advance toward the program above indicated. In many rural counties there are an increasing number of private or semi-public associations and agencies seeking support from the general public through personal contributions or through the county treasury. Farm Bureaus, Red Cross Chapters, County Y.M.C.A.'s, Child Welfare Committees, Tuberculosis or Health Associations, etc., etc., are all engaged in social and health work. So, too, the Granges, the Parent-Teacher Associations, the County Sunday School Associations or Associations of Religious Education, the W.C.T.U. and other organizations are interested in these same fields, even though they may not have employed executives. Yet how frequently are the leaders of many of these organizations, quite unaware of what the other is doing or how they might more effectively combine their influence toward the common goal. Notable advances have been made in Iowa and Wisconsin, under the leadership of the State Conference of Social Work, in holding county conferences at which representatives of all these private, semi-public, and public agencies can be brought together for considering the needs of rural social and health work and how they may be met. In New York, we are just beginning some experiments of this sort, but we are convinced that such conferences held once or twice a year in each county will be the means of securing a more accurate knowledge of the real needs, a healthy discussion of better methods of meeting these needs, and in coordination of effort by all these agencies, by informing their membership of just what it is all about and enlisting their united support for all movements which will promote the common welfare. The extension of services of the state college of agriculture, the state conference of social work, and the state leaders of the various organizations mentioned will open up a new field for public service by inaugurating such county conferences in which all those concerned with rural social and health work in a county, or a suitable local district, may come together for considering their common problems and planning a program for their joint solution. The American Country Life Association might perform a most useful function by assembling and circulating the experience, methods, and achievements of such county conferences, so that they may be established wherever, and note this limitation, the local situation is ripe for such an advance and local leadership is available.

A PREFACE TO RURAL SOCIAL WORK

W. W. Weaver

The latest public figures show that the rural portion of the United
States retains its vital superiority over the urban portion. In
rural families more children are born, more survive infancy, fewer
die during the years of youth or maturity and more live to advanced
years. But a surprising feature of this comparison is the sensa-
tional improvement of health in large cities during the past thirty
years, particularly in the field of infant mortality. Despite their
handicaps of crowded houses, mixed populations, and complicated
problems of sanitation, many cities are now safer places to live
than their respective hinterlands. A large share of American cities
have reached such a point in the conservation of human life that
natural increase alone annually adds a neat increment to the population. The leadership in child welfare bids fair to pass to our
large cities unless we analyze the rural situation and prescribe for
its weaknesses as we have prescribed for those of the great city.

The most paradoxical deficiency to be found among rural children,
and the one to which rural parents will react most sensitively is
the widespread prevalence of malnutrition. These cases are not
limited to the "pellagra belt." Every close observer of rural life
can relate cases of rickets in the land of sunshine, of blue-veined
temples and pallid cheeks in rural schools, of hollow chests and
protruding abdomens on the farms that glut the markets of the world
with food.

In the field of communicable disease, the technical superiority of
the urban community likewise asserts itself. Three closely related
rural problems are those of child labor, education and recreation.
The health, vocational efficiency and civic preparation of rural
children are so intimately bound up in these problems that the progress of certain agricultural sections awaits the positive appreciation of their importance. In the past legislative bodies have permitted the exploitation of children for the cultivation of cotton,
sugar beets, strawberries, cranberries and tobacco, but in recent
years there have been marked gains in the legislative provision for
child welfare. For example, compulsory education and child labor
laws set certain standards below which the preparation of a child

Rural America, January 1932. W. W. Weaver was an instructor in the
Department of Sociology at the University of Pennsylvania.

for life cannot legally fall. A positive appreciation of education
has carried the consolidated schools and vocational education into
rural communities, and with them should come more adequate facilities
for play.

The Neglected and Dependent

When we turn to special classes we find there are many children in
the country who suffer from permanent physical and mental defects.
Of these the blind, deaf and mentally ill have been taken care of
more or less adequately by state institutions, but the epileptic,
feebleminded and crippled children must await the slowly expanding
facilities which are being provided. A program of negative eugenics
would relieve us of many such cases, but such a program would have
to be carried out by the state or national government. On the other
hand a higher order of local social work will bring about a ready
identification of cases needing assistance and initiate the remedial
measures necessary. Mental hygiene work, for example, requires a
local unit for the assistance of the traveling clinic if the fullest
benefits are to be enjoyed.

There are also the dependent and delinquent children of the rural
community. The conditions revealed by the United States Children's
Bureau's survey of seven Pennsylvania counties, suggest the need for
more adequate local provisions for these underprivileged groups. The
fact that rural boys are less frequently caught in the toils of the
law may mean, not that they are less miscreant than their city
cousins, but that fewer facilities are available to help them solve
their difficulties. In the same manner unmarried mothers, expecting
little help or sympathy from local sources frequently find their way
into the cities where there is more likelihood of securing aid in
solving their problems. Few dependent children in rural districts
are now indentured or shut up in almshouses, but the agencies doing
foster home placement or offering the newer types of institutional
treatment are most often located in the cities. The Mothers' Assistance Fund and private family and child welfare organizations in
scattered communities have materially relieved some of the more
pressing problems of child dependency in certain of the counties of
Pennsylvania; but in many states almost no such services for rural
children's work are available.

In addition to these classes we have underprivileged Negro children and children of foreign parentage in certain rural communities
who must seek guidance for many problems outside their homes. The
existence of so many problems would appear to justify the introduction of some forms of specialized remedial work in rural areas.

Types of Social Work

In his work on professional social work, L. A. Halbert delineates
three types of social work with which most people in the field are
quite well acquainted. These are case work, group work, and community work. While there are significant shades of difference for each
class of work, they are basically the same in that each involves the
marshalling of social forces for the more adequate service of some
group, whether it is the relief of a family without means, the organization of a Boy Scout troop, or the formation of a community council. The question of mobilizing these resources calls for an enumeration of the resources available.

Social Resources of the Rural Community

A sensible inventory of rural social resources will begin with a consideration of the economic organization of the community, for farmers
live, eat and sleep with their work. The formal organization of
activities, where it is present, is usually represented by the
Grange, the Farm Bureau, and village organizations. While it is not
likely that one of these organizations will undertake relief work for
children, their membership usually includes the leading citizens to
whom any project for rural betterment must be sold before financial
assistance can be expected.

The officials of the local government, including the poor directors
and county commissioners are important factors to consider in laying
the foundation for a permanent service. It is these men who must be
convinced if professional social work is to be carried on in the
community. The state government helps to maintain certain services
such as "Mothers' Assistance," but the basic unit for rural work is
the county. Through its control of taxation and the institutions
for treatment of maladjusted individuals, chiefly the juvenile court,
almshouse and county hospital, the local government constitutes in
many respects the limiting factor in rural social work.

In almost any community, the school is a rallying point for social
activity. Where the consolidated school has established itself provision has frequently come with it for health work, vocational training, recreation and contacts with the home. Where the one-room
school remains the community activities depend largely upon the personality of the teacher. Where the school has a strong Parent-
Teacher Association, one will find likely material for volunteer
social workers, and capable champions of child welfare. Local
churches also frequently have leaders who will assist in carrying on
social work.

A discussion of all agencies providing social service for rural
communities exceeds the limits of this paper, but it may be well here

to mention some of the professional social work which has been introduced into rural communities. This includes the public health
nurses, probation officers, and other social workers. Frequently
the social work done in rural communities is done by representatives
of state or national agencies with private funds. Comparatively few
juvenile courts in rural districts have either psychological or
trained probation service.

One promising development in rural social work involves the employment of trained workers to supervise volunteer relief work for the
counties. Such a system may break down if the entire burden is
placed on the shoulders of one worker, but on the other hand, it
provides an opportunity to utilize one of the greatest assets of
rural districts, namely, volunteer social workers. In almost any
community there are men and women with leisure time which they are
willing to devote to helping less privileged neighbors. They are
anxious to help but have only vague objectives and little technical
skill. However, their efforts, combined with the professional experience of the county social worker, can produce a very serviceable
combination. Some can serve on committees to secure funds, enforce
laws, educate parents, and carry on office routine. Probably only a
few will be able to do case work, but if these are discovered they
will be capable of helping to reduce the load of the supervisor. It
is not necessary that this case work should be visiting. The home
which will accept a child for temporary placement, the man who will
give some time each week to a delinquent boy, or a job to an unemployed father, the woman who will take in an unmarried mother or feed
a malnourished child may each contribute vitally to the welfare of
the community.

THE CASE FOR FEDERAL RELIEF

Gifford Pinchot

Is this nation, as a nation, to reach out a hand to help those of
its people who through no fault of their own are in desperation and
distress? Shall federal aid be granted in this great national
crisis? It is not a question of ability to help. We are the richest
nation on earth. If federal aid is needed, it can be granted. Congress has only to say the word. Shall the answer be yes or no?

My answer is yes. To my mind it is the only possible answer. Prolonged study and profound conviction support my belief that federal
aid in this depression is our clear duty and our best hope of prompt
and permanent recovery. Two solid years of bad times have taught
us that we can no longer consider our condition as an unfortunate
accident which will automatically right itself if left alone. Gentle
bedside language can do nothing for us.

Our methods so far have been restricted substantially to local relief. Those in high places have continually insisted that a national
emergency be met with local aid alone. They have left it all, with
the exception of a bit of benevolent advertising, to the states and
communities themselves. To requests and plans for federal aid they
have cried "dole, dole." Why aid given by the nation should be a
dole, and precisely the same aid given by a state or a city should
not be a dole, I have never been able to understand.

Of course none of us wants the dole. None of us is in favor of
establishing any system which will give the unemployed money or even
food when work can be given instead. But that choice is not before
us. Industry and business are not giving men the chance to work.
Nor are they feeding the unemployed. We must feed them if they are
to live. We must feed them if they are to retain any confidence in
the government under which they live.

Crying "dole" has not helped the unemployed, but it has served a
very definite purpose, that of restricting relief to local sources.
Then what about local relief? In what direction has it headed us?

A nation-wide Community Chest campaign was backed to the hilt by
the most persuasive and efficient forces that charitable leaders
could muster. We can all rejoice that in many cases the quotas were

Survey, 1 January 1932. Gifford Pinchot was chief of the U.S. Forest
Service and member of the Country Life Commission during Theodore
Roosevelt's administration. Pinchot and his cousin Charles Otis Gill,
a clergyman, were deeply involved in and wrote about the country
church. Gifford Pinchot was founder of Yale University's School of
Forestry and a two-term governor of Pennsylvania

subscribed. The quality of neighborliness, the virtue of sympathy have not died out. We never feared they had. But if the full quotas aimed at were everywhere collected would they be sufficient to cover the needs of the winter? They would not. Responsible social workers tell me the quotas were fixed on the basis of what the chest managers believed that the communities could be made to subscribe. They were often small in proportion to the real needs. The people who think they can wash their hands, now that the chest drives are over, and go away on trips to Florida should think again.

Where does the bulk of local relief come from? Who carries the load? It comes from and is carried by those who pay taxes to the municipal and county and sometimes to state governments. The Russell Sage Foundation, reported for eighty-one cities, found that in past years private funds supplied only 28 per cent of the relief. Tax funds supplied the other 72 per cent. In some cities over 90 per cent came from tax funds.

How are these taxes raised? The answer is that municipalities raise their funds mainly through real estate and other property taxes. Local relief of this kind means an increase in property taxes. This increase in property taxes and the sort of enforced charity by which industry takes a day's pay out of every twenty or so in the month from workers, even from scrubwomen in offices, to help swell relief funds—that is how the program of local relief works out. Yet it is substantially true that every cent a man of small means contributes to relief either directly or indirectly through increased taxes is taken out of consumption. His buying power is immediately slowed down by exactly that much. And the slowing down of buying power means the slowing down of the wheels of industry. Here, then, is the heart of the local relief plan. By cutting down consuming power, it can only serve to further our economic maladjustment and to sink us deeper in the hole.

Now in considering what plan we are to advance in addition to, or as a total or partial substitute for local relief, it might be well for us to investigate the flaws in our economic structure which brought our present troubles upon us. There ought to be very little doubt that the largest single cause was production beyond the power of the people to consume. Through the years called prosperous, no stone was left unturned which would help perfect or increase our national productive power. Technological improvements, financial devices such as mergers, high-pressure sales campaigns, instalment buying and other credit schemes, all tended to the same end. All helped to raise production to new and dangerous heights, and to leave normal consuming power farther and farther behind.

Instead of sharing with labor the profits of increased production, industry shunted the wealth back to itself. Wage-earners were encouraged, persuaded, cajoled to spend their money buying goods. If they couldn't pay for them now, they should buy on the instalment plan. They should borrow money, if necessary. But they should buy. No real American, they were told, could be without his radio and his automobile.

And what happened to the money spent in buying? Did a reasonable part of it go back, in increased wages, to the working-man's pocket so that the circle of producing and consuming could go on? It did not. It went in staggering disproportion to dividends and capital. It went back to industry so that production might be increased, even at the expense of consuming power.

This is no wild guess. This is fact with figures to support it. Julius Klein, assistant secretary of commerce, tells us that in the decade ending in 1929, real wages increased only 13 per cent while the returns to all industry increased 72 per cent. Where did the 72 per cent come from but out of the spent wages of the millions and millions of workingmen? Dr. Klein tells us the dividends in industrial and rail stocks increased by 285 per cent, twenty-two times as fast as wages. Is it any wonder that the crash of depression came? Increased production served only to turn the national wealth into two tremendously unequal channels. By far the bulk of that wealth went back in a torrent to capital and production. A tiny stream returned to purchasing power through wages.

Was over-production and the disregard of consuming power entirely accidental? I think not. To me it is inconceivable that the great experts in business and economics who have taken over the banking, industrial and political control of the country can have been blind to what was going on. As early as 1921 the Federated American Engineering Societies reported that many of our large industries were overdeveloped: Clothing 45 per cent, printing 50 per cent, shoes 50 per cent, coal 50 per cent. Yet throughout the whole decade the Department of Commerce used every power of persuasion to bring industry to the highest point of mass production.

If the drive for super-production had been coupled with a drive for an increased return to labor and consumers the result might have been very different. If it had been combined with an arrangement for providing men discharged because of labor-saving machinery and mergers with a dismissal wage it might have been helpful. It was coupled with nothing of the sort.

What it was coupled with was a campaign on the part of the Treasury Department to reduce taxation on great wealth. That campaign was not only successful but over-successful. Not only was the excess-profits tax repealed but the income tax on the higher brackets was reduced.

Meanwhile what was happening to consuming power? What about maintaining the buying ability of those millions of wage-earners who would have to use the extra goods turned out by glorified production? Take bituminous coal. In 1923 the people paid $900,000 for a Coal Commission to direct stabilization of that industry, already in bad shape. Its report and its recommendations were killed in cold blood while the administration looked calmly on. Take agriculture. For years the farm organizations have battled in vain for the stabilization measures which were so badly needed. Take the stock market. Some years ago when speculation was getting out of hand and the Senate had begun to study the situation, the then president concisely announced that the amount of brokers loans was not too high. Never before had a president undertaken to support the stock market.

In all this record not a plan was made—let alone carried out—for stabilizing purchasing power. Not a prop was put beneath consuming ability while producing ability was being reared to such dizzy heights. Our national leaders, those same leaders who have been insisting on local relief, lent willing hands in the development of a prosperity so one-sided that it could not stand.

Before going further let us see what sort of an economic structure these men have been building—these men who have consistently opposed the idea of federal relief. By the steady drying up of the springs of purchasing power and the overstimulation of production, there has been developed in this country the most astounding concentration of wealth in the hands of a few men that the world has ever known. Here is the basic evil which has brought on the depression, and which we must guard against in planning relief for the future. Here is the evil which is protected and fostered by local-relief plans.

In 1926 the Federal Trade Commission made a report to the Senate on National Wealth and Income. They had studied the county court records of over forty thousand estates. The records came from twelve states and stretched over a twelve-year period. The counties studied had been chosen to represent not only every section of the country from coast to coast but also every sort of district from the farms to the congested cities. They found that in this sampling one per cent of the people owned about 60 per cent of the wealth, that sixty dollars out of every hundred were owned by one person out of every hundred. They found that 40 per cent of the wealth, forty dollars out of every hundred, were left for the other 99 per cent of the people. In other words, one person out of every hundred was considerably richer than the other ninety-nine put together.

They found further that 13 per cent of the people owned more than 90
per cent of the wealth. And at the other end, 77 per cent of the
people owned only 5 per cent of the wealth. Three quarters of the
people could have added up all their fortunes and it would come to a
bare twentieth of the total. In 1929 the National Bureau of Economic
Research made a careful study of all the incomes in this country for
1926. They found that four and a half thousand people received that
year an average of almost $240,000 apiece. And at the bottom of the
heap, forty-four million people had incomes of about one thousand
dollars each, or less than one half of one per cent of the separate
incomes of those at the top.

Most recent figures are yet more amazing. In 1929 the per capita
income in this country was $700 for every man, woman and child. But
according to the Treasury Department's preliminary estimate, over
five hundred persons had in that year incomes of over a million dollars apiece. Their total income was $1,185,000,000. They received,
these five hundred odd, the average shares of 1,692,000 people.

The facts of concentration alone are impressive enough. But even
more so are the indications of how tremendously that concentration
increased in the years during which it received governmental encouragement. The figures for these years tell all too vividly the story
of a nation building toward disaster by unbalancing its economic
equilibrium. On March 20, 1931 the National Industrial Conference
Board published in its bulletin figures representing the total income of the nation for several years back. In 1920 we made over
seventy-four billion dollars. In 1928 we made eighty-one billion
dollars. In eight years we had increased our income by a little less
than one tenth.

But the Treasury Department's latest annual statistics of income
reveal some particularly interesting things to compare with that one
tenth. In 1920 there were 3649 people who had incomes of over
$100,000. In 1928 that number had jumped to 15,977. It had doubled
and then doubled again and was still going up. In 1920 those people
made a total of over 727 million dollars. But in 1928, those who
had the hundred-thousand-dollar incomes and up received about four
and a half billion dollars—more than six times as much money. And
all this, remember, while the incomes of all our people increased one
lone tenth of its previous figure.

Then how about the men who receive a million a year? In 1920 there
were thirty-three of them and they got 77 million dollars. In 1928
there were 511 of them, fifteen times as many, and they got over a
billion dollars, or fourteen times as much. The national income had
meanwhile increased by one tenth. Finally look at our fellow-citizens

who get a paltry five million a year. In 1920 there were four of
them and they collected not quite thirty million dollars. But by
1928 they had added twenty-two new members to their exclusive circle,
and the twenty-six of them were forced to get along with an income
of a little over 250 million dollars among them.

In other words, in the eight-year period between 1920 and 1928,
while the total national income increased less than 10 per cent, the
number of men with incomes of over a million dollars increased over
1400 per cent, or one hundred and forty times as fast. And the
amount of money these men made in one year increased 1300 per cent,
or one hundred and thirty times as fast as the total amount of money
made by everybody in the whole of the United States. They certainly
got their share!

The same astounding concentration of wealth and power is seen in
the industrial world. A study of corporate wealth and of the influence of large corporations was published this year in The American
Economic Review. The conclusions reached are eye-openers. In 1927,
there were over 300,000 industrial corporations in this country. Two
hundred of the 300,000, less than seven hundredths of one per cent,
controlled 45 per cent of the total wealth of all these corporations.
The same two hundred received over 40 per cent of all corporate income, and controlled over 35 per cent of all business wealth. Furthermore, about 20 per cent of the wealth of this entire nation was
in the hands of those two hundred corporations.

Truly the growth of these two hundred giant corporations has been
almost beyond belief. In the ten years up to 1929 their assets grew
from under 44 billion to 78 billion dollars, an increase of 78 per
cent. The author of the study, Prof. Gardiner C. Means, asserts
that if their indicated rate of growth continues in the future they
will own within twenty years virtually half of our national wealth.
Professor Means then emphasizes an extremely important fact. He
says that in 1927, less than two thousand men were directors of
these two hundred corporations. Since many of them were inactive,
the ultimate control of more than one third of industry was actually
in the hands of a few hundred men. And according to present indications it will still be only a few hundred men who by 1950 will control half of the wealth of this entire nation.

It is this almost unbelievable concentration of wealth which has
killed the consuming power of the average millions and has brought
our misfortunes upon us. It is this same incredible concentration
which is the chief obstacle in our path to permanent prosperity.
And it is the Senegambian in the local-relief woodpile. For if we
examine statements and actions of the proponents of local relief,

we find that they weave together into a surprisingly harmonious pattern. That pattern does not spell relief for the unemployed. What it spells is persistent shielding of concentrated wealth—not relief for the needy but release for the millionaire.

The local-relief advocates are prolific in denials of any excessive distress. Yet I know that there are almost a million men unemployed in the State of Pennsylvania alone. If my state were typical of the rest of the nation there would be not far from ten million unemployed in the country.

Next we have statements to the effect that wage-earners are not so badly off because prices have been dropping along with wages. That argument is answered by the government's figures. Commissioner of Labor Statistics Stewart of the U.S. Department of Labor announced on October 1, 1931 that from June 1929 to June 1931 the cost of living went down less than 12 per cent. In the same period, he stated, the total wage decrease was about 40 per cent. Wages actually paid dropped more than three times as far as prices.

The local-relief advocates have also laid unwarranted emphasis on federal public works. Their construction program, they say, has greatly relieved distress and they point out that the number of men employed in the federal construction program last month was fifty thousand. We have had the past summer half that number employed on state highways alone in Pennsylvania. And fifty thousand is no large percentage of the millions unemployed, after two years of depression. Is it any wonder that President William Green of the American Federation of Labor calls this "only a drop in the bucket" toward relieving unemployment?

Finally, there are the plans now under way to make up the federal deficit the depression has caused.

Treasury proposals to increase the income taxes recommend that the exemptions be lowered and the base of the tax be spread. In other words, much or most of the increase is to come from the little fellows. Certain leaders, among them Senator Reed, advocate a sales tax. A sales tax is simply another way of putting the burden on small business. They do far and away the largest part of the nation's buying and a sales tax would fall mainly on them. Does a sales tax reach the hoarded millions of the over-rich? Does it take money from the coffers of the large manufacturing corporations? It does not. It is another way of seeing to it that concentrated wealth shall remain concentrated.

There is only one conclusion to be drawn from all this: the safeguarding of money in the hands of an incredibly small number of incredibly rich men. The force behind the stubborn opposition to federal relief is fear lest the taxation to provide that relief be levied on concentrated wealth—fear lest the policy of years, the policy of shielding the big fortunes at the expense of the little ones, should at long last be tossed into the discard.

In the name of those who are overburdened now, I demand that the tax rates on the upper-bracket incomes be increased. In their name I demand that the graduation of the inheritance tax be steepened. And in their name I demand that the exemptions and the lower-bracket tax rates be left untouched. To meddle with them is to trifle with disaster and to invite the depression to stay. When I ask that the top rates of the income and estate taxes be raised enough to pay for federal relief for the unemployed, I am speaking as a man directly affected. I pay an income tax in the high brackets myself. In time, a goodly share of my estate will go to the government.

I believe in levying taxes according to ability to pay. Our government recognizes that principle in its dealings with foreign nations. Why should it not do so at home? The burden of an income tax or an inheritance tax can not be shifted. It lies where it falls. The burden of a heavily graduated tax falls on the man who is best able to bear it—who will feel the loss the least. I am strong for it. I am strong for its use to help defeat that shameful situation by which millions suffer from want in the richest country in the world.

You may ask how federal-relief funds can be used. In two ways. First by supplementing the efforts of the states, cities and other municipal organizations for feeding and otherwise helping people who cannot get work. Second, to give work. There is scarcely any limit to the number of men who could be employed by the federal government in great public works of many kinds in every part of the country. Flood control on the Mississippi and other rivers, the development of inland waterways, reforestation and fire prevention, the use of rivers for water supply, irrigation and power, the checking of erosion, the construction of airports and the lighting of airways, the drainage of swamp land, the building of highways—all these and many others can be undertaken and will pay for themselves over and over again in the recreated efficiency of national life. More than twenty-four hundred years before the Christian era the rulers of Egypt were faced with the question of employing idle labor. It was answered by the most widespread and effective public-construction program the world up to that time had known. The Nile was harnessed. Irrigation lakes and canals, public buildings and monuments, entire cities, were built on a nationwide scale. Are we lacking in the vision and the courage that set a nation at work forty-three centuries ago?

The picture is now complete. Local relief means making the poor man pay. Local relief serves to weaken further our national consuming power and block any hope of permanent recovery. Local relief is part of a vicious policy to shield concentrated wealth—a policy which brought on the depression and has kept it with us for two long years. Local relief means release for the rich, not relief for the poor.

Federal relief is demanded by every principle of justice, of humanity and of sound economics. Federal relief can be raised from the wealthy so that the purchasing power of the millions of average citizens will not suffer. Federal relief can be spent in such a way that unemployment and distress will be defeated and the entire nation started well along the path to a permanent and balanced prosperity.

Best of all, it should be remembered that plans for a very considerable part of these developments are already in existence, and that work upon many of them could be undertaken with comparatively little delay.

This is no local crisis, no state crisis. It is nation-wide. I can not believe that a national government will stand by while its citizens freeze and starve, without lifting a hand to help. I do not see how it can refuse to grant that relief which it is in honor, in duty and in its own interest bound to supply.

9

The New Deal and Its Impact
on Rural Areas

On March 4, 1933, Franklin Delano Roosevelt was inaugurated as
President of the United States. His inaugural address stressed the
need for immediate action. "There is nothing to do but to meet
everyday's troubles as they come," he said to the nation. And his
actions indeed brought forth broad reforms of the social conditions
of rural areas.

On March 16, 1933, Roosevelt sent to Congress the Agricultural
Adjustment Act (AAA), which proposed a variety of means for government support of farm prices. Though amended by both progressives
and conservatives, the AAA was passed in May. On March 21, the
Civilian Conservation Corps (CCC), a law eight days later, was proposed. And on March 30, 1933, Congress passed a bill creating the
Federal Emergency Relief Administration (FERA) to distribute,
through state relief agencies, $500 million of the federal treasury
to help the needy. This historical measure broke the political resistance of those who had clung to the belief that helping the poor
was only a local responsibility. The consequences of FERA for the
spread of social services to the remotest corners of the nation have
been amply documented and will be illustrated throughout the final
chapters of this volume.

The selections in this chapter have been included as explanations,
examples, and commentaries of the measures of the New Deal and their
impact on rural areas.

The opening selection by Mary Irene Atkinson, "The Rural Community
Program of Relief," was presented to the 1934 National Conference of
Social Work in Kansas City. It is an excellent review of the status
of welfare services in rural areas after the advent of FERA. Atkinson summarizes the developments in many states as they traveled the
road from poor-law to public welfare.

The second excerpt, "The Farmer and Social Discipline," was written by Henry A. Wallace. Although the piece is rather philosophical

and reveals Wallace's continued commitment to the country life theme
of rural cooperation, it serves to summarize the basic ideas imbued
in the AAA.

It is interesting to note that during the New Deal years, many
agencies attempted to provide, in various forms, rural relief and/or
monies for farm rehabilitation. In his study of those agencies,
Broadus Mitchell explained:

> The AAA was intended to help primarily commercial farmers, those
> raising sizable cash crops. Many of these were sufficiently
> distressed, but generally they were distinguished from the five
> million families and single persons living on farms in near
> destitution. Among these were owners of exhausted or otherwise
> submarginal land, often in parcels too small to support a family;
> part time farmers whose side occupations in lumbering or mining
> had disappeared; tenants of various grades running down to crop-
> pers; agricultural laborers, hundreds of thousands of whom had
> lost a better status because of debt, through the crop restric-
> tion program of the AAA, or from the competition of agricultural
> machinery, masses of them becoming migrants; and lastly a few
> million young people backed up on the farms because they could
> no longer find jobs in the cities.[1]

Whatever help came to these last three groups of rural dwellers
came primarily from the Federal Emergency Relief Administration (FERA)
and the Works Progress Administration (WPA), and not from the AAA.
Direct relief from FERA often was combined with loans to buy seeds
and implements, measures which were labeled rehabilitation. FERA,
which had started these rehabilitation measures in the southern
states, broadened the practices in 1935, seeking to restore families
to self-support. But because many lived in submarginal lands, the
practices were often unsuccessful. Finally, the AAA and FERA began
buying these submarginal districts and transferring their dwellers
to better soils. In the following paragraph, Mitchell summarizes
the final outcomes of this resettlement activity:

> In April 1935, the several sorts of federal rural social work
> were combined under the Resettlement Administration, whose main
> duties were to relocate farmers from 10,000,000 acres of sub-
> marginal land, and to rehabilitate other impoverished farmers
> where they were if the land justified the effort, thus gradually
> getting them off relief.[2]

It is not the purpose of this volume to write a detailed critique
of the effectiveness of the New Deal legislation in relation to rural
areas. What is important at this point is to note that FERA involved

---

[1]Broadus Mitchell, *Economic History of the United States Depression
Decade* (New York: Rinehart, 1947), p. 208.
[2]Ibid, p. 210.

rural workers not only in the administration of assistance in the country, but also in the determination, study, and support of the various efforts at rehabilitation and resettlement.

To interpret the complicated New Deal governmental machinery, the *Survey* set up a department of emergency information edited by Joanna C. Colcord and Russell H. Kurtz of the Russell Sage Foundation, which published basic synopses of existing and new legislation. One such synopsis on "Rural Rehabilitation" constitutes the third excerpt of this chapter.

The fourth piece, "Farmers on Relief" by Irving Lorge, further discusses, from a retrospective vantage point, the nature of the farm population receiving relief and/or on rehabilitation. Some expected and unexpected findings are analyzed to provide "chart and compass" for future action. Although rural nonagricultural populations were not included in the sample studied, their well-being was thought to be "inseparably tied up with the success of farmers."

"Rural Relief and the Back-to-the-Farm Movement" by T. J. Woofter attempts to explain, in terms of population trends and migratory movements, the relief problems experienced by many rural areas during the first five years of the Depression.

The article by Esther Morris Douty, "FERA and the Rural Negro," is one of the few to be found which discusses the effect of FERA on Blacks. It reveals the consequences of FERA's benefits on the outdated tenancy system in the South on wages, farm employment, and living standards.

"Rural Relief Administration in the Northwest" by Raymond Thompson deals with the problems of emergency relief administration given the unique characteristics of their location. It begins to highlight the theme of "locality specific" social work for rural communities, a topic of discussion begun in those early years and continued to the present.

Two articles, one a response to the other, which appeared in the *Survey* July and October 1935, respectively, have been included. "If I Were a County Relief Director" by Paul Landis dealt, in broad terms, with many of the administrative and service problems facing those working for FERA in county offices of rural districts. Interpretation of rules, relief in kind or cash, work relief, training of personnel and safeguarding the integrety of recipients were all dilemmas faced by those pioneer rural social workers. "I Am a County Relief Director" is M. B. Stinson's response to Landis' article. Written from his experiences in a district in the Ozarks, it provides valuable advice for rural relief social workers and administrators, much of which is still applicable and valuable today.

Finally, the last excerpt is more sociological and research-oriented. "Experimental Social Science" by Mordecai Ezekiel posed many evaluative questions which had to be answered in relation to the AAA and other welfare measures of the New Deal. This article is of special significance because, although published in *Rural America*, it called for an appraisal and even a reversal of the pattern of migration which the Country Life Association had always encouraged. In fact, the article suggests that migrations from rural to urban areas might have to be facilitated. Of course, we now know that such a phenomenon was in fact the prevalent one after 1939.

THE RURAL COMMUNITY PROGRAM OF RELIEF

Mary Irene Atkinson

It will remain for succeeding generations to write the story of the last five years, with the objectivity and balance which only a perspective gained over the years can give. Those of us living in the thick of the fray can only serve as reporters who have been given a news assignment so overwhelming that the most we can hope to do is to dash off a story occasionally, covering what we think we see and hear at the moment, but by no means presenting a complete picture of the spectacle of which we are a part.

It seems desirable to organize the material contained here under four general headings, namely: (1) "Summary of Methods in Rural Communities Prior to 1932"; (2) "Changes Resulting from Acceptance of State and Federal Funds,"; (3) "Attitudes of Officials, Lay Citizens, and Clients"; (4) "Building a Long-Time Program on an Emergency Foundation."

Proceedings, National Conference of Social Work, 1934. Mary Irene Atkinson was superintendent of the State Division of Charities, Department of Public Welfare, Columbus, Ohio.

1. Summary of Methods in Rural Communities Prior to 1932
In the majority of the forty-eight states, public money available
for poor-relief purposes was administered by local officials, township trustees, county poor-boards, commissioners, overseers of the
poor, selectmen, etc., the official title varying with the geographical area, but the functions remaining practically the same. The
exceptions, of course, were those states in which county welfare
boards were not only permissible under the law but had also begun to
function. In some states having such laws certain counties had organized their welfare activities on a unit basis, while in other
counties of the same state the local poor-officials continued to administer such relief as was given.

In six states there were county child welfare boards, limited by
legislation to child care and child protection, and not undertaking
in any way a generalized welfare program.

In New Mexico, California, Georgia, Iowa, and one or two other
states, county welfare programs had been initiated in certain areas
more or less by "gentleman's agreement," for which there was no
legislative sanction. Upon the basis of available data, it appears
that prior to the participation of state and federal agencies in
local relief programs, about 35 per cent[1] of the United States had
some form of machinery for carrying on county-wide welfare activities, but that the program was not completely operative even in the
seventeen states which had made a beginning.

Because so many voluntary agencies were raising large sums of money
for the support of relief agencies prior to 1930, there was not a
general realization of the fact that millions of local public funds
were even then being spent in the country for a variety of poor-
relief purposes; that the legislative basis for such relief expenditures was in many particulars almost a replica of the Elizabethan
codes regarding the care of paupers; and that these public funds were
being administered by untrained elective officials.

2. Changes Resulting from Acceptance of State and Federal Funds
In order to secure material which would make it possible to discuss
the assigned topic from a nation-wide point of view, specific inquiries addressed to relief directors and state boards of public welfare were sent to certain states which are fairly typical of larger
areas. The first of these questions was: What machinery has been
set up in your state in the administration of state and federal relief in rural areas?

[1]Mary Ruth Colby, *Social Service Review*, September 1932.

Alabama.—In forty-eight of the sixty-seven counties of Alabama, the Alabama Relief Administration administers federal relief funds through the already organized and well-developed county child welfare boards. This, particularly, is true in the rural areas. The county child welfare board by designation became the official relief agency and has continuously carried the responsibility for the relief program. The child welfare superintendent became the director of relief and functions as the chief executive for the child welfare board. The county continues to pay the major portion of the salary of this executive.

Recently, the Federal Emergency Relief Administration and the American Public Welfare Association approved a co-operative plan for the Alabama Relief Administration and the State Child Welfare Department whereby local money, formerly paid toward the salary of the director of relief, may be transferred to the employment of a child welfare superintendent as a member of the staff which is presided over by the county child welfare board.

Florida.—The State Emergency Relief Administration has organized each county for administration of relief with a social service director in each unit and a regional social service staff for field service. Thus there is the possibility of demonstrating to the community the meaning of case work. Beginnings have been made in the direction of setting up a case committee on family relief and service for each local relief unit.

Ohio.—The legislation creating the State Relief Commission makes it possible for the county commissioners in each county to take over the responsibility for administration of relief with the consent of the State Relief Commission, regardless of existing poor-relief laws. When state and school funds are allocated to the county, townships which will have enough local funds to care for their relief cases can still operate independently. Eighty-seven of the eighty-eight counties in Ohio have been organized on a county basis, but in a few counties there are townships which have remained outside the fold.

The State Relief Commission deals directly with the boards of county commissioners in each county. Advisory county relief committees may be appointed and such committees must be approved by the State Relief Commission. Some of the counties have active committees whose recommendations are the basis for action by the county commissioners. Other counties have committees which merely "yes" the commissioners. In still other counties, committees appointed when the state program was begun have painlessly passed away. In some instances this has been fortunate, as the way has thus been cleared for organizing a more effective advisory group.

Pennsylvania.—Machinery set up in Pennsylvania for the administration of state and federal relief in rural areas is identically the
same as that set up throughout the state. In other words, by act of
the legislature in September, 1932, the State Emergency Relief Board
was created. This Board had the power to establish local administrative bodies and proceeded to select a board of seven people in each
county. It also attempted to select as members of these county
emergency relief boards people who had shown some leadership and
interest in welfare programs or community organizations; also if
a county official—commissioner, director of the poor, judge—was
likely to strengthen the Board, at least one public official was
appointed.

During the early months, local private agencies were selected by
the county boards, as the groups responsible for the actual service
to relief cases, these private organizations serving as the agents
of a county board. However, before very long it was realized that
there must be an administrative tie-up and control, and the use of
private agencies was discontinued—the full responsibility for direction, administration, financial control, and case-work service to
the unemployed on relief being controlled by the county board, which
is responsible only to the state.

Nebraska.—There have been set up county emergency relief committees in about seventy of the ninety-three counties in the state.
These committees consist of from three to five people, appointed by
the State Emergency Relief Committee. A representative of the county
poor-board usually serves on this county relief committee. This
committee is for advice and education of the local public opinion.
They do not determine who gets federal relief. This is done by the
county relief worker, who must be approved by the state administrator.
An attempt is made to have a county relief worker who is satisfactory
to the county relief committee, but in the last analysis no one can
write a federal relief order except one who is approved by the state
administrator, and the county committee has no authority to force
this county worker to grant relief.

There is a definite understanding with each county board as to
just what cases the emergency relief committee shall handle and which
cases shall be handled by the county. In general, we handle from
federal funds unemployment relief cases, supplying food, clothing,
fuel, and household supplies. In most cases the county furnishes
relief for the outdoor-relief cases who are regular clients of the
county and also supplies shelter allowance so far as it is supplied
at all to the unemployment cases. In the majority of counties medical care of the unemployment cases is also supplied by the counties,

although the relief administration is doing this in about a fifth of
the counties.

New Hampshire.—The New Hampshire relief set-up calls for eleven
major districts or county offices, with a county supervisor in charge.
Where the case load and territory demands, suboffices are also set
up under an assistant supervisor. Each office is staffed with investigators to meet the case load in so far as it possible. Each
office has a certain territory to cover. In each town there is a
local agent responsible to the district office. This agent has the
authority to grant relief or emergency relief when called upon if,
in his judgment, it seems wise. Immediately after this relief is
granted a report is made to the office. Investigators cover these
towns at least once a week and all new cases are discussed and investigated. The report is filed with the county supervisor, and a
permanent plan and budget is decided upon. This is given to the
local agent, and it is his authority to continue the aid.

New Mexico.—In each county the county unit of the State Welfare
Bureau is also the county administrative unit for federal relief. In
those counties where permanent units had not been organized prior to
the receipt of federal relief, new set-ups were instituted. The
plan for the new units was the same as for the old units, namely,
county welfare associations. The aim is to have a trained social
worker in charge of each of the units.

The impracticability of a state relief commission having to deal
with the township trustees, selectmen, overseers of the poor etc.,
became immediately apparent when we were plunged into a large-scale
relief-administration problem. Sheer necessity, therefore, has
(1) pushed us toward the goal of county unification of welfare activities, (2) made it possible to provide social service in rural communities as a substitute for the haphazard methods of the local relief officials, and (3) through the possible participation of committees of lay persons and public officials in the emergency program,
increased the opportunities for interpretation of what constitutes
a socialized public welfare program.

In practically every state the relief commissions have insisted
upon standards of personnel hitherto unknown in most of the rural
areas of the United States. Various methods have been set up to
safeguard appointments, with the result that for the first time people living in the country are being helped in their time of need with,
at least, some of the skills employed by workers on the staffs of
agencies of recognized standing in the metropolitan areas.

3. *Attitudes of Officials, Lay Citizens, and Clients*

Good roads, telephones, telegraph systems, radios, automobiles, and airplanes have reduced the physical isolation of our rural communities to a remarkable degree. But there remains a psychological isolation from much that is accepted as a component part of the urban scene. The efficiently organized social agency and the social worker trained for her job are not utterly strange phenomena to most city officials and to relief clients. In hundreds of rural communities in this country, however, the only exposure public officials and other citizens had to organized social work was through the medium of state departments of public welfare. In some of the states, as, for example, Mississippi and Arkansas, even this was lacking as there was practically nothing in the way of a state welfare program prior to the establishment of the emergency relief commissions.

As more people in rural communities had to ask for help and local resources became exhausted, the local officials had to turn to the state and federal governments. Then they began to run into a maze of regulations and standards which had to be accepted if necessary funds were to be forthcoming.

The impact of these procedures upon the local officials and the average citizen has produced a wide range of attitudes which will materially influence the development of the future social program in rural America.

In certain places there is no doubt but that the officials and many of the citizens feel that Washington and their state capital are bent on spending the taxpayer's money on a lot of useless machinery in order to give out "charity."

They are more concerned with winding up the relief business than they are in considering its ultimate merger with general relief and the development of a long-time program. They conform because they must have additional funds, but the organization which has been set up is not regarded in any sense as a permanent part of their governmental structure.

If anyone thinks that machine politics flourish only in urban communities, they are not familiar with the habits and customs of rural America. Officials in some of the smallest and most rural sections have, for political reasons, been antagonistic toward the consolidation of counties for administration of relief and the employment of training personnel from outside the locality. One state director of relief reports: "It is needless for me to say that the political set-up of county commissioners is very much against the present organizations for administration of relief but the local people, the selectmen and the recipients of aid, are for the most part co-operative."

The secretary of a state department of public welfare makes this statement: "There certainly is resistance in rural areas toward the new deal in the administration of relief. This has been expressed in a resistance to the amount of relief grants which in rural areas are considered excessive. There was even more resistance to C.W.A. wage rates, which, in smaller communities, were looked upon as inimical to the employment of necessary 'help' for farms and for borough and township road work."

The director of the social service division of a state relief commission comments as follows: "While there is still resistance to the program, yet through active use of the county child welfare boards and advisory committees of various kinds, and through constant requirements that county finance boards participate financially in the program, there has spread throughout our rural communities a wider and finer understanding of the implication of a good social-work program, and the need for such a program, even though, during this emergency, it has not been possible always to do the entire job which needs to be done in any locality."

It seems fair to conclude that the attitudes of local officials responsible for finances and for poor-relief administration and of the self-supporting lay public range from firm resistance to all aspects of the relief program to that of acceptance of the policies emanating from Washington and the various state capitals; that in spite of resistance or acceptance, people in rural communities have gained some conception of a new approach toward administration of relief by persons qualified by training and experience for the task; and that even in communities where local officials appear to be living for the day when the curtain can be rung down on the current scene, it will not be so easy to revert to the predepression techniques.

The social worker who goes into a rural community which never before has had any social service except that given by elective officials and volunteers has placed upon her an unusual responsibility. The community's decision as to whether the county relief administration should be kicked out as soon as the subdivision can be freed from state and federal domination or whether it is something to carry forward depends to a large extent upon the way in which the social worker has interpreted the program and the attitudes she has created by her own personality.

The attitudes of industrial workers in urban communities have been shaped by a variety of forces which do not operate in rural areas. Thus it is not strange that in the typically rural localities the attitude of the relief client is somewhat different from that of the city worker. It probably is also more truly what the orators

of the Old Deal call "American" than that of any other group. When
one comes to know some of these families, it is clear that there are
values in their points of view which should be conserved as we set
about the task of reshaping the social structure of this country. It
is not possible to sit in an office and pick up certain nuances and
overtones which are significant. To get these one must go to what
is still the motivating social force of civilization—the family.

As I attempted to prepare the outline for this paper, I became
convinced that somehow there should be included in it first-hand information regarding the philosophy and reactions of at least one or
two of the families, for whose assistance this governmental superstructure of relief administration has been constructed. While I
realized that I could draw no conclusions from such a limited experience, it seemed desirable to get into this Conference vicariously
a few of the people most closely affected by what we are doing.

With the case worker from a local relief office located in one of
the most rural counties of the state, I began my round of visits.
The worker had been well accepted by her families, although she is
an "outlander." Her explanation that I was visiting her and had
come along for the ride was accepted, and I was welcomed without
either suspicion or curiosity. Incidentally, of course, this attitude on the part of the families revealed the *rapport* existing between them and the case worker.

The story of the day spent in the homes of a number of rural families is too long to be told here in detail, but the following summarizes the experience fairly well:

To have lived through these last five years with less than the bare
necessities of life and still have the ability to find something of
advantage in one's own situation; to have the will to work for what
one gets in spite of the demoralization of irregular and insufficient
employment; and to regard the efforts of government to meet the relief needs of the community as an expression of neighborly concern,
in spite of the many mistakes which have been made—all this seems
to reveal an attitude on the part of rural relief clients which holds
much of promise.

Somewhere there is a balance between overready acceptance of public
relief and the abject sense of shame and degradation with which many
persons have come to our public agencies. As long as we remain so
stupid as to assume that we can solve our economic problems by giving
relief to people who want work, it would seem that perhaps in our
rural areas we have the best chance of maintaining such balance, if
our relief administration is sufficiently intelligent. The problem
seems to be how to conserve existing wholesome attitudes in rural

areas and to take advantage of them in the social planning which lies just ahead.

4. Building a Long-Time Rural Program on an Emergency Foundation

There is, of course, a common denominator in a public welfare program regardless of geographical differences. In a rural program, however, there must be certain differentiations both in philosophy and in procedures if the social mechanisms to be set up are going to accomplish anything.

I should like to get into the record what I believe to be a few significant notes based upon the social experiments carried on in forty-eight state laboratories during the last three years. These are as follows:

A welfare program in a rural community must become indigenous if it is to withstand the storms which are bound to overtake it. Unless the emergency relief administrations put down roots while still carrying on the so-called emergency activities, there can be no growth of permanent value. Furthermore, roots can be grown only when there is local participation in what is going on. Thus far, this philosophy has been somewhat conspicuous by its absence in many parts of the country.

There has been some tendency toward letting down standards of personnel selected for rural communities. A small community's attitude toward professional social work and social workers will be determined almost entirely by the type of person who comes in to initiate the case-work program. The story of how many rural communities have been improperly conditioned because the case worker was not qualified either by training, experience, or personality for her task will be a sad story when it comes to be written. Another sad tale is that of the rural community in which the relief administration lays claim to have a trained staff, but in reality is trusting the job largely to unskilled persons. In that case public officials and citizens reject what they think social work is, based upon their observations of what is happening in their midst without ever having seen the real article.

Rural communities in many of our states can never carry on a welfare program without financial assistance. Neither will they feel a proper responsibility for a structure financed entirely by state and federal funds. Joint financing on an equalization basis seems to be the answer to the financial problem. Precedents for this have been established in the fields of health and education. Participation in determining standards of administration and of personnel should be the privilege as well as the responsibility of each of the political subdivisions sharing the financial burden.

Mass movements of populations either into or out of rural communities can never be brought about by official fiat. Motivation for such movements must come through common religious, racial, economic, or social interests within the groups affected. In planning rural programs this principle, in support of which plenty of evidence could be presented, should be kept in mind. Many dreams conjured up by the knowledge that Washington is willing to put up money for rural projects can be seen walking in certain administrative centers far removed from the realities of boll-weevil, grasshoppers, corn-borers, flood, and drought.

As a result of our emergency administrations there are evidences in our rural areas which indicate the practicability of integrating the various social welfare services in one unit in the locality too small to afford specialized activities. This would seem to indicate more rather than less generalized training for rural workers and a new philosophy regarding social planning.

There has been much confusion both in our thinking and in our planning because we have thrown relief and unemployment into one hopper. In rural areas the problem is not so much one of unemployment as it is of exhaustion of natural resources, the result of world-market conditions, oversupply and underconsumption, and many other deep-seated economic factors which do not fall within the scope of this paper.

There are always present in any rural community long-time social problems with which, as previously indicated, only about 35 per cent of the states had equipped themselves to deal prior to the depression. It is fair to assume that many communities will make the cutover from an emergency relief administration to a long-time welfare program if there is sufficient leadership from the top and proper participation from the local communities. But unless each community recognizes that it is facing two separate and distinct problems, it will not be able for a long time to evolve a realistic method of solving its difficulties.

Someone has said that life itself is a concession to improbability. It seems not too fantastic then, to hope, that under the leadership of the New Deal rural America will become something more than a place from which to move.

THE FARMER AND SOCIAL DISCIPLINE

Henry A. Wallace

For those of us who are disillusioned about the virtues of laissez
faire and who shun the doctrinaire, whether of the "left" or of the
"right," this is an age of unpleasant alternatives. If we insist
upon examining every economic theory in the light of the facts about
us, and if we insist upon steering our course by those facts, then
our days are full of obstacles. The luxury of pure abstraction, the
pleasures of logic untempered by reality, the blissful singleminded-
ness of the man with a cut and dried economic creed—none of these
can be ours.

Unpleasant Alternatives
It is peculiarly true in agriculture that our choice is between unpleasant alternatives. Apparently we have to choose between low
prices, which are unbearable, a reduction in production, which is
distasteful and enormously difficult, and a general lowering of the
tariff, which is politically difficult. In other words, we have to
choose between doing nothing, which is unthinkable, and stepping on
many tender toes, which is no particular pleasure for any of us.

Under an attitude of drift, of trusting to luck, no one is required
to worry about the implications of individual behavior, and no one
is expected to pay any serious attention to the consequences of whatever great economic forces may be at work. The moment a society
abandons its childlike faith that things will always turn out for
the best because they always have—more or less—that moment is the
signal for difficult alternatives to crop up. Economic anarchy, we
agree, is not to be endured; we turn our faces from it; but are we
ready and willing to undergo the severe intellectual training which
collective striving for economic order entails? If our minds are
ready, are our hearts?

To many persons it is a depressing thing to have to be concerned
with the implications of what they do; but as I see it that is the
least price we must pay for modern civilization. Concern for the
effect of individual behavior upon the group is a condition of any
modern economy.

Rural America, January 1934. Henry Agard Wallace was Secretary of
Agriculture and actively involved with the Agricultural Adjustment
Administration when this paper was written.

The AAA No Bed of Roses

When I say that our choice is more often than not between relatively unpleasant alternatives, I am speaking, as you may have guessed, from experience. The Agricultural Adjustment Act, which no one has ever characterized as a bed of roses, is nevertheless in my judgment the only immediately available alternative to an utterly impossible situation in agriculture. Yet the Act has put us up against one obstacle after another. It will continue to do so. There is nothing to be surprised at in that. That has been true every step of the way in man's conscious attempts to become civilized. If we have perspective, we know that in the mind and heart of mankind there are potentialities that have never been tapped.

It is about one of those potentialities that I wish to speak today. Call it, for lack of a better phrase, social discipline. I mean by that a willingness to modify individual behavior for the larger purposes of society. It is really enlightened selfishness, for in any enduring civilization the welfare of the individual is, in the long run, identical with the welfare of the group. Without the emergence of a very real social discipline, I do not see how we can continue to face unpleasant facts and distasteful alternatives, and consciously undertake a course which we know will be difficult. Is there, then, any hope that such a discipline is in the making in America?

I am not prepared today to answer that question with a flat yes or no; I wish merely to describe what has been happening in one sector of our recovery program and to speculate on its significance.

The campaign of the Agricultural Adjustment Administration to reduce wheat acreage will serve for illustration. Without going into the facts of the world wheat situation, with which this audience must be familiar, you will recall that during the summer we offered the wheat farmers of the United States an opportunity to unite in a voluntary effort to reduce the acreage of the wheat crop to be harvested next summer. Our goal, in line with the London wheat agreement, was a 15 percent reduction under the average harvested acreage of the years 1930-32. To farmers who contracted to reduce their wheat acreage, when and if required, by not more than 20 percent for 1934 and also 1935, the Adjustment Administration agreed to pay benefits from funds collected by a processing tax on flour. These benefit payments were to be made on individual allotments based on the domestically consumed part of the grower's average production, the base period being 1930-32.

The Wheat Campaign

In announcing the plan we said: "In general, the plan is intended to obtain for the wheat growers who will cooperate with the Agricultural Adjustment Administration by agreeing to adjust production, a sum equivalent to the parity price on that portion of their production which is required for domestic consumption. This sum will be made up of two parts: (a) the prevailing market price at which the grower sells his wheat, and (b) the payment made under the Act. The income of the grower will be independent of the prevailing open market price or of the world price at which the surplus sells. . . . By adopting this plan, the Government of the United States will possess the power to bring about acreage adjustments in 1934 and 1935 to conform to whatever agreement may be reached between wheat exporting nations at the London Conference."

This plan, as many of you know, follows very closely the outlines of the voluntary domestic allotment plan for wheat as it was presented last winter by Mr. M. L. Wilson. Wheat growers utilize the centralizing power of the Federal Government to do something they could not successfully do as individuals; at the same time the plan is voluntary, not compulsory, and to an uncommon degree it depends upon an effective democracy. The contract the individual grower signs is not something to be lightly entered into: it may require keeping land out of production not only for the crop of 1934, but for the crop of 1935, if the world wheat situation compels it.

In the discussion of the domestic allotment plan a year ago, many serious difficulties were anticipated by those opposed to the plan. The proponents were generally willing to admit that some of these difficulties would arise, but they did not believe them insurmountable. Much of the discussion centered around the idea of giving farmers individual allotments based on past acreage or production, and the idea of expecting them to police their neighbors' claims and performances under the contracts.

A Detailed Plan

In an exhaustive critique published about a year ago it was argued that getting the statistical basis for the individual allotments would be an enormous job, and it was doubted if it could be done in time to affect planting this fall; or if it could be done, the expense in some counties would exceed the benefits. Again it was suggested that the job of checking up on the reduction actually made would prove not only onerous, but even dangerous in some communities. The local committeemen, it was predicted, would not be likely to serve more than one year, if that long.

These criticisms, let me add, did not come from sources unfriendly to the farmer; they were simply based on the assumption that man is exclusively an economic being, and that human behavior in the future is invariably predicated on human behavior in the past. What was is, and always will be. I never have understood why so many economists could be so cocksure that human nature is impervious to change, for there have been many periods in history when human nature has undergone very significant changes, and there is ample reason to look for further changes; to admit the possibility, however, may play havoc with one's basic economic assumptions. Just the same, I want to advance the suggestion that though man is in some part an economic being, he is also a social being.

Early last summer when the wheat plan was formulated and announced, it is probably true that the thing that attracted the attention of the average grower was the prospect of benefit payments, one of them to be made this year. The problem of the surplus, the necessity for combining in a common effort, no doubt seemed wrapped in vagueness; the offer of cash was clear-cut and compelling. I see nothing in this to be shocked or surprised at. When a man's children need shoes, when his wife hasn't had a new dress in four years, when his farm may be slipping out of his grasp, he has very little patience for long-winded dissertations on the supply and demand of wheat in Australia and China; he wants some sure prospect of cash income, because he must have it to live. And so the first thought of many growers undoubtedly was, "Let's get all we can out of this."

Motives Vary

When the county production control associations were organized, and the county and township committees selected, interest continued to center on how long it would be before the Government checks came along. That interest was soon complicated, however, by the announcement of State and county acreage allotments, and the necessity for figuring individual farm allotments. Checking back over his acreage and production during the previous three seasons, relying upon memory or figures scratched on the granary door, many a grower had a difficult job on his hands. Even a thoroughly disinterested individual would have had.

The first individual estimates, naturally, were not always made with their relationship to the county allotments firmly in mind. There were at least five factors operating to discourage accuracy: there was in the first place, the honest inability to recall accurately the production and acreage of former years; second, in some counties reliance upon assessors' estimates was unfortunate, for the reason that the assessors had accounted for only three-fourths of the average section of land in wheat; third, in the newer parts of the wheat belt government statistics were not as accurate as in the older parts; fourth, there was the feeling that since everybody was likely to over-estimate, I might as well follow suit, much as the

banks, in subscribing for Government bond issues, ask for two or
three times as much as they expect to get; and fifth, in thousands
of instances there was the pressure of a misery-ridden family to
consider.

Publicity Helps
The rather intense light of publicity was focussed on the individual
estimates when they were published in the county newspapers. You
can imagine that that issue of the county paper was read from cover
to cover. When Bill Jones, who estimated his past average acreage
at 100 acres, saw by the paper that Jim Brown, his neighbor, estimated his at 120 acres, when Bill reckoned that Jim had no more
wheat land than he did, somebody was sure to hear about it. That
"somebody" proved to be the county allotment committee. On an average there were 100 to 150 complaints of this sort in the big wheat-
producing counties. That would involve perhaps 10 percent of the
farmers in the average county.

Curiously enough, this experience jibes almost exactly with the
experience Stillwater County, Montana, had in the first year it
tried the plan of letting farmers act as their own tax assessors. As
M. L. Wilson has described that experiment, a man ran for county
assessor in that county some years ago on the pledge that if elected
he would eliminate the two deputies employed to help the county
assessor and give the farmers a better assessment as well. On that
popular program he was elected, and he immediately set out to make
good on his word. At local meetings throughout the county he presented a two-point program. First, he explained that in order to
have fair assessments each farmer must list all of his property, because each taxing unit had designated a budget and must raise so
much money, and therefore any farmer who failed to turn in all of
his property was dodging his taxes and they were being paid by his
neighbors. Consequently, if a farmer who had 50 head of cattle turns
in for tax purposes only 25, then part of his taxes are being paid by
his neighbors who listed all their property. The farmers understood
and approved the principle involved.

The assessor's second point was that the process of assessment
could be simplified by letter each farmer assess his own property.
When the farmers' estimates were received at the county courthouse,
however, they would be published in the county paper for everyone in
the county to see. Enlightened self-interest would thus be given
powerful support.

Check and Double Check

In the first year of the self-assessment plan in Stillwater County complaints were registered against 150 of the 1200 farmers in the county. Some of the complaints were "spite work." But the next year, and ever since then, there have been very few complaints and very little police work for the county assessor to do. In fact the plan has worked well enough so that counties using it frequently show more cows per farm, more brood sows per farm, etc., than do neighborhood counties using the old system of assessment. When and if the time comes to make individual allotments to wheat growers next fall, it will be interesting to compare our experience then with our experience this past summer and fall.

After the publication of individual allotments this summer, in some counties the total of these was greater than the total allotted the county on the basis of our State-Federal statistics. The first impulse of the growers was to say the Government statistics were wrong, and for two or three weeks the county allotment committees were on a hot spot. A series of deadlocks seemed to threaten the success of the whole plan. Accordingly the officials of the Adjustment Administration decided to go out into the field and get at the root of the trouble. If there was overestimating by farmers and underestimating by the Government, the obvious thing to do was to find out how much of each there really was. Surveys of enough sample acreages to check on the accuracy of the estimates clarified the atmosphere a great deal. The next step was to discuss the problem frankly with the growers in local meetings. If carefully checked Government statistics showed a base wheat area of 100,000 acres, while growers' estimates showed an area of 120,000 acres, it was plainly up to the growers to revise their estimates. The base figure for the county, as determined by impartial Government statistics, would be made as accurate as possible, but once that was done it was up to the growers to adjust their estimates to it.

Neighbor to Neighbor

Wheat growers in counties where that sort of problem cropped up talked it over in meetings and back home with their neighbors. The feeling that the Government was wrong was dissipated by the sample surveys and by the reasonableness of the Federal, State, and local administrators. The consciousness that within each county the administration of the plan was, after all, up to the growers themselves, prompted them to try to figure their own way out of the difficulty. Aware that individuals who had overestimated their acreage were encroaching on the rights of their neighbors, the local committees determined to meet the issue squarely. This they did in a

variety of ways. In some counties they called the township committees in, put the township totals on the blackboard, pointed to the
overrun in the estimates, and asked for volunteers to obtain revised
estimates from the growers. In some cases township allotments were
made. In an eastern Montana County another criterion was chosen.
There the producers pointed out that for years the state college had
been saying, as a result of its researches, that the average farm in
that region ought to have about 65 percent of its crop land in wheat.
Why not use that as a guide in revising the individual estimates?
The committee agreed it was sensible, so that the growers who showed
less than 65 percent of their crop land in wheat were permitted to
increase their wheat acreage estimates, while those with more than
65 percent were asked to reduce theirs.

This sort of thing went on in hundreds of counties and involved
hundreds of thousands of farmers. In the midst of the process, there
is some reason for believing that the first and all-engrossing interest in the Government checks gave way to corollary interests which
had a very direct connection with the problem of the world wheat
surplus and the desirability of collective action. Despite the understandable concern with case benefits, despite the conflicts and
temporary ill-feeling these may have engendered, the conflicts were
settled and the conditions of the wheat plan were met by the growers
themselves. It was a thoroughly democratic process, and to everyone
who participated there came a genuine sense of accomplishment. I
truly believe that many of these men learned, perhaps for the first
time, what is involved in making individual interest coincide with
group interest. And having identified themselves with the group,
there doubtless came to them some vision of power that resides in
group action.

Voluntary Action Necessary

The task of adjusting these allotments out in the counties could not
have been done by Government agents. Yet the plan as a whole could
not have been inaugurated without the use of the centralizing power
of the Federal Government. The majority of wheat growers, I suspect,
are now aware of these two points, and my hope is that they will
realize how much a part of the Government they are, and how much the
Government is a part of them. Certainly our greatest hopes for democracy lie in such a realization.

There were other results from this first stage in the wheat adjustment campaign which ought to be mentioned in passing. The fact
that the rights of the tenant were specifically protected in the
contracts, and by the Government, contributed to the belief that the
program was impelled by a sense of social justice. The fact that

11,000 farmers served on the county and township allotment committees has revealed the existence of a rich source of local leadership. Finally, the practical way in which members and leaders of rival farm organizations worked side by side in the campaign, merging their own programs in this common cause, is a distinctly hopeful note for the future.

The Test of the Program

The test of the wheat program in the eyes of the average person, I suppose, will be whether or not it actually does reduce acreage and production by 15 percent. The evidence thus far leads me to believe that so far as the growers who have signed up are concerned, they will meet their obligations to the letter. But what is perhaps of more importance than the attainment of a specific acreage goal, these cooperating farmers have demonstrated their willingness to undergo a certain amount of social discipline for the larger purposes of the group. It may be that the demonstration will be forgotten, yet I think that unlikely. The farmer who has a piece of wheat land which he must keep out of wheat, has before his eyes a constant reminder of his sacrifice; in his benefit payments, and in the higher wheat price which he has some prospect of expecting, he has the effect of his sacrifice.

It is true that the real problem may come in areas where wheat is not the major crop, and where less than an overwhelming majority of producers have agreed to cooperate in the plan. The December 1 crop report shows that although the main wheat-producing States have done an excellent job of reducing winter wheat acreage, several States east of the Mississippi have increased their wheat acreages. Granted that this is in the soft red winter wheat area, very little of which is ever exported, and granted that a diversified area is not likely to give up everything else for wheat, the question remains: will the growers of a big wheat State with a good sign-up permit the growers of a less important wheat State to sabotage the program? The benefit payments and the concept of parity in the Adjustment Act protect the cooperating grower to some extent against the activities of the non-cooperators, it is true, but situations are possible when only a complete control of all wheat acreage may suffice, at least in the judgment of many growers. Such control would be possible, it seems to me, only if the overwhelming majority of growers possessed an extremely active and acute sense of social discipline. Governmental fiat is no substitute for that.

The county production control associations, not only those that deal
with wheat but those concerned with cotton, corn and hogs, and others
that might be organized, are in many respects the most interesting
features of these emergency adjustment campaigns. They are intensely
democratic, and they are proving to be effective instruments of self-
government. In them, as I see it, lies whatever possibility there
may be for the development of a genuine social discipline. If the
farmers themselves felt the need for a more complete control of production, it would be relatively simple in any farming county for the
wheat association, the corn-hog association, and any others there
might be, to be merged into one production control association for
all the major farm products of that county. A member of such an
association might then sign just one contract covering his whole production schedule. And if anything like this ever did come to pass,
the people in that county would begin to think, not simply of wheat
or cotton or corn, but of all the important adjustments agriculture
as a whole must constantly be making.

Maybe you will decide that there is no possibility of such a development; maybe you will decide that a planned agriculture is a dream
born of the emergency, to evaporate when the emergency disappears;
maybe, therefore, as a friend of mine has expressed it, you will decide that we shall return to the blessed condition wherein the only
thing needed will be good outlook reports.

This last alternative is in my judgment the least probable of all.
Some degree of planning seems requisite if our civilization is not
to smash. That is quite as true whether we choose the nationalistic
course, the international course, or some combination of the two.
If we decide, as a result of vigorous, courageous public debate the
country over, to adopt the nationalistic course and wish to stick to
it for at least 10 or 15 years, then a huge area of farm land must
be kept out of cultivation, certain processing and handling trades
will have to adjust themselves to it, and consumer purchasing power
will have to be kept at a level high enough to support it; each and
all of these operations demand planning. Or if we decide for the
international course, then there will have to be radical lowering of
many tariffs, high-cost industries will have to be eliminated, and
foreign purchasing power will consciously have to be increased; this
too requires planning. The middle course, which might call for the
buying of some land to keep it out of production, a less radical
lowering of tariffs and a more moderate readjustment in industry—
this course, like the other two, just as plainly calls for planning.

Planned Economy—Social Discipline

Just as plainly a planned economy can get nowhere unless it is backed by social discipline. In some countries, there is a kind of social discipline in existence, but it is imposed from above. We are a democracy, and we propose to remain a democracy. The only possible kind of social discipline in a democracy is one that is imposed upon the people by the people themselves. Such a discipline can result, I am convinced, from the ceaseless action, reaction, and interaction of one individual on another, from the very tangible feeling of give-and-take which develops among the individuals of a group which is on the march to a common objective.

This presupposes a social machine. I have always thought of the Agricultural Adjustment Act as fundamentally just such a machine, and I have said repeatedly that it had no chance at all of functioning unless the human minds and wills and hearts which comprised it, really wanted it to function. A machine made of human material demands certain types of plasticity as well as tenacity, however, and this sort of human material is vastly different from the little hard human particles which have been so characteristic of the past.

There is nothing sacred about social machinery. It will and must be modified and improved from time to time. If there arises a social discipline which can provide the motive power for the machine, there will still be the necessity that this discipline be continuous, that it be of such nature as to be continually modifying itself to fit a changing environment and a changing task, and that, finally, it have the power of reshaping and strengthening itself for the new tasks.

In speaking of the psychic qualities necessary to operate a complex piece of social machinery I am reminded of some comments made by Dr. Max Sering, the patriarchal professor of agricultural economics at the University of Berlin. It was my pleasure in 1930 to drive with him in an automobile in some very heavy traffic. He had not been in America since the early eighties, and he commented on what an extraordinary advance in social discipline had been made by the American people as a result of the necessary give-and-take growing out of the myriad kaleidoscopic changes of infinitely varied automobile contacts. I agreed with him and thought of the way in which some of our more irascible drivers used to shake their fists and shout at another driver who had presumably committed some unforgiveable sin. Nowadays there are literally hundreds of thousands of automobile accidents annually, but when we consider that our cars travel probably fifty billion miles a year, the marvel is that we do not have more accidents.

The extraordinary thing is the adaptable good humor with which the American people have been able to meet each other in this problem of getting along expeditiously and smoothly in our crowded cities. Though there are still plenty of conflicts and misunderstandings, yet the traffic does move with remarkable celerity. I am inclined to agree with Dr. Sering that a people which can so rapidly learn the discipline necessary for operating 20 million swiftly moving vehicles, can learn to work together in attaining a great variety of social objectives. It is all a question of desire.

I do not wish you to read too much into the account of the wheat campaign I described earlier; I intended merely to speculate on the possibility of social discipline, you know, not predict the date and force of its coming. And my purpose in discussing it at this meeting, after all, is primarily to direct your attention to a potentiality that economists usually overlook.

Social Sympathy—Social Justice

Many of you will be quick to remark that there are possibilities of evil as well as good in social discipline, and I agree. It is the function of the Federal Government, in normal times as in times of emergency, to keep before the people the broadest possible picture. Government cannot serve the selfish interests of one class at the expense of the general welfare without betraying its true function. It may be the duty of Congressmen as individuals to speak for specific selfish local interests among their constituents, but the Administration, if it is to do its part in perfecting an enduring social discipline, must use its powers whether dealing with farmers, with wage earners, or with business men to keep each within the bounds dictated by the general welfare. If some one class has long been exploited so that we have a dangerous lack of balance in the social organization, it may be necessary for Government to encourage the backward class to bring about that degree of activity which is necessary for social balance.

So far as agriculture is concerned, we have found from experience that certain regions and interests have been in the habit of running to Washington too frequently, whereas others have perhaps not come frequently enough. It is essential, let me repeat, that as we grapple with the broad economic forces which sweep over our world, that farmers more and more feel that they are a part of the Government, and that the Government is part of them. It follows that we need to develop an attitude of disinterestedness much as does the highest type of sportsman who plays the game well, not primarily in order to win, but in order to command admiration for honest, courageous effort from an audience possessed of a broad social sympathy and a deep sense of social justice.

RURAL REHABILITATION

Joanna C. Colcord and Russell H. Kurtz

After eight months of experimentation, the Rural Rehabilitation Division of the FERA is ready for its 1935 offensive on rural distress. At a series of regional conferences in September, state administrations were given the details of a revised and elaborated program.

The fundamental objective of the RRD is "to make it possible for worthy destitute farm families now eligible for relief to become self-supporting on a plane consistent with American standards and insofar as possible on their own farms." But the program proposes to reach beyond that group and render rehabilitative service to other rural dwellers who are not farmers. These are the relief families living in non-industrial towns of less than 5000 population, and "stranded populations." In June it was estimated that there were, all told, 1,200,000 "rural" families on relief, half living on farms, and half in villages. This number has undoubtedly increased since as a result of the drought.

That part of the program which applies to farm families has been most thoroughly developed. The RRD recognizes that there are three classifications here: hitherto self-sustaining farmers now in distress; farm tenants and share-croppers; and displaced farmers who have not completely lost touch with the land. For these families it is proposed:

To make such seed stocks, farm animals, equipment, buildings or land available as may be required for subsistence purposes.

To provide the services of trained specialists in agriculture and home economics to aid in formulating plans for subsistence farming and home-making operations and in supervising the execution of such plans.

To provide supplementary employment in private industry or on public work-relief projects if and when necessary to complete the budgetary needs of these families.

In selected cases, to offer service in debt conciliation, procurement of credit, and relocation on better land.

Survey, October 1934. This piece was part of a series of information articles published as part of a column, "Unemployment and Community Action," during the Depression years. Joanna Carver Colcord (1883-1960) was a social work graduate of the New York School of Philanthropy in 1911. She was Secretary of the New York Charity Organization Society and the Minneapolis Family Welfare Association. She was director of the charity organization department of the Russell Sage Foundation (1929-1945). Russell H. Kurtz was Colcord's associate at Russell Sage.

It is conceded that subsistence relief must be continued in many cases until rehabilitation has progressed to a point where self-maintenance becomes a reality. Such relief, however, together with the capital goods and supplies provided for rehabilitation purposes will, in most cases, be charged against the family to be repaid later in cash, kind or work on public-works projects.

Village families on relief will be aided on the same terms, although wholesale transfer of urban families to farms is not contemplated. Rather, they are to be urged to stay where they are, since it is admitted that America already has enough farmers. Most of these village families, says the RRD, "can and should grow subsistence gardens, and they may participate in work-center activities or labor and commodity exchanges. In general, however, the objective for this group should be rehabilitation by means of employment in revived dormant industries or in new industries or on public-works projects."

It is recognized that complete rehabilitation cannot be accomplished overnight and that the methods employed must vary from state to state. State ERAs, it appears, are to be given some latitude as to the extent to which they use the various methods and devices in their programs.

Subsistence gardens. These are considered fundamental to any plan of rural assistance. The RRD holds that a home garden is a possibility for almost any family living either in the country or in rural towns, and urges state ERAs to "refuse to extend relief to any family failing to plant and properly care for an adequate garden when the facilities therefor are available."

Organized rural communities or *community farmsteads.* In cases where it is deemed advisable to transfer stranded populations or selected urban families to the land, it is urged that such transfers be effected by establishing "organized rural communities." These communities are to consist of several hundred families each, carefully selected for adaptability to the type of life contemplated. Each family will live upon a small tract of land large enough to allow it to produce its own subsistence food. It is anticipated that additional budgetary needs will be met by supplementary employment in "handcrafts, trades, industries and professions." Not more than 35 to 40 percent of family income is expected to accrue from subsistence-farming operations; supplementary employment must provide the remainder.

Community work centers. Each organized rural community is expected to develop a work center where facilities will be available for the profitable use of the spare time of the residents and neighboring relief families. Such activities as food-canning and conservation;

laundering; refrigeration; making household furniture, wearing apparel and bedding; construction and repair of farm machinery; and production of articles that may be disposed of to advantage, are suggested. Provision of resources for community social life and recreation are also urged.

Commodity exchanges. In order that rural families and community farmsteaders may have an avenue for disposal of their surplus commodities and labor, ERAs are asked to develop exchanges in each community. It is pointed out that the facilities of the Federal Surplus Relief Corporation are available to assist in the transfer of local surpluses on an interstate basis.

Industrial employment. The RRD concedes that "there must be employment; there must be a cash income in addition to the food, shelter and other prerequisites which a rural home can give. Where that employment will come from, how it will be organized and supported, constitute one of the most serious public problems before America today." It is suggested that small local industries be encouraged by the purchase of their products for relief purposes, thus aiding them to become established or revived within the community.

Public Works. Suggested as another source of cash income are public works and work relief. Such projects as water conservation and supply, construction of recreational facilities, control of weeds and pests, forest conservation, erosion control, and advancement of health and sanitation are presented as possibilities.

Debt adjustment. Many rural families are on relief as the result of unfortunate debt situations. Recognizing that rehabilitation can not be undertaken until these debts are cleared up, the RRD stresses the need for an aggressive policy in adjusting them, either by conciliation or by resort to bankruptcy. Government farm credit is to be utilized where available. Agreements between farm owners and the AAA have provided avenues for forgiveness of tenant debt in certain circumstances. The RRD is firm in declaring that "debts must not be allowed to follow and embarrass clients."

Relocation of families. In the process of rehabilitation some families will have to be moved from their present homes to new locations. Instances are: farmers on sub-marginal land, "stranded populations," and selected urban dwellers desirous of undertaking subsistence farmsteading. The RRD advises thorough study of each case of proposed transfer, individual or group, in order that it may be successful by the following tests: adaptability of family, need for moving, cost, income possibilities in proposed new environment, and outlook for permament rehabilitation. Here, too, it is recognized that "the one great problem will usually be the matter of supplementary income."

Family service. Families are to be nominated for rural rehabilitation by the case worker in the relief division of the ERA, but their
acceptance for care depends upon the approval of the RRD staff. After
acceptance they will be entitled to specialized services recruited
through the RRD office including guidance in home economics and agriculture, aid in debt adjustment, procurement of new credit, and vocational instruction. Each local RRD director is expected to employ a
home economist who will share with the relief case worker the responsibility for the family's ultimate welfare. County extention agents
of the Department of Agriculture will provide technical leadership
in establishing sound farming procedures. Through local committees,
other agencies will be enlisted as needed.

Sale of products. It is recognized that many village and farmstead
families will, in the progress of their rehabilitation, produce surpluses of food and other marketable commodities beyond their subsistence needs. The RRD urges that effort be made to dispose of these
surpluses through barter at the community exchange or by transfer to
the RRD itself in repayment of the stake secured there. However,
while commercial sale of farm products from subsistence plots is not
contemplated, no such restriction is recognized on those products
coming from farms where rehabilitation on a commercial level is the
goal, "except insofar as AAA policies should be observed." It is
likely that local RRD officials will require further clarification of
this policy before they can make application of it.

Land purchase. Funds for the purchase of sub-marginal land in
eight major sections of the United States are about to be spent with
the aim of withdrawing poor lands from attempted agriculture. Through
work relief they will be transformed into national parks, forests,
Indian reservations and bird sanctuaries.

Eighty thousand rural families were on the rehabilitation rolls
September 1, according to Lawrence Westbrook, RRD director. Most of
these have been placed on farms which have been leased until the end
of next year, with the privilege of purchase on long-time terms. The
movement has reached largest proportions in the south, notably in
Texas, Mississippi, Alabama, and Arkansas. The investment per family
in these states has ranged from $86 to $126, including land lease,
supplies, equipment and livestock. Total RRD expenditures from March
to September 1934 approximated $10 million.

FARMERS ON RELIEF

Irving Lorge

In becoming accustomed, as we have of late years, to line graphs representing unemployment of workers, decline in wages and in purchasing power, number of industrial failures, foreclosure of farms and
hundreds of equally depressing indices, we have become inured to the
human tragedies they chart. The descending curves from 1928 through
1935 depict more than an abridgement of physical and economic values.
Huddled on the sheer slopes of these graphs were human beings—men
and women and children—without jobs, resources or hope, people whose
deprivations were aggravated by the hostile natural triumvirate of
drought, dust and flood.

Of all the federal alphabetic agencies designed to spell restoration and recovery, none was more certainly directed to save human
resources than were the Federal Emergency Relief Administration and
its successors, and none affected more individuals as individuals.
In the beginning the attempts at rescue were haphazard, often providing straws instead of buoys. The history of the emergence of
plans for human reclamation is gradually being recorded in a series
of research monographs of the division of social research of the
Works Progress Administration. The eighth study, Farmers on Relief
and Rehabilitation, records the operation of the rural relief and
rehabilitation program.

In this study, Berta Asch and A. R. Mangus show that "farm families
that received public assistance under various federal relief programs
were only in part victims of the depression." More than a million
farmer and farm laborer families needed and received relief grants
or rehabilitation advances under federal programs. Taking a sample
of 138 agricultural counties as of June 1935 as representative of
the nine agricultural areas in which farm relief problems bulked
largest, the monograph surveys the extent and causes of farm distress,
relief and rehabilitation programs, types and amounts of relief, social characteristics of relief recipients, employment in relation to
the land, factors in production, and programs of reconstruction.

The June 1935 farm relief load varied widely among states. In New
Mexico, the Dakotas, Oklahoma, and Colorado the incidence of relief
and rehabilitation included more than a fifth of all farmers; and in
Kentucky, Florida, Idaho, Montana, Minnesota, Pennsylvania, Arkansas,

Survey, November 1937. Irving Lorge was on the sociology staff at
Teachers College of Columbia University. He wrote *Rural Trends in
Depression Years* with Edmund de S. Brunner (1937).

South Carolina,and Wyoming more than 10 percent of all farmers received such aid. These fourteen states contained only one fourth of
all the farms in the United States in June 1935, and yet contained
over half of all farmers receiving relief and rehabilitation aid.
Look at the distribution of these states on a map, and you will see
the effects of drought, dust and floods in 1934. If there are gaps
in the succession of the states, if some states have heavier relief
loads than others under the same unfavorable conditions, it must be
remembered that relief programs varied from state to state. The
monograph points out that relief policy was more liberal in some
states than in others depending upon administration, standards of
living, prevailing crop and employment status. Variation in relief
load does not correlate highly with relief need. This single point
should be a first guidepost to a planned program for the conservation
of human resources.

Most of the employed as well as the unemployed heads of farm families on relief rolls received work relief rather than direct relief
in June 1935, a fact which shows that many of them were normally full
time farmers forced to seek aid because of drought, dust or flood or
were part time farmers whose auxiliary sources of income were wiped
out by the depression.

The amount of relief in June 1935 averaged $13 for farm owners,
$12 for farm laborers and tenants, and $9 for croppers. Negroes in
agricultural groups received smaller relief grants than whites.
Farmers on rehabilitation received advances averaging $189 which
varied from $31 in the spring wheat area to $416 for the whites in
the western cotton area.

The farmers receiving this relief, the authors indicate, did not
differ markedly in age from all farmers in the United States. The
trend of relief from February to June 1935, however, shows that
younger farmers and younger farm laborers left relief rolls more
rapidly than older recipients. The average age of farm owners was
46.5; of farm tenants, 37.9; and of farm laborers, 36.1 years. Unfortunately, the authors did not average their data to show the age
distribution of the other members of the households. For, if they
had, it would have been shown that there were more persons under ten,
and from ten to fourteen years of age in the rural farm relief population than in the total rural farm populations in 1930. An independent study shows in this relief population a ratio of 1858 children under ten years per thousand women aged twenty to forty-five
years, as contrasted with 1604 in the total rural farm population in
1930.

The size of the household was probably greater than the figures
reported since many households with only one worker were found fre-

quently in the lower socio-economic group of farm laborer. Non-family men were relatively more frequent in the lake states cut-over area, and non-family women in the eastern cotton belt. To some extent these non-family households show the extent of migration of farmers and farm laborers during drought and depression years. The migratory trend is as much an effect as it is a cause of the need for relief.

About three fourths of the heads of farm households on relief were farmers by usual occupation, the rest were farm laborers. Tenants other than sharecroppers constituted more than half of farm operators on relief, owners about a third, sharecroppers about an eighth. In general, the situation of croppers was more precarious than for other farm operators, for sharecroppers were not able to remain on the land to the same degree as owners. While farmers and farm laborers were leaving the open country, non-agricultural workers were moving to the marginal farms. Part of the relief load was composed of workers trying to farm poor soil which could not support them.

The greater economic resources of owners and tenants, as compared with those of sharecroppers and laborers, were reflected in the length of time elapsing between the loss of their tenure and the time of their appearance as relief recipients. Displaced laborers received relief three months after loss of their usual employment; sharecroppers after five; tenants after seven; and owners after thirteen.

Farm operators on relief operated smaller acreages than all farm operators reported by the 1935 agricultural census. The small acreages show that relief recipients included a larger proportion of chronic or marginal cases. This marginality was further indicated by the lack of livestock and poultry necessary for self-support. The great majority of these relief farm operators reported more than ten years of farm experience. Of course, experience does not indicate expertness.

As a matter of fact, it is probable that the more expert farmers in need of relief were placed on rehabilitation rolls. Rehabilitation farmers came largely from open country areas, where, in general, they operated larger farms than relief operators. An indication of a greater expertness as contrasted with experience is evidenced in the fact that the proportion of farm laborers among rehabilitation clients was smaller than among relief families.

These facts, showing the type of relief and rehabilitation recipients, lead up to Prof. T. J. Woofter's excellent chapter on Programs of Reconstruction in which he reviews the need for reconstruction of American agriculture in terms of human values as well as of natural resources. He suggests reform of the tenant system, arrest of the increase of tenancy, the need for rural rehabilitation loans, guided migration and cooperative farming, especially for small farms. He points out that measures for agricultural reform cannot be expected to yield immediate results.

It must be kept in mind that the monograph deals only with farmer operators on relief or on rehabilitation. Important as is the situation of relief farm operators, the group consitutes only 42 percent of all heads of rural families on relief in June 1935. The other rural relief recipients do not live on farms; they live *off* them. The situation of the rural non-agricultural relief recipients is inseparably tied up with the success of the farmers. The recovery of the farmers must be related to the restoration of the agricultural service area.

If one were to cavil at any aspect of the study, it would not be with what is in it, but with what is left out. Too much emphasis seems laid on the farm operator household head, not enough upon the family for which he is the breadwinner. The factors causing a farm operator to go on relief also affect his family, especially his younger children. When one considers the average age of the relief and rehabilitation farm operators, it becomes evident that immediately after the world war, they were in the twenty to thirty age group. In 1920, when demand for labor, as well as wages, was at a peak, many of them sought immediate cash income instead of planning for the future. The resulting lack of economic security, the meanings in relief and the lack of realistic education should be weighed for relief children as well as for relief heads.

Berta Asch, A. R. Mangus, and T. J. Woofter have produced a very significant contribution to an already significant series of social research documents. The appendix on Methodology of Rural Current Change Studies gives the basis for the careful sampling procedure used in the collection of the data. The glossary giving special meanings for terms used will do much to dispel misinterpretation.

As Professor Woofter points out, "The administration has been groping through an unprecedented situation without an adequate chart or compass." The monograph is, in a sense, both chart and compass for the future—a future in which it is hoped that intelligent planning will prevent another toboggan of the social-economic charts and graphs.

RURAL RELIEF AND THE BACK-TO-THE-FARM MOVEMENT

T. J. Woofter, Jr.

A canvass of the information on rural occupational shifts reveals
that the shift toward farming has been for the past five years and
may continue to be for a number of years to come the most important
rural shift, and it is also apparent that this shift is intimately
related to rural relief problems.

It is pertinent to ask at the outset why there should be a rural
relief problem peculiar to this depression and relatively unknown in
other depressions. In the past bread lines and soup kitchens were
characteristic of cities and rural relief was almost negligible.
Although a relatively new phenomenon, rural relief reached distress-
ing proportions at its peak. In March of this year—the high point—
there were 2,000,000 families on relief and rehabilitation in rural
areas. It is the thesis of this paper that this situation, in part,
grew out of a back-to-the-land movement and a cessation of the previous movement away from the land.

To focus the problem still more clearly the rural relief load was
not by any means a farm operator load. There were, in March, 1935,
about a million rural non-farm cases, about 300,000 farm laborers
and about 700,000 farm operators. Most of this 1,000,000 non-farm
group had no real agricultural experience. They were miners, lumbermen and villagers. They, of course, were subject to the usual hazards of other industrial employees.

The question still remains, however, as to why so large a group of
farm operators had to seek relief—why men who had access to the
land could not feed themselves. This situation is analyzed in the
report on Six Rural Problem Areas issued by the FERA in December of
this year, a report dealing with areas where relief loads had been
high and where FERA had spent over $200,000,000 for relief up to
November first of last year.

The contributory causes of distress in these areas need not be
elaborated at too great length here. Briefly, they were the drought
and wind erosion in the wheat areas, erosion and loss of supplementary occupation in the Appalachian-Ozark and Lake States regions and
exhaustion of the soil and cash crop restriction in the cotton areas.

Social Forces, March 1936. Thomas J. Woofter, Jr., was Professor
of Sociology at North Carolina University. Woofter had done extensive research on race relations before becoming coordinator of rural
research for the FERA-WPA in 1935.

These are not entirely depression phenomena. They are factors which have been at work for years. Without being realized they were gradually creating rural slums which were vividly brought to the nation's attention by the piling up of relief loads. One factor which the writer feels has been insufficiently emphasized is the increasing population pressure on the resources of these areas for the past five years.

The population situation is well known to rural sociologists but a review of its outstanding trends will lay the groundwork for understanding occupational trends. It is almost trite to say that the rural districts are furnishing most of the natural increase in population for the nation. In 1930 the ratio of native-white children under 5 to 1000 women 15-44 years of age in the rural farm population of the United States, was 529, and in the rural non-farm was 463, and the urban was 292. This is obviously a rate insufficient to replace the population of the cities which must depend for their increase on the rural areas. In a section like the Southern Appalachian Mountains the excess of births over deaths was more than two per year for each hundred inhabitants. This means that if the population of the Appalachian region were undisturbed by migration, it would increase more than two per cent a year. No such actual increases took place, however, for some years. In fact the population of this area as a whole was almost stationary up to 1930 indicating that the 2 per cent natural increase was drained off by migration to the cities or industrial areas. Up to 1930 this same rapid natural increase was evident to a lesser degree in practically all of the rural areas of the nation, and seemingly was more pronounced in the poorer rural areas than in the more prosperous. The area mentioned, the Appalachian, is one of the most pronounced in natural increase. The Lake States Cut-Over region is the closest to it, and other poor areas stand out similarly.

Rural sociologists are also well aware that after 1930 rural increase continued but the migration trends from country to city practically ceased and in some areas were actually reversed. The calculations of the Department of Agriculture show that in 1930, the first year of the depression, migration to and from farms about balanced. But in 1931 migration from the farms decreased a half million below the predepression level, while migration to the farms continued at the old level. In 1932 there was a further drop of nearly a half million in the number of migrants from farms, while migration to farms diminished only slightly. During 1931 and 1932 the farm population increased 750,000 by immigration. But in 1933 migration from the farms increased slightly, while that to the farms decreased greatly, with a resultant net migration from the farms of about

227,000, and 1934 saw a further net increase in cities and towns of 211,000. Thus, the net increase in the first two years was 750,000 and the net decrease in the second two years nearly 450,000, leaving a gain of movement to the farms in the four years of about 300,000 people.

The work of Bushrod Allin for the Study on Population Redistribution also shows a marked change in the channels of migration. He classified the counties in a number of states according to their agricultural income and by computations from the State School Censuses concluded that before 1930 many of the poorer rural counties had been losing population rapidly and the richer counties not so rapidly, but since 1930 the poorer counties had increased in population at a much more rapid rate than the richer counties.

The reason for this return to the poorer farming sections rather than the richer is twofold. In the first place, it is a movement back home. The people moved out of these areas from 1920 to 1930 and when urban income failed, home was the place with which they were most familiar and where relatives could help them. In the second place, the land in the more prosperous farming sections is held more closely and the chance for finding an idle farm and a vacant house is not so great as in an area which has been losing population. We may conclude then, from such facts as we have about population trends, that there is unmistakable evidence of return to the land and that both the return movement and the damming up of the natural increase of the population has been more pronounced in the poorer agricultural areas than in the richer. Of the two, the unabsorbed natural increase seems more important than the actual return movement.

Another and corroborative set of facts is furnished by the 1935 Agricultural Census which indicates large farm increases in most of the country, the exceptions being in a few highly commercialized areas. The national increase in farms from 1930 to 1935 was from 6,289,000 to 6,812,000—an increase of about a half million farms or over 8 per cent. This count also indicates a more rapid increase in poorer areas than in the prosperous areas, i.e., while most of the states as a whole show a total increase in farms the county figures show varied trends with more rapid increases in the poor sections. However, there is one type of farm increase which is not in all cases a movement to poorer sections. This is represented by rapid farm increases around industrial cities which, in most instances, is a movement toward part-time or subsistence farms. There was, for instance, over 100 per cent increase in the farms of Jefferson County, surrounding Birmingham, Alabama, and similar growth around a number of cities.

The AAA has been vigorously accused of displacing people from the land but since the census figures do not support this accusation we evidently have the anomaly of the increase of people on the land in spite of the restrictions of cash crop production. This simply means that the pressure of population is greater than the pressure of the restrictions of the AAA and, of course, it also means a difference in the type of farming which is conducted by these new farmers.

In the case of tenants and laborers it also probably means the difference in the type of person who is absorbed by agriculture and the type who is displaced. In other words, there has been a marked displacement of tenants in the South who have gone on relief without any net decrease in the number of tenants, which means that the five-year increase in population has probably supplied a younger and more vigorous group who have displaced the less fortunate, without any reduction in the net total.

The farm increases confirm the population data in the conclusion that increases in agriculture have been most rapid in those areas least capable of supporting the larger population.

We may now turn to consideration of a more specific group—viz., the farm operators who have been on relief. Their number indicates that all this shift to agriculture was not successful. At the peak of relief loads in March 1935 there were over 700,000 farm operators who were on relief or rehabilitation.

It is, perhaps, no mere coincidence that the number of able bodied farmers on emergency programs slightly exceeds the increase in farms added between 1930 and 1935. In other words, it seems that the pressure of population on a static agriculture has added 500,000 farmers who have not been readily assimilated by agriculture and have gone on relief. Of course, we would not go so far as to assert that these new farmers and the unsuccessful farmers were the same individuals.

The problem of farmers on relief was also largely concentrated in poor land areas with the exception of New England.

There is also an indication in the relief statistics that many of the farm clients were not experienced in farming but had shifted from non-agricultural to agricultural pursuits. In February the relief statistics showed 12 per cent of the rural workers whose usual occupation had been non-agricultural now employed in agriculture as against less than one per cent whose usual occupation was agricultural who were employed in non-agricultural occupations, and the statistics of June show much the same situation.

This shift was also more pronounced in the Lake States Cut-Over region and the Appalachian-Ozark than in other regions. In the Appalachian-Ozark region 25 per cent of the relief clients with previous non-agricultural occupation were currently employed in agriculture and in the Cut-Over region 22 per cent.

This shift represented the change within the relief rolls from non-agricultural to agricultural occupation and does not represent the entry into farming of young adults since the definition of usual occupation in these studies is so framed that such cases would be excluded. On the other hand, it represents a bona fide shift of people who had actually been employed in non-agricultural pursuits to agriculture. Not all of this shift, however, had come about by movement from town to country, much of it was merely a shift of source of income without change in residence. Coal miners in the Appalachians and lumbermen in the Cut-Over areas merely started farming on the land which they already occupied.

Thus, from four independent sources we have evidence of a pronounced and unguided back-to-the-land movement. These facts are the piling up of population, the return from city to country, the increases in farms and the shifts within the relief population. It is also clear that it was what Mr. Carter Goodrich calls a back-to-the-worst-land movement. To quote Mr. Goodrich further on this subject:

> I believe that it would be most unwise to try to hold the population in the areas which people have characteristically found during the depression. It would seem to me very unfortunate to try to induce people to take deep roots in these localities, to tempt them to home ownership, to try to get them to settle down, in the kinds of areas to which a disproportionate amount of the depression migration has been directed. Whatever direction migration in the future should take as a long-run matter, it seems to me clear that it cannot be the direction that migration has taken during the depression. Even if you believed that in the long run agriculture would have to support a larger proportion of the American population than it has in recent years, you could not believe that it should support it on the kind of land that the depression migrants have had to choose. There may conceivably be a case for the "back-to-the-land" movement. There certainly cannot be a case for the permanent desirability of a "back-to-the-worst-land" movement.
>
> Attempts to make the migrants take deep root in these communities are not likely to succeed. In a number of these states, where we have been able to get evidence, these particular counties began to lose population even between 1933 and 1934, with what little pick-up there was then. You are not likely to succeed in planting them there, and it is more important to say that it would be tragic if you succeeded.

One may say, by way of parenthesis, that this is a sad commentary on all of our agitation for a planned economy. If planning is to take a realistic view of trends as they actually are, it must recognize this piling up of population in the poorer areas and replace this unguided movement back to the land with efforts to promote population increases in agricultural areas more capable of sustaining a

decent standard of living, otherwise we shall continue to increase
rural slums and multiply rural misery.

Let us now review, briefly, the effects of governmental programs
and of such rural recovery as we have had on the situation as it has
been outlined. As to the activities of FERA. The 1,900,000 families
who were on rural relief in February were reduced by October to
1,000,000. The rural non-farm load (including laborers) declined
from 1,300,000 to 700,000, almost a 50 per cent drop. This leaves
700,000 non-farm cases to be cared for in the transfer of unemployables back to the states and an absorption of employables into the
Works Program. This is not without the realm of possibility of accomplishment, but probably will not be accomplished without suffering
in individual cases where states are slow to assume this burden and
where works projects are not skillfully distributed.

As to the 700,000 farm operators—it was for them that the rehabilitation program of the Resettlement Administration was designed. Resettlement now has some 320,000 clients, about 250,000 of whom were
selected from farm operators on relief, and in October, 300,000 were
still on relief. It is now proposed that an additional 150,000 to
175,000 clients be transferred from Relief to Resettlement. It is
not without the bounds of possibility that the 300,000 farm operators
who were left on relief in October will be cared for by broadening
of the Resettlement program and by employment on the Works program.

Another planning activity of fundamental importance is that of the
Land Policy Section which is charged with the responsibility of planning the optimum use of the land, retiring submarginal lands and encouraging the resettlement of the better lands. The planning activities of this agency have made considerable progress notwithstanding
the fact that they were confronted at the outset with the task of
analysing and interpreting a mass of basic data. In action, however,
the program has been delayed by the unavoidable slowness of government in financial transactions. In the first phase of the recommended program, however, all of the 10,000,000 acres recommended for
retirement have been optioned and half of the acreage optioned has
been purchased.

The actual ending of the rural distress by the emergency agencies
cannot be accurately forecast because of the difficulty in forecast-
ing the situation as it may develop this winter. There is considerable evidence that if there are relief rolls to absorb able-bodied
but needy people there will be considerable accessions to these rolls.
During the period June to October there was a reduction of 400,000
cases in rural relief in spite of the opening of 460,000 cases. This
means that some 860,000 cases had to be closed to effect a net reduction of 400,000. We thus see that rural relief is a shifting

kaleidoscopic problem. Families do not stay on until permanently rehabilitated, they shift on and off, and there are new cases who lose out and replace some of the closed cases. As Harry Hopkins recently said, "We still have a relief problem and cannot laugh it off."

We may, however, say that the farm distress has been greatly reduced and that we may reasonably hope that the major part of it which is represented on the relief rolls will have been alleviated by next spring, or perhaps, next fall, except where nature brings new calamities of drought or flood. Of course, major alleviation will have been accomplished by transfer to the resettlement and the works programs and the question remains as to the permanency of these benefits.

However, this only takes care of the emergency situation and does not allow for the more fundamental problem of the inevitable expansion of rural population. This is the challenge to students of rural life to be met in this generation. Can we so reconstruct agrarian culture that it will provide a satisfactory life for a large number of people despite restrictive tendencies in commercial farming and increased productivity per man? There are some evident processes involved and some which must be discovered as we go along.

One thing evident is that some of these newcomers on the land will have to pioneer. In past depressions, when the pinch was felt in eastern areas, many families simply moved west and pioneered on a more or less self-sustaining basis. What is necessary now is pioneering on an intensive rather than on an extensive basis. More subsistence farming is indicated which may or may not mean a lower standard of living. Certainly a fair subsistence with a small amount of cash income would be preferable to the present standard of living of many cotton and tobacco tenants, of many mountain farmers, and of many dwellers on sub-marginal lands.

Another step indicated is the need for more coordination between the philosophy of the AAA and that of the Resettlement Administration. The program of the former is now preventing the expansion of cash crops in spite of population expansion and the program of the latter is putting more people on the land for their livelihood.

Still another plea which I would make is to so adjust emergency programs that farmers will not be taken away from the land, and consequently be caused to lose their agricultural assets. The Works Program is difficult to adjust to farm operation in that it is a full-time program. Unless the farmer who abandons his land for a Works Progress job is thereby enabled to save up enough money to resume farm operations on a sounder basis, the prospects are that while his Works job may carry him through the winter he will be little better off, if not actually worse off, July first than he was before he accepted employment in the Works Program. There is now evidence that the Works Progress Administration and the Resettlement Administration are facing the problem of coordinating their programs to avoid tempting farmers who should be rehabilitated on the land into the Works Program with temporarily higher wages. While in most cases the decision will have to be reached on a basis of the situation of the individual family, still the predominance of pressure should be exerted on the side of persuasion of farmers to stick to the land and conserve their agricultural assets.

An important omission in this discussion, which you will have noted, is the topic of birth control. This omission is deliberate for two reasons. First, we know the glacial slowness with which social phenomena like birthrates change, and second, if all births ceased tomorrow a sufficient number of young people would mature for the next twenty years to constitute a problem of occupational adjustment. In other words, the maturing people who will constitute the problem of this generation are already born.

In conclusion and above all, we need widespread dissemination of knowledge as to population trends and agricultural opportunities so that this misdirected back-to-the-poor-land movement may, insofar as possible, be redirected.

This is in large measure the responsibility of research workers both in the content of their studies and in the method of presentation. In large measure the facts about population increase and movement and regional agricultural possibilities are extant in sufficient volume to serve as a basis of intelligent guidance. What is needed is the presentation of these facts in such convincing form that the administrators and field workers in action agencies and the educators can translate them to the people so as to influence population distribution and occupational choice.

FERA AND THE RURAL NEGRO

Esther Morris Douty

Disastrous as the depression has been on the economic life of the
Negro there is reason to believe that in rather unexpected fashion
the business of relief, deplorable as it is, has brought changes in
his condition and outlook in some rural areas of the South which may
have far-reaching effect.

Take, for example, the situation in one of the poorer counties in
the Piedmont district of North Carolina. Its rolling red clay hills
have never produced abundant crops, and only occasionally has its
small "sand-country" section, part of the old bright tobacco belt,
yielded a fair return to its cultivators. Industry has scarce touched this country. Three textile mills, a furniture factory, and an
excelsior plant, together with a few scattered sawmills, offer to
the native population practically the only alternative to farming or
personal service. Of the county's 21,171 inhabitants, 6904 are
Negroes, most of whom wring from the harsh soil a meager living as
tenant farmers. In 1932 about half of the Negro population, 3214 in
all, received their living or at least part of it, from relief funds.
During 1933 the same proportion continued to receive either relief
allotments from federal funds or fairly adequate wages from the CWA.
The rest remained on the farm or hired themselves as servants to the
more well-to-do whites, meanwhile keeping a watchful eye on their
neighbors on the government payroll.

This government support, free from any strings and extending to
such a large proportion of the Negro population, has had certain
definite results. It has produced, curiously enough, a slight rise
in living standards. While standards are still wretchedly low, they
are better than many of these Negroes knew during the prosperity era.
No longer does Sam Johnson, colored, "chaw wheat bread only on Saddy
nights." Government flour has taught him to scorn his familiar corn
pone and to eat hot biscuits and light bread on the most ordinary of
days. Indeed, the southern rural case worker hears time and again
the complaint, "Miss, I ain't got nary a drap o' flour in the house
—nothin' but cornmeal." Sam's children may once have run uncom-
plainingly about in tattered shoes and overalls, their only possessions in the way of clothing. Now they are exhibited to the case
worker with, "Jes' look at that chile's shoes, an' he ain't got a

Survey, July 1934. Esther Morris Douty was a case worker with the
County Board of Charities and Public Welfare in Chapel Hill, North
Carolina.

change o' overalls to his name." And, justly enough, Sam's children get their "stout" shoes and change of clothing.

A highly successful canning campaign has done much in a dietary way for Sam's family. Sam's wife now adds some canned fruit and vegetables to the monotonous and unhealthful fare of fatback, sweet potatoes, biscuits and molasses. There is hardly a farm family, white or colored, on the relief rolls which has not received instructions in canning. The canning of fruit and vegetables was indeed compulsory for those farm families who wished to remain on the welfare list. The county's Farm Plan has aided a large proportion of the relief families to plant an almost adequate supply of vegetables for home use. Families on the Farm Plan were also required to sow wheat, an unusual procedure for many a colored tenant farmer. The raising of cows, hogs and chickens has also been encouraged. In this respect the family of Sam Johnson, Negro tenant farmer of 1934, is considerably better off than the family of Sam Johnson in 1928 with ten or twenty acres of cotton or tobacco and a small corn patch.

This somewhat better balanced diet has, of course, been an aid to health. The federal relief worker, moreover, keeps a close lookout for sickness in the family, and, wherever possible, provides medical attention. Thus, many a Negro who in former years would have passed from birth to death without entering a physician's office now comes to the Welfare Agency with the plea, "Miss, I get dizzy spells in my haid, an' I kain't work. Will you sen' me to the doctor?" In the important matter of childbirth, the doctor, paid from federal relief funds, often replaces the ignorant and dirty midwife, a fact which should have some bearing upon the maternity deathrate.

Sam Johnson, colored, is rapidly becoming conscious of the fact that he is a citizen of the United States. Some more affluent member of the Negro community who subscribes to a newspaper reads therein that the government is sending a large shipment of pork or butter or eggs for the needy of the county. Whereupon every Negro on the relief roll, and many who are not, eagerly awaits the "Meeting Day" (welfare distribution day) when he hopes to secure his share of the commodities the "guv'ment is sending to us pore folks." Not infrequently the case worker who, after investigation, turns down a request for relief hears the indignant protest: "The guv'ment sen's you-all money to help all us hard-up folks. I'se jes' as ontitled to it as the nex' one." The far-off federal government is losing its distance.

But probably the most fundamental change has come from the fact that the FERA has given a measure of independence to a group tied for generations to the white landlord by the urgent need of food and shelter. Many a landlord, because of this, opposes relief for any but those actually on the verge of starvation. One landlord frankly voiced a current attitude: "I don't like this welfare business. I can't do a thing with my niggers. They aren't beholden to me any more. They know you all won't let them perish." To a large degree this is true. Many a Negro feels that if his landlord is unfair or unduly harsh, he can leave and shift for himself. The Welfare Department will feed and clothe him in all likelihood just as well as his landlord. Many individuals undoubtedly take advantage of this situation, shrewdly realizing that the landlord is no longer the arbiter of life and death in rural areas.

Some of the landlords, of late, have begun indirectly to cash in on the FERA. They refuse to furnish their tenants anything but a house, land and perhaps a team. Rations are often no longer mentioned in the contract, and the landlord will not stand good at the store for so much as a sack of flour. "Why should I feed my tenants," a landlord asked the other day, "when the Welfare can look after them? After all, I pay taxes. Other farmers are taking advantage of this federal money. Why shouldn't I? I need all the money I can get for myself." Another landlord will say, "Sam, you'll have to get your food from the Welfare this year. I can't carry you; besides, if the Welfare furnishes your rations, maybe you can work off last year's debt to me." Argue as the case worker will, the landlord stands pat. His tenants can move, feed themselves, or get help from the Welfare office. Since a landlord who will "carry" his tenant is difficult to find, moving rarely helps the situation and as the tenant often cannot feed himself, the burden falls on the local relief agency. Although this attitude of the landlords is socially irresponsible and economically warped, it serves, nevertheless, to weaken further the chain binding tenant to landowner.

Bound up with these changes is a common complaint. "The niggers ain't worth a damn any more. Ever since federal relief and especially the CWA came in, you can't hire a nigger to do anything for you—the men nor women neither. High wages is ruinin' 'em." There is more than a grain of truth in the foregoing statement. Relatively high wages are undoubtedly ruining the colored folk—ruining them for a quiet acceptance of sub-subsistence pay, and ruining them for months of labor with only debt at the end of the year.

Perhaps the situation in this county is not typical. It may be that within its boundaries the Negroes receive more generous treatment than elsewhere. Perhaps in other sections the plight of the colored tenant is worse now than it was before the depression. But here at least something is happening.

It is impossible to say what the results will be, although several
interesting possibilities suggest themselves. For large masses of
Negroes living standards have risen slightly and the domination of
the landlord has been weakened. These developments may make the
Negro less willing to supply a considerable part of the labor force
in a pauperizing tenant system. Large numbers may, it is true, become permanent charges of the community, and, in time, unsuited for
economic activity. This would be a negative and unfortunate reaction.
But the Negro may, on the other hand, find some way of cooperating
with white tenants and workers to reconstruct his economic life on a
basis that will provide decent living standards to all who perform
useful labor. It is this reaction for which we hope.

RURAL RELIEF ADMINISTRATION IN THE NORTHWEST

Raymond Thompson

The farmer, so-called stump rancher, and small tract owner in the
northwestern states each presents a special problem in relief administration. Many of these people are peculiarly isolated and their
standards of living have been lowered in a marked degree during the
past few years. To treat these distressed families with any degree
of fairness and to render them any constructive service is one of
our major endeavors in Idaho.

The county is divided into seven zones. All our aides work directly
out of the central office, and each aide handles both urban and rural
cases. The urban families are located in or on the outskirts of our
county seat, a city of 10,000 population. Each zone worker is
assigned a maximum of 125 cases, with a large percentage of rural
cases.

To illustrate some of the more perplexing problems we are confronted
with it is necessary to refer briefly to the rural development in
our section spreading over a period of years. Topographically our

The Family, June 1935.

county is quite rough and not over a third of it is tillable soil. The hills and mountains were formerly heavily timbered and it was really the lumbering industry that enabled the first rural settlers to become established here. Their dependence on the lumbering industry was marked by at least two direct benefits: First—if they had any merchantable timber they had but to log off their lands and haul the product to the mills. Second—if they had no timber it was very easy to secure employment in the sawmills or logging camps. In either case hard money was available with which to buy seed and implements and lumber was cheap and easily procured for building fine houses and barns. It was a poor man's Paradise, and in the natural course of events our particular county gained the reputation of being one of God's own garden spots.

But the modern sawmill is a greedy monster. One by one the giant Idaho pines fell; disastrous forest fires helped to speed the day of reckoning. So—here we are! a few sawmills working part time. Yesterday a man approached our assignment clerk for a work ticket.

"The night shift shut down a week ago. After the first I've got to have relief again."

The relief worker questioned him. "How long did you work at the sawmill?"

"Two months and a half—at $3.60 per shift, five nights a week! I paid my water rent for last year—it was $8 an acre for five acres. I owed for my seed and for some hay I had to buy last winter."

"What about your crops?"

"Crops! What do you think I am—a farmer? I've got one acre in alfalfa, an acre in potatoes, one and a half acres in pasture land and the balance in a small orchard and garden. If prices were good I could sell my surplus produce and perhaps pay for my water and taxes. But what about clothes and flour and coffee and sugar and— and—I tell you—we small tract owners have got to have some employment for cash! That's what brought us here. We're millworkers— we're not farmers! We settled on these tracts to make a decent home for our children, where they can have plenty of fresh air, fresh milk, and fresh vegetables. But you can't make a living off a five-acre tract—and forty hours' work a week for eight or ten weeks out of the year is not enough work. You fellows have got to help us out or we'll all move into town!"

Move into town! When we have a definite program that is supposed to rehabilitate stranded families already in towns, by moving them onto small tracts of land! Some food for thought in this connection, even if the stranded town families have had previous farming experience.

When does a so-called stranded farmer or rural dweller become eligible for relief? When he has sold his last sack of oats? Killed off his last hen? Butchered his last pig or cow?

I have in mind a particular case—a small tract owner who applied to us for relief.

Jack Jones had received some relief work the previous winter, but his neighbors had complained so bitterly about it that the county commissioners, who were furnishing relief money on a co-operative basis with the state and federal governments, had Jones removed from the relief rolls.

When I first talked with him, he was just about ready to run me off with an axe, but being a natural born "listener" I stuck and let him talk it out. Finally we got down to bedrock and he commenced to show me his little place. First he showed me his hen runs, which contained 200 very fine laying hens. Then he showed me his garden and a small alfalfa patch in a corner of which was a Jersey cow, staked out to pasture. The little place was ideally kept and showed not only much hard work, but considerable careful planning.

"Now, come into the house," Jones requested, "I want you to meet my wife."

Well, I wasn't surprised to "see without looking" that the little farm house was just as well ordered as the farm itself.

"And here's our books! Look at this record on our White Leghorns. Here's what the feed cost and here's the figures on the eggs we sold! Of course we have plenty of eggs and vegetables but that $9.32 you see there is the net profit for last month from our eggs. Could you manage on it, Mister? Remember, there are seven mouths to feed!"

I did some swift mental arithmetic. Supposing this man were refused relief work? Inside of sixty days, as his hens were already going into a moult, he would be selling them to buy flour and sugar! Well, I am glad today for the stand I took. Now, eighteen months later, Jack Jones is still standing squarely on his feet. We have had to lend him a helping hand occasionally, but he still has his laying hens, and he will be one of the easiest to rehabilitate, gradually and surely.

To pioneer in relief administration is rural sections such as ours requires not only vision but a great deal of moral courage to back it up. Where to start? —where to stop? —remembering always that it is much easier to start a ball rolling downhill than it is to stop it.

At the present time we have here in northern Idaho a heavy program of forestry work during the summer months, instituted largely as a relief measure by the present federal administration. This forestry work is divided into two main groups, one of which we call Blister Rust Control and the second group Emergency Conservation Work (Civilian Conservation Corps). This program has been a great benefit to our rural people because it has taken the place largely of the lumbering activities referred to previously. Many of the men and boys in our rural families are expert woodsmen or leaders for members of the Civilian Conservation Corps, and receive special consideration from the regular Forestry Service which has direct supervision of Blister Rust Control work.

What I am getting at is this: without some assurance of cash work for several months during the year, the average tract owner or small rancher in this section cannot make a decent living. The seasonal forestry work takes care of a certain percentage of these families. So do the restricted sawmill operations. (The national forests are permitted to market only a certain amount of timber each year, usually on an open bid to competing sawmills.)

Lest we become too enthusiastic over the combination of a tract owner-forestry worker combination, we had better consult some figures. A close check on the actual wages of mill owners and forestry men over the past three years discloses these facts: Only 15 per cent earned more than $600 during the year (or an average of $50 per month income if it were spread over twelve months); 30 per cent earned between $400 and $500 and the remaining 55 per cent less than $400 during an entire year. Even where this income is augmented by vegetables grown on the tract or small farm, even where there is no fuel to buy or rent to pay other than taxes, there is still need for careful planning on the part of the family, and much thoughtful help from the social worker, to keep families self-sustaining.

While helping in setting up the F.E.R.A. in an adjoining county this past spring, I came across these startling figures: out of 482 relief cases, 95 were old men, unemployables! Too old for the forestry work, too old for the sawmills! And this is not uncommon in northern Idaho.

One day while driving between certain county relief headquarters, I picked up an old man who was hitch hiking along the road. At first I thought he was just a typical "roadster" but as we traveled along he came out of his shell of reserve. It appeared that he was an old pioneer of the very country we were traversing, and he talked familiarly of certain spots as being "where the old trail to the

Palouse first went through here" and "where old man Rogers built his first mill."

"Thousands of old fellows like me are roaming the west! We're still good men, too," he asserted rather pathetically, "but the woods is lousy with gyppos (small contractors) and the Forest Service can't use us as they've got a million youngsters on their waiting list!"

A short time ago one of our workers complained of the difficulty in visiting some of our old bachelors who are receiving small relief allotments. "It required seventeen miles of a round trip up a mountain gulch to locate old man Welch," the report read. "Right across a little clearing another old bachelor lived. They're both past seventy. What do you recommend? Shall we or can we force them into a poorhouse? They've lived in the hills all their lives. They kill a little game and catch a few fish. And that Beeson family—there's eight of them! That man just won't believe me when I tell him that valley is snowbound normally any time after November 15th!"

These cases are not extreme. We're recommending to our social workers that they try to induce some of these old bachelors to move into quarters where three or four of them can be together. And we're checking up on all vacant farm houses and unoccupied lands—partly as an aid to our rural rehabilitation program, and partly as a straight relief proposition. Here, in mid-summer, we're planning for the coming of winter as much as possible.

Are we having any success? Some—very gratifying. One stump rancher first applied for relief better than a year ago. He had invested a few hundred dollars in his place and bought a truck on time.

"I can get by if you'll help me out a little until I can finish paying for my truck. There's lots of wood but I can't make a dollar out of it if I lose my truck!"

Less than a week ago this man came in to see what we were doing on the rural rehabilitation program.

"Bought your winter's wood yet?"

"I've got 780 cords cut and piled in cordwood lengths," he boasted.

Yes, we're pioneering in a country where they pioneered before. Our distressed people are marvelous and courageous as a people. We will win out yet.

IF I WERE A COUNTY RELIEF DIRECTOR

Paul H. Landis

If I were a county relief director I should try to be as good as the best I have met, and in months of traveling about from one rural county to another I have met many kinds, good, bad and indifferent. I have met the kind who sends Honest Ole, a respected citizen, out of the office storming, "I'm not a pauper and I won't be made one. You'd think a man could at least get a hearing;" the kind who can say "No" to Chiseler Joe with complete finality no matter how loud his protests; the kind who, hearing of a family slowly starving in proud despair, brings them help with a quiet reason that leaves their dignity intact.

During my study of rural relief administration and its techniques in the mid-west dry-farming country I watched a varied procession of human beings come and go through the county offices—some brazen, some bitter, some tearful and broken. It is a region where since the autumn of 1933 as many as 75 percent of the people have turned to relief for their very existence, though in previous years relief was unknown to them. And I have come to the conclusion that nowhere in this whole business of relief does its administration call for more courage, discrimination, imagination and downright character than in these hard-hit rural districts. The majority of the people on relief there have the sturdy qualities that are the warp and woof of our American tradition. To help them in their extremity by methods that would shake their morale or weaken their self-respect would be little short of tragedy.

And so, if I were a county relief director I would try to get beyond irritating personalities and to see my job whole in relation to the entire community and its mores. I believe that most of these rural communities need a good deal more respect for relief, per se, and for its administration, than they now have. With such a large proportion of people on relief there is a tendency to easy acceptance, an attitude of "get my share" that is demoralizing. Relief should not be a disgrace, but it should not be a matter of keeping up with the Joneses. By building on such standards as I could find, I should certainly try to develop individual and community attitudes

Survey, July 1935. Paul H. Landis was Professor of Rural Sociology at the South Dakota State College in Brookings and later on at the State College of Washington in Pullman. He was author of *Rural Life in Process* (1940) which contains four chapters on rural social welfare.

which would keep from my office the stream of people whose chief reason for applying for relief is that the Joneses are getting it.

I would not sit behind my desk, if I were a county relief director, and duck responsibility by taking refuge in rules laid down by a higher-up. To say "I'm sorry, but that's the rule" is a weak defense, and that desk is no place for a weakling. I have seen that defense used again and again by directors under fire from pressure groups, from influential tax-payers and from disgruntled clients,— and I have never yet seen it accomplish anything constructive. I do not believe that directors with a sound philosophy and a flexible imaginative program need it.

I believe in work relief with cash pay for its effect both on the individual and on the community. But I believe in real work in which a man can take an honest satisfaction, not the kind that is patently time-killing, just a joke alike to the worker and to the tax-payer. Unless a director has enough imagination and resourcefulness to build up a real work program which commands respect he had better stick to the dole. It, at least, is what it is and makes no pretensions.

As to whether the dole should be in cash or in kind, I should do my best to have that choice freed of rules and left to my personal judgment, case by case. Every experienced director knows that most of the people now on relief are wholly capable of managing their own affairs within the limits of their allowances, but he also knows that there is a sprinkling who can't, who never have and never will. For them it is easy come, easy go. They have no personal responsibility and the only way we can be sure that they and their children are fed and clothed and sheltered is to provide the actual food, clothing and roof. It is unfair to blanket both these groups, the responsible and the irresponsible, under one rule. The decision as to cash or kind should always rest, I think, with the relief director and his local committee. Cash can be one of his most useful tools in preserving individual values, and kind can be equally useful in checking abuses. But we need them both.

If I were going into a run-of-the-mill county as director my first act, after I got the lay of the land, would be to call the social-work staff, case-work supervisors and investigators into counsel to try to impress on them my own firm belief that about the most important job in the United States these days is to maintain the self-respect of our people who are on relief through no fault of their own. These years will determine the life philosophy of parents and children long after emergency relief has become history. We must not break down pride and individuality by making relief too hard, nor encourage insufficiency by making it too easy. We must counsel and guide where we can but we must not expect to change human nature over night. Incidentally, for the benefit of those who didn't know it—and there are always a few—I would suggest that a case worker does not enhance her prestige among farm folk by saying that she has never milked a cow, cranked a Ford or changed a baby's diaper, or by registering surprise when a mother says she's never heard of vitamins and of course the children have always slept in their underwear, and their father before them.

In appraising the investigating staff I should remember George Olson and his overalls. I traveled with him for a few days in a remote county, and his overalls came to be for me the symbol of the remarkable way he kept in touch with the actual feeling of his clients. People asked for George, waited for him, liked him, and trusted his decisions. If I were a county director I would wish for a whole staff of George Olsons and would take my chances on giving him the essentials of case-work technique. A man with George's quick and sympathetic understanding of the temper and circumstances of his clients has a start that will quickly overcome the lack of technical training.

I remember a case worker too, Mary Johnson, a college graduate with a course or two in sociology, who had what I'd want for my staff. After two weeks training in an emergency "school" she was sent into a district settled by German and Russian wheat farmers whose tar-paper shacks bore mute evidence of the odds against them. That girl had probably never been off asphalt paving in her life, but such was her spirit and her understanding that she won the confidence and respect of people who had hitherto manifested only suspicion and hatred of the whole relief outfit.

You can't define the qualities that set George Olson and Mary Johnson apart from the others in the field—you can't write a manual around them—but every one who deals with the human equation knows what I mean and recognizes the qualities when—all too rarely—he meets them.

In rural and primary-group settings the patterns in regard to conventions of conduct are few and ready-to-wear and no matter how perfect your professional techniques you cannot go against them and survive. Reasonably or unreasonably, a worker in these country districts is judged by externals and you can save yourself some bad headaches by accepting that fact. For instance, living at a hotel is apt to draw the suspicious comment of tax-payers, especially if they themselves happen to be sleeping on straw ticks. Better take a room in a private house. A shiny new car is no advantage to a relief worker, either. Better stick to the old one, and don't worry if it gets good and dirty. I've heard a good many investigators criticized for wearing fur coats, but knowing our northern winters I'd hesitate to bar them out. However I should certainly ask my young lady workers to forego rouge, lip-stick and finger-nail enamel while in the field, and to do their cigarette smoking, if smoke they must, very very privately. If these seem like sumptuary regulations I should ask my young ladies how they would like to have Mrs. Astorbilt, in sables and diamonds, drive up to their doors in a Rolls-Royce, and with lifted lorgnettes inquire into every detail of their private affairs.

When it came to the district case-supervisors I should, if I were a county director, avoid back-seat drivers, the kind who run their districts from a desk, are jealous of authority over their underlings and free with advice to their overlings. I believe that the best place to improve the technique and shape the philosophy of the investigators is right on the job, and the more my district supervisors got out in the field the better I would like it. You cannot understand community morale and the factors that strengthen or weaken it until you get close to where it is bred. And you don't get close to it sitting in an office figuring academic budgets for farmers.

A county relief director has a thankless job. All day long he must listen to tales of woe. He must combine the qualities of Job, Solomon and Sherlock Holmes and must take the gaff for anything that goes wrong in the entire relief administration from Washington down. And if funds are cut off by the state relief administration he stands a good chance of being hanged. He's in a hot spot all right. Thank God I'm not a county relief director.

I AM A COUNTY RELIEF DIRECTOR

M. B. Stinson

When we think of a rural community we think of a more or less independent and disorganized group of people relying on the bounties of
rain and sunshine for livelihood. However, here in the beauteous
Ozarks is another group, frequently found as relief clients, whose
reliance has for generations, been on another bounty of nature,
euphoniously known as Grandma. This group is accurately described
by the word "tie-hacker," which you will not find in the dictionary
but which means a man who lives by a special skill in the manipula-
tion of the broad-axe.

The tie-hacker has a rugged philosophy gained through contact with
the big lumber entrepreneur and through the necessity of keeping
body and soul together. His philosophy is that any tree from sapling
to virgin pine which has no visible owner (by visible, I mean one
looking at you over the sights of a shotgun) belongs to "Grandma."
Grandma is a kind old lady and wants to see the boys get along, so
she does not mind if they cut enough of her timber to furnish their
week's supplies. The week's supplies include, of course, a small jug
of Bill Jones' spiritus frumenti.

But Grandma is getting old and her benevolent spirit faileth. Her
bounty is no longer so easily obtained. At one time her trees were
stately pines and oaks, the forest primeval. Those are the good old
days that the tie-hacker is fond of remembering for he was then a
forester and a lumberman, or even a sawmill operator.

Now Grandma could not forever stand this maltreatment and exploitation by her sons. But when her big trees were all gone the boys got
out their broad-axe and went forth as hackers of ties. Naturally
they took a tumble down the economic scale for ties are not as profitable as board feet of lumber. But they were still able to earn a
living of sorts and to drown their sorrows on Saturday nights.

Then before they knew it the supply of timber large enough for ties
was depleted and they had to eke out an existence from the sale of
mine props made from three-inch saplings. Times were now tough. The
children went without shoes. Maggie wore her calico dress on Sunday
as well as every other day. Bill wore his overalls till they looked
like a crazy quilt. The small patch of land he had cleared back of

Survey, October 1935. M. B. Stinson was director of the Wayne County
Relief Administration in Greenville, Missouri.

his cabin still furnished beans and corn but what was he to do for "bread-stuff" and "grease."

The final straw on the back of the proverbial camel was the purchase of the last vestige of timber by the federal government. The government was convinced that prosperity could return to the hill country only with the return of the timber stands. Small saplings must not be cut for mine props but must be allowed to grow into trees. Grandma had relinquished her title and Uncle Sam was the heir apparent. Signs were posted everywhere. Cutting in the woods was now stealing. Detection was certain, conviction swift and sure, and punishment not to be laughed off. The poor lumberman, tie-hacker, mine-prop cutter was no longer an "honest Abe" but an outlaw in his own home and community.

But Uncle Sam did provide a substitute for Grandma. He sent The Relief. At first it was misunderstood and its representatives treated with cold scorn by the leaders of the community. What about it, they asked. Were these folks who had let their bills run at the store to be handed out a living for the mere asking or for scratching the surface of a county road with a pick or shovel? Oughtn't they to be treated like Old Man Jones' hogs? Old Man Jones, it seemed, had a bunch of hogs which roamed the woods, hustling nuts and acorns for their living. But when nuts and acorns became scarce, Jones had the boys throw a dozen ears of corn down by the gate for the hogs to find. Thereafter the hogs just laid around the gate with no effort to find supplementary food. Plainly they were being pauperized. So Jones told the boys to leave off the corn and sick on the dog to drive them back into the woods to earn their own way.

This crude and homely philosophy, "root, hog, or die," was wholly typical of the average citizen's idea of relief in the hill country. But as time went on and prosperity did not turn out to be just around the corner, the community attitude changed. Sam Wood, who owned a chain of stores, saw that if he was compelled to carry a fourth of the families in the county on credit which he knew was not good and another fourth on credit which was doubtful, he himself would soon be on the rocks. The doctor saw that although babies continued to arrive and old people to get sick and die, he was running up a bill at the grocery store with no very bright prospect of paying it. Thus people began to see that relief was necessary to everybody's welfare whether they were on it or not, and that the community must receive assistance from sources outside itself. But the philosophy of the tie-hacker and of Grandma still remains. The tie-hackers have no scruples about relief; no consciousness that it is wrong to accept if they have other resources. The government took away their livelihood when it took over Grandma so the government must furnish them a living. This attitude, right or wrong, is the county social worker's problem in this part of the world and explains many of his headaches.

The relief man must have a long and willing ear for all with a tale to tell. He cannot always avoid interviews by telling people that their visitors will attend to their needs. They demand to see the "head man" and they have small faith that their case will reach him unless they themselves present it. He cannot always dismiss the client's own idea for his salvation however wild it may seem. He must go over these plans and show the client, if he can, where reason breaks down. He must show him that oftentimes a loan for a horse through rural rehabilitation may put him in worse shape than before; that benefits with a string to them may turn and bite him and that most benefits, unlike gift horses, should be looked in the mouth.

The rural social worker cannot always take the attitude that a belligerent individual is one with no possibilities. Often those who kick the loudest and longest are the ones who will make the most of themselves if given an opportunity. One of the best rural rehabilitation clients in our county was one of our worst pains in the neck when he was receiving general relief.

The county relief worker must remember that he is at the head of what is probably the biggest enterprise in the county. An organization spending $10,000 per month and directly affecting eight hundred families is at all times a mark for criticism both just and unjust. His connection with the government, however he may try to be nonpartisan, must nevertheless make him and the position he controls a target for the slings and arrows of ambitious politicians, who, whether we like it or not, are a vital part of our present system of government. He must remember that his county committee is representative of the citizens who will still be there after the relief worker has moved on to other if not greener pastures. Lasting contributions are made through organized effort, rarely through the drive of any one individual. Education of political leaders is essential to lasting attainments in social work.

Yes, it is a hot spot all right, but also a very interesting spot. Other pioneers were in hot spots. It was ever thus. Yes, thank goodness, I am a county relief director.

EXPERIMENTAL SOCIAL SCIENCE

Mordecai Ezekiel

Public agencies under the New Deal are engaged in what might properly be called experimental social science. The wide-spread operations under the Agricultural Adjustment Act involved coordination of the operations of millions of individual farmers and of thousands of marketing agencies. The creation of subsistence homesteads, the rehabilitation of workers, the inauguration of rural work centers, the operations in the prevention of erosion, the withdrawal of submarginal land, and the rehabilitation under more favorable circumstances of stranded industrial populations and stranded rural populations, all these programs involve definite action which affect the welfare of individual men. These operations constitute a gigantic series of social experiments. To be most effective these experiments must be carefully weighed and appraised. The effects and the results of this action must be considered not solely from the point of view of any one social science alone, but from a point of view which gives simultaneous consideration to all social elements involved. Economics, sociology, legal institution, and natural forces—all must be clearly recognized and dealt with if any adequate appraisal is to be made from the scientific point of view of the work going forward.

The major challenge to social students therefore is to make such concrete studies of the success or failure of the various New Deal activities as will help reveal the successful, indicate the failures or the points at which satisfactory progress is not being made, and will suggest changes which need to be made in the present programs to make them work better. If the social scientist is to really meet the needs of the present emergency his analysis will provide a constant guide and appraisal on which to base successful modification in the present program. This result can only be secured if cooperative projects are set up in which not merely one line of specialists but all the various social scientists involved cooperate and contribute to the result. The actions taking place today cover a field as broad as human life. The scientific analysis brought to bear upon it must be equally broad or it will give only a partial and distorted diagnosis and prescription.

Rural America, May 1935. Mordecai Ezekiel was an economic advisor for the U.S. Department of Agriculture.

I can mention a number of specific problems on which definite appraisals are needed to aid in the future work of the New Deal activities. Under the AAA, for example, we need to know what is the real effect of the production control programs on the welfare of individual farmers and farm workers. There has been much propaganda as to displacement of tenants under the cotton program, but so far as I am aware, no one has actually measured how many men have actually been displaced. For that to be done we would have to study individual farmers, tenants, and laborers, determine how far low incomes due to drought or low yields were responsible for their leaving the farm, and how far they had been attracted to the towns as a result of relatively high CWA wages. We would have to study the plantations as a unit to see whether the tenants leaving the plantation had been replaced by other tenants or if there had been a net reduction in the number of tenants. We would have to determine what the tenure status of each individual tenant or worker had been before the introduction of the AAA program, and if any changes had taken place after its introduction. Finally, we would have to determine whether the men shifting to the relief rolls in the towns had been completely displaced from the farm or whether the landlord was simply refusing to accept the responsibility of "furnishing" them through the winter, and had sent them to town to live on relief until time to put the crops in in the spring. Definite studies along these lines in picked sample areas would do much to dispel the present fog in discussing what effect the AAA had had upon the displacement of tenants and farm laborers.

A parallel problem is what has been the effect of the AAA programs on the income of individual farmers. How far have the incomes of tenants been increased and how far the incomes of landlords as compared with previous incomes? What has been the effect of the cotton and other contracts on the incomes of share tenants, cash tenants, croppers? Has the disparity in income among the farm groups been increased or decreased? What we need here are carefully worked up frequency tables showing the distribution of income in various counties prior to AAA programs and under the AAA. Definite facts here will throw much more light on the results of present policies than will any amount of argument.

Another aspect of the AAA program involves what is known as "agricultural freezing." How far have systems of farming on individual farms been distorted as a result of the AAA? How far have changes in methods of farming or intensiveness of operation on individual farms which farmers otherwise would have made, been prevented by these programs? How far are the blanket reductions tending to prevent individual shifts in the systems of farming? All of these problems are amenable to definite study on the ground in individual cases. Programs for future improvement could be much more effectively drawn if the individual facts of the present program were known.

An entirely different aspect of the AAA program is its possible bearing on the question of landlord-tenant relations as a whole. We know that in the past, especially in the South, the normal customs in the operation of plantations or rented farms have been such as to result in low production on the farms as a whole, and in practically complete poverty for most of the tenants. We know that the landlords have been discouraged from attempting to improve the farm or living conditions of the tenants, and the tenants have had no encouragement to improve their own conditions. We know that in many cases excessively heavy charges have been levied by the landlords for financing the individual tenants and for the supplies the tenants have to purchase at the landlord's store. But we know also that the landlords have suffered severe losses where the tenant was unable to pay the landlord and left the plantation, leaving the landlord to pay the loss. As a whole, these landlord-tenant relations appear to have developed in such a way as to encourage thriftlessness and discourage any real effort toward increasing the standard of living. The landlord does pay close attention and give close supervision to the effort of the tenant to produce the cash crop. Beyond that most landlords pay little attention to seeing the tenant pays attention to growing food and feed crops for himself. How far are such conditions typical? What can be done about it if they are? To answer these questions we must study the social and economic institutions which are responsible for the conditions, the state laws as to the ownership of improvements in the property, the local conditions as to leases, and the possibility of developing longer lease systems, or a system of land tenure, which would give some incentive to the tenant who desired to improve his living conditions. Changes in the AAA rules and regulations which would encourage better farming or which would insure that tenants received the use of the land they were supposed to use, and were encouraged to produce feed crops on that land, might be found desirable. Perhaps even ownership of tenant farms by a public or limited corporation like the "Fairway Farms" corporation in Montana, which would experiment with improved methods of tenant relations, would encourage tenants to raise their own status. Any one of these methods may be used in attacking the problem. Here, as in other parts of the New Deal, it may be possible to set up experiments where various problems of this sort can be treated in practice to see how far it is practical to apply ideas of this sort. At the same time there is need for careful case studies of individual plantations covering a range of different methods of

tenant-landlord relations. In many cases public spirited landlords
have done their best to improve the status of their tenants. Studies
should be made of the methods they have used and what success they
have attained, in comparison with other methods of tenure and results
secured on average plantations, and those below average in this respect. Such comparative studies of results secured under various
methods of plantation operation would throw much light on this problem, while careful studies of any experiments in tenant relief which
may be made would also be required to make the most effective use of
the experience obtained.

The problems of rural poverty as a whole are ones to which rural
sociologists and other rural social students must give serious attention. We know that continuous relief payments have a tendency to
break down the individual's morale. Rural rehabilitation which has
been proposed as a substitute for it is itself subject to severe
question, because in many cases it involves placing the relief clients in the rural districts on farms so small there would be no opportunity for them to support themselves by their own efforts in
agriculture, while the prospects for part-time industrial employment
in such communities are as yet unproved.

We do know that over a long period of time a great many farm boys
must shift from farming into other industry because of the limited
demand for farm products compared to the relatively elastic demand
for industrial products. Such a shift has always taken place in the
past. This is the trend which prevailed from 1800 to 1929. From
1929 to 1933 it is true the trend was the other way, but one may
venture the guess that there is more reason for the century-long
trend to reassert itself than for the temporary trend during the depression to be continued.

What can rural social sociologists do, however, to stimulate this
flow of workers from farms to industry? One approach would be to
study what has happened to previous emigrants from farms to industry,
to determine what occupations they have gone into, what success they
have made, whether they were well prepared for those occupations,
and how they could be better prepared. Perhaps a considerable part
of our agricultural extension activities should be devoted to preparing young folks for city employment rather than assuming that all
of them should remain on farms. Possibly some scheme should be
worked out for public agencies to take part of the responsibility
for transfer of excess population from farms to industry, and to
help the young folks making the change to best fit themselves for
their future urban work or industrial work, and to locate the most
attractive new occupations.

We know that higher standards of living always involve much more increase in industrial consumption than in agricultural consumption. If we are ever to establish as a result of the New Deal a continually rising standard of living for our people as a whole we must continually expand our industrial and other urban industries and services much faster than we expand agricultural production. The economic need for the transfer is therefore apparent. What rural social scientists need to do, however, is to work out the ways and means by which the movement can be most effectively brought about with less loss and with less unhappiness for the individuals concerned.

Finally, I think that we may study our social institutions, schools as well as others, to see if our whole American approach has not placed too much attention on production and too little attention on consumption. Our vocational education has placed effective training in the technique of production within the reach of all. How much attention have we given to training either young or old for wise and satisfactory consumption of what they produce? After all, prices, profits, and incomes are merely means to an end. Satisfactory living is the human end to which all our economic readjustments should be directed. Here too there is room for us to study what we are doing in education, in social institutions, and in cultural development, and to suggest ways and means by which these may be made more effective and more conducive to a really abundant life for everyone rather than being determined merely by the unplanned growth which has characterized so much of our past development.

10

The Nature and Methods of Rural Practice

The debate as to whether the application of the basic principles and processes of social work in urban and rural settings was different or the same seemed to have started shortly after World War I. The increased social work activity in rural areas resulting from Depression problems and New Deal legislation served to intensify a discussion of long standing.

There were essentially two opposing camps in this debate. One, perhaps best represented by Josephine Brown and Josephine Strode, argued that rural social work was unique, if not in essence, certainly in form. The other point of view, argumentatively and strongly represented by people like Carol L. Shafer of Wisconsin, opposed the need to "categorize workers into an urban and rural species." Shafer denied that geographic locale was a determinant of uniqueness of method. Problems for the likes of Shafer were universal. "Rural and urban, between which the border is never certain, are only two determinants among many others of greater strength. The uniqueness of the individual and differential treatment are principles of case work which need no redefining for the rural field."

Besides discussing the essence and definition of the social work method, rural workers talked about the "locality specific" nature of rural practice. Rural settings differed greatly from region to region, from state to state, and often from county to county. It was contended that they differed in topographic and other geographic characteristics more than cities would ever differ from each other. And while most workers agreed on the locality specific nature of rural practice, whether that practice had to be undifferentiated or specialized was another point of contention.

It is apparent that rural workers were actively engaged in defining their identities during that golden rural social work decade. Articles in journals making public the various points of contention were abundant. Forums on rural issues were held and rural workers began to feel that they had to influence the training of future practitioners. This dialogue on training, which eventually focused on the issue of undergraduate versus graduate preparation for the rural field, culminated in the formation of the National Association of Schools of Social Administration in 1942, with strong support from the land-grant colleges and universities. Thus rural workers were deeply involved in the generation of the dispute about national standards for training and accreditation which lasted till the formation of the Council on Social Work Education in 1952.

It is the purpose of this chapter to illustrate, through appropriate readings, the discussions about the nature of rural practice during the late twenties and thirties. Besides the argumentative chapters spicing the literature of the period, there were also many papers, more descriptive than controversial, which attempted to capture and explain the rural technique for those practitioners whose need for guidance was too great to engage in heated (though often semantic) debates. This chapter commences with the descriptive writings and proceeds to the controversial ones.

The first article is a rather late example of the writing of this period. Esther E. Twente of the University of Kansas presented "Social Case-Work Practice in Rural Communities" at the 1938 meeting of the National Conference of Social Work. Although in her title Twente, in the style of the period, uses the term "case-work" to mean social work, her description of rural practice from the vantage point of 1938 is broad and firm in terms of the need for governmental sponsorship of rural services. It is important to note that Twente's listing of situational limitations in rural practice is still valid and appropriate in the 1970s.

In 1933, *The Family* published an article by Wilma Van Dusseldorp on "The Development of Social Agencies in Rural Communities." Van Dusseldorp wrote about the major blocks facing workers attempting to develop services in the rural milieu. She emphasized the commonalities of rural and urban practice, highlighting the importance of worker adaptability, genuineness, and ability to understand the rural mind.

In "The Contribution of Rural Sociology to Family Social Work" Gertrude Vaile discusses the need for rural workers to appreciate the contribution of sociological studies of rural life. Vaile's presentation highlights the problems of a period of rapid change in the country. Free rural delivery, better roads, etc., were beginning to accelerate environmental changes. Yet, as she pointed out, rural workers needed to be aware that "attitudes change much more slowly than the conditions which created them." Rapid changes, she suggested, have also created "significant trends towards social strati-

fication. Those members of the community who reach out . . . have
inevitably less and less in common with those neighbors whose interests remain more limited." Many would argue that paved roads, cine-
matography, and television, just to mention a few factors, continue
to create similar problems among members of remote communities.

"Social Work at the Grass Roots" by Eileen Blackey deals with the
problems of rural relief work. Blackey is fully aware of rural cultural patterns and amalgamates in a single article the problems
facing clients and workers from the perspective of the state of
Florida.

In July 1933, E. L. Kirkpatrick wrote "A Farm Philosophy" for the
Survey. Kirkpatrick wanted to underscore the positive aspects of
country living in a world which was turning overwhelmingly urban.
His article elucidated a letter of response from Miss Jean Paton of
Madison and a consequent reply by E. L. Kirkpatrick, who was by then
Rural Relief Advisor for FERA. All three stages of the lively dialogue have been included. The picturesque written exchanges on rural
life, which would continue to appear in the *Survey* for a few more
years, had thus been launched.

The pieces of professional wisdom perhaps best remembered by those
who worked in rural areas during the Depression and the New Deal
were those published in the *Survey* from October 1938 and authored
by Josephine Strode from Kansas. Strode's articles were folksy and
plain-spoken, and they had lasting appeal among rural practitioners.
Strode was not engrossed in method but in rurality, and in contrast
to Josephine Brown, whose training showed in her writing, Strode was
able to remain "one of the group" in spite of her training. Strode's
articles, cast as letters to Miss Bailey, the *Survey*'s itinerant observer of social work in the country, were a treasure of humor and
reality. Many of them appeared under the main heading of "The
County Worker's Job."

Five of Miss Strode's articles as well as the brief editorial
which preceded them have been transcribed. "Rural Social Workers Do
Everything" deals with the "undifferentiated" reality of practice.
"Publicity by Way of the Barn Door" is concerned with ways of bringing about knowledge of programs in the country. "Learning from the
Job" is a self-explanatory title. "Beef, Prunes and Ink Blots"
makes fun of much of the theory on child development learned in
schools of social work, and the final piece, "Swinging the Depression" offers suggestions for relating to the youth of rural counties.

In 1933, Josephine Brown wrote *The Rural Community and Social
Casework*. In this book, which became classic and to which the interested reader is referred, Brown stated that although the basic

casework method is universal, it required adaptations when applied to the rural locale. It was important for the worker to know the specific characteristics of her own rural setting, although Brown offered from her broad experience a number of valid generalizations.

In May 1938, *The Family* published "The Application of the Basic Concepts of Case Work to Rural Social Work" by Grace Browning. Browning's thesis was similar to that of Josephine Brown. A year later, "This Rural Social Work" by Carol L. Shafer appeared in the *Survey*. Shafer bitterly denied that the so-called differences cited by Brown, Browning, and others, warranted the emergence and teaching of a new practice labeled rural social work.

Thus, through discussion and debate, we arrive at a group of articles having to do with the locality specific nature of rural practice. This theme had appeared in the twenties, and was similarly stated throughout the thirties. "Along a Country Road" brings forth Alice Gray Hickox's description of practice in remote Vermont. "Truly Rural" by Elizabeth E. A. Gissall describes her experiences in rural Missouri. From the Northwest, Samuel and Jeanette Gerson wrote "The Social Worker in the Rural Community" and from Liberty County, Georgia, came an account by Mary L. Rogers of social work among the Geechee appropriately called "Geechee Case Record." These were but a few of the examples which populated the literature of the period.

In 1933, Josephine Brown clearly expressed her bias for a generalist worker in *The Rural Community and Social Casework*. Brown's book was amply read and discussed by her contemporaries and generated a lot of response from the opposing point of view. The last two excerpts, one an intriguing poem by Marilla Rettig and the other an article by E. Kathryn Pennypacker, illustrate the nature of these responses and demonstrate the tempo of the argument.

But in fact, Josephine Brown's and Josephine Strode's statements favoring undifferentiated practice were so well-founded on the nature and elements of rural life that by 1940 no rural practitioner was arguing any longer the appropriateness of undifferentiated rural practice.

And so it is that in 1974, Leon Ginsberg was able to state without fear of contradiction "that the social worker in rural areas has to be a generalist" and that he or she "cannot get by with the specialist cop-out of urban areas."[1]

---

[1]SREB, "Educating Social Workers for Practice in Rural Settings: Perspectives and Programs" (SREB, Atlanta, Ga., 1974), p. 6.

SOCIAL CASE-WORK PRACTICE IN RURAL COMMUNITIES

Esther E. Twente

Even though the general term, social case-work practice, has much
the same connotation for different members of a group of social workers, it becomes rather important to define the use of the term in
its specific application when one wishes to speak of it in a rural
setting. As has been said again and again by those interested in
rural social work, generically, there is no difference between rural,
urban, or any other kind of social case work. The actual performance
of the worker, however, is definitely affected by the forces existing
in a rural area. The nature of these forces is such that it becomes
difficult in rural communities to assign the term social case-work
practice to a particular piece of work under consideration. In an
urban community the field of social case work is rather clearly defined: Both agency and worker have a definitely assigned place; in
a rural community where social case work programs of necessity are
undifferentiated, there is no such clear demarcation of place of
either the agency or the worker. In primary groups, such as one
finds in the rural areas, the relationship of worker and agency is
informal. There is no very clear distinction as to what the worker
does as a citizen and what he or she does as a social case worker.

Just to say that case-work practice, either good or bad, can be
called such when the rendering of the service is on an individualized basis is insufficient. When the wife of Farmer Jones visits
the sick neighbor twice a day in order to bathe her, clean her
house, and possibly prepare meals for the young children, she is
rendering a service—a social service on an individualized basis;
yet as a neighbor she is not likely to be able to approach viewing
the problem in terms of the total personality of the sick friend,
and with her limited experience in training and meeting social problems she will not have the capacity to begin to see the family in
relationship to its whole environment. In other words, she can
scarcely be said to be doing social case work. Neither does the
social worker who gives relief on a budgetary basis and, therefore,
in terms of individual needs necessarily engage in social case-work
practice. The worker may budget the needs of the individual but

Proceedings, National Conference on Social Work, 1938. Esther
Twente was Executive Secretary of the Ford County (Kansas) Chapter
of the American Red Cross and later on, Assistant Professor in the
Department of Sociology at the University of Kansas, Lawrence.

make the experience decidedly a destructive one for the client, i.e., the relief is not given in terms of the emotional needs of the client. Furthermore, an absolute criterion for social case work cannot be found in the degree of training of the worker. It is conceivable that there may be much question about a certain service rendered by the professionally trained person, while the work done by the un-trained worker may be definitely an evidence of good social case work.

When one thinks of social case-work practice in rural communities one first thinks of the factors existing in rural areas which affect the performance of the worker. These factors have been analyzed to some extent from time to time by different authorities.[1] Briefly, they are both of a physical and of a non-physical nature. The physical factors may consist of long distances; bad roads; car trouble; inclement weather—snow, sleet, ice, rain, excessive heat, excessive cold; isolation of clients; isolation of workers; necessary detachment from other workers, books, magazines, etc. The physical factors may have to do with lack of office equipment and facilities and lack of satisfactory housing conditions for both client and worker. In the middle western states and probably in other sections of the country also, it is still a rather common occurrence for a social worker, when he or she goes into a small community, to find that it is difficult to locate a house in which there is an extra room, and particularly one in which there is available a bathroom. It may even be a greater problem to discover a landlady who considers it necessary to have hot water for bathing purposes more than once a week. If the social worker happens to be a man with a family, he may have even greater difficulty. Housing for clients in small towns and rural communities is often a very serious problem. Not only may the houses which are available be most unsatisfactory—and unsatisfactory houses in rural communities can be found in sections other than in the South, even though *Tobacco Road* and *Faces We Have Seen* have made us particularly conscious of conditions there—but sometimes there just are not enough houses to go around. We have had quite a number of instances in certain parts of Kansas, when county directors of necessity have hesitated to authorize the return of residents because there simply was not a decent place vacant in the whole county in which the family could move if it did return.

[1] Wilma Van Dusseldorp, "The Development of Social Agencies in Rural Communities," *The Family*, March 1933; Josephine Brown, "The Rural Community and Social Case Work." Published by the Family Welfare Association of America, 1934; Grace A. Browning, "The Application of the Basic Concepts of Case Work to Rural Social Work," *The Family*, March 1938.

Long distances may on the surface seem of minor importance with good roads, fast cars, and telephones available. That is, we think they are available. The good roads, even very good ones, cease to be good when ice covers them for six weeks at a time as happened in the Middle West two years ago. Not all roads are good, even in fair weather. Those which lead to where the social worker needs to go are often narrow, rocky, hilly, and crossed by streams. It is difficult not only for the social worker to get to the client, but it is equally or even more difficult for the client to get away at any time from his own surroundings. Several years ago in one of the middle western states, not Kansas, the attention of the writer was called to a family living eighteen miles away from the county seat. The little one-room shack in the middle of the woods was fourteen miles away from the nearest telephone. With difficulty the writer drove within two miles of the shack. She plowed the rest of the way on foot through blackberry briars, mud, and chiggers. When she got there the mother was desperately sick, just preceding a confinement. Since there was no other car within walking distance and the nearest neighbors were several miles away, the best time-saving procedure seemed to be for the worker to rush back to town, make arrangements for hospital care, and lead an ambulance back to the scene. All this was done at top speed, yet the woman died that night after she got to the hospital. The only way to get her to the ambulance was to carry her for a half a mile, put her on a lumber wagon for another mile and a half, and finally into the ambulance.

The isolation of workers—although this has become a much less serious problem since the introduction of the federal and state programs, with workers in each county and supervisory staffs visiting county offices—has its effects. Small salaries, which of necessity are inadequate as long as the prevailing standard of salaries of other officials and public servants such as teachers, probate judges, ministers, and doctors are small in most rural communities, make impossible the buying of an adequate number of books and magazines and prohibit the attendance of workers at more than occasional conferences and at schools of social work, even for a quarter at a time. The social worker in the rural community, therefore, has less opportunity than the urban worker for keeping informed of the developments in the field of social case work. Moreover, lacking the stimulus of contacts with other workers with professional interests, there is danger that the knowledge possessed will not be put to the best use and that the worker will let herself drift into a rut. The stimulus which comes from association with other workers with similar interests seems to have particular value for the worker in public assistance programs, whose duties in the last few years have consisted to a very large extent of doing a mechanical job, or one which has a tendency to become mechanical, of filling in forms and making reports. The pressure of high case loads adds to the dilemma.

In an urban community typewriters, files, and even stenographers are considered a part of every office equipment. Not so in rural communities! A farmer is not as likely as a businessman or a professional man, or even a laborer, to see the need for these facilities. He is not acquainted with these tools. He is accustomed to working with the plow, harrow, tractor, horses, etc. Many farmers, even with all the splendid encouragement from farm bureaus to the contrary, do not think in terms of keeping books—except perhaps on the calendar on the wall—and it is difficult for them to see the actual need for all of the paraphernalia in the office of the social worker. The result is that the typewriter, usually a secondhand one, may not work very well and the files have a tendency to consist of makeshift arrangements. Steel files with locks anywhere, especially in rural communities where everybody knows everybody else, are a joy to behold! Many a social worker undoubtedly has had a vision of a tornado striking in a rural community where files are without locks and keys. Perhaps it is fortunate that up to this time large case loads and inadequate stenographic services have made impossible the keeping of detailed records. Nevertheless some of them, even now, if they were blown over the countryside, would cause havoc in a community for many years to come.

The nonphysical forces, as has already been indicated, are closely related to the physical forces and to a degree are dependent upon them. Thus, isolation is a result of bad roads; long distances; lack of telephones, cars, railroad facilities, etc. The attitude of the public, which in turn affects the adequacy or inadequacy of the material facilities available to the worker, is dependent upon the personal experiences of the individuals who make up the public. It may mean that the relatively greater isolation of a rural community makes board members, interested citizens, and clients alike either more dependent or more independent, depending entirely upon other factors operating in individual instances. Close association with nature and time for contemplation while riding on the plow may make for more imagination or for greater inertness, again depending upon the individual personality. Hardships resulting from dust storms, infertile soil, poor crops, and low prices may make for greater courage or for more acquiescent acceptance.

Case-work practice in rural communities is both hampered and enhanced by the forces affecting it, hampered through the lack of resources, at least of the kind known in the cities, enhanced by the close natural relationship between client, worker, and community.

Clinics, psychiatrists, specialists of all kinds, hospital facilities, and specialized educational opportunities are likely to be lacking, at least to a certain degree, in a rural community. On the other hand, there is the opportunity for the worker and community to get together more quickly and more closely on a working basis, and it is possible in a shorter time, because of the less complex situation, to work out a better relationship between client and community. Prejudices may be strong and they may have to be broken down, but real interest is never lacking. Moreover, the community can see much more easily how certain conditions and certain lacks which exist affect the individual client. In a more complex society these effects are not so evident, and even with intelligent leadership it is more difficult to bring client and community together in such a way that will profit by the relationship. Case-worker practice in rural communities is affected primarily by the factors which affect the material resources of the client and the personal resources within himself, and which affect a change within his environment as well as within his own emotional self, by the personal and material resources of the the worker, her capacity and skill in working with the client and the resources upon which she can draw, and the possibilities for establishing an effective relationship—one which is dynamic and productive between client and worker, client and community, and worker and community.

To what an extent then do we have social case-work practice and what is the quality of the practice in rural communities? A few general observations will be made in so far as rural communities in our country as a whole have developed case-work programs. Specifically, the conclusions are primarily based upon the situation in one state—Kansas.

That federal relief, social security, and the child welfare service programs have boosted social work in every rural community is obvious. Whether administered ably or poorly, effectively or ineffectively, every community in this country, no matter how benighted or isolated, has felt the effect of these service and relief programs.

That in the future rural social case work has to be performed primarily by public agencies rather than by private seems to be the opinion of most people working in the rural field. Few rural communities, if any, can afford to pay for two good social case-work agencies. Since public relief is administered in each community in this country, it would seem, as was pointed out recently by R. C. Hobson in his thesis *Public Welfare in Petersburg*,[2] that one good

___

[2] Raleigh Colston Hobson, *Public Welfare in Petersburg* (Va.), thesis for Master of Science Degree, College of William and Mary, 1938.

public agency in a community is better than two poor agencies, one public and one private. The establishment of one good public agency presupposes, however, that the citizen who would otherwise be a member of a local private agency needs to be encouraged to support and aid the public official.

There have been those social workers who have expressed doubts as to whether or not social case work is or can be administered in public assistance programs or by any public agency. They have said that some factors within the nature of the public programs themselves—the legal restrictions, the need for getting the same information about everybody, the emphasis upon forms—all help to make the individualization of client, the primary principle of social case work, difficult if not well-nigh impossible. A day in a local office, when one sees a man of over sixty-five finally get an opportunity, after perhaps waiting two weeks or more until the worker can "get to him," to fill out or get filled out the many forms which will make it possible for him finally to get his old age assistance checks, makes one wonder how much concern and how much understanding there is for and of the man himself. He is practically lost in the maze of detail. Even the most sensitive, imaginative kind of social worker must have a tendency to forget the individual for the vast number of forms and the amount of mechanical routine. Yet in an organization of public relief, a short time before the social security titles were put into effect and when mechanical detail played almost as big a part as now, a client made this statement to the worker: "I cannot talk to my husband because he worries. I cannot talk to my neighbors and my family because I will not tell them my business. When I talk to you, it is like I talk to myself and I feel better when I have said it. Always you let me plan, myself. If I think anything is good to do, you help me to try it."

The foregoing statement was made to a social worker not professionally trained, yet one senses in the statement elements of good case-work practice based upon a large amount of understanding of the needs of the particular client and based upon the ability to treat upon the basis of the woman's own needs. There was individualization in a public relief program by an untrained but not an unskilled worker. That gives a bit of hope when one studies the extent and quality of case-work practice in a state which has few social work programs other than those introduced by the state and federal governments, and which has among those who are practicing social case work a low percentage of members in the American Association of Social Workers.

The reading of a dozen case histories in different child welfare units in several states leaves little doubt in one's mind that social case work can be practiced by public agencies working in rural com-

munities. One finds in those records excellent work with children—
children with problems having both physical and emotional causes.
One sees in those units in rural communities a recognition of the
needs of the individual in terms of his total personality in his
total environment.

A social case worker, who for the last ten years has worked with
a public agency in a county in another state, expressed herself emphatically when she was asked whether or not it was possible really
to do social case work in a public agency under the auspices of a
board of elected officials. There was no doubt in her mind after
her years of experience that there are opportunities for social case
work in rural communities in a public agency. As to the public officials she said: "I should have faith at any time in a public official when it comes to a question of having a real interest and concern in the welfare of the people in his community. They are his
neighbors and his friends." Even though some local elected officials
in Kansas have shown greater understanding and more concern for the
welfare of the people in the community than others, the social workers in the state again and again have expressed appreciation of the
very genuine and intelligent interest of the elected county commissioners in the social welfare program in the counties and in the
state. Given frank and detailed information as to the existing conditions in the community, the public officials can generally be
counted upon to do their share.

As one reads case histories in rural communities, one is impressed
with the differences in social resources between small and large communities. Some workers seem to be greatly hampered by the fact that
there are not available, either in the immediate area or at times
even in more distant areas, such facilities as clinical and hospital
services. Some seem to be very much thwarted because there is no
psychiatrist on hand; others, on the other hand, find that by using
the resources which exist in the rural community—the teacher, doctor,
minister, county commissioner, and other genuinely interested citizens—they can go far in treatment, particularly if they couple these
local resources with other resources which exist in the state and
which are available, if only used. A worker in a rural community who
has had experience in a large city agency is likely to find that the
rural community does not present such a big problem of lack of resources, but rather a problem of learning how to use the resources
available. Resources in rural communities must first be recognized
as such and then they must be used in the most effective manner.

Ideally, social case-work practice in rural communities as well as
in any other kind of a community consists of services rendered on the
basis of an individual need, a need established on the foundation of

fact carefully accumulated and evaluated. The service is rendered through the individual rather than for him and takes into consideration his need in terms of the "organism-as-a-whole" in its multiplicity of experiences or in its environment. It is based on an effective client-worker relationship. In all rural communities known to the writer, conditions exist which limit the execution of the casework function in terms of its maximum possibilities. Some of the situations which make for these limitations are as follows:

1. The necessity for exercising authority, at least, more than a minimum amount of authority, in any form. The giving of relief on an eligibility basis or the work with a delinquent child through the juvenile court are both examples of situations which give the worker a place of power.

2. The necessity of treatment in terms of the needs of all the clients in the agency as well as in terms of the needs of other individuals comprising membership in the community. In a public agency where intake cannot be limited and where funds are likely to be inadequate, the worker must consider in determining the amount of relief or other services given the client, the need of the other clients in the agency. Furthermore, the standard of living of those who are contributing to the funds which take care of the relief and service needs in the community must be taken into account. In many rural areas, farmers who are paying taxes which help to take care of the health needs of those on relief are themselves neglecting their own teeth, eyes, or tonsils, because they have insufficient funds to pay for the necessary services.

3. The requirement of treatment without adequate resources. In a rural community it may be impossible to provide certain facilities for vocational training which is important if the work with a certain individual is to be most effective. The rural case worker may minimize the result of the lack of certain resources by making the best use of those available—yet there will be deficiencies which cannot be met. A dearth of necessary office equipment, including a capable stenographer, may be a part of the inadequate resources.

4. The necessity of treatment by a worker with too large case loads. The case-work function cannot be carried out in terms of its maximum possibilities when case loads run as they still do in areas where distances are time consuming, up to one hundred and fifty cases per worker per month, or higher!

5. The requirement of treatment by a worker with insufficient knowledge and skill. In rural, as well as in urban communities, because of the rapid increase in demand for social case workers and the newness of the profession, it is necessary for many agencies to

be served by inadequately prepared workers both from the point of view of experience and the development of well-integrated personalities. The rural social-work job demands the very best in quality of workers if good results are to be obtained. In fact, the rural worker needs to be, even more than the city worker, a regular paragon of virtues: resourcefulness, initiative, knowledge, skill, humor, tact, and poise.

All the five factors mentioned above exist in most rural areas at the present time. The extent to which they exist determines the limitations in the field of social case-work practice. If one thinks in terms of concentric circles, with all the limitations included in the outer circle, it becomes obvious that much practice in the field of rural social case work is toward the periphery of the circle. It is possibly true that proportionately these limiting factors exist to a greater degree in the country than in the city and that more work is done in the external boundaries of the circle in the rural than in the urban communities. There is, however, enough rural social case practice, much of it done intuitively, to be sure, to show that there can be such, and enough approaching the center of the circle to demonstrate that with more skilled workers who know how to work with the client and who know how to make use of the resources available, as well as to create new ones, it will be possible gradually to move farther away from the periphery toward the middle of the circle. Certainly there is a challenge to the worker who likes the smell and feel of the soil and all that goes with it, and who has imagination, resourcefulness, and a willingness to work twenty-four hours a day. Few fields offer anything like it.

THE DEVELOPMENT OF SOCIAL AGENCIES IN RURAL COMMUNITIES

Wilma Van Dusseldorp

As we use the word "development" in the subject of this discussion,
I am sure that, theoretically at least, it connotes to all of us a
process of expansion—of evolution. Few of us could improve upon
Webster's definition—"to make active something latent," "to unfold
more completely," "evolve the possibilities of." I am sure all of
us mean the gradual unfolding of latent ability and resources, but
in discussions of the subject with fellow workers from time to time
I have not been at all sure that the process we call development did
not actually result in being a succession of quickly injected "one,
two, three, and four" approved by "authorities of national reputation," and if the application of these "proper stimuli" did not produce "desired results," there was bound to be something wrong with
the community!

Much has been said about the differences between social work as it
is done in the city and social work as it must be done in rural
areas. Workers enumerate characteristics of the rural community as
causative factors for the differences they see. It cannot be denied
that social forces responsible for molding life in sparsely populated
areas are different from the social forces operating in more densely
populated areas; yet, so far as I have been able to observe, the
chief difference lies in the degree of genuineness of the social
work applied—more specifically, in the genuineness of the ability
of the social worker operating. Given a social worker who is genuinely a successful worker in the city, he, or she, will be a successful social worker in the rural districts. One worker may not like
the country and will prefer to work in the city, whereas another
likes the country and prefers the rural district in which to practice
social work, but that is a different matter. Preferring the city,
if he has the ability to be a genuinely good worker in the city, he
also has the *capacity* to be a good worker in rural areas, for the
difference lies, to my mind, not so much in the difference in the
environmental elements of city and country (for, as a matter of fact,
cities in widely separated areas present an equally great variation

The Family, March 1933. Wilma Van Dusseldorp was, after 1935, on
the staff of the Social Security Board. She was a member of the Sub-
committee on Materials from the Rural Field of the American Association of Schools of Social Work.

in environmental factors) as in the worker's ability shrewdly and clearly to pick out the factors with which she has to deal and to adapt herself quickly and graciously to them.

Every one of twenty or thirty workers in a small city may have a number of shortcomings as social workers, but working elbow to elbow the effect of the inelasticity of one is cancelled by the imagination of another, the influence of one worker's racial or family prejudices may be cancelled by the efforts of other broad-minded workers, and together they may still succeed in developing a program of social work which, though it might be improved upon by better prepared and selected personnel, will stand. But any one of the same workers standing alone in a rural community might throw overboard, in a short time, all possibility of establishing social work in that community for a period of many years; and I should not be inclined to blame the community, but would lay the causative factors at the feet of the social worker who lacked the ability to understand and wisely respond to the total social forces in the rural community. I have known workers capable of seeing and enumerating the social forces but incapable of thoroughly understanding and successfully reacting to them.

As Miss Cannon pointed out in her discussion of the social workers' shortcomings in adapting themselves to the staggering job of helping the unemployed, a doctor does not say, "This is not medicine I am practicing because the patient is too sick."[1] I believe she might also have prophesied that no doctor would say, "I can not practice medicine in this community. It is too full of sick people who are extremely stubborn." Yet social workers have been known to say, "This community is too ignorant to appreciate real social work," or, "This community is too poor for social work," "This community is too backward and self-satisfied," and so on. They might truthfully enough have said, "This community has not the financial resources with which to support a social worker of its own," or "Since the financial resources of the community are limited and health problems great, it might be best to have a health program first if they can not have both"; or "So little social work has been done here that the people do not know what a social service program might do for them." However, too often we are forced to admit that the social work this or that community has been exposed to has been so unwisely done that the community has decided that it could get on better without so troublesome and expensive an accessory. Consulting some of the leaders in those communities, we are likely to hear that the

[1]"Fear Not the Future," *The Family*, July 1932, p. 141.

social worker each had was "highly trained," but she tried to make them do too many things they did not believe in, so they do not like trained workers. Some of the most intelligent leaders might add, "without putting forth any or enough effort to give us information about fundamentals which might have helped us to understand what she was trying to do"—granting, of course, that she was trying to guide them in the right direction (about which there might also be some question).

Rural communities are said to be "very provincial." I wonder about that sometimes and recently, when reading a magazine article, the name and authorship of which I can not now recall, I decided that according to the author's description of provincialism, the accusation may be entirely false. The author said he knew of only two kinds of provincialism—one typified by the self-centered New Yorker who doubted the value of any product which happened not to have passed through the bottleneck of New York City, and the second typified by the average American citizen found in all other parts of the United States who questioned the value of his home products because they had not passed through the bottleneck of New York City. Now, I am pretty sure I am safe in saying that, generally, the rural citizen does not much care whether or not a new idea came to him through the bottleneck of New York City; in fact, I believe he likes his home grown ideas pretty well, but to him the test of the value of any idea is, "Does it work?" And the rural citizen applies this acid test to social work.

The job of "developing" social agencies presupposes the existence of something to be developed—the presence of basic material with which to start. In the rural community, just what constitutes this basic material? People, of course. People who, because of their particular occupations and habits of life, have possessions, material and spiritual, which they believe it is to their interest to protect to the best of their ability; who, because of their occupations, because of extremely intimate and open association with other personalities having similar interests and characteristics, have developed particular habits of thought and action. Life has not imposed upon rural people the strongly competitive issues in rapid succession to which city people have had to learn to adapt themselves. We say the ruralist is slow to think and act. If one's thought is less frequently pierced with new ideas, and less frequently pressed for hasty reaction, it is not surprising that deep and well worn grooves of thinking grow. No mere swift, fresh breeze, however exhilarating it may be momentarily, is likely to uproot the ideas traveling through those deepening and well worn grooves.

It behooves the social worker to understand thoroughly and sympathetically the processes of mind which have developed as a result of rural living. Criticism, however subtly offered, is recognized and resented, yet the uncritical approach is often extremely difficult if not impossible to achieve, unless the worker understands the point of view of the ruralist and the forces which have operated to create it.

A rural volunteer sought the advice and guidance of a visiting social worker (who was reputed to be trained and experienced) about a widow with children who was chronically dependent upon the community. The volunteer stated emphatically to the social worker that she had definitely decided that the only thing to do was to give the widow assistance in moving to a distant city so she could get factory work and thus be able to support her children. The social worker could not conceal her agitation over such an unorthodox suggestion and proceeded immediately to "tell" the volunteer that it was not "ethical" to send dependent families from one place to another without providing for their security; and that, further, it was each community's responsibility, anyway, to support its own dependent people through its poor relief funds or through private charity.

At the close of the interview the volunteer was only more discouraged about her job, and not a little skeptical about the helpfulness of social workers. Later the visiting social worker revealed that she thought the "poor, limited" volunteer "hopeless" because she questioned and resisted every suggestion the social worker had made.

A few months later it happened that the local volunteer was interviewed by a state field worker who was seeking information about the community in behalf of a special case on which she was working. At the end of the conference the volunteer had the courage in spite of the previous rebuff to present her still dependent widow's situation in the hope of securing help in moving the widow to the city:

"Mrs. Allen and her children really should move to the city because there is not one thing she can do to earn her living here. She is continually begging," the volunteer stated with emphasis.

"Has Mrs. Allen ever lived in the city?" casually inquired the social worker.

"No, she hasn't, but she's bright, she can catch on to city ways quickly."

"Does Mrs. Allen want to move to the city?"

"Well, I don't know. I've never asked her." The volunteer was herself obviously astonished at this revelation.

"Does Mrs. Allen have any kinfolk in the city?"

301

"No, not that I know of. Her people and her husband's people have lived around here since the eighties when their grandparents came here from North Carolina."

"Is Mrs. Allen particularly unhappy here?"

"Oh, no. I think she likes it, but she can't get work enough to make a living."

"In what part of town does she live?"

"Right on the edge. She rents a little cottage with four lots of ground she once used as a chicken run. She raised a lot of chickens after her husband died, thinking she could make something of it, but her chickens all died off. There are several mulberry trees on the place and the chickens got sick and died from eating sour mulberries and then the place is run down, too. The rats got lots of the little chickens. She had a cow she had to give up. Couldn't get feed for it, it seemed. As a matter of fact, I don't believe she has paid any rent since her husband died, but her little boy runs errands for the landlord to sorta make up for it."

"She has a sense of honesty, then, hasn't she?"

"Oh yes, she's been a good intentioned woman in her time. She's hard working in a way."

"How many children has she?"

"Four, I believe. The oldest girl must be about fourteen, then there's a boy twelve, and a couple of little girls."

"Mrs. Allen has a garden, no doubt."

"Only a little patch. She doesn't like gardening much. Her husband always used to do that and all the outdoor work. But she keeps a clean house."

"If she should move to the city, what do you suppose Mrs. Allen would think about having to get up at five o'clock in the morning in order to prepare breakfast, dress the children, keep up their clothes for school, travel five miles to work on a trolley, not to get back home before five-thirty or six to do all of the housework at night?"

"Well, that would be hard for her to get used to. She probably wouldn't like that either."

"If Mrs. Allen's ability to keep her family together and educate them depends upon her willingness to make sacrifices and the doing of things whether or not she happens to like them—like having a garden, and so on—might it not be easier for her to do the hard things right here at home where people know her and where she knows people? She would probably have to have a great deal of encouragement to help her over the hard spots. If she never did the gardening, or the bargaining for feed for the cow, she probably needs more than encouragement—knowledge about how she can manage—which you people would gladly give to her."

"Oh sure, we'd do all we could, and of course it does seem the sensible thing to try."

This is not the complete interview, of course. Inquiry about relatives, the health of the family, a discussion of Mrs. Allen's particular temperament, suggestions of possible contributions in money and service from the church groups opened up innumerable avenues of new thought and encouragement to the volunteer and served as a challenge to her to see how much she might really accomplish in spite of past effort and failure. Service from the State Department made it possible to extend similar help to this same volunteer in behalf of fully thirty families over a period of two years. By that time the volunteer had become convinced that the community should have the full time service of a professional social worker.

If in this particular community there has been "development" of social agencies—using the word "agency" in its broadest meaning of help or aid—it has been due to a willingness on the part of local leaders to accept errors in their methods of work and in their thinking about social problems as a basis upon which to build and from which to depart in evolving a new and broader understanding of social problems; it has been due to a willingness on the part of the social worker to use the most interested and best equipped people available, however limited they appeared to be in their vision and capacity to learn; and above all it is due to an assumption that, however inelastic and unimaginative these leading people might have been, they were nevertheless eager to improve their local conditions as far as they could be helped to see a way of improving conditions. But they had to be shown.

There are very able people to be found in the rural areas who may not have taken in the past a very active part in local social service but whose interest and activity can be aroused when they are assured that effective leadership is available to them.

One college bred woman living in an isolated mountainous section was very skeptical about the possibility of much change in the community in which she lived. Most of the residents were laboring people of little education and with a great resistance to change in their habits of living. Five miles back in the mountains there lived in a one room log cabin a seclusive native with his seven children, ranging in age from three to seventeen years. Not one of the children had ever been in school. The wife and mother had been taken to the state hospital for the insane two years before when highway workers had observed her roaming the hills and valleys day after day, dragging the children with her and had reported her to the county ordinary as a "wild woman."

No one had bothered to try to do anything about the man and the neglected children. The poorer people were not alarmed about the situation. Better able people doubted if they could have any influence over a superstitious mountaineer who would be impervious to suggestion. This well educated woman was disturbed about the situation but the only solution she could think of was to surprise the father one day by taking out against him charges of neglect of the children and have the children committed to institutions. She had taken steps to carry out this plan only to learn that there was no institution in the state to which these children could be sent.

She came to the state department. Discussion of the situation helped her to muster enough courage to visit the man and talk over with him the whole matter of the neglect of the children. To her utter amazement he became interested and, though he was shy and somewhat suspicious of her interest, since she was the first person ever to be concerned about his plight, she gained his consent to look up relatives with whom the matter of providing more adequately for his children might be discussed. Most of the relatives were far away and very poor. She approached a fourth cousin who was the community druggist. He had known about the family and had no suggestion to offer about how "all of those many" children might be provided for, but would talk it over with his wife.

A year later the mountaineer and his seven children occupied a three-room house owned by the fourth cousin and located near his home. All the older children were in school. The fourteen-year-old girl was being taught housework by the wife of the fourth cousin. A local mission church supplied all the clothing needed for the children so that they might attend school regularly. The father was working in the village saw mill.

The cousins and the local volunteer assisted in this new and bewildering undertaking by supervising the spending of the income for the needs of the family, taking care to inform both the man and the oldest girl about the steps they took. Two years later the family was managing its own income and family affairs. The oldest children, two boys, did not remain in school. They got jobs but remained at home. The rest of the children did continue their schooling, and after the first year, which was especially difficult for them, they took pride in their attendance and progress.

Time after time when the discouraged relatives were about to give up the ingenuity of the volunteer came to the rescue, not to force the relatives on, for that she never did, but to encourage and to bring new relief in service and material assistance which gave the

relatives—less resourceful and buoyant than she—new light and hope
with which to carry on. There were something like a dozen interviews
between the state worker and the volunteer over this period of two
years, and many dozens of letters.

Today, four years later, this same volunteer has effected adjustments for at least ten families in her local mountain village,
through the application of the principles she learned in her work
with the mountaineer and his seven children.

Developing a state program of social work in a rural state, community by community, through the services of a limited staff of experienced workers, is slow, but its value lies in the firmness of the
foundation built, through the development of leaders who grow, experience by experience, error by error, success by success, and who
are assisted through interview and correspondence with the district
field worker.

All through this discussion we have been dealing with the processes
by which growth in volume of understanding and work may be achieved
when conditions are primitive, territory great, problems many, and
related professional services in fields such as health, specialized
education, and institutional care for groups of afflicted people, are
all extremely limited compared with the need for them. It is true
that the avenues, through which a lone social worker serving an area
with a population of 500,000 progresses, are necessarily different
from those adopted by a worker who may serve a restricted area and
who may have at her finger tips resources in health and education as
well as a large percentage of wealthy and educated people. But,
though the avenues through which workers having such different fields
of responsibility may differ, the responsibility of helping her population grow, evolve, from one level (the one on which she finds them,
incidentally, not the one on which she wishes they were) to a higher
one is still before her. And can a worker help her community, however large or small, to achieve this growth with substantial security
unless she be supported by an ever-increasing number of intelligent,
informed citizens in the community back of her? How can they become
thoroughly familiar with the aims and methods of genuinely good social work in a surer, more direct way than through planned participation?

THE CONTRIBUTION OF RURAL SOCIOLOGY TO FAMILY SOCIAL WORK

Gertrude Vaile

The contributions of rural sociology to family social work are great, both in factual information and in some interpretations. And they suggest the possibility of further contributions that the family social worker needs.

Family social work is concerned with family situations in which there is "some deviation from the norm,"[1] and the family and the individuals concerned are unable by their own unaided efforts to achieve satisfactory conditions of life and personal relationships.

But how may one deal intelligently with deviations from the norms without an understanding of the norms? Studies of rural sociology have gone far to make possible an insight into norms of family life in general and rural family life in particular, and to give an understanding of the cultural environment of material conditions, customs, traditions, attitudes, and personal associations which have largely shaped the pattern of family life and which continue to affect it.

Perhaps the greatest contribution of sociology lies in that detailed, many-sided analysis of the rural culture within which the family life is set and which the social worker needs to know if she is to be intelligent in working with rural families. Any rural social worker who has not had good courses in rural sociology needs to do considerable reading covering the following subjects: the economic foundation of the rural community life, based as it is on the single occupation of farming and services to farmers; the way the family farm system brings the entire family into participation in the occupation, with all that that may mean for good or ill to the members; the standard of living ordinarily achieved on the farm; the effects upon the family and its members of living and working in family isolation on separate farmsteads; the significance and present extent of the development of modern means of communication and its effects upon family and community relationships and personal attitudes through the increased breadth of social contacts; the relations between the open country and the little town and what they

The Family, June 1933. Gertrude Vaile was a close associate of Josephine Brown at the Family Welfare Association of America. Vaile continued her advocacy of rural sociology as important subject matter for rural social workers while Chairman of the Sub-Committee on Materials from the Rural Field of the American Association of Schools of Social Work.

[1]*Social Case Work, Generic and Specific:* A Report of the Milford Conference. American Association of Social Workers, New York, 1929.

may mean to the life of each of the two parts of the rural community; the major rural institutions, the church, the school, the agricultural and civic organizations, the local government.

Another great contribution of rural sociology to family social work lies in the analysis and clear portrayal of the distinct outstanding types of family life which grow out of such cultural environment.

The first type pictures the solidarity of the rural family, with its united purpose, its sharing of interests and activities, the possible beauty and intimacy and personal security, the more significant part that the father through his constant presence may take in the family life, the educational value to the children in the all around development of head and hand and heart and healthful activity in the free air under the watchful guidance of their parents.

But there is also the darker companion picture of the same scene, and we see how that very family solidarity may stultify the growing personality and bind it into a family tradition of life and work not suited to the gifts and tastes of the individual; we see how the mutual responsibility and participation of all in common activities may overburden young children and leave tired mothers little time or strength to develop the finer sides of the family life.

The background for both these pictures is the isolation of the family on the farm, where they develop many fine virtues, but where interests and ideas tend to be narrow because they have few contacts with other people—and those are mainly with people very like themselves.

Then there is that other and newer picture, showing the farm family living on or near the hard surfaced road, reading daily the city newspaper and current magazines brought by rural delivery, receiving up-to-the-minute news by radio of weather and crops and world affairs, in personal touch with distant friends and business associates by telephone, transporting products long distances for better markets and shopping in urban centers. The young people go to the movie or dance twenty miles away and all the members of the family, like those of city families, are free to follow their own lines of interest and find their friends on the basis of congeniality and not of mere propinquity; the whole family enters into associations with farm people and others than farm people for a wide variety of purposes.

There is a darker view of this picture too, for, as sociologists have frequently pointed out, attitudes change much more slowly than the conditions which created them. The farm parents whose early attitudes were set in the days of the horse-drawn vehicle and the isolated farm neighborhood may differ widely from those of their children growing up in the days of the automobile, the radio, and

the movie. Indeed, so rapid have been the outward changes that attitudes of different members of the family may be as sharply conflicting as those with which the urban worker is familiar in the case of
some foreign born parents and their American born children.

Without the help of rural sociology the inexperienced rural social
worker, whether urban or city bred, probably starts with some preconceived idea, tending toward one or another of these patterns
(often the earlier ones), but with little appreciation, if she is
city bred, of the implications of the pattern as affecting the work
at points trivial and vital. She may be slow to grasp the thought
that she must deal with the father on the details of family life
that the city worker commonly discusses with the mother; or to modify
her house-keeping ideas for reasonable application to conditions of
no modern conveniences and a world of other work for the housekeeper
although she is at home; and to re-examine intelligently the problems
of budgeting and thrift when most of the living is or could be produced at home and cash is limited, uncertain, and comes generally at
long intervals. And she may be vastly puzzled to reorganize her
traditional idea of rural neighborliness. Repeatedly rural social
workers have expressed to the writer their surprise and disappointment in not finding the neighborliness which they had expected. Were
they right in expecting it? Has anything happened to it? Or were
they simply blind and did not know how to find it? The answer is
probably "yes" to all those questions.

Rural sociology partly answers these questions with a further,
very important contribution to the social worker in the study of
recent social change in rural life. A study by Professor Bruce Melvin of *The Sociology of a Village and the Surrounding Territory*[2] is
illuminating. The study includes the village of Marathon with a
population of 953, a smaller nearby village, and the country around.
One hundred and forty-six of the 358 country families lived on hard
surfaced roads while the remaining, approximately 60 per cent, lived
on dirt roads. While automobiles, telephones, and radios were numerous, yet about 29 per cent of the open country families had no automobile, 41 per cent no telephone, 70 per cent no radio. (This is a
dairy region in the near vicinity of Ithaca and Binghamton.) All
homes were reached by rural delivery, but 25.4 per cent of the open
country families reported no reading, and another 27.4 per cent reported the combined amount for the whole family as less than an hour

[2]Bruce Melvin, *The Sociology of a Village and the Surrounding Territory*. Cornell Agricultural Experiment Station, Bull. 523, May 1931.

a day. As Dr. Melvin points out, "Those doing no reading are the ones most likely to have no telephones or radios and to be found on dirt roads, shut away from the world during the winter and spring by mud and snow. The outlook on life of people so restricted must be limited, their knowledge of affairs scant, their conversation can only be on personal happenings, and their associations are inevitably with those who are similarly situated." And it may be added that probably the same ones who lack all these means of communication lack also accessible and vital church opportunities. "The three churches of the open country which are not wholly abandoned are doing very little," says Dr. Melvin. All are served by non-resident preachers.

These radical changes in the opportunities for communication and the differences with which families are able and inclined to take advantage of them are bringing about significant trends toward social stratification, as Dr. Melvin points out, which the social worker needs to understand and which explain some of the greatest difficulties of her work. Those members of the community who reach out, as opportunity opens, to larger interests and wider associations have inevitably less and less in common with those neighbors whose interests remain more limited. And so it comes about that the more the lagging members of the community lack the broadening influence of the long distance contacts, the more they lack also the stimulation of the best of the old time, frequent, face-to-face contacts with neighbors of strength and vision, and so the social gap grows wider.

Both in order to render effective service and to seek intelligently the co-operation needed from all forces of the community, the social worker needs the help of rural sociology in understanding all types of rural family life. She deals much with those lagging families of archaic type on the more isolated farms. Such life at its worst makes possible a neglect and abuse of children, and also of the woman, a sordidness of life and utter loneliness that would be practically impossible in an urban community. And she deals not only with such backward families, but with families of every sort, since sickness of body or mind, material misfortunes, children orphaned or awry, lack of knowledge of needed facilities for meeting special needs may occur in any social status.

Rural life includes not only life in the open country but also in the country town. On the whole, there seem to be a larger number of families who need the help of social work in the village than in the country, although it may be partly because village people have been quicker to recognize their need. It is also partly because the widows, the aged, the incapacitated drift from the country into the village where conditions of life are somewhat easier, help more readily at hand, and incidental opportunities for partial self-support more available.

Sociological studies have given exceedingly helpful information regarding village institutions and the trade and organization relations between the village and the open country, but most studies that have been directed to the life of the village itself have seemed to be concerned with the bony skeleton, perhaps the muscles, but very little with the inner spirit of the life itself in the village. Text-books of rural sociology are full of helpful discussions of the effect of country conditions upon the attitudes of country people and their personal relationships, but the attitudes of village people and their personal relationships seem only very recently to have received much attention from sociologists. Poets, novelists, and occasional magazine writers have turned the light of their genius on one aspect and another of small town life, but always they leave the rest of the picture dark or out of focus. Neither *Main Street* nor *Friendship Village* is a convincing portrayal of life as a whole in a small American town.

Such a book as *Small Town Stuff*,[3] with its analysis of personal life and relationships within the little town, should be a real boon to rural social workers. The major difference between family social work in the urban and the rural community is probably not, as some have supposed, a difference in the organized resources available but in the unorganized resources of personal relationships.

A social worker was much concerned about a deserted family in a country town of about a thousand population. The man had deserted before and had been brought back by the town. He was a man of slight build, a good voice, and rather gentlemanly manners, who had always wanted a "white collar job" but always continued to do miscellaneous manual labors which he hated. On this occasion it was learned that he had gone to a neighboring city where he was working as a salesman for a patent article of household convenience. But he sent practically no money home and the county continued to support his family. After long patience and futile efforts to get any response from the man, the worker finally, on a visit to the city, called upon the man's employer. She found him interested and responsive to her presentation of the problem. He said the man was doing well and suggested that he would transfer him to the district around his own home, where he could live with his family and be at much less expense. It was untouched territory and the man should make a good

---

[3]Albert Blumenthal, *Small Town Stuff*. University of Chicago Press, 1932.

thing of it. The worker returned to the little town and reported with joy to several people who had been helpful in planning for the family—only to have her ardor dashed by each in turn. They all said in effect the same thing:

"He won't come."

"Why not?" asked the worker. "It seems just the sort of thing he has always wanted."

"He knows better than to come."

"But why?" persisted the puzzled worker.

"He can't sell anything around here."

"What do you mean? Don't people think he is honest?"

"Oh yes, he is honest enough. They don't like him. They don't think he will use his money for his family if he gets it. If he cares anything about his family let him make good where he is and send his money home. He can't sell anything around here now."

And they were right. The man returned but not to try any salesmanship. He took odd jobs for a while and deserted again. Probably it was inevitable. But to the urban bred young worker it was a startling idea that the man's personal relation to his community was such that he could not be permitted to make good at the job that seemed such a wonderful find for him.

Social workers may be conscious of the difference in social relations in the large and small community but for lack of adequate knowledge and philosophy about them they may sometimes be timid and clumsy in their approach. The use of the case committee for consultation and aid in difficult cases is an illustration of this. The purpose of such a committee is the same in every community, namely, to secure the thought and participation of representative persons particularly well qualified to be of service in the solution of family and community problems, and to do this in a way that shall always safeguard and build up the dignity of the family concerned. But the methods of functioning of the urban and rural committees at their best are at almost opposite poles in technique. In the city the case committee discusses the problems impersonally without using the family's name and the members of the committee are in honor bound not to mention outside of the committee room anything that is said there. In the rural community, many urban bred workers do not dare to use a committee for fear of gossip, yet without one their work will always be thin, detached, and unstable.

A particularly successful rural social worker, when asked her experience with case committees, replied that she could not get along without one. The members were invaluable in advice and interpretation and endlessly resourceful in developing means of help for families. When asked whether she discussed the families by name she laughed outright and replied that if she did not the committee would all be guessing and that would be worse. As to the problem of keeping everything confidential she replied, "I do not try to keep it confidential. I just try to lay on their souls our responsibility for the family and the idea that if there is any occasion to speak of it, or if we hear it spoken of, it is our obligation to see that what is said is true and helps the family." She thought the best case work she had ever done had been done not directly with the families themselves but with the community, to affect attitudes toward certain families. And then she added, "Of course you have to be careful who is on the committee, and there are some cases that I would not bring before a committee, because the family's troubles probably are quite unknown and should not become known."

The participation of members of the small community in the efforts to help ill-adjusted families to better relationships within the community is a basic problem of rural social work and calls for more light from sociological studies, showing the social forces at work in a variety of American villages with different racial stock and occupations, history, traditions, and leadership. Although small towns have essential characteristics in common, as clearly brought out by Mr. Blumenthal in *Small Town Stuff*, yet the rural worker quickly discovers that every little town, even within a single county, is as different from every other as families are different from each other. Things can be accomplished in one that are impossible in another because the inner spirit is different.

Mention must be made of one other contribution which social workers need from rural sociologists and which they have not yet received in large measure: studies of the administration of rural government, meaning in this connection not elections and politics as such, but the services which the people expect from the officers whom they have elected, and the relation of public officials to the lives of private individuals.

The mayor of a village of two hundred people telephoned the county attorney to ask his advice about what could be done in the case of a sick old man who needed care but refused to call a doctor or tell who his folks were. The county attorney referred the matter to the newly installed social worker, who immediately went out to see the mayor. She found him much concerned about the old man who was very sick with diabetes. Neighbors were caring for him but could not do it adequately and none of them had "nerve enough" to insist on getting from him the information that would make better care possible. The mayor had called the town council to consider the matter but they were baffled. The record is a very charming glimpse of neighborly and official responsibility and of the way in which a social worker, coming in objectively, can sometimes open the way for effective neighborly service.

Repeatedly has the writer seen a village mayor show such solicitude about the needs of some family, or perhaps put a recalcitrant citizen on probation and personally try to make him go straight, or call attention to a neglected child in need of care. His official responsibility seems to lay upon him a personal, paternal responsibility for the welfare of the people within the town. Other officials—county attorneys, sheriffs, county commissioners—not uncommonly perform their functions in that same way, assuming a social responsibility as inherent in their office. They have been elected by their own neighbors to perform certain services for the community, and they fulfil the duties in a personal and neighborly way. Reading a large number of rural social case records in which this quality appeared I found nothing to suggest any self-interested political motive in such action. It was all simple and natural because the relationships themselves are simple and neighborly. But one could see with startling clearness how devastating might be the political consequences when the small community pattern is transferred to the metropolitan ward where personal relationships are not really close and official responsibility is not rooted in neighborly responsibility. Sociological studies would help to discover the real elements of vitality in local units of government as they function in the lives of the families and individuals in the community, and would greatly help the family social worker.

The contributions of rural sociology to family social work are rich and fundamental—in the detailed analysis of the various aspects of rural culture within which the family life is lived, in the special portrayal and interpretation of patterns of family life growing out of such environment, in the studies of social and material change now going on which profoundly affect the group and family life. It has also made helpful contributions for the understanding of life in the village, in which the larger part of family social work lies at present. But further contributions are needed by the social worker for insight into village life and for understanding of rural government and its relations to the rural people.

SOCIAL WORK AT THE GRASS ROOTS

Eileen Blackey

The distressed farmer, as he comes to the relief office is more than
himself; he is the personification of all the people who have molded
him, their economic and social struggles and their resulting philosophies. The rural family in the far West, or in New England will
reflect the early development and thinking of those areas. So too,
in the South. The rural worker there needs to be keenly conscious
of the factors contributing to the status of the southern cracker,
the share cropper, the tenant farmer, the corporation farmer, and
the Negro. There is no sense of ownership here and little incentive
to reach for other goals; there is only a year in and year out struggle for a bare subsistence.

The background of an area is largely responsible for its attitude
toward relief. Unless a worker understands the derivation of these
attitudes she is apt to become confused and ineffective. Some of
the southern states had their first introduction to social work
through the FERA. There was no community consciousness of social
work because there were no social agencies. Therefore, when it was
necessary for the federal government to take over the relief program,
there was often defensiveness, misunderstanding, and lack of interpretation.

At the beginning of the program in Florida, there seemed to be in
some sections even a patriotic connotation to being on relief. One
client of long standing objected to being removed from relief because,
he said, he'd answered the first call and had been on ever since.
One old fellow confided that he wasn't quite sure about "all this
relief"—he'd been on two years and he wasn't savin' anything and he
wasn't gittin' anywheres and he didn't know as how it paid. Other
clients look upon relief as a family pocketbook in which they have a
just share and, whether they are eligible or not, they present their
claims.

These comments seem humorous but they represent a hurdle for the
social worker. The rural client is actually bewildered by the pater-
nalism which has surrounded him and his family in his quest for help.
The relief setup has been primarily for the urban client, whose
skills the works program has to some extent capitalized. The farmer,

Survey, September 1935. Eileen Blackey was Director of Training,
Social Service Division, Florida Emergency Relief Administration.

314

however, finds himself in an unfamiliar setting when taken from his land and given a work card.

In the past, periods of stress made themselves felt largely in urban centers and their adjacent communities. If the farmer felt the pinch of need the fact that at least there was enough to eat kept the family off the relief rolls. But the present distress has penetrated to practically every farm home and the rural family has been caught in the maelstrom. Through the very necessity of sitting in an agency waiting-room or standing in line for commodities or attending a medical clinic, the rural person has been made "social work conscious." When life was going along at a tempo familiar to him, he was an individual concerned largely with his family, his land, his crops, and his occasional trips to town. Through his very isolation he developed a philosophy which met his own problems in his own way. He shared few confidences, and sought little advice because time and distance forbade. He emerges now, from a lifetime of such mental and emotional experiences, with a rather set pattern of behavior which is baffling to us, primarily because it is new to us. The farmer as he appears at the relief agency is often shy, awkward, ill at ease. His inarticulateness is apt to appear to us as stupidity. Or he may be ultra-cautious in his approach—naturally suspicious of an organization about which he knows little. He seems stubborn, unwilling to give information, unable to grasp the significance of his situation. It is not unlikely that he will call forth our irritation rather than our understanding unless we are alert to the things that have made him what he is.

Two factors have characterized the difficulties of the rural relief worker's job: the nature and extent of the relief problems and the necessity for placing effective tools as quickly as possible in the hands of untrained people. After an interview with a supervisor or director, an applicant for a job is likely to find herself on the staff of a relief agency, for which in all probability her previous experience has in no way prepared her. If she is fortunate she receives a week or two, or possibly three, of training in the fundamentals. The chances are, however, and this is more accurately true in the rural communities, that she is put under the tutelage of someone already so overloaded that what she absorbs is largely her own responsibility.

The rural social worker is confronted with a real dilemma in knowing how much of a family's welfare is her responsibility when there is no one else to take it on. It is not unusual to find many rural areas untouched by social work organizations or, for that matter, by community organizations. Thus the rural worker may be called on to provide for the health needs of families, while school attendance also frequently becomes her concern. She finds mental hygiene problems, acute or of long standing, and securing treatment or institutional care becomes part of her service. Whether she is equipped for it or not, emergencies arise where she must participate in removing children from the home, and in institutional placement of delinquent or feebleminded members of a family. She needs careful guidance on how far she may go in any given situation. At the same time, and above all, she should be convincing the community of the need for the social services on a permanent basis.

A second essential which the inexperienced rural worker must grasp is an understanding and appreciation of the individuals to whom her job relates. This involves an understanding of the underlying factors in the motivation of behavior. Clients and workers alike find themselves dependent on basic equipments in life—physical, mental, social, and emotional. The worker's skill comes in estimating a client's capacity so that she does not impose her own level of equipment on him or underestimate his ability to work out his own difficulties. The need of individuals for economic and emotional security is no less important than their equipments. If a worker cannot understand why a client has a blustering, bullying attitude; if she does not sense what has made a man cling to some physical ailment as a way out; if she fails to recognize the satisfaction which comes from living in the past when the present has nothing to offer—then she can in no sense help the person beyond the mere handing out of the relief voucher. The therapeutic value of being a good listener has been another definite lesson for the new worker to learn. She must recognize, however, that a client who discusses his innermost problems does not necessarily want anything done about them. The privilege of unburdening himself to someone who, he feels, understands, is in itself an emotional catharsis.

The so-called "behavior" of persons asking for help has been one of the difficult obstacles for rural relief workers, most of whom have been born and brought up in the judgmental and moralistic atmosphere of a rural community. For untrained workers to accept the fact that relief is based on eligibility and not on how people behave is in most instances extremely difficult. In such situations workers may feel that they have attained a degree of objectivity, but find their emotional equilibrium upset by the appearance of an unmarried mother, a prostitute, an alcoholic, or an ex-convict. Their proximity to the rural situations has undoubtedly made for a sympathy with and an understanding of rural problems which an urban worker placed in a rural area would have difficulty in assimilating. At the same time, however, this places the rural worker in the position of making decisions concerning people she has known all her life and who insist on looking upon her as a personal friend rather than as a professional worker. She finds herself in conflict and may become too lenient or too severe in her judgments. It has seemed advisable in many instances to shift a worker to a section of the county or district where she was not so well known.

Another dilemma of rural relief work becomes apparent when we realize how difficult it is to secure workers for rural areas where life is more or less stagnant and lonely. One cannot insist on too rigid professional standards here, or there would be no workers. The rural community has for years been forced to submit itself as an experimental ground for untried teachers and ministers or as the final resting place for those whose best years are over. Some of the same feeling seems to prevail concerning rural social workers. The trained worker is reluctant to go into an isolated county not so much because the job itself is undesirable but because the rural community does not offer her, as an individual, sufficient social and cultural stimulation. Previous to training, she is more receptive to a rural job. This appears to be an argument against training people for rural placement. It is not that, but is rather a plea for the utilization of capable, if untrained, workers who are willing to adjust to rural conditions until such time as the importance of skilled social workers in rural districts is more generally recognized.

Work with rural families in the present catastrophe has made relief workers aware of the dignity of small things. The rural worker has been forced to keep simplicity in her technique because of the inaccessiblity of anyone to whom she could delegate responsibility or with whom she could share it. When a worker is the only human being whom an isolated farm family sees, she has much to contribute. When the mother of that family dies, it is the worker who secures lumber for the coffin, who calls for volunteers for its construction, and accompanies the family to the grave. Later, with the home demonstration worker, she teaches the father how to cook for his children; to stay on his patch of land and maintain some semblance of a home for his children is his only choice. There is nothing intricate or analytical about this worker's treatment. She meets the situation on the family's own level and in so doing brings about, perhaps, more material and emotional rehabilitation than would be possible through any other approach.

While the urban family offers ample opportunity for constructive work with its various members, it is the utter lack of everything which connotes a happier existence that offers the rural worker her challenge. She must be familiar with every possible opportunity for

her family. Adult education classes may mean the thrill of learning
to read and write, the blossoming of a talent or a hobby, or possibly
real vocational rehabilitation. Limitless possibilities for service
to families through home demonstration workers, parent participation
in school activities, agricultural extension service, nursery schools
and churches are all present, and unless the rural worker is aware
of them and can use them effectively she is neglecting fertile soil.
The effort in all these extra curricular relief activities has been
to divorce them from relief and to think and act in terms of community sponsorship. It takes skill on the part of the worker to present
activities to the family in this light for many clients are extremely
sensitive to participation in anything which savors of "relief."

Bringing to the family an interest in their own home through simple
beautification and improvement is another angle of the rural worker's approach, though it is frequently difficult for her to see that
only such progress as the family wants to make will be of lasting
value. She often finds herself upset at the squalor, the lethargy,
the emptiness of the lives into which she steps, and in her eagerness to improve conditions, may urge the family beyond its willingness and capacity to change. To insist on cleanliness, for instance,
may bring temporary response to her as an individual or to the agency
as the controller of the family destiny, but visits two or three
weeks later may reveal the same old state.

The rural worker can be promptly discouraged if she expects changes
to occur early in her work with a family. She must look for her reward, if any, in what may seem to be pretty trivial efforts of the
family to better its own condition. She needs most of all to rely
on the strengths within the family group and in her ability to capitalize them. Time and again parents who have brought children to a
story-hour sponsored by the recreational division have asked to stay
and listen; the stories are as new and enchanting to them as to the
children. A worker was attracted one evening by a huge bonfire in
one of the fields. She found Negro mothers and fathers gathered
there playing the games which the children had learned in their day-
school playground groups. When children in their eagerness for play
make jumping ropes out of grapevines, baseballs out of inner tubes,
and whittle bats from old boards some of the numerous starting
points for a rural worker becomes apparent. There is romance in her
job if she can only see it.

A FARM PHILOSOPHY

E. L. Kirkpatrick

Some time ago I talked to the president of the Student Section of
the American Country Life Association about the need of some sort of
a philosophy for farm life. I asked her, a junior in home economics,
an energetic and intelligent young woman, what she thought teachers
and students might do about it.

"Teachers could dig around and find something that's right with
farm life if they would," she said. "We farm boys and girls go to
college with a lot of sentiment for country life, but we soon learn
about all the things that are wrong with it—wrong with the farm,
the neighborhood and the home town. Those of us who have any notion
of getting ready to live on a farm when we go to college get it
knocked out of us before we finish. Why don't we make it the subject of our next conference?"

With that suggestion we went to work, officers of the Student
Section, and members of the Student Advisory Committee of the American Country Life Association, of which I happen to be chairman. We
held a preliminary meeting of representatives of a dozen colleges
and came to the conclusion that what we needed to discuss was Basic
Elements of Rural Life. That was too large and general a topic,
however, and these student delegates broke it down into seven questions for discussion.

When the conference was held there were three hundred students representing colleges all the way from Kansas, Wisconsin and Michigan,
New York, Tennessee and the parts between. They manned their own
conference and to the adults on the side-lines they seemed really to
be going somewhere. Here are the questions and the answers as they
formulated them:

1. To what extent does farming provide steady work as compared
with other occupations?

Farming escapes unemployment difficulties. The farmer is never
out of work. He and his family have a steady job. This is indeed
reassuring when millions of industrial workers are out of employment.

Survey, July 1933. Ellis Lore Kirkpatrick (1884-1964) was Professor
of Rural Sociology at the University of Wisconsin and later at
Marietta College in Ohio. Kirkpatrick was a sponsor of the youth
section of the American Country Life Association. He also spent
time studying rural youth at the American Council on Education.

There are few bread lines or soup-kitchens in the open country. The farmer may not get much for his products but he usually has something to eat and always some way to occupy his time.

2. To what degree does the farm provide a good living on a moderate income?

The farm provides a better living than is enjoyed by urban families on equivalent incomes—shelter and good wholesome food at any rate. Comparable studies made by the U. S. Bureau of Labor Statistics and Agricultural Economics show that farm families eat more meat, eggs, milk, fruits and vegetables than workingmen's families, and thus are well provided with vitamins. People with larger incomes in the city set a better table, of course, but the majority of urban families are in the workingman's class and do not fare as well as farmers, generally.

3. In what respects is the farm a superior place to rear children?

The farm has many advantages in the rearing of children. Among these are greater physical strength, freedom from dangers of traffic and the like, better opportunity to use time effectively, greater diversity of tasks, and direction or guidance from closer association with parents. The country has the more wholesome social and moral background for children. The farm child is usually better trained in initiative, ability and dependability.

4. In what way does farming promote cooperation in family life?

The nature of farm work, with common interests and objectives, work and play together at home, and group participation in church and social activities, makes for cooperation in family life. Members of the family are more likely to be pals and partners on the farm than in the city. Farm conditions make it necessary for members of the family to work together. The family farm is the foundation of American agriculture.

5. What are the most satisfying community activities in rural life?

The most satisfying community activities are those in which as many persons as possible in a given area participate. These include educational, religious and social affairs, such as club meetings, play days, picnics and visiting in the rural areas. The open country is still characterized with satisfying group activities according to recent studies. To quote from one of them:

"Mr. Getman is an active organization leader and supporter. He is one of a group of farmers who helped organize the Equity, the Jersey

Breeders' Association, the Farmers' Club and the Orchard P.T.A. He
attends practically all of the meetings of the organizations with
which he is affiliated and serves on committees several times during
a year. He likes the Farmers' Club best because of the opportunity
it gives him to work with his neighbors. He helped promote this
organization because of his interest in the community. He does not
find his work in the different organizations burdensome and gives
community picnics as his favorite form of recreation.

"Mrs. Martin is affiliated with seven organizations. She attended
seventy-three meetings and served as president of the Upton Mine
Homemakers' Club, the Monona Community Club and receiver for the
Royal Neighbors. She joined the Homemakers' Club for social times
and for the opportunity which it gave to learn. She regards her
work with organizations pleasant and satisfying."

6. In what ways does farming afford opportunity for satisfying
leisure?

The farm affords more opportunity for leisure than does the city
generally and more than is appreciated by farm people at present.
Any one who is as free as the American farmer can, if he will, live
a zestful and creative life. The farmer's work with "living, growing, blooming and bearing things gives him an advantage over the
person who is dominated by the presence and pressure of lifeless
products and deadening mechanical work." Farmers could just as well
have less of the "unable-to-get-away" delusion and more of the "take-
a-day-off" spirit. They need less of the traditional contempt for
any one who does not work incessantly.

7. What effect does farming, dealing with nature, have on one's
philosophy of life?

Farm life, dealing with nature, affords an opportunity to meditate
and thus determine a wholesome philosophy of life. Its environment
teaches responsibility, obedience to nature, the laws of life. Rus-
kin once said, "There is no wealth but life." If this be true the
farm is a place of wealth, for it deals with life·—plant life, animal
life, human life. Farming, as a vocation, tends to bring out qualities of originality, courage and management in a rural civilization,
in contrast to a lack of the development of those qualities in the
routine and directed factory and commercial life in the city.

These same young people will hold their conference this year at
Blacksburg, Virginia, August 1-4, to discuss Basic Elements in Relation to National Policies Affecting Rural Life on the same realistic
lines as last year. I for one plan to be there.

SEVEN ANSWERS

Jean M. Paton

To the Editor: After reading Dr. Kirkpatrick's "Seven Points" in
the July Midmonthly, one is inclined to wonder how any of us urban
dwellers can bear to continue our present mode of existence, and why
there is not an immediate rush to the farm. May we not be allowed
to take up these points separately in an attempt to deny the idyllic
nature of farming?

He says that "the farmer is never out of work"; is never unemployed.
Our urbanity suggests that employment implies full monetary return;
and can anyone say this is the farmers' happy state? Busyness and
employment are two different concepts in the modern exchange economy.

Secondly, "the farm provides a better living than is enjoyed by
urban families on equivalent incomes, shelter and good wholesome food
at any rate." Can this be considered an optimistic situation? The
misfortunes of city-unemployed do not minimize those of the farmers.

Thirdly, "the farm has many advantages in the rearing of children."
Granted, but there are disadvantages. Is "freedom from dangers of
traffic and the like" enough for one to pull out of the bag to offset the lack of good schools, avocational opportunity, concerts and
libraries, to mention only some of the city child's advantages? I
also doubt that there is "greater diversity of tasks" on the farm,
unless the uniqueness of each cow before the milk pail is something
more alarming than I had ever supposed.

Fourthly, "members of the family are more likely to be pals and
partners on the farm than in the city. Farm conditions make it necessary for members of the family to work together." But does this
forced association necessarily lead to congeniality? It must be more
than stated as a generalization before we can believe it.

Fifthly, "the most satisfying community activities are those in
which as many persons as possible in a given area participate."
While hardly denying the beneficient influence of any trend toward
solidarity, one questions whether a mere numerical criterion here is
appropriate. The farmers' need of association, furthermore, is far
less a product of social feeling than of the sterility of their long-
vaunted independence.

Sixthly, "the farm affords more opportunity for leisure than does
the city generally, and more than is appreciated by farm people at

Survey, October 1933. This letter by Jean M. Paton was written in
response to the preceding article by E. L. Kirkpatrick, "A Farm
Philosophy."

present. Any one who is as free as the American farmer can, if he will, live a zestful and creative life." I am sure that no modern social worker will lay the blame for dissatisfactions on deficiency of "will power." That good old catch-all is out of date. We must go deeper than calling the farmer a stubborn creature if we really want to help him. The farmer is not a free man because the determination of his income, and therefore of his cultural enjoyments, is far from him. A union member in the dullest factory routine has more freedom. And as to what leisure a farmer possesses, surely dull winter days in the company of Sears Roebuck catalogues and a barren interior are as different from a creative environment as the bare rooms of an un-employed family are from the comfortable den of a professor. When will the professors take inventory of their material "props?"

Seventhly, "farm life, dealing with nature, affords an opportunity to meditate and thus determine a wholesome philosophy of life." It is true that some of us, at times, go out into the open fields with questionings as to ultimate realities. We seek a philosophy in quietude. But the answers to be found in mortgaged fields, with their fullness of insecurity, will be of the nature of escapes from reality. There might be much potency in a certain such outdoor activity on the part of farmers. Let them go out into their fields, not only to plow them under the broiling sun, but to ask themselves what it is that the professors are trying to put over on them, and why.

As Samuel Johnson once said, "You never find people labouring to convince you that you may live very happily on a plentiful fortune."

BASIC ELEMENTS OF RURAL LIFE

E. L. Kirkpatrick

To the Editor. Miss Paton's retort to the "7 points" in the July Midmonthly Survey seems to be based on the notion that I had set up

Survey, November 1933. In the polemic style of the period, this letter was Kirkpatrick's response to Paton.

a straw man for college students who are concerned with rural life. My only intention in submitting the article to the Survey Associates was to try to inform thinking readers of the deliberations of approximately three hundred students who had conducted their own conference at Bethany College the preceding October. It avails nothing to argue the question of which is worse, to be unemployed in the city or to be underpaid on the farm. Likewise, it is futile to argue rather than to discuss the question of whether the level of living of the city's unemployed is lower or higher than that of the open country's underpaid. Since the July Midmonthly came out, I have had the opportunity of working with the Federal Emergency Relief Administration and I am convinced that both of these levels are much lower than they should be. I pass, therefore, to the larger aspects of the whole issue.

In August 1933 rural-minded students from a score or more of our leading colleges met in another four-day conference session at East Radford, Virginia, to re-discuss the basic elements of rural life in relation to national life. They reiterated their emphasis on points like the "7" referred to above and asked seriously, "Why have we in college been taught to see everything wrong and little or nothing right with rural life—the farm, the home town, and the rural communities? There are good points—desirable things—about farm life as well as city life; and we propose to help thinking students see them."

Furthermore, during the time intervening between the two Conferences I visited about thirty-five colleges and universities in which I reported to ten thousand students in assembly groups and classes the findings of the former Conference, namely, the "7 points" and asked for reactions to them. The only outstanding adverse response came from a mature student who rose to inquire emphatically, "Now what are you going to do about the price of eggs for the farmer? You know he is getting only ten cents a dozen, don't you?"

Seemingly, to me, serious-minded college students in rural life are appreciating, as never before, at least in their generation, that country life has some things which are worth saving.

SOCIAL WORK AT THE GRASS ROOTS

"Out in the country—in the county seats and villages and crossroads
—that's where things are happening in social work, where it's being
hammered into forms as indigenous as buffalo grass in Kansas."

Josephine Strode, dropping into the *Survey* office one hot summer
morning, knew all about Kansas and its buffalo grass. She had spent
the depression years helping plant modern social work practices in
the windblown soil of the dust bowl. Now, with a brand new M.A.
from Northwestern University tucked into her brief case, or wherever
one keeps degrees, she was back on what she admitted was her favorite
subject.

The editors of *Survey Midmonthly* did not need to be convinced of
the impact of rural needs on modern social work. They knew that
down at the grass roots in every state in the union a new application
of accumulated experience, principles and practices is under way.
They knew too that social workers everywhere sense in the unfolding
situation an outstanding challenge to their philosophy and techniques. Last year the editors, aided and abetted by the American
Public Welfare Association, sent out one of their number to observe
just what was happening in the highways and byways at that crucial
point where benefit meets beneficiary, the real test of the efficacy
of all our striving toward security for the individual. The results
of those observations were published in a series of articles, Miss
Bailey Says. . . .

Meantime the editors were "spearing around" for material of direct
service to the growing number of extraordinarily eager workers in
the rural field. Material was not easy to find. Workers were somewhat inarticulate, their problems not wholly clarified, their practices not wholly adjusted to the realities of their setting.

"But," we asked Miss Strode, "what do rural workers actually do
that is different?"

That was enough. "Do? Do? They do everything and most of it
without benefit of anything but their own integrity and ingenuity."
And reaching into a plump brief case she brought out a sheaf of
paper which looked like a questionnaire but was in reality a list,
pages long, of "duties" that county social workers may and frequently
are, called upon to perform. "It isn't what they do that worries
them," she insisted, "but how to do it better."

Survey, October 1938

At this point the editorial instinct asserted itself and presently Miss Strode had agreed to write an article which would pose the problems of rural workers, and the methods by which, more or less isolated as they are from the professional associations enjoyed by their urban colleagues, they are endeavoring to raise the level of their work. Then, to our surprise, she dived again into her brief case and came up with a manuscript which, a fortnight later, was to blow a good lively Kansas breeze into the National Conference of Social Work. Asked to contribute something on publicity in rural areas, workers in thirty-nine western Kansas counties had pooled their experience and observation, had prevailed on Miss Strode to ghostwrite a paper for them and had appointed Helen Maxwell of Grant County to present it at a session of the Social Work Publicity Council.

We didn't need to wait for the conference to know that this paper was "*Survey* stuff." Promptly and firmly we pinned it down for future publication—and went on from there. What about the education of workers on the rural jobs? What about group relationships in country districts? Miss Strode, out of her experience, her knowledge of the realities of rural work and the ambitions and aspirations of the workers, had answers, not always final as she was quick to point out, but answers indicating the forces that social workers themselves are exerting to nourish a native growth at the grass roots.

The upshot of that summer morning confab was a scheme for a series of articles to run in *Survey Midmonthly* on the process and problems of social work where the county is the unit of administration and practice runs out over the back roads to the villages and remote farms. The backbone of the series will be a number of articles by Miss Strode, their content already suggested in this overlong foreword. Her present article, cast as a letter to Miss Bailey, *The Survey*'s itinerant observer of the social work scene, sets the stage for those to follow. First of these will be Publicity by Way of the Barn Door, drawn from the paper which Miss Strode "ghostwrote" for the Kansas workers to send to Seattle.

These scheduled articles will deal with the realities—and humors —of the day-to-day job and the practical methods that are growing out of experience. Along with them and supplementing them will be articles by other authors—we call them "backlog articles"—which will delineate the applicability of fundamental social work philosophies, techniques and aspirations to practice in the rural field. Such for example are two articles on the much discussed subject of in-service training by Josephine Brown, once field secretary of the Family Welfare Association of America, but associated since their inception with the FERA and WPA. The first of Miss Brown's articles will be found in this issue; the second, in November.

Finally the editors of *Survey Midmonthly* have a scheme, not yet fully fledged, to bring into their pages more and more live material from workers themselves, material hot from the forge so to speak. More about that next month.

This then is *Survey Midmonthly*'s special project for the months ahead: to examine, evaluate and pass on to its readers the new adaptations of social work practice that are being evolved by social workers themselves in the county welfare offices up and down the country. These offices are today's laboratory of social work methods from which will come the shape of future social work practice in a great sector of American life.

AN OPEN LETTER TO MISS BAILEY: RURAL SOCIAL WORKERS DO EVERYTHING

Josephine Strode

Dear Miss Baily: It's open season, now, on the range. The quail fly in coveys over the sagebrush and, for a brief time, the cans of surplus beef rest on the commodity shelves gathering dust.

While the cans rest, and my '28 jalopy cools its axles behind the relief office, I thought I'd write you an open letter which would give me license to take a few shots on behalf of rural social work.

Ever since 1933, when we set up our first orange crate to file instructions from the higher-ups, we rural workers have been listening to city social workers tell us *how* to do, and lately some of us have been wondering if they mightn't like to hear *what* we do!

Of course, you understand, we're not big game hunters in the field of social work theory, but we figure we've bagged some pretty good ways of doing things, just from having to do them.

It's funny, but when most people think about rural problems they

Survey, October 1938. Josephine Strode, social worker with the Kansas ERA, was author of *Social Insight through Short Stories* (1946) and co-author with Pauline Strode of *Introduction to Social Casework* (1940) and *Social Skills in Casework* (1942).

usually think of land, crops and cattle. Millions are spent every
year to conserve material rural resources, but how we crowd every
dollar that's spent to save human resources! Folks don't seem to
realize that rural people count up to almost half the population of
our country, and that this rural half has its problems of unemployment, family life, housing and health, and its own youth worries,
too.

More than two million farmhands have lost their jobs permanently,
and those who still hold on make less in a year than unskilled workers in the cities. One machine now shells as much corn in an hour
and a half as a farm laborer could, by hand, in twenty days.

More than three fourths of all rural people carry water from wells,
have outdoor toilets, use kerosene lamps, have neither bathtubs nor
showers, neither electricity nor radios.

Doctors in rural areas are growing older and fewer, while health
problems multiply. Recent graduates of medical schools do not come
to rural districts.

Lack of jobs, delayed marriages, loafing, drinking and petty gambling are boring at the lives of rural young people. Between two
and three millions of them are dammed up on the home farms, with
neither opportunities nor facilities to train themselves for new
occupations, nor incentives to follow their parents' way of life.
The outlets they find for themselves bring complications into family
situations which probably are not unique to rural life but which are
certainly baffling.

Now, of course, a rural person goes at his problems in his own
peculiar way. I recall old Tim Smithers, who lived on a ranch in
an arid district, seven miles from the nearest well. For years he
carried water in barrels loaded on his old ox-cart. One day someone
said, "Tim, why don't you dig yourself a well nearer home? Seven
miles is a mighty long way to draw water." "Well," replied Tim,
"there aint much difference; it's just as far down as acrost."

Rural social workers, too, must go at their problems realistically
in terms of the situation, resources available, and their own abilities. Because rural work is different—and it really is, Miss Bailey
—I was glad to know this past summer of a job analysis being made
of the duties of county social workers in rural areas. I received
a copy of the check list of duties which I understand was sent to a
number of rural county directors in all the states. I suspect that
a good many others were as surprised as I was when I counted up how
many of these duties were a part of my daily work. I'd never really
thought about it before.

This list had 528 duties a county social worker might have to do.
When I finished checking I found I was doing 371 of them. I felt a

little ashamed to have to check so many, and I know that I don't do any of them as well as I'd like to. Yet the fact remains. I actually have 371 duties which I must do myself, or must see to getting done.

Let me run over a few of them, starting off with case work for all the welfare services—including old age assistance, aid to dependent children, the blind, crippled children, maternal and child health, direct relief, WPA, CCC, NYA and transients. For these we have the duties of intake, home visits, case records, budgeting, correspondence and treatment.

Then there are community contacts with school and church people, government officials, county commissioners, bankers, editors, the Rotary and Kiwanis clubs, the Masons, the Farm Bureau, and chamber of commerce, the Red Cross chapter, and the PTA, as well as women's clubs and client groups. And that isn't all of them by a long chalk. A county worker can't turn around or open her mouth without making a community contact, and if she doesn't realize it at first she soon will.

Also, we who are responsible for the functioning of the office must hunt for office space—often catch-as-catch-can in rural parts—must equip it with desks and chairs, must set up our own filing system, hire and train clerks, and supervise and train case work assistants.

Finally, we must be available for conferences with supervisors and state and federal officials, must attend training institutes and prepare regular weekly, monthly and yearly statistical and narrative reports, to say nothing of special reports.

As I said before, I checked 371 duties on the list sent to me but the more I think about it, the more I realize that the actual number of tasks is many times 371, for the simple naming of any one duty does not give a picture of the actual work involved in discharging or even in tackling it. One duty brings on a whole flock of others which by no stretch of the imagination can be foreseen.

For example, in the matter of correspondence for aid to dependent children, take just one case, call it the Smith family. There were eight dependent children, none of whom had been registered at birth. To get the births legally verified and so to establish their eligibility for ADC it was necessary to write twenty-six letters and they couldn't be form letters either. Each one had to be framed to meet the mind of the person from whom we wanted the information. It took us from September 7, 1937 to May 10, 1938, to round up all the verifications of birth of those eight Smith children, all of whom had so undeniably been born.

Then, consider the matter of verifying the age of Sarah Jones, applicant for old age assistance. But I won't take your time to tell that, Miss Bailey. You can imagine, though, our dismay when our letters and visits turned up ten different ages for her, when all we wanted was a verification of one age.

In the matter of community contacts, I had to make twenty-two in one month in order to get one child to a hospital for needed treatment. These contacts included clinics, hospitals, doctors, relatives, landlord, the chairman of the Red Cross chapter, the Sunday School superintendent, a county commissioner, the treasurer of a Bible class, the rural postman, a Traveler's Aid worker, a bus company, and so on. Many of them were necessary to raise $15 for the expense of the trip to the hospital, and several of them to secure the consent of the parents for the treatment.

In addition to all the regular services, we have many miscellaneous duties, including that of arranging for county burials. One cold morning I was routed out of bed about four o'clock by word that the night watchman for the last shipment of government pigs had had a stroke and had fallen into a pen. The whole thing was pretty awful and in the midst of all the horror the undertaker had to be persuaded to make a reduced price for caring for what was left of the watchman. Rural work brings an acceptance of the hazards of life, and we learn to do what we have to do.

Rural social workers long have felt the need for special skills to help them not only with case work but with office management, personnel supervision, publicity, writing, community organization, budgeting, clerical procedures and group leadership. Skills for us, however, must be based on an understanding of the realities of rural life. For example, the rural county director must know the essentials of clerical work since rural districts seldom can produce any trained or experienced office workers. I remember when Mamie Lou came in to do our filing: she was not stumped by her new job; she simply lumped all correspondence in two files, labelled starkly, Mail We Sent, and Mail We Got. When any letter had to be located, the trick was to remember whether it was "Sent" or "Got."

As to group leadership, I don't know of any book that could prepare a social worker for the kind of things we meet in a rural community. Books give us philosophy, of course, and an idea of basic techniques, but it takes practice and quick thinking and gumption to start with to adapt them to our circumstances.

One bitterly cold night I went out to Prairie View, a little settlement on the edge of our county, to talk over certain new government regulations. The meeting place was an abandoned one-room depot where a pot-bellied, hot-blast stove furnished the heat. A table for me was at one end with chairs in rows down the length of the room. As the hot-blast stove went into action, the people near it began to mop their faces, while those near the loosely boarded walls were blowing on their chilly fingers. Soon there was much moving about and changing of seats and, of course, inattention. I was slow to comprehend that this was a cooperative demonstration of sharing the heat and the cold. I despaired of the success of the meeting until I thought up a group technique of my own to keep people hot and cold in the same places at the same time. We moved the chairs into a circle around the stove, and thus achieved some integration, a uniform heat-in-the-front and cold-in-the-back condition, which is the best you can do with a hot-blast stove.

While individual rural social workers are contributing valuable techniques in their own situations, these are not known generally by rural social workers as a group. To retain the best in developing practice and to evolve better and more scientific procedures, we must engage in that good old-fashioned, sometimes belittled, business of cooperation.

We need to pool our experiences. The greatest contribution to interpretation of the needs and skills of rural social work will undoubtedly come from the workers themselves. Some of them already have developed techniques for reducing burdensome routine and detail, others have worked out office forms, plans for study groups, and programs of in-service staff training. Our days are too busy, our lives too full of pressing obligations, to tackle every problem in a trial and error fashion. We need the benefit of the experience of other rural social workers, both successes and failures.

We could profit from an exchange of ideas on the best books for rural workers. We'd like to hear from workers who have honestly read and applied the material they have found in professional literature. Eventually we might arrive at a worthwhile "five-foot shelf" of books for rural social workers. Recently I attended a meeting of a newly formed association of rural workers who were trying to decide what books would be most helpful to buy with their limited funds. One worker read over the titles of a number of books advertised and reviewed in *Survey Midmonthly*, hoping that someone present might be able to advise which of the books would be helpful in the particular problems of the group. It was possible to tell these workers about many government bulletins and other pamphlets with material that bears on their area of work. I wish that we might have clearer and more comprehensive descriptive statements—reviews if you like—of such bulletins and pamphlets so that rural social

workers could determine quickly which ones are most practical for
their purposes. A lot of time and effort is spent now in "spearing
around."

Another thing we need is ideas and suggestions for programs for
client association meetings, for young people's forums, for "Old Age"
parties, as well as lists of simple games and other aids to rural
good times.

I am convinced that the stuff of real literature is present in the
happenings in rural social work and that this should not be lost to
our culture. The workers sense the drama and the significance in
this day-to-day work, and talk about it among themselves. But they
are chary about writing it down—or perhaps too busy. Is there not
some way to encourage them to write realistically about rural life as
they are experiencing it, and of the job of rural social work as it
is developing?

Finally, the question arises, how are we to achieve this contribution and cooperation by rural social workers? You, Miss Bailey, always understanding of client problems, will appreciate our need.
Could you persuade the "powers that be" to give the problems of rural
social work a little space in *Survey Midmonthly*? Couldn't you ask
the workers themselves what are the things they find most difficult
to cope with and then give us a chance to discuss them in our own
way out of our own experience? Somewhere, between the skyscrapers
of urban social work, there must be a place for us to conserve our
grass roots!

But now the glory of a prairie sunset fills the sky. I declare
I've written more than I intended, but you know how it is once one
gets going. Let us hear from you, Miss Bailey!

PUBLICITY BY WAY OF THE BARN DOOR

Josephine Strode

> This is the second of a series of articles by Miss Strode on
> "the process and problems of social work where the county is
> the unit of administration and practice runs out over the back
> roads to the villages and remote farms." Material for this
> article was contributed by workers in thirty-nine western
> Kansas counties and was written originally by Miss Strode for
> a session of the Social Work Publicity Council at the Seattle
> meeting of the National Conference of Social Work.

When a teacher of social work first came to our district she asked
us what books we had for study. Did we have Social Diagnosis?
Changing Psychology in Social Work? The Art of Helping People Out
of Trouble? We did not! Did we have *The Survey* or *The Family?* We
did not! Finally in despair she asked, "Well, what books do you
have?" In the middle of a general silence one of our members spoke
up. "Lady," he said, "there's one book we all have that you can
count on, and that's a Sears Roebuck catalogue."

So it is now, when we are asked about our publicity methods. Probably a good many unorthodox particles of hay stick out from them,
but for all that we know that publicity for Main Street is not so
different from that for Fifth Avenue. The catch is in knowing how,
when, and where to put the emphasis.

This matter of emphasis recalls a story about William Allen White.
It seems that at a dinner party someone told of a family, in the
covered-wagon days, that was spending the night in Missouri before
going on to Kansas. That night when the child in the family said
her prayers, she concluded with "Good-bye God, I'm going to Kansas."
Mr. White took up the challenge. What the child very likely had
said, he insisted, was, "Good, by-God, I'm going to Kansas." Just
a matter of emphasis.

The welfare services for which rural social workers seek publicity
are essentially the same, of course, as those in urban areas; and
rural publicity has the same two-fold aim of bringing information
to the people and of promoting their understanding of the program,
thereby insuring their cooperation with it. Likewise the tools of
publicity are essentially the same in rural areas as in urban centers: talks with individuals, speeches, newspaper articles, radio,
community councils, case committees, reports and so on. How those
tools are used constitutes the distinctive difference between rural
and urban publicity, a difference that grows out of the very nature

of rural existence itself and what it does to the minds and life of
the people. Before a rural social worker attempts to plan or to engage in publicity she must be very sure that she understands clearly
the basis for and the nature of rural consciousness and rural conduct.

An important consideration in any program of rural publicity is
the tempo of rural life. Things can't be done in a hurry. Farmers
are accustomed to waiting six months or longer for a crop. In western Kansas, we've been waiting six years!

When the county commissioners come to town to consider welfare
matters, or any other county affairs, they drive in, stop at the gro-
cer's to leave their milk and eggs, drop in at the corner drugstore
for a chin with the boys, leave word at Aunt Mary's about coming out
to dinner next Sunday, and finally, around ten or eleven o'clock,
turn up at the courthouse. Here sitting around a big table—or like
as not, in the small counties, around a big pot-bellied stove in a
room over the hardware store—they prop up their feet for leisurely
consideration of any matters needing their official attention. But
they're in no hurry about it. Frequently there'll be silences of
many minutes, broken occasionally by such general remarks as "Well,
looks like another Methodist crop this year." (To the uninitiated, a
Methodist crop is one which is saved by a "sprinkling.") Townspeople
come in and out to swap bits of news and ask questions; it may be an
hour or so before the commissioners get around to the business of
the meeting.

The wise social worker with a proposition to put before these men
learns to take it easy and to wait. If she has the "feel" of the
tempo of rural life she'll enjoy the leisure, the humor, the back-
chat, and be so much a part of the situation that the commissioners
will not be conscious of her as an outsider. But let her get fidgety
or restive, or press her point by talking too much, and her proposition will not get a hearing let alone approval. It will die aborning.

I recall a man from a large midwestern school of social work who
came out to us to supervise. He was quick-thinking, executive, and
accustomed to pushing his program and getting things done. Before
his first meeting with the commissioners we cautioned him about taking his pace from theirs and he really tried to slow down. But the
experience was painful for him. He was amazed to discover how long
county commissioners can "jes' set."

What this man didn't appreciate, of course, was that the commissioners weren't "jes' settin'." They undoubtedly were "sensing" him
out just as surely as if they had asked him a flood of questions.
He was accustomed, probably, to getting acquainted with people by
talking with them, but rural people appraise a person by means of

some inexplicable feeling about him. The farmer learns to feel things about the weather, his cattle, his crops, the land, and the winds. They can't talk to him, so he has to sense their meaning. Likewise with people, the farmer is deliberate and slow in his approach to acquaintance. He gets to know people largely through his feelings for them and the reaction of his organism as a whole toward them. His silences are as pregnant with meaning as his speech and he is not impressed by a flow of words. It takes few words, simple, direct, meaty in substance, and based on good hard facts, to touch him.

A recent book by Stuart Chase, The Tyranny of Words, surely illustrates a point about rural people. He says that for words to have any real sense to a listener they must have "referents," that is the listener must be conscious of the thing or happening to which the words refer. Anyone who has listened to the talk of rural people knows how rich in referents their words are. I remember hearing a county sheriff say that he couldn't walk "hawk and buzzard." It took me some time to figure out that one. You see when a hawk attacks, he darts straight, swift, sure, direct to his prey. A buzzard, however, circles slowly in great deliberate circles, descending gradually on his prey.

Publicity experts stress the importance to interpretation of knowing the language of a community. The problem goes deeper than that in a rural community, because in order to understand the speech, you have to know the life.

Rural people are upstanding, accustomed to dealing with their own problems. When your nearest neighbor is ten or twenty miles away, you think and act for yourself and you learn to be mighty resourceful about it. Just the same we social workers, it seems to us, can learn a lot from the way these people help themselves and each other. Cooperation and interdependence are the very fabric of their life.

As Josh Lee says, "Folks that have lived on oxtail soup and beef tongue to make both ends meet" are pretty apt to have something worthwhile to contribute to the business of budget-making. A farmer who has had his living wiped out by a summer of drought, or his cattle frozen in one cold night of winter, or his stand of wheat eaten up by grasshoppers is going to be able to stand up under the shock of learning the limitations and restrictions of the welfare program. Furthermore, he usually can give the worker some mighty good pointers on how to eke out county allotments, whether of work, commodities, or money.

Not only is the rural citizen capable of solving his own problems but he so has the habit of thinking things out from scratch that he wants to know all the facts on which our social work policies are based. It is not enough to tell him that because of the financial condition, relief allotments can be only so much. He'll want to know all about that financial condition, how much it is and why it is, and how come it isn't enough. Living kind of simple, as we rural folk do, our mental apparatus isn't very complex, and we think pretty much in terms of the ABC's of everything. Like children we ask plenty of direct questions because we want to know all about things, and we've got plenty of time to find out.

Because of their roots in our democratic pioneer life, our rural people dislike class distinctions and anything that makes for differences, such as strangeness in dress or speech, or in ways of doing things. They are particularly sensitive to insincerity or artificiality. A worker from the state office once came out to a far western county in Kansas to persuade the county commissioners to hire a trained social worker from "outside." This particular county is in the heart of the dust bowl. Heavy black blizzards are almost daily occurrences in the dust season, and the morning on which the state worker arrived at the county seat was the morning after a particularly heavy, dirty storm. Coming in on an air-conditioned train, the state worker was turned out all in spotless white. The chairman of the county commissioners, an ex-cattle baron and ranch owner who had ridden the range as a cowboy from Denver to the Rio Grande, tells the story:

> Here, she comes along, all purty as my wife's pet duck after a swim—white shoes, white hat, white dress, everything white! "My good man," sez she, "my good man, can you tell me where I'll find the chairman of the county commissioners?" Me—there I was black an' dirty from the dust, sweepin' up the hallway of the court house so folks could get through the dust without wadin'. I looked like the janitor would'a looked, I reckon, if we'd had one! "My good man," sez she again, chokin' on the dust I was raisin' with my sweepin', "where would I find the chairman of your county board?" I never stops sweepin'; an' raisin' more and more clouds of dust, I sez to her, "I jes' been up to his office, Ma'm, and he ain't there!"

When a rural social worker understands somewhat the pattern and psychology of rural life, she can use some of the usual channels of publicity. In leadership at community councils she keeps to the spirit of rural living. Her speech, dress, and tempo of activity is gauged by the place, the people, the occasion. She is frank, sincere, detailed, thorough, vivid in her presentations. She leaves the responsibilities for decisions with the people, and, if she is intelligent, furnishes just enough leadership of an inconspicuous sort to get them working together cooperatively.

In newspaper and radio publicity, the social worker bears in mind the feeling of rural people toward too much talk. In regions where practically all the people have suffered severe hardships, pathetic case stories are in bad taste. Tragedy and pathos come close to all of them, and they are not accustomed to talking about their own troubles or feelings. Rural people are like the two Englishmen who, in silence, were viewing a sunset in the Alps. Finally one of them said, "Not a bad sunset, that." "No," said the other, "but no need to get so bally sentimental about it."

There is really very little that a rural social worker actually can say in words to get help for tragic cases. Some of us have found the best way to gain the cooperation of a group is to ask some member of it to drive out with her to the home of the particular case. Not a word need be spoken; once the case is seen the neighborly response is immediate, substantial, heartwarming. The technique may not be according to Rule No. 711, but it gets results.

There are times when cases need to be interpreted to the rural community as a whole, but as a rule case committees, as city social workers know them, have not proved successful. The reason for this, it seems to us, is that the community as a whole is in itself a natural case committee by reason of everyone's intimate acquaintance with everyone else and with everything that goes on in and around the town. Some of our workers do their best case committee work at women's clubs, sewing circles and card parties. When a group of women meets to sew for missions, or whatever, the history and conduct of some of our problem clients are discussed with a freedom which would startle an orthodox case committee. By being present at some of these gatherings, the social worker can, if she is skilful, drop a word here and there and lead the gossip around to points that she wants to emphasize.

It is generally good strategy for rural social workers to confer with people in the fields or in their homes, rather than to try to get them into town for committee meetings. A man on our staff used to carry his lunch in a paper package when he went into the country on visits. He'd eat it while he talked with a farmer in the field, or while the two of them sat and talked on the porch at noontime. The quiet of the leisurely country noon hour is conducive to the discussion of pressing problems with a minimum of words. Here again "jes' settin'" isn't all it seems to be.

Frequently we secure our best cooperation through indirection, by personal contacts or friendly services. One of our county directors got an operation for the mother of the town twins by spending the evening in the swing on the mayor's porch, talking town gossip with the mayor's wife to the music of the katydids. Another worker won over the local newspaper by writing the obituary notices for the editor.

Some of our social workers have cashed in on chance happenings, taken with good will and humor. One of them still laughs about the day when a big burly farmer barged into the office with blood in his eye. He'd come after a work order, and was going to get it or "break every winder and pipe in the d____ building!" Wishing to appear at ease until the man had finished his tirade, the worker teetered back in her chair. Zoom! the chair shot out from under her and she folded up between the wall and the desk. The man laughed, and she laughed; and after he had helped her up, they laughed some more. He apologized for scaring her and listened to what she had to say. Since then they've been the best of friends, and the man is now a staunch supporter of the welfare program.

A rural worker must have not only a clear social philosophy and know her social work techniques and programs but, if she is to interpret those techniques and programs and gain support for them, she must be knowledgeable about the physical setting and the state of mind in which they must be rooted. She must know more than a little about plowing, planting and marketing, about the granges, the 4-H clubs, the cooperatives, and the farm labor movements. She must know a combine from a threshing machine, a go-devil from a disc. She must know the life that goes through the barn door as well as what passes through her office.

It is said that when prosperity comes back, it will come through the barn door. Certainly, if rural social work publicity is to succeed, it must approach through the barn door of reality.

LEARNING FROM THE JOB

Josephine Strode

Out in the cornfields of case work practice, rural social workers are learning on the job. They are learning how to do from having to do, which is true education. Their learning, however, springs from

Survey, December 1938.

experiences and a way of life very different from those of the urban
social workers. It is the difference of the rolling sweep of countryside, fenced in by winds, sky and sun, and the constricted tenements, walled in by the smokestacks of industry and serried by tragic
deprivations and disease.

Our very approach to our day's work is different. See the city
social worker breakfast on coffee and toast, as often as not at the
corner drugstore, then push her way into a crowded bus or street
car—lucky if she can grab a strap before someone else gets it.
Watch the rural worker, on the other hand, as she breakfasts on liberal country fare—we still like our hotcakes and sausages and do
not hold very much with the notions of "continental breakfast"—
before she pushes off down the road in her old jalopy.

When the urban worker reaches her office she, likely as not, must
wind through a maze of windowless partitions, until she comes to the
stall devoted to the segment of social service which is her job.
Here she concentrates on the specific difficulties of the clients
that fall within her segment, somewhat as a scientist scrutinizes
the specimen under his microscope. She will not, it is true, think
of her client apart from his family and possibly his setting, but
her concern seldom goes beyond that. The problems of community interpretation and cooperation, and of administration of policies and
procedures are dealt with largely by executives located in other
stalls remote from the scene of her day-to-day job. She has little
to do actually with the framework within which she functions.

The rural social worker has no segments in her job. She must be
administrator, community interpreter and organizer, as well as case
worker for a multiplicity of social services. As a matter of fact,
rural workers say they have so many things to do that by the time
they have figured out how to do them, they have no time left to
analyze what they are doing. In other words, they say, they have
so much to think about that there is seldom time to think what they
are thinking about!

That is one of the reasons, I believe, why rural social workers,
out on the firing line of challenging, pioneer jobs, hesitate to
contribute to formal discussions of social work to the extent of
their practical knowledge and ability. Analyses of theory, piece by
piece, bit by bit, leave us pretty cold. "So what?" we ask ourselves, as we turn back to figuring out how to get old man so-and-so
to patch his roof before winter—meantime taking no part in the conversation. Another plausible reason why we have been backward in
putting ourselves forward is, I believe, the growing emphasis on the
importance of professional study at a school of social work. Now
any rural social worker worth her salt would like nothing better

than to get away for a year of two of study, but given the circumstances of her life and the exigencies of her job she might as well reach for the moon. Just the same, the constant hammering on the *sine qua non* of formal professional education does get under our skin and often leads us to hold back in the presence of our presumable betters.

No school or college claims to accomplish the entire education of any individual student, and no school of social work claims to furnish the complete training of a social worker. The best that any school can do is to equip a worker with tools which are not ends in themselves, but useful only as they serve the situations to which they are applied. Delicately wrought tools wrongly applied are sometimes much less useful than "homemade" ones. The young worker whose psychiatric conjectures raised a fine lather of possibilities as to why Mellie Griffiths was always too early or too late for appointments failed to discover the simple fact that Millie had no clock.

In the rapidly changing world of social work, formal professional education—and this is not to belittle it—cannot be geared to equip all social workers with all the knowledge and techniques needed to administer the broadening area of social services in varying situations. A large part of the education of social workers today, even those coming out of the professional schools, must and does take place on the job.

To make this education on the job valuable both to worker and work, we rural workers must shed our inferiority over lack of formal training and turn our minds to the meaning of all that we experience as we go along. Only thus will we acquire the judgment and ability to decide and act in terms of situations, in short to shape our tools to our necessities.

When a worker thinks through the reasons for success or failure in a situation, she begins to shape her tools. I recall a worker in our county who, after many successful meetings with a community council, was suddenly faced with failure. The people were quiet; discussion lagged; there was none of the usual cheerful, hearty give and take. Puzzled, she suddenly realized that all former meetings had been held in the school assembly room, while this one was in the church. The people were not accustomed to participating in what went on in church and the worker had not been able to break through this conditioning. Thereafter, you may be sure that in arranging a meeting she considered the possible effect of environment—which is a good group work tool for any social worker's kit.

A rural social worker who was unable to get the interest of his community group told me how he finally figured out the reason for his failure. He knew all about the value of cooperation, and the necessity of carrying the community and the county commissioners with him, but his most ingratiating efforts fell flat. It was only as he thought through his failure that he realized he had been trying to carry the group along in *his* way, instead of facilitating the group thinking from which—and only from which—could come true group decisions. He was able to see that there could be no sense of real participation in any group that merely followed his or any one person's ideas. Thus from studying through his failure, this worker arrived at sound conclusions as to the value of group interaction and its product, creative thinking.

In addition to critical analyses of experience and performance, we rural workers need to be critical of reading material. All too frequently we accept the printed page as a guarantee of infallibility. When we find that our experience does not coincide with the professional text, we are apt to assume that we are at fault. We need to have confidence in the value of our own experience, and to have the courage to test social theories critically in the light of it.

A study group of rural workers found that the method of having reports on books brought in by individual members was unsatisfactory. The members listened to the reports but did not seem to reflect on them, or to relate the content to their own experience. As an experiment each member purchased a copy of the same book, so that it could be studied critically page by page. They took six months to read and discuss one book on interviewing, but every meeting was an exciting event with every statement of the author analyzed and sometimes challenged, and every theory examined in the light of experience. New theories were tested in practice, and reports made on the results. I suspect that few social work texts ever have been analyzed and tested more rigorously by students and practitioners. I always have wished that the authors of that particular book might have sat in at the dissection. It would have been by way of education to them, as it was to the study group.

In spite of many limitations in the way of formal educational resources, rural social workers have rich opportunities to learn. There is something so real and simple, and yet so wise, about rural people that every contact with them is instructive—yes, even in such a matter as courtesy. A rural worker conferring with a county commissioner noticed a blackened pipe on the floor beside his chair. She called attention to it, thinking he had dropped it. "Let it lay, Ma'm," he said, "I'm sore tempted to smoke if it's in my hand, and I don't want to do you the dishonor of smoking in your presence."

Sage counsel and good technique may be gained from clients who have
had to think through their own situations for many years in the face
of almost insurmountable difficulties. At a meeting of social workers, which had been announced in the local papers, a client appeared
—a tall, rugged, weather-beaten, old ranger. "Ladies," he said,
"pardon me, but I heard about this meetin' where you're thinkin'
what to do for us folks on relief. It come to my mind that the best
way you folks could help us is to get us together, and then help us
to figger through for ourselves."

Aware of rural people's sensitivity to artificiality and unneighbor-
liness, the rural worker easily learns to watch his own "little ways."
The man from the city who hung a "Do Not Disturb" sign on his office
door for several hours every day, in order to work uninterruptedly,
soon found himself the object of a buzz of gossip and learned to do
his work with all doors and even windows wide open. The district
worker who installed a buzzer signal system in his office, discontinued it when he saw that it affronted the democratic sensitivities of
his helpers.

Because of the multiplicity and complexity of their duties, rural
social workers learn to share and delegate responsibility. In order
to survive in their jobs, they must have the capacity participation
of their staffs. Take the matter of office management, for example.
A county director found herself so swamped with office detail that
she was able to do little else. Her three office assistants, local
highschool girls, showed small interest and less responsibility in
their work. But when the director put the office problems before
them as a group responsibility and invited each girl to contribute
to their solution, the young workers responded. In a short time
the office management required little more than general supervision
from the director.

Because rural life is elemental, the rural worker learns to think
in terms of pretty basic values. There is the matter of local
leadership, for example. A city worker may go through life believing that leadership rests with certain traditional "key" people;
prominent business men, newspaper "philanthropists," big contributors, scions of "old families," high officials, and so on. Nothing
can happen without those certain people, she holds, while at the
same time admitting that very often not much happens with them. In
rural parts, however, leadership never is static. Of course, education and position carry prestige and the cultural pattern of a particular group often has weight. But the reactions of the led are
clearly in evidence in rural communities and often create a shift
in leadership values to which the social worker must be alert if
she is to capitalize them.

When a state supervisor asked a county worker to call a meeting of the "key" people in the community to discuss certain policies, the rural worker asked, "Key to what?" The banker is an important person and no doubt holds the "key" to a lot of farm mortgages, but the farmers themselves are the important "key" to their own problems. The president of the Ladies Aid Society in the county seat is not a "key" to what the farmers' wives think and feel.

As her education on the job progresses the rural social worker discovers that the artistry of leadership lies in ability to let initiative unfold in a group, within the demands of the situation. She may call a meeting and present problems, but she will not expect dominant personalities to push her program, nor gain objectives for her. She will let leadership, whether it be of ideas, mores, individuals or groups, arise naturally in the situation, within the self-determined objectives of the group itself. If she furnishes any personal leadership, it will be in the form of a contribution from her experience and understanding.

We rural social workers have to get our social work education more or less on the run, out of the job itself, by reflection on its whats and whys, and by continuous critical examination of our own functioning in relation to the feelings and attitudes of clients, co-workers and community. We do not have to go away to school to get it; it is right under our noses from morning till night. In our daily experience is the stuff of real education, with the key to its acquisition our own capacity to know it when we see it, and to take it, even on the run.

BEEF, PRUNES AND INK BLOTS AND OTHER ASPECTS OF
AID TO DEPENDENT CHILDREN

Josephine Strode

As a county worker with 371 assorted social work tasks crowding my
waking hours, I decided to take time out for a little serious thinking about the sixty dependent children on our roster who were eligible for that species of aid promised them under the Social Security
Act. What was being done for them? What could be done for them?
They couldn't vote, they had no lobby or means of organized pressure,
no notion at all about the efficacy of "telegraph your congressman
today." Yet here they were, sixty children for whom I, by reason of
my job, had definite responsibilities. Sixty children living with
anxious mothers or harassed relatives in dug-outs, in crumbling sod-
dies, in wind-scoured shacks on the edge of town or on debilitated
farms. Sixty children with inadequate food, insufficient clothing,
no medical care, no suitable recreation, and without the security
in their environment needed for their mental and emotional development. What could I do for them? I made up my mind to examine the
whole problem and situation as realistically and objectively as possible, and not to spare myself.

Was I honestly doing anything more than giving out the just-enough-
to-keep-'em-alive beef and prunes? On the level, was my case work
skill anything more than a pleasing bedside manner in the bestowal
of an inadequate relief allowance? With all my bundle of good intentions and my professional social work training, was my only ges-
ture one of welcome to a small, uncertain spot in the public relief
picture? Was I anything more than a dispenser of a palliative something, to which I added weak exhalations of my own personality when
confronted with obvious material and emotional needs? Was my job to
shake up bromo-seltzers of case work theory and methodology to ease
client tensions, the while my eyes and mind were closed to social
ills and remedial inadequacies? In other words, was I providing any
degree of leadership to help these sixty children gain their rightful
heritage? With my own personal inadequacies, the limitations of
rural social resources, the restrictions of governmental agency regulations, and all the hazards and insecurity of economic and political
changes, was there anything to do over and above the routine job of
establishing eligibility to receive a few dollars a month for beef
and prunes?

Survey, March 1939.

In facing the situation, I was determined not to overlook anything to help me do my job better. I got out the notes I had taken in a course on Child Care and Development, and scanned the headings: "Children's feeding problems in relation to food aversions in the family;" "Thumb sucking from the psychiatric angle;" "Child training for international intelligence;" "A comparative study of fourteen socially well-adjusted children with their maladjusted siblings," and so on. I was annoyed; how could all this gear in with the needs and problems of my sixty dependent children? After all, they had no food aversions, except aversions to having too little. I sighed as I thought of the professor with the aloofness of mind and the time and wherewithal to make an extensive comparative study of fourteen socially well-adjusted children and their not so well-adjusted sisters and brothers, but all of them probably with plenty to eat and wear.

I returned to my notes. Surely I would find something helpful. What's this? Oh yes, ink blots! The Rorschach method of personality description. Not so long ago, it seems, one Rorschach, a Swiss psychiatrist, developed a series of ink blots which he used as basis for a "descriptive dynamics of personality." When a subject comes to the examiner, he is handed, one at a time, ten large cards with meaningless blots of varying size, form and shadings of color. As the subject describes what he sees in the ink blots, the examiner takes down every word he says and notes his non-verbal responses. If the subject sees only outline or color there is a certain conclusion as to his personality; if he sees shadows or animal forms the examiner is apt to spot insecurity in his emotional pattern.

This was too much; I closed my notebook. From the thumb-suckers of Riverside Drive to personality descriptions via the ink blots of a Swiss psychiatrist was a long and diverting jump, but I still had the survival problems of my sixty children. It came to me then, with blinding clarity, that I had large ink blots of my own—dense, black ones—to resolve and interpret in addition to the fairly simple beef-and-prunes outline of mere existence for these dependent children.

There is little in published material on child welfare to prepare a county worker for the menacing ink blots which confront and obstruct when she would reach out to do something constructive for dependent children. This is true particularly in such matters as housing, foster-home care, education and recreation, and in efforts to secure the necessary community understanding, cooperation and support; and such material as there is offers less, I fear, to help the worker hold on to the vision, as she looks at these ink blots, of a square deal for all dependent children.

Take, for example, the matter of housing for dependent children in a rural county. The romantic glamour of pioneer experience still hangs over many of our worst dwellings. That dark, crumbling, smoke impregnated soddy, housing the eight Timken children, was built by the parents of the present chairman of the county commissioners, and he himself was reared in it. While he admits the possibility of deterioration, it is hard to make him face the evidence that the best of virgin-sod bricks may have a way of crumbling after years of drought and strong prairie winds. He has a sentimental fondness for the house and thinks the Timkens are privileged to be living there.

The more abstract, psychological factors involved in crowded living are even more difficult to convey and interpret to matter-of-fact rural neighbors. Through many hardships they have learned to make the most of bad situations, and to them it seems personal weakness on the part of the social worker to want to change the environment of relief clients rather than to insist that they rise superior to it.

The difficulty here, as ever, is what we can do about it. Looking back over my own attempts to "rouse" the community, I can see that most of them were of the "tear-jerking" variety, the "ain't it awful the crowded way they live" sort of thing, which raises nothing but a lot of emotional calluses on the community conscience.

A method of handling the question of living accommodations for her clients, good because it worked, was figured out by a lone county worker in the Southwest. Being extremely knowledgeable about her community, she made a spot map with every tenant house and farm indicated. In an index file was information about each place, the exact number of rooms, windows, leaks, barns and hen-houses, and the fair rental price for any given place. When any house was vacated, clients in less desirable dwellings were notified; single old ladies in big houses were informed about small houses and big families about larger ones. Demands made of landlords had to be respected because the social worker and the clients stood together in refusing to rent until necessary repairs were made. The social worker conferred with landlords in the matter of rents and did what she could to insure clients' ability to pay. All of which may have violated some theory of the clients' responsibility, but it sure did improve housing conditions for them. As an unexpected by-product the people in the community took cognizance of what she was doing, notified her of vacancies and helped her with recalcitrant landlords.

County workers out on social work frontiers have to make adaptations of their skills to fit pioneer situations. When grass roots are too tangled and tough for the plows of urban social work methodology, we get us a pickaxe and tackle our job realistically. We learn to improvise, to initiate, to change and adapt. Our aim is to achieve with professional conformity if possible, but achievement comes first and if we cannot have both, conformity must go.

In the matter of foster-home placement for our dependent children
we thought to do orthodox case work in securing the best possible
social and emotional environment for them. It was Mrs. Hawley (grain-
elevator Hawley) who gave the first blow to our naïveté. Finding
Mrs. Hawley "over-protective," with strong, unconscious needs for
dominating people and situations, we concluded that she was an "emotional hazard" for little Hubert, her second cousin's child whom she
had "taken in," and we advanced cautiously to remove him from her
influence.

"Well! Of all things!! The very idea!!!" She, Mrs. Hawley, the
widow of pioneer, grain-elevator Hawley, had never heard of such a
business! Just barely in time we remembered that anything unusual in
a small community achieves the status of "national," almost religious
significance. The matter of young Hubert easily could become the
subject for a general town meeting. We saw that if he were removed
summarily from the home of Mrs. Hawley her friends and sympathizers
would rally 'round in a way to make it impossible to do anything
further for Hubert, or for any other children for that matter.

We of the social work staff remained undaunted although our tongues
fairly ached from holding them. We knew that mischievous, noisy,
so-called problem children are hard to keep in foster homes. Foster
parents, as a rule, prefer a docile, quiet child of inoffensive be-
haviour, such as Hubert was fast becoming under the eagle eye of Mrs.
Hawley. We recalled that Hubert had not always been so subdued, and
while I would not say that we set out deliberately to change his
conduct pattern, well, we plotted.

Our professional conscience was clear, however, for had we not
learned in a course in psychiatry that excessive docility has serious
implications, that the "holy terror" who makes his needs and wants
known has thereby achieved a sort of adjustment, while the quiet,
retiring child, introvertive, anxiety-ridden, turns aggressively not
against society but against himself, inducing sickness, poor school
achievement, and worse. We saw clearly that unless something was
done soon for young Hubert he undoubtedly would become a serious
personality problem. With active cooperation from his kindergarten
teacher, and from a few well-selected hoodlum pals, Hubert soon became too much for Mrs. Hawley. She herself came one day to the welfare office to insist, no less, that Hubert be removed from her home.
And for proof that all the efforts on Hubert's behalf were worthwhile, one has only to see "Bert," now on his Uncle John's farm, as
lively a young rascal as ever was.

This business of caring for dependent children is a serious one,
and there is no end to the learning how to do it. There is, for
example, the kind of information we should have before we even think

of placing a child in a foster home. We should know something about his past and present physical, emotional, mental and social life, and the same things about his real parents. We should know about his relationships to his brothers and sisters, and about the behavior patterns laid down in his early conditioning experiences. And then, of course, there is the new home where the entire family must be studied for their probable influence on the child, and their potentialities for helping him emotionally, intellectually, and physically, particularly in their capacity to give him a sense of security, a real feeling of belongingness, free from intense emotional conflict and from tensions due to the worries or anxieties of the foster parents. Perhaps we can't do very much to shunt worry and drive fear from the lives of our dependent children, but if we understand their need for emotional security we sometimes can find ways of fortifying them.

Often because of environmental or social lacks, the rural child presents unique problems. Isolated as so many farm children are, there is grave danger of personal stagnation and even degeneracy, unless stimulating and compensating factors are a part of their experiences. Sociologists have shown how even comparative isolation produces a sort of gelatinoid mental life, which is sometimes mistaken for deficiency in innate intelligence. Unless children are provided with stimulating play and social contacts, they do not achieve the personal growth and develop the creative ability which normally might be theirs. If it is not possible for farm children to have the experience of working and playing with other children, provision should be made for stimulating toys, books and other educational materials. Sometimes, it is true, extreme passivity on the part of country children when play or play materials are presented to them is not due wholly to lack of social experiences. Lack of proper and sufficient food, poor health, affection denied or rejection by parents may be involved.

It is really all very difficult. Sometimes when we think we have figured out a good way to achieve some objective for a dependent child, community pressure or the rules of the agency present obstacles. It never is easy and the best we can do inevitably falls short of what we want and even know how to do. But we are a tough lot, we sod-busters of social work, and little by little our continuing experiences are helping us to improved ways and means of doing more for these children than merely passing out beef and prunes.

But now my time-out for thinking is up, and where have I gotten? Not very far I'm afraid, except as I have fortified my faith that our contribution to this hard perplexing problem must come from our own ingenuity, the quality of our understanding and our never-say-die-ness. To which I would add my conviction that the best interests

of dependent children at the present moment demand that we put aside
notebooks and psychiatric formulations, quit peering at ink blots,
and lift up our voices.

The Social Security Board recently has recommended that federal aid
to dependent children be put on a 50-50 basis, which should bring
milk and, perhaps, cod-liver oil to the beef and prunes account of
your dependent children and mine—over half a million of them—in
the hummocks of the Southland, in the timberlands of the North, in
the mining districts of the East, in isolated counties and in crowded
cities. Children can't vote, but they all have congressmen and so
have you and I. Now is the time for us all to use a technique not
mentioned in any book on social work, nor referred to in any course
on child welfare: Buttonhole Your Congressman! Send a Wire!!

SWINGING THE DEPRESSION WITH THE KILLER-DILLERS, HOT-SHOTS,
AND ALLIGATORS

Josephine Strode

There's a "Hot Club" of young people in our county, and we social
workers are learning to "swing it." As they say, we're in the groove
with the killer-dillers, hot-shots, and alligators at every jam session and jitter-bug jamboree! Yes siree! We've trimmed the long
hairs from our case work methods and gone modern! In plain English,
for those who have a BS (before swing) social work education, we are
streamlining our thinking and our techniques to keep up with the
young folks.

It was a crumpled piece of paper, dropped by Ernie Padgett, which
started it all. As far as young people were concerned, we had been
worrying along in a kind of primordial haze of good intentions and
case work compunctions. We had the habit of excusing ourselves; we
were busy enough administering benefits under the Social Security Act
to little children, the crippled, the blind, and the aged. Anyway
the young folks seemed to expect nothing from us, in fact they rather

Survey, April 1939.

seemed to avoid us, slipping out the back door as we came in the front.

The piece of paper Ernie dropped, and neglected to retrieve, opened up a new world to us social workers, filling to overflowing some of the wide open spaces in our thinking, and causing us painful professional qualms.

It happened the morning Ernie came into the relief office to get the surplus commodities for his mother. We talked a little as he waited for his bundle. He said he sure wished he could get a job, a real job; NYA work was all right, he guessed, but it wasn't real work, and he couldn't seem to take any interest in it; jobs sure were scarce, especially in small towns, and even farmers didn't want a fellow any more. For my part, I contributed the cracked-phonograph-record kind of counsel we turn on for the young, trite admonitions about patience, perseverance, ambition, starting at the bottom, working hard, and if at first you don't succeed, try, try again. The arrival of Ernie's package terminated our dialogue—to our mutual relief. There had been no real conversation, no social interchange; realistically we were poles apart.

Yet I was more than vaguely disturbed; clearly we were failing to meet the challenge of youth's need for guidance and leadership. Bewildered and confused by my own inadequacy, I absent-mindedly smoothed the piece of paper Ernie had dropped. Then I read:

KING CONGO AND HIS CATS AT MACLENNEY CORNERS
Meet His Majesty at Saturday's Jam Session

Out of the world you'll go, jitterbugs and alligators, when that killer-diller King Congo and his Rhythm Cats get into the groove and go to town. Are you hep? His Majesty plays it solid, jive, and schmaltz. Even tin ears ride his hot-licks when he barrel-houses. Long-underwears forget their long-hairs when the King tips his ride-men behind the skins to get the clambake moving with his riffs.
Stop being an ickie, a turkey, a noodler. Pick a cute number, truck to Maclenney Corners and lose that beat feeling!

What was this? Where was I? Yes, this was my desk so it must be I, and there was Mamie Lou at her desk! I turned back to the bit of paper; I read it again, and then again. I called to Mamie Lou. "It's swing talk," she giggled, "about the dance Saturday night," and when I asked her to translate it all for me, she said: "Jeepers creepers, don't social workers know anything about swing? Don't they ever go scooter-poopin'?"

Later that morning we gathered at a staff meeting to talk it all over. Our preoccupation with the problems of the very old and the children had been complete; we had not realized how great was our

unawareness of young people, how far we had drifted away from them
and they from us.

We had read about Youth with a capital Y, about their unemployment,
their restlessness, their delinquency, their drinking, their gambling,
their delayed marriages, and their submergence in the unreal world of
the movies, the radio, and the pulp magazines. We had not realized,
however, the extent of their escape from reality into a dream world,
where even the language was unique. Laughter died in our throats as
we considered the serious implications to the rising generation in
our community of this withdrawal from the actualities of life.

We decided to delay no longer, but to accept the challenge of Youth,
and to tackle the problems of young people in our own county with a
view to doing something constructive for them. To start, we set ourselves three tasks: to study the whole situation with regard to
young people; to review our own local situation; to attend that jam
session of King Congo and His Cats Saturday night and bring our BS
(before swing) education up to date.

We went after the facts about young people and found that there are
twenty million of them in the United States; one sixth of our population, according to the 1930 Census, is between sixteen and twenty-
four years of age. The American Youth Commission tells us that of
the ten million youth who reached employable age during the five-year
period from 1929 to 1934, five million were still unemployed in 1935.
As to the number of young folks now unemployed no one really knows.

A rural expert tells us that by 1940—and that's only next year—
there will be a million more young people in the rural districts
than the million or more who we know were dammed up on the farms in
1930. This does not count the 900,000 or more rural youth who, according to the indication of present trends, will have migrated to
cities and towns during the decade.

Exhaustion of timber and minerals, decline of soil fertility, erosion, regulation and quotas, as well as technological developments,
have reduced the traditional opportunities on the farms, and the
great majority of rural youth have not had the opportunity for education and industrial training to fit them for other occupations. According to studies made by experts, 75 percent of all youth do not
receive anything which could be called guidance, and yet, admittedly,
there never was a time in history when they needed intelligent guidance more than they do right now.

The social problems of youth are largely the outgrowth of lack of
economic and educational opportunities. One large problem which
right now looms with threatening consequences is the use of leisure
time. What are the millions of unemployed and out-of-school youth

doing with their waking time—say sixteen hours a day, 112 hours a week for each one of them? We could find no study which gave us even a ray of light on the mystery. Nor could we find that anyone has presented a plan for constructive use of these hours, the potential value of which is being lost forever to our needy civilization.

The National Youth Administration, in its June 1938 report, states that there is an appropriation of $75 million to care for a possible 600,000 young persons for the year ending June 30, 1939. Of this number 326,644 are needy students, leaving 273,356 youth from relief families to receive part time employment at an average monthly earning of about $14.71 a month (NYA figure for May 1937). The U. S. Employment Service registered in the one and a half years to January 1936, 1,883,000 young people under twenty-one years of age, and found jobs for 831,000 of them—the lowest placement rate for any group aided by the service.

We are prone to think, or rather give it as an excuse for not thinking, that the government is "taking care" of "needy" people, yet these federal services for young people, including the CCC, which offers many boys the temporary opportunity for healthy activity, help not more than probably one fifth of the total of our unemployed youth.

The larger and more important labor unions are not admitting apprentices, and there seems little indication this bar will be lowered in the near future. Some unions, admitting apprentices, charge fees which prove virtual bars; others have fixed the entrance age for apprentices at twenty-one years.

Youth must be turned from the mirage of civil service as an opportunity for one and all. When as many as 200,000 file for a single clerical examination, it would seem that the very heavens must open to strike us in the name of Guidance for Youth. We can't all work for the government and continue to be the democracy we prize. One saving thought is that our youth are seeking security, the security of a job, and are not motivated by a desire to increase the reach of the long arm of government.

In our local situation, what did we find? I must admit that we did more talking about what we do not have then about what we have. We do not have educational facilities to teach new industrial and other occupational skills. Our highschool teaches the traditional academic subjects, year in and year out, and aside from one venture with an anemic commercial course, nothing else. Yet we need in our community carpenters, electric repair men, garage mechanics, a veterinarian, bakers, milliners, landscape gardeners, nursery men, an optician, dressmakers, confectioners. You can't get homemade cake or cookies on our Main Street, except three or four times a year when some church society has a food sale; if your radio or refrigerator needs repair you must wait for an electrician from the nearest city. Our automobile accessory shop recently hired a salesman from a city sixty miles away, when we knew of at least seven young men who could have filled the job satisfactorily if they had been given a six-months course in merchandising and salesmanship. Housewives who want new shrubbery or plants for their lawns or gardens write to mail order concerns, or travel miles to neighboring counties to get what they want.

For the first time we were doing some real thinking about our local employment situation, and we realized that a thoroughgoing study should be made of the opportunities for our youth, the training needed to fit them for these opportunities, as well as of the aptitudes, potentialities, desires, and ambitions which are the contribution of the young people themselves.

To date there has been little attempt to relate school experiences to the life situations which rural youth face today. This also is true, apparently, of schools in metropolitan centers, where greater school funds permit of wider curricula, for Homer P. Rainey of the American Youth Commission tells us that society's efforts to bridge the gap between school and employment for students are not successful, the wasted years extending from two to five.

And for the leisure time of our unemployed youth, what did we have? We have nothing in our county in the way of organized community recreation for any of our young people, and the consequence is that they seek artificial and commercial amusements at nearby towns. The unemployed youth seek the same, regardless of whether they can afford it, or take to the open road, with their thumbs as their passports.

The churches, the Grange, and the Farm Bureau are falling short of enlisting participation of the mass of rural youth. Prof. Paul H. Douglas pointed out some years ago that such agencies as the YMCA, the YWCA, the Boy Scouts, the Girl Scouts, the Camp Fire Girls, and some church organizations do little for rural young people; his conclusion was that what is needed is a special leisure time program for rural boys and girls, rather than the extension of the work of these agencies, which neither traditionally nor practically are geared to fit the rural scene. Also, we know that, proportionately, few of the children from rural families ever get to highschool, or benefit from 4-H club activities.

In our county we found that we had assets in the persons of our highschool principal and three of the teachers, who all were anxious to do something constructive for our young people. We promptly invited them to meet with us. They brought along what books they had on guidance for youth. Carrers, Opportunity, Vocational Hygiene, and Guiding Our Children were some of the titles. We read from several of them. They were as far removed from the realities of the life situations of our young people as fairy stories. Is it sense to tell a young man who has never tried himself in a job and who has been looking for work—any kind of work—for two years, that he must analyze his aptitudes and interests (which he can't do anyhow without professional help), that he must only take a job which he is sure he will like, which promises steady employment at a living wage, and which offers opportunity to win promotion? Of what help to a young man or woman today is a volume of success stories of the hardy individualists of our pioneer days? Life situations are different today; we no longer can truthfully tell youth that "if you put into your job enough energy you need not worry about the results," that early to bed and early to rise will make you wealthy, or that if you study hard, wash clean, and keep your shoes shined, you will "get there." These and other such formulae have a hollow sound, for we hear the echo as reality laughs.

Young people today want to chew on the red meat of reality; they want a vital job of real work, not made work, whether it be slicing meat, laying rails, selling cheese, or polishing doorknobs. They want the chance to try themselves, to feel their occupational muscles, to use their powers on legitimate, needed tasks.

This is the way our talk ran on at our second meeting. It is remarkable how much clearer thinking becomes and how new ideas pop out when you sit down in a group and, laying aside your cloak of mental conditioning, attack a problem directly and four-square. And we did not spare ourselves. Did we really know what our young people wanted? Had we talked to them, individually or in a group? After all each one of our unemployed youth was a distinct individual. Did we know all the characteristics, the potentialities, the aspirations, the background, the record of each one? We did not. Had we talked to any of their parents about them in a constructive fashion? We had not. Did we even know how many unemployed youth, between sixteen and twenty-four years of age, we had in our county? We did not. In fact the more questions we asked ourselves the more we showed ourselves up. We had very little to be proud of as far as our young people were concerned.

We were on the spot; there could be no turning back now. For the next meeting we decided to bring in some of the parents and a few of the youths themselves. And, if we were going to tackle the problems of jobs for our boys and girls, we must invite some of the business men, like Mr. Simmons of the lumber company, and Mr. Harkness of the electric light plant, and representatives of organizations such as the school board, the Chamber of Commerce, the Rotary Club, the American Legion, the Woman's Club, the churches, our Consumers' Cooperative and the law in the person of the county judge, or the county sheriff.

We are making progress. We no longer gaze vacuously at unemployment statistics, nor shake our heads over the problems of Youth with a capital Y. We now have a Youth Council in our county and we are going to do things for our 124 unemployed out-of-school young people between sixteen and twenty-four years of age. We have plans, also, for community recreation facilities for all our youth. Each unemployed youth is now registered at the office of the Youth Council, and we have a committee at work on a canvass of job possibilities— where they are, what they are, where others might be if our youth had special training, and where they are not but might be and why. With the report of this committee, we feel sure we can win the support of the school board in the interest of industrial and trade courses in our highschool. This will take funds, of course, but the prospects are good for the passage of the Thomas-Larabee Bill now in Congress. This bill would appropriate $899,705,000 for the next six years to bring equality of educational opportunity to the children and young people in all the states by means of grants-in-aid for the improvement of public elementary and secondary schools, for adult education, for rural library service, and for a wide range cooperative educational research and demonstration.

In our county we are attacking ourselves on our own frontier; people talk about the passing of American frontiers, and the end of challenging pioneer days. By taking our heads out of the clouds of economic theories and generalizations, and facing our own situation, we have found that our frontier is right before us and that the enemy facing us is not the Red Indian but our own mental inertia. We still have resources in America, and the greatest are the vast unexplored areas of cooperative action. A new world of culture stands before us with an endless challenge to creative thinking and enterprise. The frontiers for our young people are new and uncharted, but the demands still are for courage, ingenuity, versatility, cooperation and service. We must help them evolve weapons of achievement and give them through intelligent guidance and leadership, confidence and assurance that together we can "Swing this Depression."

To return to the education of our social workers, with their BS training, we went to that jam session, the jitterbug jag, on Saturday night. We were fearful that we might run into some erotic or neurotic manifestations, but it was all quite the contrary. Speed, dash, and good humor were everywhere apparent. The dancing was swift and

strenuous. It was as though the young people sought to shake off
their troubles in a mad frenzy of physical exertion. A placard advertising songs gave us a clue to the escape from reality the young
people sought:

TRY TUNE TONICS

Sing and swing yourself out of your depression; let swing solve
your problems; let it fix your emotions and change your whole
outlook on life; here's a melody for every mood. Are you wist-
ful, are you worried, are you nervous, are you beat? Let Doc
Swing prescribe a musical pill.

We could see nothing particularly harmful in the demonstration of
swing at this jam session; it was merely an escape pill for youth
from life situations which, given their lack of guidance and education, they were unable to face realistically or to deal with confi-
dently. On the whole, we concluded swing is no more harmful, and
probably a lot healthier, than youth's identification with the unreal
world of the Hollywood stars and the ether waves. While we adults
have been gazing starry-eyed at the alphabet constellation in Washington, detached from the realities of our own home towns and counties, the song writers and masters of swing have captured the minds
and feet of our killer-dillers, hot-shots, and alligators for a good
share of their waking hours.

We've got a long way to go to do the right thing by our young people, but on the basis of what noodling we've done, we'd make you hep
that if you start a representative youth council in your county, with
everybody pulling and planning to give your youth a square deal,
you'll be in the groove. When your staff holds its weekly hash
sessions, play your facts on the nose, and whether you shag or peck,
suzie-q or truck—or lay an egg—you'll be giving off the works with
your young people, and together you can do better than "Swing the
Depression," you can swing at it with a good left to the solar plexus
and mow it down.

THE APPLICATION OF THE BASIC CONCEPTS OF
CASE WORK TO RURAL SOCIAL WORK

Grace A. Browning

The rapid development of rural social work in the last few years has offered an abundant opportunity for social workers with a zest for pioneering to test the application of their basic concepts in a variety of settings. Temerity characterizes any attempt to generalize in a field as vast as that of modern rural social work. The very term "rural work" may conjure up for one individual the farm-tenant sections of the south, for another stranded mining communities, lumber camps, abandoned oil fields, the dust-bowl area of the southwest, or the open farm country of the prairie states. One may visualize the cultural life of the French fishermen along the quiet bayous of Louisiana; another, the migrant Mexican laborers in the cotton and beet fields, or some of the primitive Indian cultures of the western states.

The social case worker in any of these areas is practicing a profession that is not static, one in which her concepts may grow and change continuously and from which she selects skills adapted to the needs found in the particular administrative setting. She adds to these selected skills a knowledge of the cultural and economic factors that affect the particular section and an awareness of individual and community limitations. The end result is case work, modified and adapted certainly, but still case work, an "individual approach to human beings in trouble."[1]

Basic to case work is a concept of limitations. One of the greatest difficulties experienced by the rural worker is involved in an understanding of that concept. Since most rural social work at present is practiced within the framework of public welfare, there are

The Family, March 1938. Grace Browning was a native of Geary, Oklahoma. She was the daughter of a country physician and had an early introduction to rural practice. She worked with the Provident Association in Oklahoma City, the Red Cross in St. Louis, and the Oklahoma State Department of Welfare. She was an instructor at Tulane and Pittsburgh and Director of the Indiana University Division of Social Service. She was the author of several books, among them *Rural Public Welfare: Selected Records* (1941).

[1]Bertha C. Reynolds, "The Social Case Worker's Relationship to Clients When the Community Demands Action of a Definite Sort," *Collected Papers on Relationships in Short Contact Interviewing,* National Association for Travelers Aid and Transient Service, 1934.

certain inescapable legal and administrative limitations. If categorical funds are more nearly adequate for the aged, less so for the
children, and completely lacking for yet other groups whose need is
great, the handicap to a well rounded job is evident. The restrictions imposed by so-called administrative economies which necessitate
high case loads and superficial work are likewise limitations. One
of the earliest lessons relearned (if it has been forgotten) by the
worker who goes into rural work is the fact that she cannot, as representative of her organization, progress more rapidly than the
community in the acceptance of responsibility. If no more responsibility is felt by the state for the care of the aged than is covered
by the "Dun and Bradstreet" financial investigation which a state
governor recently declared to be all that was necessary, the worker
employed by the state will be faced with needs she cannot meet. She
may have to confine her efforts to making that investigation as pain-
less as possible and then proceed to interpret to those in authority
the need of other services.

Then there are limitations imposed not by the administration but by
the environmental setting. Such are the infrequent contacts with
clients because of distance or of roads which are impassable at certain seasons, and the frustration caused by an economic poverty to
which case work is not the answer. Coupled with these may be a paucity of community resources which in some areas is appalling. The
urban worker who may visit several families in the same tenement and
a dozen or more within the same city block is apt to forget that
there are remote, rural sections which may be reached only by boats
through the swamps of southern states; mountain areas where half a
day or more on horseback is necessary to reach the home of a single
client; and large western counties where scattered families may live
fifty miles or more from the county seat town. In such counties one
visit may involve travel by automobile, on horseback and on foot.
In one county on the Oklahoma-Texas line, there are three distinct
districts—one, the "mountains," another the town (the county seat),
and the third, the "mud-line," a name used to designate the land
along the Red River, populated by Indian, Negro, and white tenant
farmers.

The worker who can calmly call the city ambulance to transport an
emergency case to the public hospital may not know that there are
many midwestern states in which persons sick enough to require hospi-
talization may have to be taken two hundred miles or more to a state
hospital because the small, poor county has none and no funds remain
to pay the private hospital even if one is nearer. A county worker,
a few months ago, took a child in her own automobile (because there
was no way to get an ambulance), one hundred and eighty miles to the

state hospital for treatment of what the local doctor thought was a brain tumor. Upon arrival at the hospital a diagnosis of spinal meningitis was made.

In addition to such practical limitations are those involved in the rural client's frequent inability to accept assistance with anything except material needs; his tendency to reflect community attitudes and to regard the worker's role merely as that of an investigator in whose hands lies the important decision regarding his eligibility to assistance. The difficulty of the worker in establishing herself in any other role is increased for the worker who, because the local board insists upon the employment of local persons, is assigned to work in her own county or town. The worker who may be sent into a county from the outside often finds it easier to establish herself as an expert in meeting social distress than does the local merchant's daughter, even when each has had the advantage of professional education.

The problems found in rural social work, just as in any other setting, are both individual and social and, as has been said many times, the case worker—urban or rural—must see a differential approach to those needs that require a control of the environment and those that require individualized treatment. Some will be met by skilled use of natural and community resources while others, arising from conflict with the environment or within the individual, will require a high degree of awareness of emotional factors.

In a recent child welfare conference in a midwestern state, the discussions centered around the problems confronting representatives of the Children's Bureau, the Indian Service, the State Health Service, the Crippled Children's Commission, and the Department of Public Welfare in a five-county area where co-operative health and child welfare demonstration units are in operation. The area comprises five of the poorest counties of the state, located in the foothills of the Ozarks, and occupied largely by a tenant-farm population including many poverty-stricken, pellagra-ridden whites and Indians. In case after case referred to the child welfare workers for service by baffled county judges, health service doctors, and members of the public assistance staff, the social situations involved lack of ambition, illiteracy, disease, housing, neglect of children, and "chronic" dependency. Further inquiry almost invariably revealed lack of opportunity for education, absence of adequate health services when first needed, and years of existence on incomes far below what is needed for health and decency.

One such family consisted of a father, mother, two aged grandparents, an unmarried aunt, and two little girls, aged ten and
three, living in a one room log cabin with a dirt floor. The
mother had tuberculosis, the grandmother was suffering from
heart disease, the aunt had Malta fever, the three-year old girl
had hemorrhoids and the father was acutely ill. The housework
was being done by the grandfather and the 10-year-old girl, who
was an arrested case of tuberculosis. The family had never had
an income except the small amount earned by the father from
seasonal farm labor and "odd jobs."

The welfare files in these counties are replete with similar case
stories. Obviously the social worker must view with unclouded eyes
such situations; must realize that, when deep-seated economic and
social factors are involved, skill in dealing with emotional disturbances will not be her most frequently used tool. She must remain
unconfused in her conviction that public assistance may alleviate
and case work service mitigate the individual need, but that the
basic problems will not be solved without social action. She will
utilize to the maximum both community and state resources for medical
care and for meeting economic needs. She will support efforts to
obtain adequate facilities. At the same time, she and her organization will join other social forces in working toward a long-time
educational and economic program that will lift the children and the
children's children of her clients to an opportunity for self-maintenance.

Overwhelming as these environmental factors sometimes are, the
rural worker will not lose sight of the fact that case work is desperately needed in the rural communities and that problems of individual disorientation are apt to be more conspicuous and more acute
because of the economic, cultural, and social pressures of the rural
community.

While in a few rural areas and especially among certain racial
groups the unmarried mother, for example, may enjoy a social status
no different from that of her married sister, in many villages dominated by a rigid conventionality she may suffer from an internalized
conflict vastly accentuated by the attitude of the society in which
she lives.

Recently a county judge (also the juvenile court judge) referred
to the attention of the case worker Marie, aged 15, whose commitment to the state training school had been requested by her
grandmother. Marie was "dating" a married man, staying out late
at night, and sleeping all day. Neighbors of the grandmother
declared she was "bad" and importuned the court to send her away.
Marie revealed much pent-up feeling against the tyranny of her
grandmother who tried to make her conform to the standards of
her own time; against the lack of home privileges, and against
being deprived of pretty clothes. She wanted nothing so much as

to leave home, find employment, and through distance and financial independence escape the condemnation of her grandmother's friends and contemporaries.

In another community was found a 12-year-old boy who had only a rudimentary knowledge of reading and writing taught him by an almost illiterate mother. He had been excluded from attendance at the school where his brothers and sisters were students, because of his dark skin and wavy hair. The mother contended that the child's father was of Spanish ancestry. The unhappy boy refused to go to school with the Negro children and was meeting his own needs through "anti-social" behavior.

The rural social worker, of course, finds that in some communities tradition and custom have remained more adamant than in others and that some of these pressures have social value. Abbé Pierre in speaking of his native Gascon village says:

Of course we have our stubborn customs handed down since the night of time . . . but because our customs are different from those of Paris, does that make them any narrower? For instance, does one cease to be provincial merely because he uses an electric light? Your citizen of the world who is at home in every place is apt to miss life's deeper loyalties. . . . That my fellow-villagers resent innovation may be an evidence of our great strength rather than weakness. Such provincialism as is ours has its recompense.[2]

Like Abbé Pierre, we find that there are factors in many rural communities which tend to solidify family life, to deter certain disintegrations, and are, therefore, the allies of the social worker.

But social and cultural pressures are not static in the America of today and we must not yield to the temptation to over-emphasize the rigidity of rural customs and the narrowness of rural life as contrasted with city life. True enough, there are here and there isolated sections, still pools, characterized by odd sects or racial groups such as are portrayed in Lyle Saxon's *Children of Strangers*.[3] There are also lonely ranch homes and remote farm sections cut off from social advance by the lack of roads and by their poverty. Into the thinking of such communities the radio and the movie have scarcely penetrated but these sections are not typical of the largest part of modern rural America. Those persons who gained certain impressions of rural life from the sociology of twenty-five years ago must be reminded that the social distance between generatio:.s is great. It was Novy, the young Tennessee mountain girl, who commented cryp-

[2]Jay William Hudson, *Abbé Pierre*. Appleton, 1922, p. 56.
[3]Houghton Mifflin, 1937.

tically to her neighbor as she applied her make-up: "Ain't it a
sight? Me a-usin' a lipstick, an' Mammy—her a-usin' a snuff-
stick!"[4]

The application of the fundamental concept of self-help in rural
areas is probably more universal than that of almost any other concept. The newness of case work practice means that no pattern has
been set by well meaning "charity visitors" of "doing for" the client.
A high premium is placed by the community on self-reliance and independence. Even where the staff members of the rural agency have no
professional training, they are usually influenced by state supervision in their approach to the establishment of eligibility and
utilize the case work principle of participation by the client in
establishing his claim to assistance. The trend is toward the frank
explanation by the worker of the legal basis of eligibility, followed
by real participation of the client in assembling the necessary data.
Aged persons are busy the country over communicating with relatives,
employers, ministers, family doctors, and old friends in an effort
to gather the information needed to obtain old age assistance. Inmates of county almshouses are re-establishing old relationships and
helping work through plans for their own care outside of institutions.
Blind individuals are arranging their own transportation through
friends and neighbors to the eye specialists for examinations, and
mothers of dependent children are gathering birth and death certificates with a view to obtaining aid.

The influence of the state supervising agency, usually the state
department of public welfare, is definitely seen in the procedures
used by the local units in the administration of the public assis-
tances. Even if such procedures were not utilized because of a conviction that they were sound, they would be necessitated in many
areas because of the numerical inadequacy of the staff and the im-
possibility of finding time to do for the client anything he can
reasonably well do for himself. The trend is away from the antiquated method of the poor relief system—which frequently offered two
alternatives: meager relief in kind, or care in an institution—
and toward a more constructive method of administration of assistance.
Certain mandatory requirements of the Social Security Act—such as
assistance in cash, given with regularity and based on individual
need—and the availability of federal and state funds have made it
possible to put into operation some of the case work principles which
without such leadership would have taken years to accomplish in some

[4]Anne W. Armstrong, *This Day and Time*. A. A. Knopf, 1930, p. 83.

jurisdictions. A better administration of public assistance under
plans that have been approved by the Social Security Board is influencing the administration of local general relief funds in some areas
because of the effective demonstration of a method better than that
of the old poor relief authorities.

On the other hand, while accepting readily the principle of self-
help, the rural community is less apt to recognize the client's
right to live his own life. Rural case records are filled with evidence of the inflexibility in attitude of board members or laymen
toward the man who does not accept work at any wage, however inadequate; toward members of certain races; and toward individuals who
are in conflict with the mores of the group. Many a county director
has had difficulty obtaining the approval of the local board on an
aid to dependent children grant for an unmarried mother or in convincing them that members of one race require assistance based on the
same standards as those of another. One of the most difficult problems in interpretation to the rural community has been that of why
old age assistance should be granted alike to the man in need, who
has "paid taxes for years and been a good citizen," and to the man
who has always been a "ne'er-do-well" in the eyes of the community.
There is more than a trace remaining of the attitude typified by a
small town minister who refused to approve giving clothing to a certain family because the children did not attend his Sunday-school
with regularity.

It is often difficult for untrained workers and for boards in rural
areas to understand any necessity for the worker to obtain social information or even to make an investigation of the needs of families
whom they have "known for years." An E.R.A. scholarship student in
one of our southern states related some of her experiences in taking
over a county relief office. One of the first records she picked up
consisted of only a face record card and one sheet of paper. Across
that otherwise blank page, in the handwriting of the administrator
(who was her predecessor), were the words: "I say let them starve."

We err if we fail to realize that many of our clients other than
the younger generation have reluctantly accepted the limitations of
their own environment. A few weeks ago a recipient of Old Age
Assistance travelled by bicycle some twenty-five miles to the public
welfare office to ask permission to move from a rural community to
an urban community across the county line. Apologetically he explained that such a move would add greatly to his happiness as he
desired to make church connections where the minister held *liberal*
views, he wished to be near a good library, and he coveted an oppor-

tunity to attend adult education classes which were not available in the county.

Under the more flexible new state legislation which makes no mention of local settlement for purposes of assistance this move was permissible. If only other deeply entrenched community attitudes and prejudices could likewise be legislated away!

It is sometimes very difficult for the local worker, with community prejudices infringing at every point, to maintain the non-judgmental attitude so necessary to good case work. She may be sorely tempted to moralize or to coerce the non-conforming client into the accepted community pattern. But one of her most important functions is the modification of the attitudes of parents, teachers, judges, and laymen in rural communities toward the person whose path to self-expression may conflict with established ideas and practices. This role is no different from that of the urban case worker, except that the rural client's deviation may be more conspicuous and the impact of his community's attitude correspondingly harder. On the other hand, the judgmental attitude of the rural community, the tendency to attempt to control the lives of clients through the weapon of the assistance grant, and the frequent punishment by the community of the "transgressor" often make more satisfying and necessary the case work relationship to the person in conflict with that society.

That this relationship must of necessity remain similar to that of a neighbor and friend who is more understanding than the others, rather than develop into the strictly professional relationship possible in certain urban agencies, is indicated by the circumstances of rural life. Just as the rural doctor is still the general practitioner and family doctor, often mixing family counsel with scientific treatment, so is the rural case worker often an integral part of the client's somewhat intimate community. She must, however, distinguish herself from other members of the community through her ability to achieve a non-moralistic attitude, if she is to do a sound piece of work.

There has been much discussion of what is needed to make a successful rural social worker. It has been suggested that case workers with a capacity for rural adaptation can be just as successful as those born or brought up on the farm and that case work must merely modify its approach in terms of cultural and administrative conditions. But may we emphasize that, in addition to adaptability and resourcefulness, there is much actual knowledge that is essential to equip a worker for an administrative setting which involves so much lay participation, for the constant integration of case work with

other community services, and for the constantly patient interpretation of this art called case work?

A working knowledge of county government, taxation, and the economic and cultural factors operating in any given rural area is necessary. Easy converse with the value and kinds of crops, with live-
stock and other resources of importance to the clientele of the
agency, is almost as essential to the rural social worker in establishing client and community relationships as a knowledge of the
social factors in disease is to the medical social worker. It is
both difficult and dangerous, if all these remain to be learned on
the job.

The rural social worker must not only be able to establish a satisfactory relationship with clients, but if she is to be successful
there must be, as Miss McCord has pointed out, mutual acceptability
of worker to community and community to worker.[5]

The capacity to adjust happily in the rural community where assigned is most essential.

> Recently in one of our rural states, an "out-of-county" director
> was appointed because there was no local person available who
> met the qualifications of the state department. One of the
> local county papers leveled an attack upon the new worker based,
> first, upon the fact that she was not a "business man," and
> second, that she was not a local person. This courageous worker
> paid an immediate visit to the editor to become acquainted. The
> facts that she had chosen to live in the county seat of 200,
> without even the convenience of running water in her house, and
> had placed her child in school there, were pointed out. She was
> able to convince the editor that she had really adopted the new
> community and she thereby won his support to her program.

Many excellently qualified workers have been rendered useless because of their inability to win acceptance in the community. This
ability to get along well with the local board and the community at
large, as well as with the client group, is indispensable to effective rural work.

The rural worker is perhaps fortunate that practice in her field
has necessarily lagged behind experimental practice in urban communities and more protected settings. She has thereby been spared what
has been characterized as the "silly season"[6] in case work practice
and has escaped many of the "fads, eddies, and flurries" against

---

[5]Elizabeth McCord et al, *Social Work Practice in Three Rural Counties*,
F.E.R.A. mimeographed report, Employment Division, Works Progress
Administration, 1936, p. 11.

[6]Gordon Hamilton, "Basic Concepts in Social Case Work." *The Family*,
July 1937, p. 147.

which Mary Richmond warned us some years ago.[7] Because of the necessity to carry ever with her a critical and sometimes diversely opinionated community, she tends to bring to bear in her work only those concepts and procedures that have been tested and found good. Needless to say, she should possess far more skill than she often can use in present settings. Only through knowledge and skill can she make the differential approach—decide what to treat, how to treat, and what not to treat. That adaptation of case work concepts for rural practice in its present stage is essential cannot be denied. This adaptation is necessitated, however, not by any lack of universality of the concepts but rather by certain practical difficulties which may obstruct the application of some of them.

Many of the limitations with which the rural social worker is hedged about have been mentioned above. May we emphasize that, because of the limitations imposed by the social and administrative settings, the lag of practice behind knowledge, and the pressure of community and client for the elemental services, it is more difficult and in some areas impossible for the rural worker, however skilled, to deal with internalized factors except symptomatically? The rural worker in such areas just now is very busy with the attempt to interpret the need for and to make available the requisite food, shelter, and medical care. She is concerned with the removal of the aged, the mentally ill, and little children from almshouses, and with protective services to all groups. She is confronted with the cumulative effects of long years of neglect and inertia on the part of the community. As the first "trained worker" to enter the county, she may find herself submerged by cases referred to "try her out"— the most difficult social situations, which have been town or county "problems" since time immemorial. She may be met, on the other hand, by fear on the part of the county officials that she will find more need than can be cared for, and that the demand for welfare services will outstrip their ability to pay for them. A state legislator charged on the floor of the House during a recent session that the child welfare worker was hunting up children all over his county to place them on state funds—in a state where 80 per cent of all state funds were earmarked for the care of the aged, and .5 per cent for child welfare!

[7]Mary E. Richmond, "The Concern of the Community with Marriage," *The Long View*. Russell Sage Foundation, 1930, p. 615.

There is, however, a hopeful note in all this. There is now in almost every county in the country at least one worker whose job it is to know and care what is happening to the aged, to the children, and to the families of men out of work. If competent professionally, this worker will freely interchange the technics of social case work, social group work, and social action. And time will show results! There is no more challenging field open at the present time for the resourceful and courageous social worker. The recent developments in the field of federal responsibility for public welfare have placed at her disposal resources heretofore unknown in many localities. With funds for health services, vocational rehabilitation, the care of crippled children, and public assistance to several groups, new vistas are opened. No longer is the rural worker completed isolated. New ideas are being transferred from county to county and state to state through state supervision and federal consultative services.

A changing public attitude is likewise encouraging. A few years ago a rural public accepted quite apathetically in many areas such situations as Miss Armstrong portrays, in which a father mercilessly beats his 14-year-old daughter who is slowly dying of untreated tuberculosis.[8] Neighbors look on but do not interfere. That acceptance of such conditions and reluctance to interfere are becoming less common is evidenced by the way in which the workers in the program of Child Welfare Services are being welcomed to communities hitherto untouched, and by the myriad situations referred to them for care. The interest of lay members in the community, their intelligent service on advisory committees, and their fine support of new social services in many areas are gratifying.

In many new state departments of public welfare, it has been encouraging to note the similarity of thinking between lay boards and professional staffs in the desire to individualize, in so far as time and staff limitations permit, the needs of the thousands of individuals under care of public assistance programs. The growing recognition by many local public officials of the need for so-called environmental case work service in their own counties is likewise indicative of a changing public attitude.

Is it not to be expected that this appreciation will progress to a rural public awareness of the need for treatment of unadjustment resulting from inner tensions, and that the rural worker by her acts of definite service in connection with environmental problems will open the way to a wider opportunity for the treatment of individual factors which bring about conflict?

[8]Armstrong, op. cit.

THIS RURAL SOCIAL WORK

Carol L. Shafer

In times past a few social work adventure stories were heard from
the rural field; but now a new call rings out. "We are doing social
work, not just relief work, out here in the country. We have hundreds and hundreds of different duties. New philosophies and new
practices must be developed. Help us formulate them." The profession
rushes to the rescue. The rural social worker is on the map.

I often have wondered what it is that justifies a categorizing of
workers into an urban and rural species. Having worked in both city
and country I never have been impressed by a wide variation between
them. It has been said that the rural field requires a readaptation
of fundamental social work philosophy and techniques, "a new application of accumulated experience, principles and practice is under
way." Yes, a new application is under way, but does not that process occur everywhere and constantly? Is it not one of social work's
middle names? To maintain that the rural field is unique in its
needs and treatment requirements seems to me an unworthy position,
needlessly dissipating our efforts. Why take two winding roads to
see the view that the top ridge-drive reveals in splendid panorama?
The arguments which uphold this division are usually traditional
assumptions, not clear candid camera shots of modern experience.

Rural social work, I have been told, differs because of the country itself. "Look at the great distances, farms far apart, dinky
isolated villages. Why wouldn't social work on those God-forsaken
prairies and mountains be different than on Halsted Street, Chicago?"

Well, what is a "rural" area? A morass of controversy catches anyone who tries to define it in terms of culture, economic or political organization, or characteristics of inhabitants. Population density seems to be the most widely accepted measure, so the census
bureau's definition shall suffice for this discussion. Rural is all
open country and all villages under 2500 in population. However,
the questions which I want to raise apply also to the less restricted
meaning of the word.

Is every locality of this designated density so similar that social
work in these areas can be set off and taught as "rural social work?"
"Rural" is not just an eighty-acre farm tucked between hills and
snowed in every winter. It may mean the Bad Lands of North Dakota,

Survey, May 1939. Carol L. Shafer was a social worker in Menomonie,
Wisconsin.

a New England village, or the hills of Kentucky. It includes farms, stores, schools, churches, factories, mines, railroad yards, homes of every type. Everywhere under 2500 population covers such an assortment of localities that only the most ruthless of clerical minds would slip them and all their people into the same folder.

"Look at the great distances." Great distances and isolation are less typically rural than is commonly believed. Distance is no longer measured by miles, but by minutes by auto, hours by plane, or connections by wire. It is fifteen minutes by auto from the edge of this rural county to the hospital in the center. To drive from South Chicago to St. Luke's or from lower Manhattan to the Orthopedic Hospital on East 59 Street takes longer than that. Here indeed is the individual who lives today as far removed from the outside world as did the early homesteader. Surely on the basis of geography and time it is ridiculous to say: "This is the way to help people in villages and country and that is the way to help those in cities."

"People are different in the country," the argument goes on. "They are naive, gullible, even ignorant. But what can one expect with their environment? Cultural opportunities are nil. Living alone always does things to people. Everyone knows the farmer is a strong individualist. You can't tell him anything. It takes a special technique to work with him."

Living alone usually does produce strange individuals. But who lives alone today? One may find a trapper in the woods, a village witch, a poet in his garret, or a maiden lady with seven dogs in some rear apartment, but few people in city or country really are isolated unless they want to be and work at it. It is true that country residents seem to differ from city dwellers in the type and number of their contacts. Intimate family contacts are likely to predominate in small places; casual contacts in large centers. But how chart the influence of these contacts upon the life of an individual? How weigh them? How many secondary equal a primary? What is the average number of each per individual in city and country? It becomes apparent that generalities on this matter can be sounded only by the sweeping-statement addicts.

"Cultural opportunities cannot compare with the city," they say. Yes, I agree. But who takes advantage of these opportunities whether urban or rural? To the destitute and low income groups wherever they live cultural opportunities seldom are available. Public schools are everywhere, but the country boy quits the grades to work on the farm and the city boy leaves as soon as he procures working papers. Relief families, city or country, have few newspapers and fewer books; only the exceptional one possesses a library card. The theatre, the

lecture, the opera and the concert hall are all out of price range
of the poor, while radios and movies of more doubtful cultural value
are about equally available to the low income groups in either city
or country. Museums and exhibits are urban advantages, but even when
free they are not frequented much by people who could never afford
training in the arts. Too many of us, city or country folk, never
will experience "finer" enjoyments in living because our teachers are
poverty, drudgery and ignorance.

The notion that rural people are strong individualists is a superstition, however traditional. The old romantic picture of the farmer,
a solitary Millet figure standing on his freshly turned field, a
philosophical union between earth and God, must be put in the attic
and a Thomas Benton mural, crowded with brawny men and whirling machines, hung in its place. The farmer depends upon much more than
God's weather and his own strong back. He studies and experiments
with crops, fertilizers, balanced diets and pedigreed stock. He must
know markets, AAA brochures and Farm Union advantages. Farmers loaded
with debt (and most of them are) or the farm laborers, have even
less economic freedom than city workers and scarcely more opportunity
for independence. The farmer is no longer an individualist, but is
dependent upon outside help, influences and events—and well he knows
it. Furthermore, not all rural people are farmers: they are ministers, teachers, lawyers, doctors, shopkeepers, mill and factory hands
and workers in countless other trades. They cannot be lumped together by occupation or characteristics of naïveté, unrefinement or
stubborn individualism.

"No matter what you say," city friends maintain, "problems in rural
areas are different. No slums, no organized vice, plenty of fresh
air and helpful neighbors. Don't tell me the problems are the same."

Let us look at these rural problems and see if they belong in a
separate category. Two years ago I made a thorough study of all the
relief cases in a midwestern rural county and discovered almost every
form of illness and misfortune. About 41 percent of the families
were dependent chiefly because of economic difficulties; 22 percent
because of ill health; and 37 percent for reasons broadly classified
as social. No, misery takes much the same form regardless of city
limits.

Jobs are lost in city and country. John Kaczmarek is out when the
steel plant shuts down; Pete Johnson when the creamery fails. Marie
loses her job when the Broadway restaurant closes; Jean when the
Willow Springs tea room loses its summer tourist trade. Little businesses go in the red on Main Street as well as on Fifth Avenue. And
the "farm problem" (a broad wave of the hand should accompany such

phrases) is in principle very similar to any small business. Much
of the social worker's bewilderment has resulted from a strange belief that a farm is made up of brooding hens, seeds under ground and
other incalculables. I've found it about as hard to evaluate the
stock of a farm as that of a secondhand store in the city, and easier
to subtract the milk check from a budget than to deduct cash received
from transient roomers in a casually run urban lodging house.

Swoops of fresh air, gallons of milk, rosy-cheeked children, Paul
Bunyan men pitching hay, and a horse-and-buggy doctor appearing heroically in the middle of the night—this is the common version of our
"healthy" countryside. County nurses say otherwise. Our nurse is
haunted by pasty-faced youngsters, "Right in this dairy county, too.
You know they actually sell the milk and feed their children canned
stuff." No slums? There are Dogtowns and river flats. There are huts
with chicken roosts, straw beds and tin stoves scrambled together;
tarpaper shacks in swamps, housing seven or more; condemned hotels
oozing with families and roaches; rotting privies, squalor, filth.
and disease. Grandma Beck died of cancer in the old homestead; the
village minister's daughter had infantile paralysis; the millhand's
eight children had diphtheria; that paper factory worker takes treat-
ments for syphilis; Jake was ruptured while threshing, his wife has
been bedridden since the last baby; the hired man's wife has had
tuberculosis for three years.

Economic and health problems are not all. In the country as well
as the metropolis husbands die and leave needy families, old folks
become helpless, and young people "go wrong." What consternation in
the village when Widow Lane had a baby two years after her husband
died, and when the Schmidt boys robbed the filling station and shot
a man. No one in Spring township will go near the Derber place:
Mrs. Derber is "cracked," Mr. Derber shoots at trespassers, Jerry is
a feeble slobbering hunk of a boy and Minnie, the unmarried daughter,
age fifteen, has had two babies. Young Benson is a whiz at drawing
and wants to be an architect but his father won't let him finish
highschool. Big-eyed Mabel was caught distributing marijuana among
the school girls. Her uncle formerly owned the finest hotel in the
county, but now lives in a box car and his wife calls out the police
once a month when he goes on a spree. A case count in a rural
county reveals desertion, feeblemindedness, illegitimacy, incest,
delinquency, incompatability, and on down those lists which are so
similar in city welfare departments.

Are not those problems universal? There are variations, of course,
but these are occasioned not by rough divisions of locale but chiefly
by the differences inherent in each individual and his life experience. "Rural" and "urban," between which the border is never

certain, are only two determinants among many others of greater strength. The uniqueness of the individual and differential treatment are principles of case work which need no redefining for the rural field.

"But isn't the rural worker more a community worker than a social worker?" It seems evident that the rural worker does have more community exploration and education to perform. However, every agency, rural or urban, public or private, has to know the needs and desires of its community and fit and interpret its work to the group in which it functions. Rural agencies are relatively new and small, hence much of this work falls directly upon the case worker. New agencies in cities must do likewise. It is highly probable that the size and status of the agency are more indicative of the amount of community work falling to the worker than the locality is indicative of the agency's influence.

The final argument does have observable grounds. "Well, if everything else were discounted, it remains that the social workers themselves are different in these two areas. Rural workers are relatively unskilled and have very little professional training."

Most of the rural workers I know do lack professional training. But they also possess other qualities more difficult to measure and compare. State departments long have been searching for scientific methods of evaluating their workers. If we could weigh range of experience, general understanding, emotional maturity, acquaintance with a group or community, ability to organize work, to diagnose, plan and treat, I wonder how the balance would swing between rural and urban workers. The rural worker may keep her files in packing cases, may write letters in longhand, may drive thirty miles to visit one family, but by such artificial standards we cannot judge her.

That there *are* social workers in areas of less than 2500 or thereabouts, of course I admit. They are the "rural social workers." But I submit that to set them apart is unwise and a waste of time. The fundamental principles of helping people out of trouble are as broad as human nature. The problems of the rural worker are "people's" problems, not just rural problems. The ridge road is far superior to the lower drives. It holds a strategic position, it favors us with an extended view, and it is the most direct route home.

ALONG A COUNTRY ROAD

Alice Gray Hickox

It was a sparkling winter's day in Northern Vermont. The social
worker was thoughtful as she drove the Ford between the high snow
walls thrown up by the plow. Ahead, over the tops of sturdy snow-
covered spruces rose the Presidential Peaks, white against the sky.
The scattered farmhouses along the way sheltered families nearly all
of whom were known to the social worker. Town officials, references,
clients, in one guise or another—with few exceptions she had worked
with them all. She was troubled about the lists of "paupers" soon
to be published in the various town reports. She was responding to
calls from the board of selectmen in one town and from an overseer
of the poor in another, both seeking advice and help in planning for
families who were destitute but too proud to ask public assistance.
Why did officials still insist upon printing these names? These same
selectmen had been so glad to carry out a plan she had outlined for
a family the previous winter when they had summoned her as they were
doing today. It had been necessary to force a father to accept town
assistance, a choice of having his name on the pauper list of the
town report mailed to his neighbors and fellow townsmen or answering
a charge in court of neglecting his family.

The worker drew up at a country store and postoffice, receiving as
she entered the expected cordial greeting. As she stood for a moment
before the red-hot stove to warm her hands and to chat with the
storekeeper, he said, "Well, it's some different traveling about
this country than it was those first years when you used to come with
a horse and sleigh. It must be five years or more since you first
began to come here. We've made a lot of progress. Roads open all
the year. Get most anywhere with your car now."

As she drove along she thought of the seven years she had worked
in this country and the improvements and progress made. She had been
troubled those first years about the poor little rural school buildings. Nearly all had been repaired or replaced with good modern
schools with the state's standard label over the door; proper heating,
lighting and sanitary equipment. The roads *were* better. Seven years
ago the worker would have been crazy to think of driving through this
country in an automobile in February. The veterinary passed her,
probably to test someone's cattle for bovine tuberculosis. Untested
cattle were hard to sell today while in those first years scarcely a

The Family, May 1930. Alice Gray Hickox was a District Agent with
the Vermont Children's Aid Society.

farmer in the county had a tested herd. She passed a house where in her earlier work she had tried in vain to prevent the marriage of a thirteen-year-old girl. Laws had since passed making marriage at this age illegal. In those first years probate judges were not legally permitted to investigate adoptions; now they must be investigated. Girls no longer reached their majority at the age of eighteen. And so on.

She was exhilarated with these thoughts and the beauty all about her when she arrived at the cozy little inn where she was to spend the night. She liked this little town and had acquired speaking acquaintance with most of the village people. While the hotel proprietor made a wood fire in her room she paid a visit to a farmer a mile or so beyond. Less than a year ago neighbors had complained that the year-old baby had a bad case of rickets. In a family of eleven children, father, and mother, the worker had found much to do. She had taken the baby to a distant hospital and later to a temporary boarding home. The other children were physically examined and given prescribed treatment. The boys were sent to Boston to a study home, the father and mother examined and the mother given a necessary operation, a little girl taken to the preventorium. The extreme filth was cleaned up and the place kept in greatly improved condition, diet advised, and so on. The father of this family was a sensitive, educated man. A siege of pneumonia two years previously had taken his courage and loosened his grip on things so that he had sold off his stock, thus lowering his income. The social worker on this occasion conferred with him and his wife as to how he could restock his farm, pay his taxes and again find a financial footing sufficient to care for his large family. With the assistance of insurance nearly due, a forest of pulp wood to be cut, and a financially able sister to back a note, arrangements were made for a new herd of cows which, with the farm, will enable this family to be self-supporting.

Further on up the river, in a settlement hardly large enough for a town, a young mother with four children lived in a tiny house close to the road. Left alone, a girl in her teens, she had married her cousin who never properly supported her and the children. There had been a divorce, with alimony which had never been paid. This mother was about to have an illegitimate child. She refused to apply for town aid and become one of the "paupers" in the town report. The family was destitute. The overseer was powerless to assist with town funds without formal application. The social worker interviewed relatives who took the children for a few weeks; arrangements were completed for nursing and medical care for the mother away from home; warrants issued for the arrests of the delinquent father and of the confessed father of the child to come.

374

Still further on, up at the Canadian border, the social worker visited a family of father, mother, and thirteen-year-old daughter. Three years ago this mother was living immorally, frequenting line houses and neglecting her child. The father had left years ago when, upon his return from the World War, he found his wife living with another man. The little girl was committed in court to the children's aid society. After some weeks this mother had come to the district office asking just what would be expected of her before she could have her child again. She was told that until she had lived properly for at least a year the matter would not be considered. At the close of the year she had returned to her husband, had been living a decent, straight life. The child was placed with her parents under supervision. A year and a half have passed since then and this family has been doing well. There have been storms. Catherine has been saucy. She has brought up the past and blamed her mother, but the mother has not returned to her old life and the society has transferred Catherine's custody to her parents.

The social worker visited and disapproved a prospective foster home; called upon three little sisters in a boarding home, and endeavored unsuccessfully to locate a man for a Boston agency. She turned the Ford toward the district office. She had travelled many miles. Her route lay through another section, no less familiar. She passed more little standard schools; travelled through smooth, well ploughed roads with similar white snow-walls. She felt the same friendly security as she passed home after home familiar to her.

Her thoughts dwelt upon the week's work and the variety of contacts —the storekeeper; the county judge who signed the warrants and discussed the progress of the children's aid society; the doctor, the overseer of the poor; the game of bridge at the inn with the new young doctor from New York, his wife, and the contractor on the pulp job; the cattle buyer consulted in connection with the new herd of cows; the poor little old lady interviewed for the Boston agency who had been so glad to sell the old-fashioned mirror; the farmer and his wife denied the little girl they wished to take because of the presence in the home of their own feebleminded son; the wife of the inn proprietor who had been such a helpful friend all these years; the little girls in the boarding home and the kind foster mother.

She thought of the wonderful response of the farmer with the eleven children. How discouraged the social worker had been a year ago with the dirty home and the pinched, poverty-stricken little folks, shunned in school and in the social functions of the village! How interested the cattle buyer had been! The judge had mentioned the change in the family. The children were playing happily with others at school. What an effort that mother and father must have made!

What a response to the case work effort expended! And that last
mother who returned to her old neighborhood and bore unflinchingly
the criticisms of her neighbors and even of her own child.

The social worker again considered her seven years. Was she giving
a quality of service in proportion to this response? She thought of
the long list of appeals on her desk at the district office, so many
of which she was forced to refuse because of limited resources, and
she wondered how many of these would have made similar progress. How
could she bring a better social consciousness to these fine country
folk who accepted her so simply as their friend? What a challenge!

TRULY RURAL

Elizabeth E. A. Gissal

Case work has always been a series of adventures, but perhaps the
most exciting adventures which come to the St. Louis social worker
are the trips she makes in the course of her work into rural Missouri.
For five or six years now visitors of the St. Louis Provident Association have been making field trips 150 to 250 miles to different
parts of Missouri to learn the background information about families.

Of course, a beautiful spring day when the dogwood is flowering on
all the Missouri hills is the most entrancing time to make these
trips, but visitors have developed such an interest in going that it
has become a real privilege and mere weather can neither make nor
break the trip.

For most of us, rural background has a rather vivid meaning of
chickens and cows and meadows and fields. But what a contrast to the
Ozark farm. As one of our students reported after her trip to the
hills, "My memory of rural life was colored by what I knew of northern Ohio, where the commercial and truck farms are very different
from the small, poverty-stricken, and forlorn patches of planting up
and down the lopsided hills and valleys of Missouri. In Ohio, paved

The Family, July 1933. Elizabeth E. A. Gissal was a social worker
with the St. Louis Provident Association in Missouri.

and improved roads are taken for granted, but here we drove over narrow, muddy, rutty trails and forded small rivers in our car because there was no bridge. The live stock—poor lean cows and mules—wandered along the roadsides rather than grazing in fenced areas. There were no large barns, no granaries, no silos, no comfortable farm homes—only small desolate cabins, often windowless and floorless."

The student's picture is only half the story. The Missouri Ozarks, gently rolling up hill and across valleys, covered with pines and scrub oak, are to the nature loving but city bred eye beauteous and inspiring; but much of this land is marginal and this is a real explanation of the unproductivity of this countryside and its resultant poverty.

Not only is the countryside poverty-stricken but each community has a certain isolation and aloofness which the case worker must understand if she is to appreciate even partially the terrific adjustments for these hill people as they come to the city. It is a real experience to enter a small Missouri village of 200 or so people, and hear the whisperings and commotions caused by your innocent question of where Annie Jones lives. The hesitancy with which each question is answered and the suspicions with which your every move is followed are a challenge to the case worker to learn more and more of these queer hill people—so like the city person physically and yet so vastly different emotionally and culturally and traditionally.

Thus the field experience may give a kaleidoscopic view of elemental emotions, primitive practices, and fundamental hill philosophy.

When a case worker has followed a high ridge road where skilled driving of her car is a dire necessity, she comes upon a small log cabin with newspaper wall covering, crude handmade furniture and perhaps straggling corn in the front yard. She is greeted by two dogs and all the family—grandfathers to baby grandsons. In the very hospitable homes she may be invited in and perhaps offered a dish of blackberries swarming with flies and served with quaint lead spoons. On the other hand, she may be so little understood that she is commanded to stay outside and given only a curt yes and no. But inside or out she learns much of the people. "We ain't seen a nickel of money in two years, mam," they say. "We'd kill her if she'd dared come back. She made her bed and we warn't ever goin' to lay eyes on her agin." One lanky mountaineer tells us about his runaway daughter, while his wife behind his back cautiously asks us to take some sorry looking chestnuts along to the girl. If the man grows loquacious, he may even tell us about the neighbors: that Jake Wilson's boy had got blood poisoning from a rusty nail, and a live chicken cut open for a poultice is the best remedy and would we believe our eyes but that boy's foot has turned eight chickens green.

Sometimes we feel a lack of imagination among these people—they guess the glorious sunset is all right, they eat such meager and unvaried diets of beans and cornmeal cakes and dried meat, they have so little decoration in their homes or clothing. Does this lack go back again to the poorness of land, which even in good times was failing to give them enough living to pay taxes to get schools? For we do find that the schools are remote and usually inadequate. Lack of education and poverty may be the strong contributing causes for the poor dietary habits and low housekeeping standards which become such a problem to the worker when transplanted to the city.

The vista of understanding includes also glimpses into rural industries of which we know so little. A man has told us he works in the timber and we are surprised to find he is rail-splitting as truly as in Lincoln's day. The hills dotted with bent-over figures digging tiff, a porcelain appearing substance found in sections of the Ozarks, are a new sight, and the rustic tiff-mill where the product is sold is a contrast to any mill we have ever seen. In the little towns the coming of the shoe factories has caused a real revolution, for the shoe workers with sudden money in their pockets have become the town aristocrats. The lead mining section with its capitalistic overlord, visibly responsible for the whole community, is a revelation.

The administration of law in the rural communities is revealing too. We are barked at and almost shooed from the office by the county clerk from whom we request a marriage verification and cannot understand his attitude until we learn that he has not been paid for eighteen months because the county has no money.

Each trip back to these country villages gives new understanding and sympathy. We become friends with the village hardware dealer and the country doctor, the filling station boys and the restaurant keepers.

Case workers in any state would probably find great value in learning what particular brand of rural background characterizes their clientele. Our experience has shown that rural life in northern Missouri with its farmers is as great a contrast to that of the Ozarks as it is to that of rural southern Illinois with its miners. We have perhaps emphasized our Ozark experience because in the St. Louis case load we have a larger proportion of migrants from that vicinity than from others.

Experience obtained from these visits to the country has stood us in good stead in our present situation when we are helping people in larger numbers than ever before to return to the farms. The adjustment back to the land is going to be just as hard as the adjustment to the city has been, but is one that many of our clients look forward to having and seem to welcome. One man who had been in St. Louis for eight years had an opportunity to go back to a cabin with a patch owned by his wife's mother. His city possessions were almost useless to him down there in the hills some hundred and twenty miles from St. Louis, and we found him bartering his fountain pen for a yellow cat, a long electric light cord for a saw, and two men's hats for a churn. He is using an old recipe for making yeast of fermented peach leaves and oatmeal and has, for the time being, developed a great happiness in his simple life in the hills. What conflicts will arise for him as he begins to miss electric lights and radio, corner groceries and movies, running water and street cars, is a matter of conjecture but may again create a situation which requires case work treatment.

From the point of view of St. Louis and its relations to the smaller communities in answering inter-city inquiries, there are both advantages and disadvantages in sending case workers directly into the communities. The advantages are probably obvious. The case worker is able to obtain much more complete information than the correspondent—an untrained person. She becomes acquainted with the correspondent and may both interpret the service to him and gain enough of an acquaintance with him to bring back to the inter-city department a more complete evaluation of his personality, his position in the community, and ways of using him. We have had incidents when the correspondent, a banker, has passed on our letter to the rural mail carrier, who passed it on to the family, who, after they had read it, sent back some word to the banker. Such occurrences might have been prevented if a worker were able to interview the correspondent directly and give him a clear picture of the value of a more confidential relationship.

Then too, the case worker may develop new and better correspondents in the community. We have one instance of a splendid piece of work done over a period of a year and a half by a volunteer in a town of 200. The visitor had found that the only correspondent in the county lived 20 miles from this village but, through a school friend, she learned of a university graduate who lived right in the town. The woman had had no social work experience, but the visitor called on her and secured her assistance in locating a deserting husband. They talked with him together and secured money from him. Later, though letters and long distance telephone calls were necessary, continuous support of the wife was maintained and the eventual reconciliation of the family worked out through the activities of the volunteer who, as one may guess, soon became a favorite correspondent.

Another more general advantage of visiting in a community is the chance for interpreting the case work job, perhaps giving to rural communities a greater desire for case work service and an idea as to how it can be worked into the county program. With the use of federal funds and the development of local committeemen, it seems more than ever apparent that the city worker has a real interpretative job when she goes to the country.

When visitors have gone into communities without first getting in touch with the correspondents, we have had some difficulties, as the correspondent has sometimes become annoyed because the visitor did not call on him while visiting in his community and he felt that the organization either did not appreciate what he had done or did not trust him to do the task the visitor had come to do. However, if the case workers visit our correspondents when they are in their vicinities, we feel that this country visiting will become a constructive rather than destructive part of our inter-city services.

These trips are usually made in automobiles belonging to the organization, and over week-ends so that they are partly on the worker's time and partly on the agency's. Although the motive for making the trip may be to consult old employers or locate missing relatives, the more valuable results are certainly the intangible—the understanding which seeps into the visitor's thinking and becomes part of her future knowledge, and the stimulus to learn more and more of the habits of people who may at once be so like us and yet so different.

THE SOCIAL WORKER IN THE RURAL COMMUNITY

Samuel and Jeanette Gerson

In no subject now claiming the attention of the public does the time-worn cliche have more of a strangle-hold on modes of thought than in the consideration of farm problems. In no field of endeavor is the social worker more beset by preconceptions or misled by false assump-

The Family, January 1936.

tions than in the field of rural social service. One has always
heard the hardy merits of the farmer's life extolled, his pioneering
spirit vaunted. One is constantly assured that "a man can always
make a living on the land." Not long ago, in a transcontinental
train, we were told by a man who felt he had his hand on the pulse
of the nation that a "back to the land movement" was the only thing
that would save the country.

Then we have the happy assumption that where there are wide-open
spaces there is no overcrowding—that country people are healthier
than city dwellers, that there may not be much money but there is always enough food on the farm. Statistical evidence to refute these
theories is being gathered rapidly, but it has not yet become common
knowledge. It is, however, necessarily a part of the orientation of
the rural social worker. As industrial conditions, hours of employment, and wages are part of the framework within which our urban
families must construct their lives, so a knowledge of rural social
and economic problems is essential to successful social service in
the country. The limitations imposed by psychological and economic
determinism are as grim and unyielding in the country as in the city
—only the conditions are different.

There is one more set of false assumptions that should be mentioned
before we go on to describe some experiments in orienting the rural
social worker. They may be summed up in the belief that, having a
knowledge of rural life in one section of the country, a worker is
thereby qualified to undertake social service in any rural area. With
all their variation, cities are standardized in comparison with rural
areas. The conditions facing the farmer of diversified crops in Ohio,
the truck farmer of New Jersey, the corn farmer of Iowa, and the
wheat farmer of the Dakotas are different in important ways. Doubtless the south, with its plantation system, presents another set of
problems. Out on the High Plains we have the "dry farmer," the farmer
using irrigated lands, the sheep rancher, and the cattle grower.
Climate plays a leading role in this drama and cannot be removed from
the cast of characters. The social worker needs to know what it
means to say that the mean annual rainfall at Bismarck, North Dakota,
has been about 16 inches, whereas in Illinois it runs about 37 inches.
This meteorological figure is illumined for the social worker when
she visits the "dry farm," where water is being hauled twenty miles,
where there is no milk cow and no vegetable garden. It is further
illumined when she discovers the large proportion of "lifers" in
western prisons who are serving terms for murders over water rights.

In many eastern states there are genuine rural communities with a
community life highly developed and an asset to the imaginative social worker. On the High Plains, the homes tend to be scattered over

too wide an area, often having fifty miles of deeply rutted cowtrail
between houses. This is a handicap in rural organization which is
being partly offset by emergency relief road building.

There is another handicap against which work projects are powerless,
the deep traditional dislike of the cattleman for the sheepman—the
remnant of old frontier feuds which have left bad feeling where one
would expect that misfortune would have brought folks together.

Thus the rural social worker is faced by a bewildering set of problems in addition to those which are basic in human life everywhere.
What can she do? Must she become a rural sociologist, agriculturist,
nutritionist, nurse? Are her problems insuperable? Is it any use to
try?

Except in a few states where rural social work got a head start,
the rural worker has at her disposal few of the technical resources
that the urban worker takes for granted. There are often no free
clinics. There may be counties containing no doctors. There are few
rural nurses or school nurses. Health officers are likely to have an
extremely restricted view of their job. Schools are distant and
often impoverished, offering only a few months' study under conditions which have entrenched the little red school house in song and
story but made the gaining of an education an endurance contest with
poverty, bad weather, and lack of resources. Of psychiatric and
child guidance service there is none. State institutions are likely
to be over-crowded, and so able to give care only to those in desperate need. They have no field service for prevention or after-care
supervision. Some states do not have an institution for the treatment of tuberculosis.

Many things are lacking, but the rural worker is not wholly without
resources if she knows where to look. If she is entering upon her
new field, she will find important leads in Josephine Brown's book,
The Rural Community and Social Case Work. Discussing the resources
listed in this book with groups of rural workers, we have been able
to add to the list. The emergency relief and rural resettlement services have developed within themselves staffs of specialists to whom
the social worker may turn. No, social workers do not need to turn
agriculturists, but they must learn the ABC of farm life, must learn
to speak, read, and write the language intelligently. A worker who
points to a field of flax and remarks to her farmer-client, "What a
nice field of wheat," is not likely to gain his respect. A social
worker of mid-Victorian turn of mind has made herself notorious over
the length and breadth of a western state by referring to "gentleman-
cows."

The agricultural college extension worker, the county agent, and the representative of a farm organization can give the rural worker important background information and can set her right on the details of farm life. She has much to learn from them, as they have much to learn from her. Successful rural work in pioneer states has been marked everywhere by an enthusiastic give-and-take between the two groups. In Montana, we have gained much for the service by putting rural rehabilitation workers through a social service orientation course, and including in our social workers' field training instruction by teachers from the agricultural college. There should be no conflict between two services which have a common goal, and certainly the mind of the rural client should not be confused by exposure to two conflicting programs. It is also necessary for the social worker to make the acquaintance of farm-loan agencies and other state and federal departments which have contact with her client. These agencies can be of inestimable value not only in assisting her in understanding her client's problems but also in the complex matter of estimating farm resources in making up the farm budget. Cash income is a relatively unimportant item among the resources of a farm family. The rural social worker must be able to think in terms of pounds of potatoes and tons of hay.

Historically, the social worker should know the conditions of settlement of her area. In the west, a knowledge of the land laws under which a large section of the population homesteaded is important. She should know what it means to "prove up" on a homestead; and why, although 134,313 homestead claims were filed between 1910 and 1918, there are at present only 47,000 farms in Montana. She must know the importance of water and large acreages of range grass. She must know the general conditions under which irrigation is the key to success. She must know the difference between cattle growing on the open range and dairy farming. She must know the significance to the sheep rancher of the lambing season and the time of shearing. She should be able to identify common grain varieties and common breeds of poultry and livestock. She should know just a little about normal yields and prices, just enough to know to whom to refer the farmer for advice.

One of the first lessons a rural worker in this area learns is not to venture out in her district between September and June without a shovel and a gunny sack, to enable her to dig herself out of snowdrifts in which she might easily freeze to death in her car before anyone else came along to pull her car out.

It is of the greatest importance to teach the rural worker to obtain an accurate description of the location of her clients' homes. The urban worker who goes by street and number has no problem of this

kind. Rural workers must get the legal description of the location
of the property as well as directions for reaching it. The worker
often starts out on her first visit with a description of this sort:
"ten miles east and then down the coulee and over the creek"; or
"follow the road that circumvents the hill, until you reach a big
rock, then turn to the north." Two devices have helped rural workers
find their way about their districts. One is the use in the office
of a county surveyor's map on which the homes of clients are accurately spotted. The second is a special tab inside the case record
folder given directions for reaching the home. The single address on
the face sheet is often far from sufficient.

This is the setting in which the social worker finds embedded her
client's problems of social adjustment. Imagine a family that homesteaded in Montana under one of the earlier homestead laws which
granted a tract of land to any adult citizen who would improve it and
live upon it for five years. In many cases the odds were against the
settler. He came west from the wooded country his parents had
cleared, rejoicing in the breadth of the land, the absence of forests
to be cleared and stumps to be grubbed out. He staked his claim and
built himself a sod house or a dugout which was to be used only a few
weeks until another house could be built. He tried to farm land that
should have been left a cattle range. He was beset by drouth. There
was no money and no timber for the new house. About his one-room
cabin lay miles and miles of bare, rolling prairie without a tree.
"Nothing to hide behind," moaned Beret in *Giants in the Earth*. Nothing but the prairie, endless and austere as the sea. Your homesteader
won his bet and made the land his own. But after he had acquired it,
he could not make a living on it. It is his married son, now with
seven children of his own, living in the same one-room dugout, who
is the 1935 client of the social worker. Here the word "emergency"
in the name of the organization that has come to the homesteader's
rescue has an especially ironical ring.
This is a typical picture insofar as a single case can ever be
typical. It is repeated in hundreds of case records. Let me quote
from one:

> The house was half dugout and the rest was made of native stone
> which the family had shaped out of the rocks on their own land
> . . . . This house, window sashes, doors, and all cost $76.50
> and took the boys three months to build. It is a brave attempt
> but unfortunately faces the west and is beaten by the prevailing
> winds. . . . It is unfortunate that this family seem to know
> nothing whatever about ranching. Their two horses and cow were
> dying for lack of feed and there is no water on their land, mak-
> ing it necessary to drive the stock one and a half miles to
> water. The family have been advised to move back to Colorado
> where the mother, who is a widow, was receiving a mother's pen-

sion. They have refused to move and are sure that they can make a living with a dairy herd on this place which is 63 miles from the nearest market. They will probably never make a living on the land, as it is definitely submarginal.

The worker commented, "It is a shame to find such energy and ambition bent in the wrong direction. We (the rural rehabilitation worker and the social worker) were invited to luncheon but did not eat with them as they obviously did not have very much food."

Such a family has expended blood, muscle, and imagination for years, sometimes for two generations, gaining title to a desert. The emotional problems involved in this situation may well give the social worker subject matter for study. Even where a resettlement plan might be worked out, it is often impossible to persuade the family to move. So much of the homesteader and his family has gone into the effort of proving up that nothing is left except a passionate clinging to a hopeless life. Living in dugouts, in sod houses, in rough log cabins with dirt floors, in 'dobe huts—sometimes only with a door, sometimes with only one window—he has reared his family without comforts, often without even enough food. Nevertheless, a departure from the homestead means defeat in his lifelong struggle and renders meaningless the years of suffering and hardship.

The isolation of many rural homes in the west continues to be a problem not only in community organization but in the individual adjustment of the members of the family. Physicians and social workers comment upon the frequency of mental depression among the wives of ranchers. State institutions for the treatment of mental diseases draw a relatively large proportion of their patients from isolated ranches, but by no means does the institutional population indicate the extent of the problem. Institutions are over-crowded, and so only the most desperate cases are likely to be accepted, while former patients are sent out on parole without any supervision whatever. Sheep herders are the second class from whom the state hospitals draw their patients, since many of them are not able to endure the complete isolation of weeks and months on the range alone.

The mere visit of the social worker has meant much to these people, and it has not been accomplished without often heroic effort on the part of the worker. A Children's Bureau study of maternity care and the welfare of young children in a homesteading county of Montana, published in 1919, describes the difficulties of the research workers in reaching the homes they wished to visit. It is not so different today. Workers frequently have to stay out several days in order to visit a remote group of families. In the summer they sometimes take a bedroll with them and spend the nights in their cars. A Wyoming social worker contributed this description of one of her trips (on which she was fortunately accompanied by a rural rehabilitation worker):

> We left this house at 1:30 and continued to our next stop which was 30 miles further on. At our destination, we found the wife of our client and a small daughter home alone, and so we helped her do the chores and then borrowed her pump and tire patching to repair our spare tire. We drove 35 miles further on and spent the night with a family who had a five-room house and could put us up.
>
> The next morning we continued up toward the peak. There were at least 20 gates to open and close within the next 20 miles. On this road we visited four families living in a small group of houses on a dry creek bed. In one of them we found both husband and wife in the well they were digging. During our stay at this house it began to snow, and by the time we left, it was blizzarding. It was necessary to follow the fence line back in order to keep on the road. It took an hour and forty-five minutes to cover the next 10 miles.
>
> The ranch house at which we spent the next night was a one-room log cabin, and I spent the early part of the evening wondering just where we all slept. We were made welcome, and I slept with a thirteen-year-old daughter. The beds were screened from view by sheets hung on wire with safety pins. . . .
>
> My total mileage for this trip was 250 miles. I had to buy a new rear axle, wheel, and tire before I reached home, and the total cost of repairs was $45.00. The mileage check I received was $12.50.

When we try to list the qualities necessary for successful social work in rural areas, the number is overwhelming. We should agree with Josephine Brown that "love of the country for its own sake is perhaps the most important of all qualifications." No worker who did not have the "feel" of the country would think it worth while to endure the hardships of rural work. The salary would tempt no one. A study made by the FERA in connection with a survey of rural problem areas indicated that the average monthly salary for rural visitors in the areas studied, exclusive of traveling expenses, was $68.78. Executive ability, initiative, and ingenuity in developing resources, and a realistic background of knowledge are of great importance. The ability to organize scattered rural groups for recreation is highly valued. Maturity is also important. Many a girlish-looking worker with real ability has been unable to command attention and respect. Appearance is even more of a factor in the country than in the city. Country people see few strangers and are quick to appraise the suitability of their attire.

The time element is a vital factor in rural social work. Recognition of its importance is closely related to an understanding of the rural client's psychological needs. There are two elements here. In the first place, the farmer wants to know "what the worker has come for." Just being a visitor isn't enough. When he knows, and accepts the errand as important to him, there is no longer need for hurry. That is to say, the approach must be businesslike, for people do not drive 50 miles just to pass the time of day. However, once accepted, the worker must not hurry this client, who does not live by the clock as city folks do, and who is likely to be reserved and inarticulate. In no field of social work is the ten-minute visit (thrust by necessity on over-loaded relief workers) so unproductive. It is necessary to be patient and listen without hurrying. Receptivity and patience are the rural worker's most effective therapeutic tools.

For all of herself that the rural worker gives, what does she receive in return? What are the rewards of so strenuous and exacting a life? To many workers, they will seem insufficient. To some, they will seem rich and gratifying. Rural work offers an unparalleled outlet for the pioneering spirit. It offers an opportunity to blaze new trails where trails are greatly needed, to live in the country in the midst of the pageantry of earth and sky, to skim along the open road with that sense of freedom that wide spaces give, to gain a sense of proportion, of one's own place in a scheme so vast. There are austere but glorious rewards. Less austere and most gratifying of all are the friendships one makes with one's clients, more slowly accomplished than those in the city, perhaps, but real and enduring in proportion to the place the worker has made for herself. To know that in some remote homestead a lonely woman is shading her eyes to gaze out at the far horizon, hoping to see the cloud of dust that marks the approach of the social worker—this is the true reward.

GEECHEE CASE RECORD

Mary L. Rogers

In none of the instructions on forms, be they FERA, CWA, ERA, WPA, or DPW, nor in any one of the books on social case work, can one find any light on the art of getting a case record from a Geechee

Survey, December 1939. Mary L. Rogers was Welfare Director in Liberty County, Georgia.

Negro. I doubt if anywhere else on earth there is a person who can make himself more cunningly obtuse than a coastal Georgian of mahogany hue. Peter shuffles into the office, and eases his rheumatic old frame into a chair. He wants a "pension," but he isn't telling too much to the Gov'mint Lady. He does not remember the ages of his children or any part of his work history, and knows absolutely nothing about his property. When it is explained that a home visit is necessary he hesitates, but finally gives hazy instructions for reaching it.

After following the directions past the big water hole, and as far as Sist' Susan Jones' fence, Worker then must pick up a guide, and go on foot through the swamp. Aunt Martha Holmes, age seventy-one, is recommended. Fleet as a deer she pads through the forest throwing news of the settlement over her shoulder as she goes, but all of it stopping just short of real information. Worker develops a steady dogtrot as she follows over bog holes, across the branch made by the artesian well, past the little white-washed schoolhouse, and on by the dim path under the second-growth pine.

Old Nancy, the Geechee's wife, is gathering wood, but agrees to go back to the house on beyond the stripped cornfield. To the side are the chicken pen and the crib of logs with hand-hewn shingles. Rose and cape jessamine bushes make a complete Geechee background for a house built of scrap lumber with a stick and dirt chimney, wooden shutters, and newspapered walls. Rotting side timbers cause the sand-scrubbed floor to bow up in the middle. Old Nancy flings wide the shutter to show a room filled with children, dogs, benches, a table and a tiny glowing stove. A chicken takes flight and dodges under the bag curtain at the end of the narrow passageway.

Old Nancy shoos dogs and children to the doorstep, and calls Peter, our friend of the office interview. Nancy claims a daughter and three children as members of her household, and gives their names and ages from the penciled flyleaf of an old encyclopedia. She interrupts here to give the children a scolding definitely more ostentatious than sincere. "Stop that lookin' at white folks whilst they's talkin'." The wind from the open window flutters the papers, the stove glows and a fly persistently returns to the nose of Worker as she takes down this information. Two of the children, Nancy says, are her daughter's. Peter explains that he does not know the name of the father—just a gentleman passing through. As to the parentage of the third child, they have no idea—it's 'dopted. A lady in Savannah just came up to Nancy and said, "Lady, don't you want a little girl?" and that is how they got her. Take it or leave it, that is all they know, and they stick to it.

The application blank fills up rapidly, but two spaces are glar-
ingly vacant—no age records for Peter and Nancy. Age records are a
complicated business for Worker for the Geechee knows only three
dates: Freedom, the Shake, and When-the-Big-Mill-Went-Broke. American history dates whirl around in Worker's head for a minute, and
finally she remembers Freedom. The Shake turns out to be the
Charleston earthquake. When-the-Big-Mill-Went-Broke is a little more
difficult, but is found by comparing it with the year that Uncle John
died. Peter remembers that his mother always told him that he was a
"hand baby" when Freedom came. Nancy was told that she and So-and-So
were "one year's chillun." She and Peter were married before the
Shake. . Peter knows that Worker can get affidavit to prove age from
his Old Master, who will remember that Peter was making syrup in the
backyard when the Young Master was born.

As to work record, no, Peter has not worked any since the Big-Mill-
Went-Broke. How did he live? Oh, he just worked on his little
"fahm of five tasks," and had pick-up jobs. A good working knowledge
of the employers in the neighborhood enables Worker to go on, "Did
you work for A. L. Brown or James Carter, or Frank Smith?" Worker
must know her trades, and the line-up of bosses in these trades in
each community. Behind Peter's last eight months of tie-cutting lie
months of woodcutting and of timber work with various employers, all
casual jobs of uncertain dates, with perhaps a year or two as an
extra hand on the railroad gang. This succession of events takes
Peter back to When-the-Big-Mill-Went-Broke. Before that, everybody
had a job, so that Worker feels that she safely can credit ten years
of continuous employment to that happy period.

A financial form hardly seems necessary in these circumstances.
But the rules require it, so Worker starts in. Has Peter any money
in the bank? He looks dazed, as if he had never heard of such a
thing. Plainly there is no use in looking for money in the bank, or
savings in the post office. Has he any insurance? Yes, he belongs
to the Good Samaritans, and pays 25 cents a month for dues. He
thinks that he will get about $90 for his burial.

Asked to list his property, both personal and real, Peter becomes
completely devious. It is fairly safe, the tax collector had told
her, to estimate the value of household goods at $15 or $25, according to the number of rooms. So that goes down. Has he any hogs?
Well, the cholery killed some, and the highway got 'bout ten. If he
counts the ones that he has in the woods, he has 'bout twelve. How
many cows? Well the railroad killed one last year. Maybe 'bout
seven, if he can call them all up.

How much property does he own? Peter puts on his dumbest face,

and says that he does not own any. When he sees that it is Worker's
policy just to sit and wait, he says that he lives on "estate property." Whose estate? His wife's grandmother's, who left it to her
children without will, and they in turn left it to their children
without will. Where did his wife's grandmother get the property?
From her Old Master, of course. How much property does he claim in
his estate? He doesn't know. One of his wife's grandmother's children is dead, but has heirs; a second child is in Miami, and a third
in New York. He doesn't know any addresses of any of them, isn't
even sure they're alive. But they may come back some time, he says,
build a house and start farming. He expects neither disagreements
nor lawsuits and cites five related families in the neighborhood who
work in one field without dividing fences, and amicably mix their
cows, pigs, corn rows, and children.

Finally, the discussion boils down to this: How much land does he
work, and how much do his wife's local relatives admit that he
claims? He gives the amount in tasks, or fractions of an acre, and
Worker figures the acreage. What taxes does he pay? His wife's
brother John handles the taxes, and he pays John a dollar a year for
his share. What is the assessed valuation of the property? He does
not know. Worker recalls a recent statement of the tax collector
that in this community wild land is valued at $2 an acre, cultivated
land at $3. Peter wants to know if he must "sign" his property to
the Gov'mint. He doesn't want trouble with his wife's kin. The
Lien Agreement has been withdrawn in Georgia and Peter is reassured.

With Aunt Martha Holmes padding along in front of her, Worker
travels back through the swamp to Sist' Susan Jones' fence. Here she
picks up her car and hurries back to her office to reduce tangled
facts to the explicit data called for by DPW forms 101, 104, 106,
112, 113 and 119 from which her DPW betters will determine the eligibility of Peter and Nancy, his wife, for old age assistance.

why i do not think i would make a good rural case worker

after reading the rural community and social case work by josephine brown

by marilla rettig

with apologies to archie mehitabel and don marquis

```
dear boss
i just finished miss browns book
and i dont wanta be
a rural case worker
on account of i dont claim
to be a superwoman or
a paragon
period
the only women who ought
to even think of this job
oughta be old maids
on account of
they are the only one
who would give a
lifetime to
a community program
and they wouldn't care
if there wasnt
any place to go
when they quit work
except home
exclamation mark
moreover
boss what worker
could possibly have
all those qualifications
laid down by miss brown
question mark
by the time she learned
how to be a bookkeeper
treasurer stenographer
file clerk statistician
case record writer
and what not
```

Survey, January 1936.

as well as public speaker
amateur farmer psychologist
fund collector and interpreter
of what the board is and does
and tactfully so too boss
and has six years in college
with courses in agriculture
and farm management just
thrown in for good measure
and three to five years experience
preferably rural
what i mean is boss she would be
very aged no less
period
and when she starts on the job boss
and carried 400 cases
and covers 1000 miles
maybe without an auto
on account of she cant
get the board to give her one
and talks the pta into
giving roller skates to the kids
and county fairs into giving
rest rooms
and the state hospital to lend
a psychiatrist
and gets papa farmer to see light
and farmers children to see papas side
too
all these she must do besides having
judgment
commonsense patience and humor
and a constitution unbeatable
and boss miss brown even
expects her to remain friendly
and to all free from prejudice
and while in rome to do as
the romans do though to
tell the truth boss there
isnt anything else to do
if she doesnt want the
romans to talk about her
and all that priceless personality
boss for a measley 2400 a year

it aint right boss really
with all that she oughta be
president at least
period
and then boss in her spare time
miss brown wants her to be an
amateur photographer or
butterfly chaser for her own
recreation
and boss while there is life
in the old dame yet i dont
wanta try it please
on account of
i cant take it

NO ONE CAN DO EVERYTHING

E. Kathryn Pennypacker

I must confess to a growing irritation with the idea that the county
worker's job is fundamentally different from that of the social
worker anywhere. My whole experience in years of work in rural
areas in three states denies that idea. Those states are on the
Atlantic seaboard, but if there is any spot more rural than Sandtown,
Kent County, Del., please lead me to it. That particular spot can be
recognized only by the gas pump in front of Sam Houston's general
store. There isn't even a crossroads to mark it on the map.

As I see it, people are people and they are "funnier than anybody"
wherever you find them. A case worker helps people by an approach
and a method which is fundamentally the same whether she is just a
human atom "in a stall devoted to a segment" of the case load of a
large city agency or whether she is the only social worker in her

Survey, December 1939. E. Kathryn Pennypacker was a social worker
in Kent County, Delaware.

county. The approach is individual and the method is, or should be, professional. Just here is where I part company with those who discuss the relative merits of training *vs.* experience for the rural worker. I don't think it is an either/or proposition: both are essential. I have a further conviction that rural social work can be carried on at a high professional level, and must be if it is to be effective.

I do not for one minute question the necessity of learning on the job and of modifying procedures to meet changing or radically different situations. But surely this is not a distinctive requirement for rural social workers. Where would city social workers be today if, under the pressure of an unprecedented relief situation, they had not learned to modify their ways of working? Is there a fundamental difference in necessary skill and knowledge for meeting the realities of a rural situation, rural clients, rural public officials and those of a city? I doubt it.

Part of any social worker's equipment is a working knowledge of the local economy, social life, school facilities, health and medical services, and what-have-you. If the worker is at first unfamiliar with all this, she soon begins to absorb it. Only a person completely oblivious to the community and the clients she is serving would fail to do so. In the city, knowledge of housing and industrial problems is essential; in the country, the problems of the farmer, his tenants and his day laborers demand attention. All the reading in the world is not as valuable to either city or country worker as the day-by-day facing of these problems in the lives of clients, be they urban or rural.

After all whom do we serve as social workers? The clients, most assuredly. The community, yes, but in a different sense. We are the instruments whereby the community helps those in need of a particular service. We serve as its personal representatives, so to speak, in giving help. We have a responsibility to the community for rendering this service and doing it in such a way that the client's needs are met insofar as the community, operating through the individual worker, can do so. It is true of course, that in many rural areas the social worker in the new child welfare services under the Social Security Act represents state and federal rather than local concern for dependent and neglected children. "The gov'ment," as represented by the child welfare worker, is pretty far removed from the bailiwick of Sam Houston, the local storekeeper.

I have small patience with the idea that "an undifferentiated service" is the most feasible way of practicing social work in rural areas. That may be because distances in rural Delaware are not so great as in western states, but in any case I believe that it is a mistake to expect a rural social worker to do everything from certifying people for WPA employment to placing children in foster homes or running parties for old folks. In fact, I hold that the case worker has no business organizing social gatherings as part of her regular job. If she wants to do it in her leisure time, all well and good, but it is a group activity that falls outside her function as case worker, even though she may be responsible for administering funds for old age assistance.

If Miss So-and-So is the only "case worker" in the county, I submit that it is much wiser for her to be responsible for services to a particular group of clients than to be at the beck and call of all the welfare services. To say that she should provide "case work service" for old age assistance, ADC, the blind, crippled children, maternal and child health, direct relief, WPA, CCC, NYA and transients, seems to me to defeat her reason for being there at all. What is this so-called "case work service," anyway? For two years I have struggled with this question in relation to other agencies that ask for "case work service" for their clients, and I have not found a satisfactory answer. Perhaps that is because my conception of case work is closely related to my conception of agency function and the responsibility of a case worker to identify with this function in order to be helpful to those needing the service of her agency. For me, case work unrelated to function means irresponsible activity and not real help.

Let me illustrate directly from my own experience. The child welfare service department of the state agency for which I work frequently is asked for "case work service" for families with children receiving certain kinds of public assistance. We have no responsibility for determining eligibility, we do not administer relief funds, we are not employes of the relief agency and, therefore, have no direct responsibility to it. The help that a family may need, aside from actual financial assistance, is vaguely felt but not clearly defined by the relief worker. She says, "My supervisor doesn't want me to touch children's cases," or "Mrs. Mapes isn't spending her money for the benefit of the children," or "She has a star boarder, can't you make her see she mustn't go on this way?" What then? How can our CWS worker be helpful? What function does she have in relation to the family? Is she to act as a detective to see that Mrs. Mapes spends her money properly or does not entertain "star boarders?" I hope not. What is it that the relief worker does not have time to do that she thinks a "case worker" can do? Perhaps she feels a need for help that her clients do not feel or even want. Perhaps she has a standard of behavior for her clients

which qualifies her willingness to give financial assistance unless
they conform. She can't "make" them conform so she asks for "case
work service." This seems more like a confession of her own inadequacy than a real need for her clients.

We rural social workers must think our way clearly out of these
dilemmas. We cannot afford to excuse ourselves on the basis of the
pressure of work and a never-ceasing demand on our time. First of
all, we should decide that there are very real limits to our job and
begin to use those limits constructively and helpfully in giving a
particular service, instead of making ourselves available to "do
everything." Only thus can we demonstrate the value of real social
case work in the rural districts. Only thus can we set a standard
of performance that will be a guide to the establishment of better
standards of service and personnel in the other welfare agencies
which are now asking us for this so-called "case work service." The
process may be slow, terrifically slow sometimes, but I believe that
it would be fruitful. The trouble is that we get caught by the desperate need for better social work services all along the line. We
are, or think we are, equipped to give them, so we make a try only
to find that we have scattered our energies and have not been particularly helpful anywhere.

In Delaware we have, in the State Board of Charities, a child welfare department with a fairly clear conception of responsibility for
the care and protection of dependent and neglected children, and
those in danger of becoming delinquent. We do not have funds to aid
children in their own homes, but we do have funds to provide foster
home care for children who need it. The Mothers' Pension Commission
administers ADC funds and "mothers' pensions." The federal government provides money for helping to administer child welfare services
in the two rural counties. Our service is set up on functional
lines and we are honestly trying to render a real case work service
to children. In so doing we find ourselves, willy-nilly, related
to relief-giving agencies, to local citizen groups, to the juvenile
court, to the industrial schools, to the public schools, to the
State Board of Health in its maternal, child health, and crippled
children's program, to doctors, hospitals, lawyers and what-have-you.
We administer an adoption law and thus find ourselves related to
maternity homes, unmarried mothers, adopting parents, orphans' court,
and so on. The variety of our relationships knows no limits except
those of the community itself and its resources for human welfare;
but our function is limited to the particular one of helping children, and of protecting them from neglect and the evils of broken
homes.

One of the most serious dangers facing the rural social worker is her inclination to take too much responsibility. I have found that people in rural communities are loathe to shoulder their share of certain kinds of responsibility, in child welfare, for example, by going to court with the social worker in a case of serious neglect of children. They may know that Josh Smith is a drunken, brutal father, that Maria Smith is "weakminded," unable to care for her seven children decently and that she sometimes runs off with other men, leaving fourteen-year old Susie exposed to attacks by her father; but they refuse to appear in court as witnesses to these facts. Their refusal seems to be rooted partly in fear of what the father might do to them if they testified against him, and partly in a conviction that the social worker ought to reform the father and make him support his family, so that the state would not have to spend money caring for his neglected children.

The social worker's relationship to this tangle of family and community is complicated. It demands all the skill that training and experience can give her; a sensitivity to the needs of the children, materially and emotionally; a nicely balanced appreciation of the responsibility and capacity of parents—or their lack thereof—for providing adequate care for their offspring; of the responsibility and resources of the community for cooperative help; of her own responsibility for helping these children. Her eyes must always be on the children; and all her relationships with the neighbors, the parents, relatives, doctors, clinics, court, and other agencies, should contribute to her purpose of helping them.

Take the care of Jimmy Smith, one of Josh and Maria's brood, caught swiping cookies in Sam Houston's store. The neighbors think in terms of punishment, specifically the industrial school; the mother loves Jimmy after her fashion; the father thinks he is old enough to be of some use to the family; Jimmy himself is scared to death and covers it up by swaggering. What is the case worker to do? Take Jimmy promptly to juvenile court and urge his commitment to industrial school? That might satisfy the neighbors, but her job is to help Jimmy. So she makes a counter-proposal. Perhaps foster home placement would help Jimmy, shall we try it? The neighbors shrug their shoulders and express doubts, but agree that at least he would be out from underfoot in Sam Houston's store. This is doubtful cooperation, but it is not opposition, so she goes ahead.

It may be several weeks or even months before she can accomplish her purpose. More than likely she will be opposed by Jimmy's parents. Active cooperation of the neighbors may be necessary to gain custody through court action. Some social workers might feel that parental consent and neighborhood cooperation should be disregarded. Jimmy needs help in a hurry, so just take him and place him. I doubt whether such a hasty procedure would help Jimmy, the family or the neighbors. How can the case worker be considered a responsible and helpful agency representative if she hastily uses authority without full regard to the individuals affected? A slow process is much more likely to "educate" the neighbors and to help Jimmy. A worker expected to do everything might not be able to wait and work and help in this way. Sam Houston wouldn't know whether to trust or distrust this "welfare lady" who does things in such a hurry. The family would most surely hate her and Jimmy might end up in industrial school after all.

It seems to me that rural social work gives a case worker an unequalled opportunity to serve community and clients in such a way as to develop a growing conviction that her services are indispensable. She never has a chance to escape from her responsibility to the community, because it knows her personally and directly in relation to the job she is doing and the people she is helping. But I think she makes a serious mistake if, in her desire to be helpful, she yields to the pressure to undertake case work service for any agency that asks for it. Humanly speaking we are limited, so are our clients and so is every one else in the community.

Rural social work, as well as city social work, involves a continuous process of helping. In the country almost as much time has to be spent in helping the community to give help as is spent in actually helping clients. But it is all of a piece and ultimate success or failure depends just as much on the case worker's skill in dealing with the interested neighbors as it does on her skill in helping Jimmy become a social being instead of anti-social. Child welfare services are in a strategic position in the rural areas for demonstrating the value of a professional job. The communities I know seem predisposed to find ways of helping unfortunate children. People cannot bear to see children starved, mistreated, or deliberately exposed to immoral and vicious influences. They seem to be reaching out for any sort of constructive help for such cases.

So let's have more training and more experience, a maximum of skill and of functional responsibility and, above all, an awareness of the strength to be derived from an identification with a limited agency function. In this way we can hope to meet some needs fairly adequately and not be overcome by a sense of failure. We simply can't do everything.

11

Training Rural Workers

The training required for practice in the rural field was a question
of concern from the times of the first Country Life Commission. The
American Country Life Association held meetings and institutes for
rural workers as early as 1910, when a summer session was offered at
the Massachusetts Agricultural College in Amherst. In 1922, Josephine Brown discussed the personal traits and technical expertise required of rural workers, hinting at the need for special preparation
for the rural field ("A City Case Worker in the Country," *The Family*,
Vol. III, No. 8). Surveys on the place and importance of rural sociology and rural economics in the curriculum were carried out in
the 1920s and early 1930s, but it was not until the Federal Emergency
Relief Act began to be implemented that questions of special training
for rural workers were seriously raised.

The administration of relief in remote counties necessitated the
employment of local personnel. More often than not, those indigenous
workers, who came from all walks of life, had little formal education.
How could they be prepared for the stresses of those demanding positions? Local relief administrators were baffled with a variety of
questions: What kind of training should be provided to relief workers? Were they, in the fashion of the day, doing "case work," and
if so, how should their natural abilities be enhanced? What should
be the duration of training? Where should it take place? Who should
be selected for it? The questions were almost endless.

Through its Division of Training and Research, FERA made available
substantial sums of money for the training of its workers. Short-
term institutes and seminars were held in rural localities. Intense
supervision was used as a teaching tool, and finally workers were
sent to the schools of social work which were generally located in
large cities, often out of their own rural states.

Out of this frenetic training activity came a number of descriptions and conclusions. The remedies were as varied as the problems,

but at least the idea that rural workers required "something special" was firmly established. A lot was argued about the validity of training away from the rural locale. Generally, research showed that any training was better than no training at all. A lot was said about offering training in the land-grant colleges and universities, which were, after all, naturals for the task. Much was argued about the level of training (graduate or undergraduate) and the content of it (general or job-related). In summary, many of the questions raised lived on in the bitter controversies between the National Association of Schools of Social Administration (NASSA) and the American Association of Schools of Social Work (AASSW) during the 1940s.

It has been mentioned before that between 1942 and 1952, there existed in the United States two national accrediting bodies for social work education. One, perhaps the better known, was the American Association of Schools of Social Work, whose members were primarily the large schools of the East. The AASSW insisted upon graduate instruction for all social workers. The other organization, the National Association of Schools of Social Administration, was formed in April 1942 by members of the Southwestern Committee on Education for the Social Sciences of the Southwestern Social Service Association. The members of NASSA, for the most part small colleges and land-grant universities, indicated the need for a new association in response to a decision of the AASSW to refuse membership to a school or department which offered any part of its social service instruction on the undergraduate level. (Clearly, this was an unrealistic decision at a time when most rural jobs were filled by totally untrained people.)

It is the purpose of this chapter to present some of the historical antecedents of social work education for rural workers. The questions raised in the 1930s have not yet been resolved. Perhaps the experiences of those pioneer educators can help us in our struggles. Because many of the important issues born in the thirties were elaborated upon in the forties, some of the pieces transcribed in this chapter date beyond the year of 1939. Those who wrote them, however, had crystallized their ideas through their Depression and New Deal experiences.

The first excerpt, "The Teaching of Rural Sociology and Rural Economics and the Conduct of Rural Social Research in Teachers' Colleges, Schools of Religion, and Non-State Colleges," was written by Edmund de S. Brunner for *Social Forces* in 1930. This article has been included to exemplify the nature of the surveys which were carried out in the thirties and which revealed the interest of social science educators in rural matters. It is interesting to note that Brunner suggested that when it comes to rural courses, "listing a subject in the catalogue does not necessarily mean that it has an important place in the curriculum." Many rural educators would echo his statement in 1979.

The second article was written by Irma Mohr in 1930. "Training Apprentice Workers in a Rural Agency" deals with the issue of inservice training, which rural agencies, unable to get professional personnel or desirous of developing a cadre of indigenous workers, chose to sponsor.

The third excerpt was published in the *Survey* in 1935. Written by Ruth A. Lerrigo, "The Test of the Training" reports the results of FERA-sponsored courses in existing schools of social work. The quoted comments of one student are particularly significant: "The fact that we did not study rural situations disturbed me" and although she concluded, as the schools would have emphasized, that "human nature is an unchanging factor and only the externals of a rural and urban community are different," one cannot help but wonder how many students are feeling equally concerned in 1979.

Descriptions of experiments for the training of relief-FERA workers were abundant. There are many articles as well as pamphlets by the FERA Division of Research from which to choose. They all describe various ways in which schools of social work and local FERA training departments attempted to tackle the development of rural workers. Two articles have been selected here. "An Experiment in Training for Rural Social Work" by Lucille Cairns describes the short course offered by the University of Missouri since 1934. "Learning with Our FERA's" by Mary Lois Pyles describes what was done at Washington University in St. Louis, and emphasizes realistic retraining of personnel from other walks of life. The Pyles' article, as well as another by Mary F. Bogue and Magdalen Peter, "Two Experiments in Training for Supervisory Personnel in New Jersey" (not included here), deal with the notion of learning from peers. In the New Jersey experiment, students enrolled in the New York School were mixed with nonenrolled workers in a single training unit. Although it appears that the potential contributions of the indigenous workers were underutilized, the idea was a novel one, worth many possibilities for the present.

In 1938, Josephine C. Brown wrote two articles on "In-Service Training for Public Welfare, The Whys and Whats" and "The Hows" (*Survey*, October and November 1938). The first one has been included. Like the articles by Josephine Strode, it was addressed primarily to administrators of remote county offices, where the needs for in-service training were most obvious. Brown stressed the educational role of supervision.

"Supervision in a Rural Setting" was a paper presented by Minnie

Alper at a session on "Supervision as One Method of Staff Development" of the 1939 National Conference of Social Work in Buffalo. Alper addressed the problems of transition experienced by "workers who have learned to practice with the use of urban resources and specialized agencies" and underscored the role of the supervisor in helping the worker become accustomed and oriented to the rural situation.

A fascinating article is that by Herman M. Pekarsky entitled "Rural Training for Rural Workers." Pekarsky indicts the field for having tried to fit the urban formula to rural conditions. He places strong emphasis on the recruitment of workers who have "a native philosophy indigenous to the soil," and it is doubtful whether he would have accepted workers who were not born in rural areas, a rather problematic generalization.

Another article containing a strong stance on rural social work is that which A. A. Smick wrote for *Sociology and Social Research* in 1938, "Training for Rural Social Work." In this paper, Smick makes it clear that he disagreed with the prevalent opinions of the period. Smick insisted that rural social work was unique and required special training which should be developed in typically rural communities. He proposed that such schools be established in the land-grant colleges which were in the position of lending their expertise in rural sociology, farm management, home economics, and related subjects.

"Training for Rural Social Work" by Hazel A. Hendricks is concerned with the appropriate content to be included in the training of rural workers for child welfare. Her suggestions give heavy emphasis to the study of social legislation and social administration.

The final selection is dated 1946 and was written by Mattie Cal Maxted, one of NASSA's early members and active proponent of undergraduate social work education. At this point in our history, rural and urban workers have accepted the advent of undergraduate social work education as a contemporary phenomenon. Historians of the rural field must help dispel this myth. Rural workers risked much enmity and criticism when they supported these ideas in the early forties. In "Don't Forget Your Country Cousin," Maxted wrote for the *Survey* the reasons which kept rural workers fighting for undergraduate education even when the cause appeared to have been lost.

We have now covered, even if in a broad, basic, and somewhat sketchy fashion, the development of rural social welfare between 1908 and 1939. I do not believe it is necessary to belabor the point. It will now suffice to say that the spirit of the early rural pioneers lives on in present issues. For how much have we done which is truly new in the rural field since 1940? Let the epilogue by Joanne Mermelstein and Paul Sundet bridge the gap.

THE TEACHING OF RURAL SOCIOLOGY AND RURAL ECONOMICS AND THE CONDUCT
OF RURAL SOCIAL RESEARCH IN TEACHERS' COLLEGES, SCHOOLS OF RELIGION
AND NON-STATE COLLEGES

Edmund de S. Brunner

Early in 1930 the Department of Rural Education of Teachers College,
Columbia, conducted an investigation into the research activities in
the fields of rural sociology and economics of the colleges and universities listed by the Department of Agriculture as having teachers
of rural sociology. The inquiry was made in order to assist one of
the projects of the Committee on Social and Economic Research in
Agriculture of the Social Science Research Council.[1] The questionnaire used was a very simple one. The correspondent was asked to
list the courses given in rural sociology and economics, the number
of hours of credit for each, and also to describe research projects
conducted "under the general supervision of the department or by the
department without or with the aid of students," since 1925.

The chief object of the questionnaire was to discover the activities of the smaller institutions though all were circularized.

This emphasis was due to the fact that it did not seem fair to
compare the state colleges of agriculture with their liberal appropriations for research under the Purnell Funds with other institutions. Furthermore, because of publication funds the work of the
state colleges is well known. All but four of these state institutions offered one or more courses in rural sociology. All of them
taught agricultural economics. Most of them had under way research
projects in this subject but nearly 20 of the states had failed to
use the Purnell Funds for social studies.

Two other classes of institutions were eliminated from the final
comparison, namely, the large urban universities like Harvard,

Social Forces, October 1930. Edmund de S. Brunner spent his early
years in Bethlehem, Pa. He had a degree in theology from Moravian
College and served for years as a pastor in rural Pennsylvania. In
1919, he began directing the town and country survey department of
the Interchurch World Movement and after its dissolution, Brunner
continued with the Institute for Social and Religious Research where
he launched his career as rural sociologist. He is the author of
The Growth of A Science (1957) and held faculty positions at Teachers' College of Columbia University.

[1] It had not been intended to publish a report of this brief study
but many of those replying to the questionnaire asked for a summary
of the findings. It is interesting that nearly one-fifth of those
making such a request failed either to sign their names or else to
give their addresses. By using postmarks and the directory of
teachers furnished by the Department of Agriculture, all but a few
of the absent-minded were identified.

Chicago, Leland Stanford, Yale, and state universities that were separate from colleges of agriculture.

With few exceptions the former group was doing very little rural work. The records of the latter varied greatly. Some took almost no interest in rural topics, leaving that field to the state college of agriculture. A few had extensive courses and considerable record of research projects especially the University of North Carolina and the University of Virginia.[2]

The Teaching of Rural Social Science

The remaining institutions reporting numbered 215, approximately half of the rest of those listed as teaching rural sociology. These were classified in three groups: Teachers' colleges, schools of religion, i.e., theological seminaries and church colleges giving pre-theological work, and all others.

Of these 32, or 14.8 per cent, had either dropped their offerings in rural sociology or had offered none. Rural sociology, however, is a more popular subject than rural economics in the institutions under consideration for more than three-fourths offered no courses in this latter subject, as Table I shows.

TABLE I

Institutions Offering Courses in Rural Sociology
and Rural Economics by Type

	Total	Offering Rural Sociology		Offering Rural Economics	
		Number	Per cent	Number	Per cent
All types	215	183	85.2	50	23.2
Teachers' colleges	69	59	85.5	23	33.3
Schools of religion, etc.	61	55	90.1	5	8.2
All other	85	69	81.2	22	26.0

This table shows that there is little difference among the three types of institutions as to the proportion offering rural sociology.

[2] Professor E. C. Branson of North Carolina reports that since 1914 his department has published three books, 26 bulletins, and 18 county surveys. Through the Institute for Research in Social Science, sixty-three other county surveys of social and economic conditions were completed but not printed.

The theological seminary group shows scant interest in rural economics though it leads in offering sociology.

Listing a subject in the catalog does not necessarily mean that it has an important place in the curriculum. Forty-three of the teacher training institutions, an equal number of schools of religion and 62 of the other institutions have only one course each. In other words, four out of five of the 215 schools under consideration offering rural sociology have only one course. A three point course is the most frequent, nearly half being of this type. One course in 10 was but one hour. Two and four hour courses were of about equal frequency, occurring respectively in 26 and 23 places.

The institutions having more than one course in rural sociology offered from 2 to 7, though most of them only two or three, and from four to eighteen hours, the maximum being attained by one school of religion and one teachers' college. The average number of semester hours devoted to rural sociology in those institutions offering courses was 3.0. The schools of religion exceeded this average by half a semester hour, the teachers' colleges equalled it, the others fell half an hour below it.

In the case of rural economics, the average number of semester hours for each institution offering work in this subject was 3.5 for the entire group but only 3.0 for the teachers' colleges. The other groups slightly exceeded the average.[3]

In the main there was, as would be expected, a correlation between the size of the institution and the number of courses offered. As a rule it was the larger institutions that multiplied courses and hours. It is apparent from the figures given, however, that in the institutions under review neither rural sociology or economics command the full time of many men. In the schools of religion these courses are frequently combined with those in rural church methods.

Research in Rural Social Science

So much for the teaching of rural social science. The inquiry now turns to the conduct of research studies. Two out of every five institutions conduct some work along this line. As Table II shows, the teachers' colleges lead in this activity closely followed by the schools of religion.

Most of this research and survey work is undertaken in connection with classes especially in rural sociology but two teachers' colleges

---

[3] In three institutions rural sociology and economics were combined in a single course. In these cases the hours were divided between the two subjects.

and seven schools of religion have courses in survey and research methods.

The studies undertaken cover a wide scope. Eleven teachers' colleges, twelve schools of religion and six other colleges conducted the more or less usual type of social and economic surveys of communities, townships or counties. The teachers' colleges showed a tendency to move from the study of the school and its pupils as such to surveys into the relation of the social and economic environment upon the school and its students. Thus studies were reported on the sociological and economic problems of school attendance, the use of leisure time, trends in population, the intelligence of the rural as compared with the urban population. The research program of one teachers' college included studies of the reading matter in farm homes and rural schools, of the distribution, professional equipment, salary, tenure, and social contribution of rural school teachers in a given area, of the type of advertising in the magazines entering the farm homes of several school districts, and of the status and distribution of the rural churches of a county. Another institution of this type studied rural social distance and the superstitions of prospective rural school teachers. Still another was studying rural taxation and a fourth had adopted the interesting device of requiring students to survey the community to which they were assigned for their practice teaching, an idea that might well be adopted by others.

In addition to church and community studies schools of religion had conducted studies of rural health, rural social work, rural lodges, rural religious education, and the attitudes of rural people.

One such institution had, at the time of this report, 10 students who were making community studies in places in which the churches that they served were located. These surveys included an historical study of the community, maps showing the distributive aspects of community life, statistical data on each family, an analysis of the major social, religious, economic, and institutional problems and finally the building of a program.[4]

Two teachers' colleges and two schools of religion cooperated with the colleges of agriculture in their respective states in Purnell studies. This is a plan that might well be extended.

The other institutions included in this survey, as Table II shows, have not done very much in the line of research nor has what they have done been of much originality. The frequent complaint is made that there is "neither time, energy nor money" for such work. On the other hand one small institution with less than 150 students has

---

[4] Chicago Theological Seminary, Chicago, Ill.

TABLE II

Percentage of Institutions Conducting Research

	All Schools Conducting Research	Teaching Rural Sociology and Conducting Research
All types	40.5%	47.5%
Teachers' colleges	55.0	64.4
Schools of religion	45.9	50.9
All other	24.7	30.4

conducted creditable studies in such fields as church and community, changes in retail trade areas and their causes, conditions in rural industrial centers, etc.,[5] which shows what can be done.

The extent to which survey and research is being used in the professional schools of the group under consideration is encouraging and a bit surprising. Unlike the colleges of agriculture most such institutions have no appropriations to cover publication. Thus it is impossible for the outside world to judge of the volume of this work. While the results of many of these studies had been built into the teaching material and while a number had served definite purposes in affecting community or institutional policy none but those immediately concerned have had the benefit of the work. This failure to publish is unfortunate but probably difficult to remedy.

This inquiry shows, however, that the teaching of rural sociology is being increasingly followed by the conduct of social studies, a tendency that is particularly marked in the professional schools. It shows also that such schools are beginning to go beyond the usual type of social surveys of communities and investigate problems. It is hoped that this tendency will continue and that ways and means may be found of giving wider circulation to the results.[6]

[5] Moravian College and Theological Seminary, Bethlehem, Pa.

[6] Apart from short summaries in the bulletins of some of the institutions, a few other summaries printed in journals of sociology and three or four bulletins nothing had been printed. A few studies were given local circulation in mimeographed form.

TRAINING APPRENTICE WORKERS IN A RURAL AGENCY

Irma Mohr

With new organizations forming in our small communities, and with
older organizations receiving a fresh impetus from the growth and
development of our rural areas, how are we to meet the difficulty
of finding trained personnel to equip these agencies? Although the
problem of securing trained workers is undoubtedly not peculiar to
rural and small town areas, it is felt much more keenly there, since
the majority of trained workers prefer the advantages of city life
and think that coming to a small community to live is equivalent to
renouncing the world. After we have educated our rural areas to
appreciate the importance of organized social work, carried on by a
trained personnel, are we to tell them that this is an ideal beyond
their realization?

How can the executive and board of directors of the small agency
meet this dilemma? Can a secretary, responsible for developing community interest, for engineering the annual financial campaign, for
carrying on a year-round publicity program, and, perhaps, for handling a portion of the case work, undertake to train and supervise
apprentice workers? Or should she throw up her hands, say that the
job is impossible without trained assistants—who are difficult to
find? We, in Montgomery County, tried both procedures, found the
second to fail, and met with some degree of success in working out
the first.

Organized in 1908 by a group of earnest volunteers, who carried
on the entire program themselves for a time, the Social Service
League of Montgomery County has had a slow but steady expansion, until its program includes, in addition to family case work, a probation department in connection with the juvenile court and a department of child placement and supervision. The county itself offers
unusual diversity both in population and in geography. Adjacent to
the District of Columbia, it extends westward along the Potomac into
the foothills of the Blue Ridge, so that on approaching from Washington, one travels first through a series of well populated suburban
communities, whose residents have business and social interests in
Washington, on into scattered towns and villages, with acres of rich
farm land lying between. The majority of our problems occur among
the farm laborers, although in the suburban sections of the county

The Family, February 1930. Irma Mohr was General Secretary of the
Social Service League of Montgomery County, Maryland.

our clients come from a wide range of occupations and of social groupings. About a third of our work is with the negro population of the county.

When a new executive came in 1926, she found an untrained worker struggling under a case load of a hundred and fifty families a month in the family department alone. The probation department of the juvenile court averaged three new cases a month, and there were forty children to be supervised in the department of child placement.

The agencies and resources at hand showed possibilities for the development of an adequate case work program. The county employed three public health nurses who worked under the direction of the local health officer, a school attendance officer (who kept in close touch with us and worked with us on a number of problems), and a nutrition worker, financed by the local Red Cross Chapter, who not only conducted classes in the schools but visited a number of families under the care of the League. The state department of health provided weekly clinics for the treatment of venereal infections; chest clinics, prenatal and pre-school clinics, and mental hygiene clinics, held monthly. A private hospital in the county offered a limited number of free beds for the use of our patients.

Our first thought was to find two trained assistants to master the volume of work but, although we were willing to pay $1800 a year and boasted of being within commuting distance of Washington, no trained workers were forthcoming. We might modify this statement by adding that one worker, fresh from a school of social work, came, saw, and left within two weeks.

Bitter experience forced us to the decision that we must have local people on our staff and that, since we could not find them trained, we would train our own. The rural community is slow to accept outsiders; although the League had been organized eighteen years, it had made little progress in the rural sections. It happened that there were two workers available from those sections and we felt they would be better able than any outsider to interpret social work to their communities. Both were college graduates, with some teaching experience, and both had lived in the county for years so that they were thoroughly familiar with small town and rural conditions.

In view of the situation which the organization faced, it was generally decided that the most important job was for the executive to build up a sound case work program. This meant an immediate emphasis on case work training. We had selected workers who already had a background in sociology and economics, so that we made little attempt to offer them more than the fundamentals of case work technique plus the realization that a case worker's training is never complete, and that the job is a constant challenge to the individual's development and growth. The training plan involved a certain allowance of time each day for reading records and for conferences and a weekly staff meeting.

The course of training (started in 1926 with the two new workers) continues today with a staff made up as follows: an executive secretary, two full time case workers, one worker who gives a third of her time to clerical work and the remainder to case work, a full time and a part-time stenographer. As our staff has increased in skill and in number, the executive has been able to reduce her share of the case work, so that at present she carries about twenty families a month. In an office log, which we kept recently over a period of two weeks, her time was distributed as follows: one fourth to actual case work, one fifth to travelling in visiting families, seeing volunteers, or attending meetings, one fifth to supervision, and one third to miscellaneous executive duties. Our volume of work for the last fiscal year totalled 407 family cases, 38 juvenile court cases and 58 children under foster care. With this volume of work, carried by a small staff, our training was necessarily planned on the basis of expediency and it suffered occasional interruptions, due to emergency situations. The procedure in training was in accordance with the following general plan:

The introduction to field work consisted in follow up visits to families where the investigation had been completed and where treatment was under way. As we gradually began building up an adequate system of record keeping in the office, we introduced beginners to the work by having them make summaries of long-time records of families which it was planned to have them visit later. Next they were given cases in which a full first interview had been obtained so that it was possible for the supervisor to outline fairly definitely with the worker the next steps to be taken. Because of the pressure of work, the workers were obliged to take first interviews before the end of the first month and to carry through the study and treatment of new cases, always however with close supervision. Since our case load totalled 150 families a month, it was necessary to assign them about 30 families the first month, most of them cases where treatment was already under way. Before the end of three months their case load had increased to 50 or more families a month. Individual conferences, held with each worker every other day, gave opportunities for reports on visits and for discussing the work for the two succeeding days. (Distances to be travelled made daily conferences inexpedient.) During the first two or three weeks the workers' interviews, recorded in long hand, were read and corrected by the secretary during the conferences. As their recording improved they were encouraged to dictate, and the stenographer brought their

records to the secretary's desk for written or verbal comments before
filing. The individual conferences related almost entirely to the
concrete family problems which the worker was attempting to treat,
but the supervisor found occasion to suggest articles or books dealing with particular problems and to discuss the wider implications
of the concrete problems.

More abstract discussions of the theory and technique of social
case work were held in the weekly staff conferences. Before starting
on their field work, our workers were given *What is Social Case Work?*
to read. For our staff conferences *Social Diagnosis* was assigned,
chapter by chapter, and discussed with the group, using the workers'
own case material for illustrations of the topics to be covered. We
also used a record from the Baltimore Family Welfare Association for
teaching purposes—one especially applicable to our situation because
it showed the utilization of community resources in organizing relief. This record was analyzed step by step and criticized from the
standpoint of its application of the technique set forth in *Social
Diagnosis*. The record was also used as a standard for case recording, since there were no records available in the office for this
purpose.

After we had read *Social Diagnosis*, we continued our study of investigation, diagnosis, plan, and treatment by carrying on critical
analyses of our own records in the weekly discussion groups. Each
worker in turn read one of her own records analyzed from the following standpoints: the picture presented of the family's background,
the picture of individual members of the family group, family interrelationships, the family's adjustment in relation to health, education, recreation, religion, and employment, the worker's diagnosis
of the problem and her plan for the family, and the methods used in
treatment, both subjective and objective. The workers also wrote
out several interviews in detail, including a first interview and a
treatment interview and these were analyzed.

Each member of the staff of course subscribed to *The Family,* and
articles were read and discussed from week to week, the workers taking turns in reviewing the article assigned for the week and in
leading the discussion. We read first articles dealing with investigation or social study, later those dealing with diagnosis and
treatment. Several meetings were devoted to a discussion of diagnosis which the workers had written.

Toward the end of the first year we began a study of the more
subjective aspects of treatment, continuing to use articles from
The Family in this connection. In the course of our discussion,
articles from *Mental Hygiene* were suggested for reading, and such
books as *The Social Case History, Broken Homes, Interviews, Three*

Problem Children, Mental Conflicts and Misconduct and Everyday Problems of the Everyday Child. Since we do not have access to a library, our reading was largely determined by what was available in the office.

From the beginning community attitudes as they related to the cases were discussed in the individual conferences with the workers, but we did not discuss the community as a whole in our group meetings until the second year of training. We then stressed community participation and education, using articles from *The Family* for this purpose. The workers again brought in their own records to show instances in which community attitudes and prejudices had seriously affected a family's adjustment, or to illustrate the use of local people in working out family plans. For instance, one of our small rural communities was greatly disturbed about a couple living in adultery, rearing a family of five children. The wife had been deserted by her legal husband and had established a home with this second man; relations were harmonious, and the children received satisfactory care. The community felt very strongly that the home should be broken up but, through a local citizen, a county commissioner, we were able to change this point of view. He assisted us in obtaining a divorce for the woman and in arranging for her marriage to the second man, thereby legalizing the family status.

Even with local workers, it was necessary for us to stress the danger of carrying our case work too far beyond the standards of the community. Early in their training our workers were given experience in presenting problems before a case committee made up of representatives from various parts of the county. In each district, we have a few local men and women with whom we can talk over case problems in confidence and enlist their help in interpreting our point of view to their neighbors. In training the workers for this method of approach, we introduced discussions of objectivity in the case worker, bringing out the effect of emotional attitudes not only in her work with the individual family but in her work with the community as a whole.

Following this study of case work in relation to the community, we returned to the study of case work processes, this time attempting to introduce something of the psychiatric approach. We studied one of the records prepared by the Institute Committee on Alcoholics and the workers then wrote evaluations of a number of their more intensive records from the standpoint of personality development. We again took up the art of interviewing, this time considering it as an attempt to change attitudes and to develop personality. That these discussions have stimulated our workers' thinking is indicated by their later records.

One of the most encouraging aspects of our experiment in apprentice training is the workers' keen desire for further training. The one high school graduate on our staff spent three afternoons a week last winter taking a course in sociology at George Washington University. Another worker attended Mr. Bruno's institute at the Maryland State Conference last year, and a third attended Miss Hamilton's extension course in case work held in Baltimore last spring. We encourage them to attend summer school and allow them time off with pay.

At one of our recent staff meetings, we discussed what we considered the fundamentals of case work. In thinking over their experience during the past two or three years, our workers agreed on the following:

(1) Knowledge of what constitutes normal social relationships and knowledge of the local community.

(2) The use of the technique of the first interview and of investigation, or social study, to acquire insight into the individual and the family, in relation to their background and environment.

(3) Treatment, following a plan based on the above knowledge, leading to the better adjustment of the individual, through participation of the client and through the use of various resources within and without the family group.

(4) Participation of the community in case work, through the use of local people to assist in carrying out the plan.

(5) Emphasis not only on method, but on what effect the method will have on the client and on the community, stressing the importance of spirit and attitude rather than technique, and modifying technique and procedure to meet local conditions.

Without minimizing the value of school trained workers we feel that the results of our experiment justify the rural community in the use of local apprentice workers. The difficulty of adjustment which a newcomer is bound to experience on moving into a small town or rural community has been eliminated for them. Because they know the background, the history, and the treasured idiosyncrasies of every village, they are more sensitive to community reactions than a stranger could be. With only four instead of thirty-four or more agencies to which we can turn for help, the use of machinery has been simplified for them. They see case work reduced to its simplest terms as the art of human relationships. By interpreting case work to their neighbors and their friends, they have certainly increased the interest of the community in our work and have helped us not only to double our financial support but to develop a more sympathetic attitude toward social work and a more ready response to our calls for volunteer service. It is impossible, however, to overemphasize the fact that our results depended not only on the getting of workers familiar with the locality, but on the correlation of theoretical discussion and field experience planned definitely for an educational purpose.

THE TEST OF THE TRAINING

Ruth A. Lerrigo

What "book learning" in the form of training in professional schools of social work has to offer the emergency relief worker was given a significant test during the last school year, when upwards of nine hundred carefully selected emergency relief workers and promising recruits attended accredited schools of social work for periods of from four to six months at FERA expense. The FERA Department of Research has reported in a recent bulletin (Series II, Number 7) the results of a careful inquiry into the results of the training program, made a month after the first group of students had completed the courses and gone back to their jobs. Returns from 244 students and thirty-six relief administrations, as well as the schools' estimates of student performance were weighed in compiling the material.

The report leaves little room for doubt that the experiment was well received by the students concerned and was a valuable demonstration of principles and practice for future emergency training programs.

The voice of the scoffer has been too frequent and loud through the land to be ignored in any consideration of the need or lack of need for professional social work training for emergency relief work. To those who may see the job solely as one of administration and business efficiency, the one valid answer, the test respected by the public, the professional schools, relief administrators and workers alike is: How does the client come off? Is he any better off because a trained or partly trained social worker "investigates" or "supervises" or "does case work" on him. To this question, then, the

Survey, October 1935.

414

judgment of the executives for whom these students returned to work is that clients did profit.

According to the summary of findings, students and directors of social service found improvement in service to families, in administration of relief and in making and sustaining satisfactory community contacts, as a result of the training experiment. State directors report that students have developed "perspective, assurance, leadership, administrative and organizing ability."

About 55 percent of the students in the group on their return to work, were promoted to positions of more responsibility than they had previously held. State directors of social service qualify the significance of this, however, by saying that the promotions of a highly selected group did not necessarily indicate that the students were wholly equipped for increased responsibilities but rather that they were relatively better equipped than other members of the staff.

A gain in general perspective and understanding of the whole relief program is the benefit most frequently cited by the students themselves. The training period varied in different schools. Only a handful felt that a shorter period than their FERA fellowship permitted would have been adequate, this feeling being dictated apparently by impatience to put what they had learned into immediate practice. Students fresh from the hectic realities of the relief field needed time to adjust themselves to the atmosphere of the class room and the conditions of controlled field work. "The first quarter was spent in 'unlearning' and getting adjusted," commented one of the students. "As a first quarter student I did little definite constructive thinking. . . . During the second quarter concepts became clearer, goals more orderly and organized, and professional attitudes, skills and spirit were born."

A general difficulty experienced by students on their return to their jobs was in re-orienting themselves to local conditions and in applying the principles they had gained to the hard realities of overwhelming case loads, inadequate equipment and so on. Many felt that the courses offered should have taken more cognizance of the actual conditions of work at this time, particularly in rural areas, with instructors thoroughly familiar with the rural scene. Many shared the feeling of the student who said:

> My work helped me to understand and meet the need of a rural community only insofar as it helped me to understand people. The fact that we did not study rural situations disturbed me until I realized that human nature is an unchanging factor—that only the externals of a rural and urban community are different, and that a case worker's resourcefulness was the only substitute for outside resources so abundant in cities.

Another student said:

> The classroom and field work can never completely meet the needs
> of any social work job. A certain amount of seasoning, practi-
> cal experience, experimenting, is necessary in every situation.
> I know that I could not have handled my present position ade-
> quately without the background of professional training. I know
> now, more than I realized while in school, what the particular
> needs of my own job are.

Of the courses taken, case work and field work were an easy first
in student rating of practical value, with public welfare administration, psychiatry and medical information coming next. Other courses
rated as of particular benefit were community organization, financial
planning, social statistics, jurisprudence, economics, social legislation and problems of unemployment relief.

Conspicuous among the questions raised by state directors of social
service out of the FERA experiment is that of the value of short-term
courses. Six months was considered not long enough, while a year,
even though it must include fewer students was preferred by twenty-
four of thirty-four directors queried. Care in selecting workers
for student fellowships was generally emphasized since the FERA experience clearly indicated that those with good job records and preferably a college degree showed the best response to the training
processes.

A probable future consequence of the 1935 FERA emergency training
program is suggested by the fact that a large percentage of the students who participated have expressed professional aspirations and a
desire to continue professional education and training.

AN EXPERIMENT IN TRAINING FOR RURAL SOCIAL WORK

Lucille Cairns

The Graduate Short Course for Public Welfare Workers was officially instituted at the University of Missouri as a C.W.A. project in the spring semester of 1934. It was the answer to the call for trained workers in the counties of Missouri. Unlike the "Come over into Macedonia" plea, the rural need had not yet been recognized by the large rural population itself, but only by a few of its leaders. Yet relief and service needs were growing at a tremendous rate. The job for the social worker, therefore, had been an intensive selling as well as a serving one from the beginning, taxing every ounce of patience, ingenuity, courage, and fortitude she—or he—had. (The counties responded less defensively to the man worker "instead of the 'ooman who oughter to be hum raisin' young 'uns and fixin' a man's grub 'stead o' tellin' 'em.") The first relief worker appointed under the F.E.R.A. remarked after his initial tour of one of the rural counties, "I'd as soon announce myself as a 'revenuer' in some places as a social worker."

Little wonder that the urban workers who had gone into counties with the pioneer spirit and run up against such resistance welcomed the suggestion of reinforcements from the Short Course, since the course was designed to attract native rural young people of university training. At the University a semester's classroom work was offered with ten hours of graduate credit. The subsequent three hundred hours of supervised field work was only a tentative part of the program at this time, and became a reality only at the close of the semester. Then eight hours of credit were offered for it, six hours for field work and two hours for special reports.

The training project was fostered by the Division of Women's Work of the Missouri C.W.A. but was worked out by the Rural Sociology Department of the University and financed and encouraged throughout by the Director of the State Relief Commission, even after discontinuance of C.W.A., and by his Field Director whose trained staff contributed throughout to the program.

The plan included the offer of 150 scholarships at $6.75 per week. Any man or woman graduate of a college or university, not over 30 years of age, a resident of any county in the state was invited to apply for a scholarship. All the local newspapers were asked to run publicity on the project.

The Family, June 1935.

Each county formed a committee made up of the chairman of the relief committee, a physician, the county superintendent of schools,
the county home demonstration agent, the county agricultural agent,
a prominent farmer, and a prominent farm woman. This committee was
asked to pass on the applicants after interviewing them personally
and reviewing their applications covering educational backgrounds,
employment history, extra-curricular school activities, reasons for
interest in social work, signed certificates from family physicians.
The committee indicated the first, second, and third choices which
were sent in to the State Relief office. The State Relief office
reserved the right to make the final selection after its supervisors
had conferred with the candidates individually. Frequently the committee's first choice was accepted. Occasionally one was discouraged
because of obvious interest in "just something to do and a chance to
accumulate college credits" without evidence of personality qualifications for the case work job. A few counties had no available college people or were not interested, so other counties were given
larger quotas. A few exceptions were made for applicants above 30
years of age. Unless the individual had had previous interest along
social lines, this increased age became a handicap. The average age
was about 27. Of the 144 applications finally approved there were a
few more women than men; the men dropped out faster for various reasons, however, so that of the 117 finally available as visitors or
assistants, about a third were men. The possible political pressures
expected in this method of selection did not materialize to more than
a negligible degree. The quality of the candidates and the high
standards of the professional group making the final choices were
safeguards here.

Many of the students accepted had been teachers. Some were unable
to get schools because of the continued closings; others were looking for broader fields of service. The group also included engineers,
architects, a nurse, home economists, athletic directors, journalists, three preachers, a funeral director, two missionaries, a number
of students just out of school without experience, a few C.W.A. workers, and a group who had done the emergency case work job without
previous training. Their degrees ranged from B.S. and A.B. to Ph.D.
and came largely from the University of Missouri and the various
state teachers' colleges, a few from smaller private colleges and
the two other universities in the state. Universities outside the
state were also represented to some extent.

The students from the beginning showed a professional attitude toward their work. As a help in their own financial problems as well
as an opportunity for developing executive and group participation
skill, some fifty of the students organized and successfully operated

independently a co-operative dining room. This did much to stretch the $6.75 scholarship. Here as elsewhere they demonstrated initiative and ability to work together. Through the community center that sprang up about the dining hall they brought in faculty members and visiting leaders to discuss professional matters with them.

They became a tribunal for their own problems and while at times were a bit arbitrary, they demonstrated remarkable understanding and ability to face the difficult situations of individual students and of the group. Some real problems of handicapping timidity and over-compensating aggressiveness received marked impetus toward adjustment. The problem of financial insecurity, the frequent anxious question from many of these young people who had never experienced vocational achievement through performance—"Am I a misfit?"—received dilution therapy from the group outside the classroom every bit as much as in the classroom and individual conferences.

The $6.75 scholarship was granted on the basis of fifteen working hours per week. This work included the mapping of county soils, each student taking his own county; research for county history; statistical assistance with a mental testing project; and some other work in connection with classes. An excellent recreational project of two hours per week under special leadership was included. The time given to work projects cut into the study time of students quite heavily, and is now being evaluated as to its justifiability.

Since the students arrived on the campus after the opening of the second semester, classes were arranged to cover subject matter for only ten graduate credit hours:

Home Economics	2
Case Work	2
Agency Administration	2
Depending on prerequisites, a choice of Sociology, The Family, Abnormal Psychology, or Social Pathology	2
Case Work Seminar and Special Investigations which later included talks by outside speakers and the Recreational Seminar	2

To the regular university faculty were added instructors for Agency Administration, Case Work, and the Case Work Seminar—practicing case workers from executive and supervisory positions of family agencies within the state.

Much as it was desired, it proved impossible to arrange field work for so large a group of students in so small a college town as Columbia whose agency loads could not warrant the absorption of so many. The Case Work Seminar was the best substitute that could be afforded pending field training or practice work later.

In planning the content of class work the Short Course faculty were early encouraged to face realistically the time limitation. An experienced training consultant warned against surfeiting with a mass of indigestible material but rather strongly urged that the emphasis be on less concrete subject matter with its rigid standardizing effects and on more stimulation toward individual, objective, and progressive thinking. This seemed particularly essential where rural workers would operate largely on their own in isolated areas. The concept for education of the group soon came to be recognized as akin to Thomas Whitney Surette's "by education . . . we mean . . . to secure and establish a set of trustworthy emotions based on clear perception of the difference between what is great and not so great . . . between the best things men have done on earth and the second and third best things men have done on earth."

The discussion groups of the Case Work Seminar were particularly planned with these things in mind. The students were divided into nine round table groups of 17 to 20 members each, meeting two hours per week. Such devices as the use of the students as group leaders and as secretaries rotating in office at stated periods; projects in self-evaluation; the use of individual conferences and agency tours—all were utilized to supplement classroom work and to approach more realistically the articulated goals of theory-practice integration, resource and relationship emphases, and individual student development through participation toward the concrete use of theory.

The weekly programs of the discussion groups were built around the social deviations of unemployment, widowhood, illness, old age, and so on. Under unemployment work relief were discussed the C.W.A., the more recent F.E.R.A. policies, personality disintegration, relief and its various aspects. The groups had been previously referred to material that would help them on their job.[1] The discussion was planned about an actual case history and brought out local and state resources or needs—financial, social, and legal. In the discussion of widowhood, the mother's allowance law was reported on

---

[1]This included *Emergency Work Relief* by Colcord, Koplovitz, and Kurtz, Russell Sage Foundation; "Man on the Hills" (C.W.A. worker's analysis of that work); *Morale,* by George K. Pratt, National Committee for Mental Hygiene; *Some Aspects of Relief,* by Grace Marcus, Charity Organization Society, New York; "Miss Bailey Says ——." articles on relief issues in *The Survey;* and the articles on rehabilitation and subsistence homesteads by Joanna C. Colcord and Russell H. Kurtz in *The Survey*'s column on Unemployment and Community Action.

and its administration checked by students in their individual home counties.[2]

Of the 144 students enrolling in the Short Course, 124 successfully finished the semester of theory and wished to go into practice work. The approval for their field training by the State Relief office coming late at the end of the semester meant speed and almost magic in the reorganization of training centers for so large a group. With the scholarship increased to $10 or $12 per week (according to rural or urban placement), the ingenuity of the state case supervisor in challenging the interest of rural communities in the training project, the assurance of assistance from the experienced urban agencies, and the enthusiasm of the young field guides, ten training centers were quickly under way. Semi-monthly meetings for the field guides, a statement of objectives emphasizing case loads of limited size, selection of cases, principles for stress, and importance of individual student conferences and weekly staff conferences supplemented by visits during the eight weeks' period by the university training supervisor, were the methods used to control the educational process.

To give the students some administrative experience, community projects were encouraged and individual students handled them through the various stages of stimulation of community interest and organization of committees to the consummation of goals. Some of the projects were a clothing bureau, a tuberculosis clinic, a crippled children's clinic, and a survey of a legal situation involving long antagonism between employer and employees of a key local industry. The administration class had done much to challenge the students' interest along these lines and the imagination and skill of field guides provided the necessary encouragement in the field projects.

Of the original 144 students, 117 successfully completed the semester of theory and the eight weeks of practice work. Most of them were placed in Missouri counties, with only a small number assigned to St. Louis, Kansas City, and our neighboring counties in Iowa. The students recognized that, while the need for their employment might be mutual—to them individually and to the community—at this point, preparation for the case work job was by no means considered complete, nor would they be thought of as trained social workers by

---

[2]One of the references used was Phyllis Greenacre's article on "Consideration of the Role of the Father in the Treatment of a Mothers' Aid Situation," *The Family*, January 1933.

the profession. It was gratifying that a large number of the group, much the majority, made inquiry regarding the F.E.R.A. grants for the fall training program. Four of the group have already enrolled on their own responsibility for further graduate work. Several others have made definite plans for midyear enrollment.

What the course has done for the students individually it is early for us to say, although we have noted the usual loss of group prejudices, the gains in self-confidence, the satisfactions in social orientation. Some of this came from the 27 who returned to their teaching or to other previous positions, or who for various reasons, illness or vocational unadjustment, did not finish the work. Supervisors have noted in the group a marked community consciousness and an ability to evaluate situations critically and constructively. The rural communities touched by the students—about 85 of the students after training there have gone back to these communities as county visitors and assistants—have indicated some growth in understanding their needs, and genuine desire for assistance through case work service.

LEARNING WITH OUR FERA'S

Mary Lois Pyles

Let us imagine ourselves back in September, 1934, or February, 1935. A hundred selected FERA workers from nine states are arriving for a semester at Washington University in St. Louis. The social work department receives them with thoughts of "Here is an alert looking group of people who come from tremendous jobs performed under pioneering conditions with little guidance. Their training has been in other fields—teaching, farming, ministry, engineering, law, medicine, bookkeeping, business, and so on. It is miraculous how well

The Family, January 1936. Mary Lois Pyles was on the staff of the Department of Social Work at Washington University, St. Louis.

they have been able to do their public welfare job. Someone thought a semester of training and experience would help them. Wonder if they thought so too?"

And what are the students thinking? "When I first received notice that my application as a FERA scholarship student was accepted, I was much elated. In the first place I was glad to realize my ambition to continue school work. Second, I reluctantly admit that I was thoroughly sick of the job I had been attempting to perform and looked forward to school as a desired change and almost a vacation. The enormous case load I had been attempting to carry, the woeful lack of facilities, the ever present petty politics, and the needless red tape had all combined to exhaust my original enthusiasm and to make my job an irksome task."

They came with varying reactions, reflecting the spirit of their communities and their own philosophies, hopes, and fears. Their eagerness for knowledge and experience, the help they insistently desired, and the development they made proved a challenge to the School and an experience of lasting value. A review of the adjustments and developments on the part of the students and the School may preserve some of the values applicable to the present developments in the field of social work. The students have participated in formulating this review of the year's experience and have given it their approval.

As we became acquainted it was found that many of the students had come not knowing what they wished to find at the School and without interpretation from the state administration as to what it desired from the period of training to which they were being sent. The case work principle that present reactions are the result of past experience took on new meaning, and we began to consider with the student his background, preparation, and present needs. All were college men and women but some had little knowledge of social science. All but eleven had been employed in FERA work, but a few were from communities in which the work was so new and so little understood that the worker came with uncertainties about the conflicting purposes and methods he had been expected to follow. A short orientation course was arranged to help the students get acquainted with their setting. At the first meetings there was explanation of the FERA scholarship plan and the purpose of the courses in Case Work, Medical Aspects of Social Work, Problems in Public Welfare Administration, and Field Work. At other meetings agency administrators led discussions on the local social work program and the set-up of the agencies with which the students were to do field work.

Reactions shown in class and field work revealed uncertainties and conflicts but efforts to understand and integrate as well. The fears of difference between rural and urban work and case work and relief decreased during the semester. As the students found familiar material in class discussion and field experience they realized that here was opportunity for help with the problems faced back home. "The mere experience of seeing an office where personnel was not crowded into hopelessly inadequate quarters, where some privacy had been preserved, and where clients weary from waiting were not jamming the doors gave new hope that maybe things can be properly organized." There was great approval of the community resources found for meeting health, educational, vocational training, recreational, and social needs. Some felt discouraged about returning to work in communities without such resources but some said, "We can work out a cooperative plan with our local doctors if we can just interpret the need and possibilities to the community and our state administration." Or, "I have a client at home who would be good at organizing a club for the young people and a cooking class for the mothers." There was a new appreciation of neighborliness and the personal resources of a family which might have been overlooked previously.

Administrative routine and use of resources were more easily assimilated and approved than some of the relief and case work practices met for the first time. Naturally there were insecurity and questions. "How can I presume to be able to help clients adjust their lives when I have similar difficulties in my own life and no one prescribes a remedy for me to offer?" Patent remedies were not found, but there was comfort in finding that this "new profession" had a body of literature, history, consciously thought-out methods, and developing philosophy and principles. Along with what could be gained from experience of others was an opportunity to learn from practice under the guidance of one with experience in helping students. Field work was found to be a laboratory in which to test out the theory learned in class, to make one's own creative contribution, and to find new material for class study. The supervisors of field work held meetings with the faculty to find ways of adapting field experience to the special needs of students enrolled for only one semester. Efforts were made to follow the direction the student wished to go, to utilize his special interests, and to consider the problems with which he was concerned. Some of the usual field work experiences and methods took on new meaning with FERA students. Group conferences meant opportunity to share experiences and find new methods to apply to problems at home as well as training in how to conduct conferences. A greater variety of case work situations

was selected for field experience because the student may have no
other opportunity of training for some time and must handle difficult situations when he returns to his job. Adjustments were made
by both student and supervisor in regard to case records. The question, "How long should a record be held against a family?" reflected
the stigma attached to relief and doubt about records. The use of
a permanent case history of more than skeleton form was not understood at first. It was necessary for the instructor and student to
think out together the values derived from case histories in terms
of better service to the family and continuity with change of workers, the material available for evaluation of treatment, and information ·for study of social conditions. The student [was] told of
the difficulties in safeguarding confidential information in small
communities and public agencies and studied ways of adapting the
case record to community conditions and the type of work undertaken.

Relief practices were of paramount importance because of the students' past experience and expectation to return to the public relief field. There seemed to be inconsistencies between case work
and relief policies. More nearly adequate relief was seen as desirable from the standpoint of living standards, health, and future
community conditions, but on the other hand, "Won't more nearly adequate relief increase pauperization?" After experience with a family
who for a long period had to depend on the agency for finances but
who had not lost independence and ambition, the question changed to,
"Is it the amount of relief or the way in which it is given that
pauperizes?" Budgets had been thought of as useless in communities
without funds to meet all needs, but students were now using budgets
to determine with the family its actual need, resources for meeting
the need, and to interpret the limitations of the agency. There
was opportunity to think out, experiment with, or at least discuss
questions that arose about various relief practices—such as the
degree of community responsibility, work relief or direct relief,
property and insurance problems, and commissary orders or cash
grants. Often no final conviction was reached but a new awareness
was developed of advantages and disadvantages, social implications
and effects. "There is help in learning what has been concluded (at
least tentatively) in a community that has long been conscious of
its social responsibility."

An understanding of case work philosophy helped work out some of
the questions about clients who lie, conceal resources, and stir up
trouble in the community. Practical value was found in approaching
difficult situations from the view of the client, trying to understand the meaning of his behavior and learn what interpretation and
re-evaluation of the situation with the client is needed. Questions

of the right to make an investigation and to consult relatives for
information or assistance were answered when understanding developed
of making the investigation with the interest and participation of
the client in order to help him within the limits provided by the
community.

After becoming better acquainted with social work practice there
were frequent questions as to "What should the public relief worker
expect of himself?" There was agreement that the primary purpose of
his job is the administration of relief, and to perform this honestly,
efficiently, and fairly to both the client and the community is
a task of true merit. But what of the other problems involved in
the economic situation? Public relief has recognized to some extent
the need to treat accompanying problems of unemployment. Public relief funds have been used to provide some medical care and maintain
educational and leisure-time projects. What the individual worker
is able to do about problems connected with unemployment is limited
only by his vision and ability and the understanding and support of
the community.

"Then doesn't that take us into other fields of responsibility?
Suppose meeting the need of the family means getting the community
to understand the need and the family a little better? Suppose the
community needs to understand the agency better?" Clearly the FERA
worker does have other responsibilities upon his shoulders than case
work alone. There are administrative details, perhaps supervision
of other workers, and always the task of interpretation to the community. The answer to many questions of how to work with the community was found in the case work method of individualizing in attempted
study and treatment.

One student found it necessary to gain an understanding of the
experience of a business man who complained of the amount of
money spent by agencies and was impatient with a family who
were unable to keep up mortgage payments on their home. "The
man informed me that the mortgage had been foreclosed after he
had been very lenient with the family, that any man who wanted
a job could find one, and that he would like to know when he
would quit paying taxes to support worthless people. He threw
this at me as a challenge and I accepted. I told him I was not
in a position to say whether the family was worthless and it
was not for us to judge, for if we had been caught by the depression in our declining years without education or special
skill we too might have to depend on someone for help; also that
as far as I knew there never had been and never would be a time
when those who have would not have to give to those who have
not. After an explanation of the agency's interest and discussion of the family's situation he helped me figure out a plan
for the couple to remain in the property until he had opportunity to use it or their declining life might end. I was convinced that antagonism is often created by ignorance and the
agency would find less criticism if we took time to let the

public know how their money is spent. This man was interested in knowing that some families are helped to preserve morale, that some return to a decent, independent standard of living, and that health needs are considered for the sake of the family and society. The agency often has problems to work out with the company this man represents and I feel that the time spent interpreting the agency to him is a good investment."

Discussion groups were organized to consider the application of case work methods to supervision and administration. There was discussion of the supervision the students had been experiencing and the administrative processes they had been carrying out, observing, and studying. Interest in present day problems of economics was uppermost among the questions of the students and this was recognized as so basic to public relief that a condensed extra-curricular class in applied economics was arranged. The group gave so much time to voluntary extra meetings that the faculty was amazed at the students' capacity and sometimes wondered about the assimilation.

The end of the semester has come and the students are leaving for public relief jobs. What can we hope that they have gained from one short semester? The School may have had little to do with some of the greatest profits. In the first place the students made contributions of their own to one another—through association with workers from neighboring states who have met common problems in similar or varying ways. There was also value in associating with groups of local social workers from both public and private agencies. The students were included in open meetings of the American Association of Social Workers and were stimulated by the social work leaders who talked to the school and other groups in the community. Perhaps it is being so close to realism, having experience from the job on which to base study, knowing the nature of the task ahead, and having only limited time, that made the group so ambitious for help and insistent upon more than is usually crowded into one semester. They have undoubtedly obtained more than usual in this length of time, though not all problems have been solved and not all questions answered. There is less asking of specific questions because there is broader understanding and stimulation to work out difficulties. There is enthusiasm for professional training in connection with public relief work and a less acute but more chronically unquenchable thirst for knowledge. Again quoting a student, "This respite from pressure which overcomes, this learning tools, techniques, and methods, this vision of what has been done and of what can be done, this view of relief as a whole has restored my enthusiasm, polished my dulled idealism, and given me a desire to remain in social work."

It has enriched the department to have an influx of 100 students from the public relief field contributing to other students and to class discussion information about present conditions, needs, practices, and difficulties. It has been a clarifying and developing process to think through with the students where case work and relief work may be the same thing and where each may make its own contribution. From the standpoint of the whole field of social work another gain has been that of interesting some of the capable workers in remaining in social work permanently. If some of the new recruits return to their former professions, social work has gained in being better understood by a larger group of people who have found stimulation and growth through studying case work philosophy and methods.

IN-SERVICE TRAINING FOR PUBLIC WELFARE: THE WHYS AND WHATS

Josephine C. Brown

In-service training is a phrase borrowed from other fields and relatively new to social work. During the Emergency Relief Administration we talked about "teaching-on-the-job," and before that, in the pre-depression era, many social agencies gave their workers "apprenticeship training." These terms were applied to very different processes, designed to meet situations which varied sharply from each other and from the situation today in personnel needs and training facilities.

There is no question but that we now need a new term, and in-service training has an extensive, if somewhat confused, usage in other fields. But recent discussions have made me wonder whether we were not in danger of putting the cart before the horse—taking the newly

Survey, October 1938. Josephine Chapin Brown progressed from caseworker in St. Paul, Minnesota, to Associate Field Director of the Family Welfare Association of America, to Administrative Assistant of the FERA and the WPA (1934). She was the author of *The Rural Community and Social Casework* (1933) and *Field Work with Public Welfare Agencies* (1936, 1938).

adopted phrase and arbitrarily applying it to our present program, instead of looking at the job, seeing just what it involves, and then deciding whether any part of it can fairly be called in-service training.

In these articles I shall try to make some such analysis of in-service training, considering here the reasons for such instruction on the job and what it should seek to accomplish; and in the succeeding article, I shall consider methods. The discussion may take us over familiar ground, for it involves an examination of the whole function of the public welfare agency in relation to personnel standards and development of the staff. And it must be borne in mind that we shall be dealing with a subject of many intangible values and uncertain boundary lines.

A public welfare agency has by its very nature a three-fold obligation: to the government which has given it legal authority and defined its functions; to the public whose money it spends; and to the men, women, and children who are entitled to its assistance. The last is the most important since it is the purpose for which the agency exists.

The first essential in doing a job well is to learn what the job is, exactly what it involves, how each part of it should be performed and the kind of personnel required. This means a careful, detailed definition of function, and an equally clear description of every type of job called for. The resulting class specifications, to use the technical term, must be very clear about personal qualities, academic and professional education and experience.

Having faced these personnel objectives, the next step is to analyze and compare the qualifications of the existing staff. The discrepancies and gaps revealed by a comparison of the two sets of qualifications will give some indication of the amount and kind of work that needs to be done in order to build up the existing staff into a staff which meets, as nearly as possible, the personnel objectives already set forth. This development of staff involves a double responsibility. The agency's part is to discover and make available to each staff member what he needs in the ways he can best use it. The crux of the matter is, of course, the extent to which the staff member applies what is offered.

What do the staff members need? In other words, what do they lack in terms of the desirable qualifications for their respective jobs?

At the risk of over-simplification I have ventured to list the most common lacks—realizing that more than one of them will apply to most staff members and that there is almost no end to the combinations of qualifications and of lacks on every administrative level.

The most satisfactory way to get at the essence of the problem seems to be to look at these needs and suggest some of the things an agency might do about each of them.

Every public welfare agency is likely to find that many of its staff lack all, or part, of their professional education.

This is the most serious lack of all and it is one which no agency training can supply. It is a deficiency striking at the very heart of the job itself. Some day it will be just as unheard of to set up a public welfare agency without a full technical staff who have graduated in their professional field, as it would seem now to staff a hospital with one-year medical students and practical nurses!

In the meantime, there are two ways in which an agency can begin to build a professionally educated staff: by giving due weight to this factor in the selection of personnel, and by granting leave with pay to selected staff members in order that they may attend accredited schools of social work. It is just as important that a worker who has had part of his professional education should complete it, as that another worker should begin his studies. It may be equally valuable to have a worker who has graduated go back to specialize in a subject which will make him more useful on his return.

It is worth noting, however, that a series of unrelated, single courses, taken under a variety of auspices and circumstances, do not constitute professional education. So often "training" is judged by the results of such scattered efforts at learning.

Probably very few of the staff who lack professional education can be given leave at any one time. This means that many, perhaps most of the visitors in the county offices, must go on doing their jobs with whatever help the agency can give them.

These visitors need help in two main areas: first, on the mechanics of the job, in planning and organizing the work; and second, in their relationships with the people with whom they are working. The last covers a wide field. It includes the visitors' relationships, attitudes and philosophy in regard to their clients, to the rest of the staff, to the agency and to the public, and the reasons underlying these relationships and attitudes. Its object is to help them learn what to do on the day-to-day job, how to do it, and why. This is the most difficult task in the entire process of staff development. It is peculiarly pressing because there are so many staff members without professional education. The problem is to give them what will help them safeguard and serve the best interests of the clients, the agency, and the public, and to do this in such a way as to develop the visitors, stimulate interest in the professional field

on the part of those who show capacity for it, and make the whole
process one of sound sub-professional instruction, no aspect of which
will later have to be unlearned.

SUPERVISION IN A RURAL SETTING

Minnie Alper

In trying to think through the purpose, scope, and content of supervision in a rural setting I have taken for granted some of the
generic concepts in supervision and have tried to separate and emphasize some of the elements that are particularly important in rural
practice. I have first attempted to analyze the effect of the rural
setting as it operates in the selection of staff. I have then tried
to define the needs of rural workers and the effect these needs have
on the content of supervision and the relationship and function of
the supervisor.

There are certain factors which tend to lower the amount of professional training of rural as compared with urban workers. State-
wide programs of public welfare are beginning to break down the fear
of professional isolation and stagnation which has operated in the
past to keep social workers in the urban centers; but the fear still
exists to a considerable extent. Salaries in rural areas must have
some relationship to salaries of other professional groups in the
communities, and these salaries have in many states compared un-
favorably with those attainable in urban agencies. In addition,
workers who have gone to rural areas have had few opportunities to
take professional courses while on the job and have had to take
leaves of absence, frequently at their own expense, to obtain any
further training necessary. Often the prospects for advancement in
salary after training seem remote and are not in proportion to the

Proceedings, National Conference of Social Work, 1939. Minnie Alper
was Superintendent of Child Welfare Services for the Division of
Child Welfare of the Missouri State Social Security Commission in
Jefferson City.

amount of money expended for education. Fear of lack of supervision and of taking on more responsibility alone than the worker has been ready to meet has also acted as a deterrent in attracting trained staffs to rural areas. On the positive side, rural experience has offered to the adventurous earlier opportunities for creative effort and for executive and administrative experience beginning in smaller and less complicated population areas than those of urban centers.

In order to attract trained workers of comparable background to rural areas it has at times been necessary to offer higher salaries than city agencies offer. In the past, social work as a primarily urban profession has drawn its practitioners from a group where interests and tastes were primarily urban. As opportunities in rural areas increase it is highly possible that a new group of workers who prefer rural living and are better adapted to it will become interested, and the problem of competition for workers in urban areas may become less acute. Because of these many forces tending to limit the professional equipment of rural workers, additional help in the form of supervision and direction is important.

As we move on to the consideration of the particular needs of the rural social workers, we at once begin to think of the problems arising out of professional isolation. In rural counties in many states it is not uncommon to find only one or two workers, at most, who have had professional training. This means that a great responsibility is placed upon the supervisor as a person who can keep the local worker in close touch with social-work ideas, developments, and ideals. It is difficult to estimate how much teaching of the social worker in urban areas is done through contacts other than those with the supervisor, through conferences and other agencies, participation in professional organizations, attendance at lectures and meetings, and informal discussions with professional friends. These opportunities for professional growth have been greatly lacking in the past in rural areas, though they are beginning to be created through programs of staff development, development of rural professional groups, and other means. The lack of competition and goal setting created by the presence of other professional persons may make for stagnation without supervision. The danger of slipping into ruts because the worker does not recognize the biases and narrowness of his own thinking applies even more to a rural worker than to an urban worker. It is easy, on the one hand, for the rural worker to develop a feeling of inferiority because of the smallness and narrowness of his experience and the lack of any measuring rod for comparing accomplishments and ideas with those of other persons; or, on the other extreme, to develop an inflated ego because of the large amount of recognition given by lay persons who evaluate the worker on the basis of personal characteristics and responses which are not carried over into the professional level of attainment.

The effect of a setting where the preponderance of opinion is that of the lay group creates the need for direct supervision to give balance and support to professional ideas which in young or inexperienced workers are often in the making and none too thoroughly and solidly imbedded in their philosophy. Almost unconsciously the impact of lay opinion tends to superficial acceptance of situations and to judgmental attitudes unless the worker is constantly on guard. Community attitudes of prejudice toward certain families, races, and problems creep almost insidiously into the thinking of even the experienced workers.

The very fact of closeness to the client and the community creates certain emotional attitudes on the part of the worker. Each case, after a fashion, is a test case, since the whole community often has first-hand knowledge of it, and many persons have formed some judgment of the situation. To make a skilled case-work study and at the same time so to interpret the findings that those interested may understand and profit is no small job. There is little salvation for the worker with muddled or unclear thinking. The intensity of feeling which a small community may develop against a delinquent child, an immoral mother, or a drunken husband is often such as to require extreme strength on the part of the worker to remember the needs of the client and to preserve his own professional integrity. The worker often carries the total burden of the community feeling against the client to the point where at times it becomes a mountain of negative feeling against the community which cannot be expressed to any local person. The need for talking to someone outside the situation, who can be trusted, who has perspective, and who can help the worker clarify his thinking and bolster up his sense of the worth of the individuals involved and the value of his own judgment, is the force which often consumes the first hour or two of a conference. At times, until the worker has had an opportunity to express his negative feelings against the community, he is not able to go on to any constructive thinking. Again, the scrutiny which the community constantly gives to the worker's personal as well as professional life serves as a repressing factor at times and makes for constraint and lack of freedom in the local setting.

The need for compromises and adaptations to the state of growth of community social attitudes due to the newness of professional social work in rural areas creates problems which the worker must meet. The ability to work toward a goal and yet to be flexible in accepting present limitations embodies a fine skill which the worker new in experience or new to a rural or public program often does not develop

working alone. On the one hand, we may find a worker antagonizing
a whole community and endangering a total program by insisting on
certain types of care before the community is ready to recognize the
need. On the other extreme, we may have the worker who accepts
without question the lack of resources and responsibility and loses
sight of ultimate objectives.

The worker must not only help the community develop an awareness
of problems which it has perhaps never recognized before, but must
also face the task of developing a sense of responsibility on the
part of the community for meeting needs and ways and means of doing
so. Until resources are available, makeshift plans and second-best
plans are often all the worker has, and at times there is no plan
at all. Often, through unavoidable neglect, problems grow greater
so that more crisis situations develop.

It may be said that professional social work is on trial at present
in the rural areas. The old order of meeting need through the efforts of interested volunteers is passing, but not without a struggle
on the part of most communities. Often the paid worker, whether he
has training or not, is considered a social worker; and the public
is searching for the skill which makes him superior to the displaced
volunteer. The supervisor, through the aid which she may give in
improving and developing the worker's way of meeting situations,
helps the worker to meet a little better the expectations of the community for a "trained expert."

Social work on a professional level, except for scattered experience in the past, is new in rural areas. Case-work techniques must
be adapted to encompass the personal relationships projected into
the professional relationship by the fact of the intimacy of community life. The neighbors know personally the clients and the worker;
the worker knows the neighbors and the clients. In the city the
worker may have confidential interviews with his client, and the
neighbors do not always know about the personal life of the client
or that the person visiting is a social worker. The social worker
is known only in a professional capacity. In the country all the
neighbors know when the social worker calls and, with varying motives,
often offer to take part in the solution of the problem. Judgmental
attitudes and biases may block the whole treatment plan. Instead of
dealing with one client in a professional relationship, the whole
community may be the client; and until constructive community attitudes are developed, case-work effectiveness is limited. The worker
of limited experience and training or the worker who has practiced in
the more protected atmosphere of an urban agency needs the help of a
supervisor who is professionally secure to be able to adapt old tech-

niques and develop new techniques as we pioneer in a new professional setting.

A special problem has arisen out of the extension of the base of rural operation from a township and county to a state and Federal level. This makes necessary the development and stimulation of professional standards over a wide-enough area to carry the program on a state and then on a national level. Administrators are responsible to the state as a whole. Coordination of activities and the setting of levels of accomplishment through supervision are imperative at the local level in order to maintain the program on a state and national level. While it is increasingly important to recognize the state-wide aspects of the job, at the same time it becomes imperative that local autonomy and responsibility not be overlooked. Through wise supervision the recognition of individual difference in communities and the development of local consciousness are fostered. The necessity for balance among the needs of the community, the agency, and the worker must be constantly kept in mind.

The executive, administrative, and interpretative aspects of rural jobs are new to many case workers, even to those with considerable experience in urban areas. In the cities the executives have had the major experience with boards, committees, and lay groups. The newness of rural public agency setting and alignments must be learned on the job and sometimes before the worker is really secure enough to take on such a responsibility. He can be helped, however, through consultation and supervision to avoid many dangers and subsequent losses to program development.

We are now ready to summarize briefly the content of supervision. The legal and governmental setting in which the agency functions must be taught. It is often necessary to give the worker of experience or training considerable orientation to the public welfare setting. For the untrained worker it is necessary to transmit not only the case-work approach and some case-work concepts as they are applied to the function of the particular agency involved, but also something more intangible, the beginnings of a professional attitude and respect for the job which may eventually lead to the desire for further professional training. Most social-work training in the past has been geared to the urban setting where there has been acceptance and development of organized social work far beyond that of the present rural setting. Workers have learned to practice with the use of urban resources and specialized agencies. When the worker moves from the urban to the rural setting he may become lost without accustomed aids and resources until he has oriented himself to his new situation and developed new skills as substitutes. Careful supervision in social work helps to bridge this gap.

Supervision needs to give, also, considerable attention to orientation to the aspects of life peculiar to the rural setting. The closeness of community life and relationships and the rural conservatism in accepting persons from outside the community are important factors. The rigid classification of social strata and classes which may be accompanied, at the same time, by an intimacy in which the town drunkard and the leading banker, who went to school with each other, may call each other by their first names, is most confusing to the urban worker. The transfer from an industrial setting to small-town and farm surroundings with all the accompanying changes in modes of living and tempo must be made. The change from a setting where man-made industry seems to rule to a place where things as natural as rain have a vital importance must be accompanied by a change in outlook and philosophy. Housing standards are different. Health attitudes developed out of distance from doctors and medical centers vary from city attitudes. The lack of organized social agencies is confusing until the worker is able to discover some of the compensating factors in the way of direct interest in the client group from neighbors, friends, social, civic, and religious groups. The social controls exercised by close and intimate associations with neighbors and friends must be discovered.

The importance of the community and its attitudes in relation to the case-work program in rural areas has been frequently mentioned. The development of boards, committees, county commissions, and other lay groups, and the ability to work with them and to help them in assuming obligation for the part of the job which belongs to the general community is no mean task and must be accomplished if an adequate public welfare program is ever to be firmly established. There is also need for the development of policies and function in relation to other social agencies, county officials, and volunteer groups. The eventual pattern which will be developed in the rural setting will, no doubt, bear marked differences from those we have known in the cities. The high degree of specialization which we have accepted in large centers will be modified in county and state programs. The worker on the county job is at present developing many aspects of the job at one time. He may be doing community organization, interpretation, family case work, and relief administration, child welfare, group work, probation and parole, medical social work, and a myriad other jobs. Supervisory help, some in the form of consultation from specialists, is imperative.

The difficulties of a scattered staff are many. The natural fear of the unknown and of authority and the lack of geographical closeness to the supervisor affect the supervisory relationships in a very real way. It may take longer to establish a relationship be-

cause of intervals of time between conferences, and relationships
are easier to disturb and destroy. On the other hand, the emotional
pressure and the need for help because of professional isolation accumulate until there is often a terrific outpouring of difficulties
and experiences when the conference begins. There is frequently a
heavy pull on the worker between his need to identify with his community and its thinking and his need to identify with his agency and
professional standards which at times seem at variance. Independence
of action and thought tempered by mature judgment is the goal of the
supervisor for workers. Because of inability to have conferences at
crisis points it is important that the supervisor permit a great
deal of· initiative to workers and that supervision be adapted to
various individual methods.

Because of scattered staff there is necessarily less possibility
for staff participation in policies. Policies made in the state
offices do not always fit local situations comfortably or well. In
addition, controls must be set up in certain danger areas for the
protection of the worker, the client, and the program. It is not
always possible to discuss policies before they are adopted. This
condition makes it necessary for the supervisor to be unusually responsive to sensing local needs and finding the common elements that
should be integrated into agency policy. It puts upon supervision
the added burden of making policies real and of helping workers develop within the limitations and possibilities of the agency.

The physical effect of long-distance travel on conferences must be
taken into consideration. Conferences following long journeys are
not particularly conducive to comfortable relaxation and concentration on the problems at hand. There is a tendency to make conferences too long and to have them take place less frequently. There
is less control over the psychological setting. There is constant
pressure to present new ideas and philosophies at a rate faster than
the worker can easily accept them. There is less control in being
able to wait till the psychological moment arrives. Philosophy in
relation to the place of the conference in a rural program undergoes
some changes. A sharing of responsibility for initiative in coming
and going and a balancing of the factors involved make for a steadier
program of supervision. Occasional visits to the supervisor's headquarters or state office seem to give the worker a more definite
feeling of belonging and a sense of the total program.

Some consideration must be given to the personal needs of the worker
in relation to the professional job. The supervisor often has too
great meaning to the worker because of the paucity of professional
and satisfying personal contacts. If the relationship is unsatisfactory the supervisor may be much more of a threat than in an

urban agency. On the other hand, it is easy for the relationship to verge too far into the personal level. Because the rural job so often involves the whole self of the worker in a very obvious way, the supervisor needs to develop a fine sense of discrimination and balance in giving professional help and knowing when to stop.

As an underpinning of the whole supervisory relationship the security or insecurity of whole agencies and programs are having their effect on supervision. In many states rural programs have been newly created or reorganized within the few years just past. The public at large is not well informed and is often critical. Many agencies are functioning under great handicaps and pressures which must be passed on through the supervisors to the workers all down the ranks. Professionally trained persons often unfamiliar with the pressures of governmental and political setting may be functioning under lay persons unacquainted with the history, traditions, and practice of social work. In many state programs the persons with social-service training are functioning in an area between the lay administrators and boards, a comparatively small group of workers with training in the field and a mass of workers who have had no professional training. We must recognize the need for a huge measure of adaptability. This total picture of the large group which makes up the usual state staff of today, reaching out to encompass the new field of rural public welfare, is an inspiring one if we keep perspective on the total situation. Each group participating in this new venture will have a special contribution to make. Pressure of case load and volume as well as emotional stress on the workers involving their total personalities in a large area of learning, of new concepts, and of constantly meeting unaccustomed problems and situations are creating a terrific strain on workers everywhere. It is through the individual supervisory conference focused by the worker on the points where he feels the greatest need for help that supervision can be of most value in giving balance and depth to the worker's performance on the job.

RURAL TRAINING FOR RURAL WORKERS

Herman M. Pekarsky

The weakness of rural social work is one of the several disturbing
realities of the American scene exposed by the operations of the
FERA. When that many-tentacled organization reached into the remote
and obscure places of habitation it found not only need for social
ministrations of every stripe and color but, more serious perhaps,
a complete lack of local awareness that anything much could or even
should be done about it. For two years in the face of local lethargy
and sometimes open opposition, the FERA pushed steadily for decent
standards of relief and of personnel. To a considerable degree it
developed personnel reasonably competent to meet the demands of the
emergency job. It could not and did not undertake to train highly
skilled social workers.

Now the federal pressure for standards is gone, but the real job
remains, requiring not only the best technical skills of social workers but the capacity to interpret and to develop pressures from within
the community, without which the job cannot be done. What rural
social work needs more than anything else right now is the right
kind of people on the job. At present they are too few for the need
and for the opportunity that is at the doorstep. Josephine Brown
has enumerated at various times the prerequisites for the right kind
of rural workers. They must have ". . . outgoing personality, insight, and vision . . . good judgment, common sense, patience, a
sense of humor, sound physical health . . . not only the highest
type of training but the most exacting personal qualifications."

Now these are the prerequisites of the ideal social worker everywhere, city or country, and of course so far as pure theory is concerned there is no difference between rural and urban social work.
But I submit that the plunge of the past two years into rural conditions has shown us that in reality there is a difference, a difference not only between city and country but between one section of
the country and another, and that the pattern of accepted social
practice, developed as it has been under urban conditions, does not
fit the present rural scene. One of our weaknesses these last years
has been the effort, sometimes a little frantic, to fit the urban
formula to rural conditions and to try to make the rural mind accept
it. And so to Miss Brown's foundation qualities for the rural social
worker I would add a further stone: a native philosophy indigenous

Survey, April 1936. Herman M. Pekarsky was Director of Social Service of the Welfare Relief Commission in Kent County, Michigan.

to the soil. In other words I would recruit rural social workers
from rural people, from those born on the soil, with an innate respect for the man who lives by it, and, except for general philo-
sophic background, I would relate their training as closely as possible to the type of rural area in which they will probably work.

That is what we are trying to do here in Kent County, Mich.; trying
to develop a training program—of necessity on the job—that will
better the workers for the immediate relief task and at the same time
prepare them for the broader undertakings of rural social work in
this section. We conceive of our program in the form of two major,
definitely related cycles. The first embraces grounding in the implications and practice of family case work, with emphasis on relief
as a case work process. It is followed, after completion, by the
second cycle which deals with the rural community, its resources,
its problems, its strengths and weaknesses, relating the subject matter of the first cycle to the discussions of the second. The whole
program is preceded by general discussions of social work as a profession and of professional ethics and advancement.

The subject matter of the first cycle is divided into four sections:

Job analysis. An evaluation of the purposes, theories and mechanics of intake; continuing contacts with emphasis on the continuity
of relationships established at intake; completion of investigation
—home and collateral calls, available records; treatment function
of referral to other agencies.

The interview. Analysis of types of interviews, their content and
technique; the sociological and psychological problems of interviewing, such as illusions, memory, suggestibility, social philosophy
and so on.

Records. Purposes and content of the record and forms and mechanics of recording.

Modes and patterns of behavior. Significant theories of personality and their contributions to the understanding of social relationships; analysis of the personality and philosophy of the case worker,
her prejudices, resistances, attitudes; mental hygiene for the social
worker—the relation of a well-rounded personal philosophy to the
strains and demands of the job.

This in brief outline is the groundwork in which we believe the
special skills for rural work should be rooted. We propose that each
worker should spend two months of the year in each section, with the
job she is doing geared into the subject matter of her study.

The second cycle is less clearly plotted than the first and has less accumulated experience behind it. Its implementation probably will be determined somewhat by trial and error. But at least we know what we are aiming for—a thorough understanding of the rural person, and of the way his mind works under the conditioning of his environment, his economic position, his social organization, his community life. The subject matter of this part of the training course would differ with different sections of the country, but there are, it seems to me, certain essentials which can be outlined. There should be, first of all, study of the history of the particular region, its economic development in relation to its natural resources and the influence of both on the influx of certain ethnic groups in its population. With this should go detailed study of the social institutions of the region and the small communities—the grange, rural school and church, women's organizations and so on—in relation to ethnic groups and their predominant occupations.

In analyzing social and educational resources, local, state and national, emphasis should be given to the place in the whole rural community of the county agricultural and home demonstration agents. The state agricultural college and the U. S. Department of Agriculture, through their extension services and publications, are resources with which the social worker needs to be thoroughly familiar in the interest of the clients. So too are the various special agencies of government recently set up—the Farm Credit Administration, the rural electrification program, the Resettlement Administration and all the rest. The rural worker needs also a working knowledge of farm management, farm economy, marketing facilities, the relation of soil productivity to types of farming and standards of living, and of farm resources to family budgets.

But all these things, important as they are, are not enough. The rural worker, if she is to be more than an automaton, must understand the rural person's psychology—why he thinks the way he does, and the influences that shape his attitudes. She must understand the pressure of local *mores* in shaping individual conduct and family life and must be aware of the potentiality of local personalities—the minister, the successful farmer, the political leaders of various persuasions—in influencing change and progress. She must learn to see the rural client as a human being with his own prides and resentments, his own strengths and limitations, and to deal with him in terms of his own outlook.

Rural social work, if it is to go forward, will have to break down, in many places, some of the local attitudes developed by relief activities. Mary Irene Atkinson has truly said, "The story of how many rural communities have been improperly conditioned because the case worker was not qualified either by training, experience or personality for her task will be a sad story when it comes to be written."

It seems to me that one of the most promising aids for the social worker in overcoming antagonism and gaining the respect and confidence of the rural community is a recreation program. And so I would add to the equipment of the rural social worker a knowledge of the principles of group leadership and of the adaptation of recreation to the rural scene, preferably in forms and through agencies already accepted by the community. We have had a first hand experience in this line in Kent County. In one of the districts the relief recipients were stigmatized and completely ostracized by the rest of the community. A leisure time program developed by the worker was successful in breaking down this antagonism and bringing the community together on a simple basis of neighborliness and common interest.

As I have said before, the implementation of this second cycle of the training program for rural workers remains to be tested by experience. In the last analysis its success in terms of results in the rural community will depend on the personality of individuals. But I am firmly convinced that its chances are improved if the training is imposed on actual experience in the realities of rural life. I am convinced too that rural social work must build from the strengths of rural life and follow the line of existing rural institutions, section by section. I do not believe that the pattern of urban social work can be laid on the rural community and be accepted by it, and I believe with Eduard Lindeman that, "Social work, if it takes its cue from the few values conserved in American rural life, will be of and by, not for, the people in need of adjustment."

TRAINING FOR RURAL SOCIAL WORK

A. A. Smick

Rural social work has received rather widespread attention on only two occasions in the history of the United States. In both instances it took a national emergency to arouse this interest. The first of these periods developed as a result of the work of the American Red Cross in rural counties during the War and post-War periods;[1] the second as a result of the experiences of the past depression and the establishment of public social work organizations in over 3,000 counties by federal and state agencies, which resulted in ". . . the greatest development of rural social work that the country has ever seen."[2]

In view of these recent developments of social work in rural areas, on a somewhat nation-wide and more or less permanent basis, an analysis and evaluation of the problem of providing training facilities for rural social workers would seem to be rather timely. In making such an analysis and evaluation, three major questions immediately come to mind. They are: (1) Is rural social work a specialized function or process that can be carried on most effectively by social workers who have had special training for work in rural communities? (2) If so, where can such specialized training be most adequately provided? (3) What should be the nature of such a special program of training?

Need for specialized training

The literature of the early post-War period, and of recent years, clearly indicates a rather general agreement among many authorities that the actual process of applying the principles and techniques of social work to a specific problem is the same in rural as in urban communities.[3] A general agreement also seems to exist to the effect

Sociology and Social Research, 22 July 1938. A. A. Smick was a Professor at the Graduate School of Social Work of the State College of Washington at Pullman.

[1] J. H. Kolb and E. de S. Brunner, *A Study of Rural Society* (New York: Houghton Mifflin Company, 1935), p. 559.

[2] Josephine C. Brown, "Rural Social Work," *Social Work Year Book* (New York: Russell Sage Foundation, 1935), p. 429.

[3] E. L. Morgan, "Field Practice in Education for Rural Social Work," *Proceedings of the National Conference of Social Work* (Chicago: The University of Chicago Press, 1927), p. 593.

that the personal qualifications needed for social work are the same in the two areas.[4] On the basis of these conclusions, too many leaders have assumed that urban trained social workers are capable of analyzing and understanding rural problems without any form of specialized training, and can therefore practice their profession in rural and urban areas equally well. I find it impossible to accept this point of view.

My stand seems to be strengthened by a rather general agreement, among students of both sociology and social work, that institutions, forms of organization, and attitudes of people in rural and urban areas are fundamentally different. As one leading authority has said,

> Social workers may be conscious of the difference in social relations in the large and small community but for lack of adequate knowledge and philosophy about them may sometimes be timid and clumsy in their approach.[5]

Prior to the experiences of the past depression, the need for specialized training facilities for rural social workers had been recognized by a few students of the problem.[6] However, the experiences in federal and state emergency agencies, and more recently in state departments of public welfare, have more definitely demonstrated the need for this specialized training. One leader in this field sounded the keynote when he concluded that "the pattern of accepted social practice, developed as it has been under urban conditions, does not fit the rural scene."[7]

Recognition should be given to the necessity of providing a specialized type of training, designed to give the rural social worker a thorough understanding of the environment in which he is to work, at the same time that he is acquiring the fundamental principles, pro-

---

[4]Wilma van Dusseldorp, "The Development of Social Agencies in Rural Communities," *The Family*, 14:20, March 1933.

[5]Gertrude Vaile, "The Contribution of Rural Sociology to Family Social Work," *The Family*, 14:106, June 1933.

[6]Howard W. Odum, *An Approach to Public Welfare and Social Work* (Chapel Hill: The University of North Carolina Press, 1926), p. 16.

[7]Herman M. Perkarsky, "Rural Training for Rural Workers," *Survey*, 72: 104-5, April 1936.

cesses, and techniques of social work.[8] This understanding cannot be obtained without a specialized program of training.[9]

Need for Graduate Schools of Rural Social Work

All recognized schools of social work are agreed that supervised field work is an essential and vital part of the student training program. There also seems to be a general agreement that the student should do his field work in the type of agency in which he hopes to secure employment, and with the type of cultural group with which he later plans to be working. In almost the same breath it has been generally assumed that a specialized training program for rural workers could be developed in an urban area, where the social agencies are highly specialized and peculiarly adapted to the needs of an urban environment.

It is rather presumptuous to suppose that a student trained in an urban environment, with its specialized social agencies, will learn to recognize and make use of the different types of social forces and resources available in a rural area. Such an understanding can be attained only if the student has a knowledge of the values, objectives, ideals, and attitudes of the people in the area in which he is to work. How often a social work program in a rural community has met with violent opposition because the worker, trained in an urban environment, has lacked this knowledge and understanding! Administrators, case work supervisors, and group work leaders, in both public and private agencies in rural areas, have borne adequate testimony to this fact.[10]

If the present demand for well-trained rural social workers is to be met with a corps of graduates who fully understand their task and are capable of utilizing the resources of rural areas in developing rural social work on a professional plane, graduate schools of rural social work need to be developed in typically rural communities.

[8]James H. Tufts, *Education and Training for Social Work* (New York: Russell Sage Foundation, 1923), pp. 122-30.

[9]For a further discussion of this point see J. F. Steiner, *Education for Social Work* (Chicago: The University of Chicago Press, 1921), pp. 86-96; also L. Cairns, "Experiment in Training for Rural Social Work," *The Family*, 16:114-17, June 1935, and E. C. Lindeman, "Organization of Rural Social Forces," *Proceedings of the National Conference of Social Work* (Chicago: The University of Chicago Press, 1921), pp. 12-21.

[10] The writer secured the information upon which this conclusion is based in hundreds of contacts made with community leaders in rural areas: while doing survey work for the United States Department of Agriculture, while assisting in making a survey of welfare resources in the State of Washington for the State Planning Council, and while serving as State Director of Intake and Certification for the Works Progress Administration in Washington.

In view of the position of leadership that our land-grant colleges have held for several decades in studying the problems of rural areas and promoting constructive programs of treatment for these problems, it would appear that they are in an excellent position to develop such graduate schools of rural social work. This would seem to be true for three reasons: (1) These colleges have made a detailed study of all phases of rural life and have a complete understanding of the problems involved and of the social forces and resources that may be used in dealing with these problems. In this connection we need but mention the research and community service work that has been done by the rural sociologists, the home economist, the farm management expert, and the agricultural extension divisions and experiment stations. (2) These colleges already have elaborate administrative setups that reach into every county and community. These could well be utilized in developing such graduate school programs.[11] (3) The people of rural areas, because of these specialized types of services that have been provided by land-grant colleges in the past, have learned to look to them for leadership.

It would seem little short of tragic if we should now fail to take advantage of the opportunity of providing leadership in this field of social work through the establishment of graduate schools of rural social work in our land-grant colleges. By experience and organization, these institutions are well qualified to meet the challenge of this new field.

Content of Rural Training Programs

The training programs of graduate schools of rural social work should be of a threefold nature. In the first place, there should be courses in the principles, methods, and techniques of rural social work, designed to give the worker a technical background and a professional approach to his work. In this group there should be courses dealing specifically with principles of case work, group work, and social organization and administration; courses dealing with the technique of the interview, the legal aspects of rural social work, and the provisions of local, state, and federal legislation for rural social work programs; and courses dealing with the methodology of applying these principles and techniques under the provisions of the present forms of organization.

---

[11] Here I refer to the work of the county agricultural agent, the home demonstration agent, the extension services of the rural sociologist, and the other services of the extension and experiment station divisions. Each could play a vital part in the development of a well-rounded program of training for rural social workers and the services of each division, well known to the worker by virtue of his training, could be utilized daily in coping with rural problems.

In the second place, a series of service or supplementary courses in rural sociology, home economics, farm management, and related subjects should be required. These should be designed to give the student a thorough understanding of rural areas, and to acquaint him with the potential contributions of the home demonstration agent, the rural extension agent, and similar public services available in most rural counties.

In the third place, there should be supervised field work in a rural area, where the student may apply his theoretical principles and techniques to actual problems, under conditions similar to those in which he will find himself when he has finished his course of training.

Some objection has been raised to a program of supervised field work in rural areas because of the supposed absence of a variety of problems, and because of a lack of specialized and representative agencies with which the student may work. In answer to the first objection, one authority has said, "It is clear that the rural field furnishes all sorts of problems which have as much educational value as do those found in the city."[12] This point of view is further substantiated by the fact that several urban schools of social work have set up field training centers in rural areas.[13] These centers were developed as a result of the recognition that students should be trained in an environment similar to that in which they would later work. Training with specialized agencies will have slight value if these agencies and their services are not available in the community in which the student is to work.

By means of a well-organized program of rural field work, graduate schools of rural social work could provide first-hand experience for prospective rural social workers and at the same time assume a role of leadership in experimenting with various types of rural agencies, in an attempt to determine what forms of organization and administration best fit the needs of the rural area. In this manner, graduate schools of rural social work could assume the role of leadership in developing social service agencies and resources that are typically suited to rural needs, just as the urban graduate schools of social work have assumed such a position of leadership in the large cities.

[12] Jesse F. Steiner, *Education for Social Work* (Chicago: The University of Chicago Press, 1921), p. 96.

[13] An example of this arrangement may be found in the Graduate School of Social Work at the University of Minnesota.

Such a development would in no way duplicate the excellent work now being done by urban schools of social work, but would merely fill a need that is recognized by many leaders, in both rural and urban social work, for special training facilities for rural social workers. Well manned and well planned, rural training centers would do much toward establishing rural social work on a professional basis. If they are not developed now, while the interest in the problem is at a high level, we may have to wait for another national emergency before we can hope to achieve such an objective.

TRAINING FOR RURAL SOCIAL WORK

Hazel A. Hendricks

Growing pains are inevitable in anything that has developed as rapidly as the field of public social service, expanded almost unbelievably in the last six years. Worst pain to spread from federal, state and local agencies to schools of social work, state universities and professional organizations is the headache caused by efforts to determine what training is most essential for the social workers that must be produced to assure the effectiveness of these services.

The problem looms particularly large in relation to child welfare service in rural districts, a service that has had most of its growth since the passage of the Social Security Act in 1935. A relatively brief experience points definitely to the fact that if children really are to benefit by the act those who carry it out, from the top administrator down to the field worker, must be especially equipped for their jobs, with professional preparation that keeps a large clear eye on the proclivities of the field.

The words "rural area" connote different things to different people. One person might see corn fields marching to the horizon;

Survey, November 1939. Hazel A. Hendricks was field consultant in Child Welfare for the U. S. Children's Bureau.

another, stony hillsides, mean in yield and size; a third, a dusty coal camp. It is obvious that in three such regions the problems of service differ widely.

Anyone who believes that the American frontier has vanished should accompany a rural social worker on her rounds. In one state within seventy-five miles of a great northern metropolitan center, he easily could come on men "swapping wives for jack-knives"; in another he could see a man who traded his thirteen-year-old daughter to a forty-five-year-old bachelor for a cow; in another, a county judge who encouraged a mother to "sell" her four children for money to pay for her divorce. In more states than one he could see dependent boys under ten committed to the state reformatory because there is no other place to send them; girls and boys of four—yes, four—to sixteen in county poor farms; children of fourteen years and under, in county jails; children separated from their families for life, placed in superficially investigated homes, suffering not infrequently from neglect, overwork, exploitation and even abuse.

The territory covered by one child welfare worker may range over twenty-seven counties. In one state the worker gets around chiefly on mule back; in another, she "poles a boat" to the homes of some of her families. Such a worker cannot draw on community resources—there aren't any.

It is popular to say that radio, telephone and good roads have eliminated distance. Child welfare workers know better. Hundreds of the homes they visit are far from paved roads. Often they must leave mule, boat, wagon or car, and finish the trip on foot, wet and muddy to the knees.

Caused by and intensifying such isolation is the frequent lack of rural free delivery service and of schools that can be reached by the children. Medical attendance is reduced to a minimum—a doctor's call costs so much that it is delayed until illness is far advanced. Churches, shopping centers, places of amusement are pathetically few.

In addition to physical factors, cultural and social patterns tend to isolate some groups. The rigid traditions and customs of the foreign born and their descendants, who even after two or three generations in this country do not speak English, keep them from mingling with "Americans." But rigid cultural patterns are no monopoly of the foreign born. In certain sections, native Americans couple inflexible religious belief with moralistic prejudice toward the ne'er-do-well, the unmarried mother and her child, the alcoholic, and the child whose "folks are no 'count."

Not all state and local welfare departments operate on the same basis, though they have common denominators of practice and function. State patterns of administrative and supervisory control vary according to the equipment and security of the executives, the realities of the local situation, attitudes, size and capacity of the staffs.

Inherent weaknesses in state child welfare programs can be corrected only by leaders with training, philosophy and experience enough to see child welfare in its true perspective and with courage enough to modify previously accepted methods which do not fit realities. What may be expected of a "trained" worker in the state program often occasions confusion. Some state departments expect too much, forgetting that a child welfare worker is after all a human being. Others give full credit to trained workers for successful undertakings. Some enthusiastically grant leaves for workers to secure additional training, while others grant the leaves with poorly concealed pessimism, or not at all.

Opinions differ as to what should constitute the training of the child welfare worker for the rural field. In general it is conceded that everyone dealing professionally with human beings should be trained along two broad lines: the acquisition of professional knowledge; the acquisition and development of working skills. But just exactly what working skills does the rural worker need and how can schools of social work define and impart them?

That is the challenge which this field offers at the present time to the schools of social work. Until they meet it, it is debatable whether newly graduated workers, with little or no experience in community organization and without previous administrative or supervisory responsibility, should attempt to perform the wide variety of tasks which confront them in rural areas. Theoretical work and carefully supervised field work, usually in urban centers, cannot prepare them for the exigencies of rural work as it exists today and for the personal adjustments that it demands. Often the county public welfare directors have had no professional training; frequently there is no county case supervisor and although the state staff may attempt some supervision, the very nature of the program makes this supervision sporadic and general. The child welfare worker must carry a case load, act as consultant on a wide variety of children's problems, develop an awareness in the community of its needs in relation to child welfare and assist in planning to meet these needs. Sometimes she must assume direction of a county office, and always she must be at the beck and call of groups which seem to have slight relationship to her job.

For all these duties the usual technical professional education is adequate. Of course undergraduate courses in economics, political science, sociology and psychology are important and necessary as well as the basic graduate social work courses, including family case work, child welfare problems, medical and psychiatric information, public welfare administration, community organization, research and statistics, with field work in family and child welfare agencies. But to these as essentials in the preparation of the rural social worker should be added the study of social legislation, social insurance, taxation, and the historic approach to social problems, public assistance and public welfare administration. Especially desirable for rural child welfare workers are studies in community organization and group work and something of the federal government's agricultural program and land policies in general.

Within the states, the responsibility for public child care is vested in state and local governments—cities, counties, and towns. Therefore knowledge of the organization and functioning of all local government agencies, not merely those with which her job gives her immediate contact, is a prerequisite for the worker with children.

If she knows where the county revenues come from, and how and for what they are spent, she may develop more understanding of the problems of the local officials, an understanding apt to become reciprocal. Her work will also profit if she learns to recognize the inherent differences in the handling of money among human beings in various sections of the country. In some areas, where topography restricted communication and transportation for early settlers, stern economy is a heritage. In others fertile land, favorable growing conditions and accessible markets have developed a freer attitude toward spending. The money attitude in any country community is part of its whole rural philosophy which will unfold before the worker as she becomes acquainted with the taboos and the honored customs of the community in which she is placed.

But the child welfare worker must also possess a broad knowledge of technique, methods and principles of public welfare administration, as it effects children—children in their own homes (where there is or is not economic need) before these homes are broken up and children separated from parents; children in foster care or in institutions. Courses in history of public welfare administration are not enough to provide skills for meeting everyday problems.

Since she always must deal with partially abstract and therefore nebulous phenomena the child welfare worker must expect criticism from laymen, particularly from those unaware of the complexity and subtlety of work with human beings. She will do well to avoid quibbling over trivial matters when, by yielding a relatively minor point, she might win cooperation for a major one.

Child welfare workers fresh from the schools often find it hard to apply their training to specific situations and to reduce their professional vocabulary to easily understood terms. Frequently when a worker goes into a rural area and meets a "real" situation instead of a synthetic one, she becomes confused and disheartened, and revolts either against the job—"This isn't really social work,"—or against her training, leading her to agree with Josh Billings that "Ignorance ain't so much not knowin' as knowin' such a lot that ain't so."

The rapid increase in demand for trained personnel in the field of child welfare has resulted in a flood of applications to schools of social work. Many of the applicants have no preparation or special aptitude for the work, only a general interest in it and a need for employment. It is clear that the schools—and they are the first to recognize it—have on their hands a responsibility for vocational guidance for undergraduate students looking to public positions in child welfare work. Otherwise they may find that their most carefully planned and ably supervised training in basic concepts, philosophies and principles is lost on a student limited and restricted by personal experiences, interests and tastes. It is the schools' job to supply the field with workers who are able to cope with economic and environmental situations; who are patient with slow progress and able to inspire confidence in their own capabilities; who have enough initiative and imagination to turn a situation's latent possibilities into account and enough self-assurance to stand up alone to complete responsibility. If child welfare workers could be given a period of protected but real experience, similar to internship, between school of social work education and full responsibility for a job, some of the problems now plaguing the field might be eliminated.

It is inevitable and desirable that new techniques will be developed during this period of sudden expansion of services to children. Old methods will be discarded, definitions will be recast. What philosophy and patterns will emerge cannot now be predicted, but in the present ferment there is promise of enrichment for the entire field of social work, training and practice.

DON'T FORGET YOUR COUNTRY COUSIN

Mattie Cal Maxted

The director of the New York School of Social Work recently remarked
that its students came from nearly every state in the Union. It is
not where students come from but where they go that counts. At the
present time they do not go to rural areas.

Driving over rough country roads in an old jalopy in all kinds of
weather isn't as easy as traveling by rapid transit. Evenings in a
dingy rooming house where one's every act is scrutinized by the landlady and all the neighbors, aren't as pleasant as those based from a
metropolitan apartment, with plenty of amusement and freedom to do
as one pleases outside of working hours.

Low salaries reflect the low esteem in which social work is held
in many sections of the country. Under the Arkansas merit system,
for example, the salary of a typist ranges from \$85 to \$105 a month,
of a telephone operator from \$90 to \$110, and that of a senior stenographer from \$110 to \$130. The range of a visitor's salary is from
\$100 to \$120 a month. But although clerical positions pay as much
or more than the visitor's positions, educational qualifications are
lower. A typist, clerk, or stenographer calls for graduation from
a standard four-year high school, for which can be substituted a maximum of two years' successful full time employment. A visitor must
be a high school graduate with two years of college, for which can
be substituted a maximum of two years successful employment.

City pastures are greener than this. The postwar prospects are
for even more lush browsing grounds. Graduate trained social workers would be less than human if they turned instead to the dry
stubble of many rural areas.

Strange Animal

Like his city cousin, the farmer must have a pretty clear idea of
what social work is if he is ever to give his support to a state
plan to employ a sufficient number of competent, well trained social
workers. He does not now have a clear idea. Social work itself was
just beginning to understand how valuable a person a social worker

Survey, September 1946. Mattie Cal Maxted holds a degree in social
work from the University of Oklahoma and a law degree from Oklahoma
City Law School (1929). She worked for the Provident Association
in Oklahoma City, the FERA in Oklahoma, and Rural Rehabilitation in
Arkansas. She was organizer and director of the social work program
at the University of Arkansas, Fayetteville. She was secretary of
the NASSA and an early proponent of undergraduate social work education.

might be, and something of the kind of training she needed, when along came the depression. Almost overnight there was need for thousands of workers and only a handful with training available. Men and women on the farms in many parts of the country had not the faintest idea of what the creature called a social worker was supposed to do.

What they've seen in the intervening years hasn't helped them much. In the first rush, people desperately in need of work and willing to tackle anything, were given jobs and then classified as "social workers." Applicants emphasized their need for a job, not their qualifications. People got the idea that any one with a kind heart and common sense could do social work and that, if necessary, the common sense could be omitted.

Many in the rural states started their thinking about social workers in the same terms as did the clergyman who wrote to Mary Richmond in 1897. "You ask me," he stated, "what qualifications Miss Jane Smith has for the position of agent of the Charity Organization Society. She is a most estimable lady and the sole support of a widowed mother. It would be a real charity to give her a job." Or in terms of public approval for the person who was "employed to distribute relief because he had failed in the grocery business."

Since then we have given the man on the farm little more that is definite and understandable about the achievements he can expect from the social worker. He wants to know what the social worker did for the Jones family? She is untrained in most of our rural states, and often her net accomplishment was to raise taxes so that the Jones family could have three more babies for the public to support. Although salaries are low, many social workers are actually overpaid in terms of their training and the quality of their work. At the present time, one third of the visitors in the state department of public welfare in one southern state have a high school education or less, only six are college graduates, and none with any social work training.

Or the man on the farm may be curious enough to want to know what a *trained* worker could do for the Jones family. And every trained social worker knows the vicious circle started by that question. What she can do depends to a considerable extent on the resources available in the state and the community. These resources do not come into being until there is a sufficient demand for them. Such a demand cannot be created until there are some trained social workers competent to demonstrate their use. And so it goes. Mr. Public is so confused that he decides that he can get on a while longer without these newfangled ideas.

Suitable undergraduate training courses in our state universities and colleges is certainly one practical way to break this vicious circle. In many of our rural states I believe that undergraduate departments of social work are worthwhile even if they never produced a single professional social worker. They serve almost automatically to develop understanding and leadership among young people who will some day be influential in the state as teachers, doctors, lawyers, ministers, housewives, and businessmen. These can be our future social worker interpreters, more effective because they are not paid social workers.

Over and over, students after a few weeks of undergraduate study comment that they never knew there was so much to learn about social work. They say: "Why, the welfare director in our county is an old man who can scarcely read;" or "There is an old lady who sits in the office and gives out a few grocery orders." During the summer terms when the classes are composed chiefly of teachers, school superintendents, and principals, they repeatedly say: "I never realized what a wide variety of activities social work embraced;" or "I did not know that anyone could do anything about such conditions. I supposed they just existed. When I get back to my county I intend to see that we get a trained social worker."

In other ways, undergraduate training can help a state "pull itself up by its own bootstraps." While, as time goes on, a few highly trained workers from other schools may be enticed to come for supervisory positions, the beginnings of the professional achievement needed to build respect and support must come from the present staff workers. A large percentage of them now feel that the standards set for graduate trained personnel are far beyond their reach. One result is to stifle ambition for any improvement. The pace set by undergraduate departments, on the other hand, is not so unattainable. Facilities are nearer at hand. Of staff members who are encouraged to begin their training in this way, many will finish and get their degree and a few will go on to graduate training elsewhere.

States Are Different
Even though it is "undergraduate" rather than "graduate," training within a state for positions in the state has certain practical advantages. The student learns about state conditions, problems, personnel, laws, and resources, with a detail that could not be the case in a school located elsewhere. Administrators often complain that workers from the graduate schools located in large cities are intolerant of the conditions which they find in states with few resources and make less effort to use the facilities that are available. Initial training in state colleges and universities also opens up possibilities for employment and advancement within the

state itself, even though students have gone on for graduate training elsewhere. Thus the home state has a better chance of keeping the "cream of the crop."

Nor does my experience bear out the objection so frequently heard, that undergraduate training lowers the professional sights of its recipients. Of eight graduates from one southern university's department of social welfare who went on to take training in a graduate school, seven probably would not have gone except for the interest created by their undergraduate courses. We need not fear that the concept of high professional quality will be undermined by those who have even a little professional training. Rather we should fear those who have had no training at all and who do not know that any is necessary.

Too often, we who advocate undergraduate training are made to feel that we are arguing for less training. But the fact is that, in great sections of our country, a high percentage of the people occupying positions classified as social work have had little or no training. My plea is for *more* training for these people and for these positions.

No profession makes progress by training a group of workers by some theoretical standard, and then trying to find something for them to do. Rather, progress comes from the reverse process. A job needs to be done. Someone tries to do it as best he can. Gradually it becomes apparent that some particular kind of training will help a person to do a better job. Thus a profession grows—out of the realities of the experience of its practitioners.

Because of the great expansion of the Thirties, the graduate schools are now remote from great blocks of these practitioners. The undergraduate school makes it possible for many of them to improve themselves, and it can serve as a recruiting station for new workers. And in our rural states particularly, it can help break the vicious circle of poor work and meager funds by leavening the lump of ignorance and misinformation about what a social worker can do to help people with their problems.

Epilogue

Rural Social Welfare, 1940-1978

Joanne Mermelstein and Paul Sundet

In popular American mythology, the war years (1940-1945) ended the "farm problem" and started rural America on the way to economic security and progress after a decade and a half of general poverty. Public assistance declined dramatically in almost all states, farm income increased, and farming took on new status as a defense-necessary industry.[1] The arms and aircraft factories paid premium wages for unskilled but willing labor. But other less positive elements accompanied the economic security. Rural-urban migration accelerated and this, compounded by the military manpower drain, foreshadowed the postwar decline of small towns with family-based businesses and growth of impersonal regional trade centers. More specific to social work concerns was the disruption of traditional culture and familial patterns. Expanded kinship relations were no longer sufficient. New responses, including day care and supportive family counseling, became part of the major formal service delivery system—the public welfare agency.

When Johnny came marching to his rural home, both Johnny and home had changed. Between World War II and the Korean conflict, substantial portions of the rural population continued to prosper economically. The former serviceman or defense worker had tasted a

Joanne Mermelstein and Paul Sundet are Associate Professors at the University of Missouri—Columbia School of Social Work. They have been involved in the National Rural Social Work Movement from its incipient stages and have authored a number of papers and articles on rural practice.

[1]Lola Dunn, "Public Welfare in 1945," *Public Welfare*, Vol. 3, No. 1, January 1945, p. 1; Jane M. Hoey, "Public Assistance in 1948," *Journal of Social Casework*, April 1948, p. 81; Wilbur Cohen, "A Salute to 25 Years of Society Security, I," *Public Welfare*, Vol. 18, No. 1, January 1960, pp. 17-28.

different life and often either sought to bring another environment home with him, or saw the rural style too provincial and soon moved, if able, to the city. For those who remained, farm yields increased and price supports were the rule. But left behind in this surge of growth was a significant number who lacked the ability and/or opportunity to take advantage of the general prosperity. And for these, the plight was worsened by the relative affluence surrounding them. Largely excluded from the postwar boom were the rural minorities, including white subcultural groups as well as racial minorities. Toward these persons, the best in rural social work began to extend both individual and programmatic help, a decade before it became fashionable within the profession.[2] And the worst in rural practice mirrored the community context of prejudice and discrimination, helping to perpetuate the conditions social work was intended to alleviate. And the record shows that no one area or region of the country could lay claim to the best nor deny the worst. All too often both were side-by-side in the same office, a situation which could only reinforce the schizophrenic image of the profession.

During the early fifties, the country was preoccupied with Communism, represented both by foreign war and allegations of domestic intrigue. But as the Eisenhower presidency progressed, rural human services continued to quietly develop through significant changes in federal law. Amendments to the Society Security Act extended new categories of financial assistance for disabled, medically indigent, and aged; impact of these programs was substantial in service-poor rural communities with their high incidence of aged. The creation of a new cabinet-level department in 1953—Health, Education and Welfare—initially promised coordinated program efforts which would address wide-ranging human problems, but the staffing pattern quickly skewed toward a metropolitan focus. And who could blame administrators for looking to the cities? Levittown was being duplicated in every large urban area; census figures confirmed the rural-urban migration as well as the changing nature of the core city. But what few realized was that as affluence moved to the suburbs, the core city was filled with rural people. To attribute the resulting problems solely to population density defies not only scientific method but elementary logic. The "disadvantaged" person in the core city and his cousin in the country not only shared the same problem and

---

[2]"Civil Rights in Social Work," *Social Work Journal*, Vol. 29, No. 4, October 1948 (special issue); *Into the Main Stream: A Survey of Best Practices in Race Relations in the South* (Chapel Hill: University of North Carolina Press, 1947).

etiology, but frequently traded places as well.[3] But programs were aimed at locations—in this case, cities—not problems, not the conditions affecting persons irrespective of where they might be found! Still and all, during the quiet fifties, both program and worker sophistication increased in rural areas and foundations were laid for innovations which would produce major changes in the following decade.[4]

When the Joint Commission on Mental Illness and Mental Health presented its report to President John Kennedy during his first year in office, the criticism leveled at the existing hospital systems was ringing. Two years later (1963), the Community Mental Health Center Act opened the door to a whole new form of rural practice. Although the 200,000 population base required in the Act clearly worked travel hardship in many rural areas, most western and some southern states were quick to seize the alternative to cold-storage asylums. And with equal rapidity, rural practitioners turned to the transplanted psychiatrists, psychologists, and psychiatric social workers for the consultation and direction which they had long heard of from their urban counterparts. And where the highly trained staffs were knowledgeable about rural life, or willing to learn, the rural community benefited. In all too many instances, however, the transplant failed to take hold. At the Annual Program Meeting of the American Orthopsychiatric Association in 1965, Dr. David Vail, head of mental health in Minnesota, described "community" as "a language in which social workers speak haltingly, psychologists stutter, and psychiatrists are dumb." Although the development of community mental health centers was and continues to be one of the signal changes in rural human services delivery, the wholesale importation of large mental hospital techniques and mentality has been a continuing impediment in rural America.

In the early 1960s, there was a general awakening of the nation's social conscience. The 1954 Brown versus Board of Education decision arose from a rural context. At the Highlander School in rural Tenessee, Myles Horton was training Abernathys and Carmichaels and Kings in the late fifties and early sixties, in techniques of direct social action.[5] The first White House Conference on Aging

[3]Walter B. Miller, "Impact of Urban Lower-Class Culture for Social Work," *Social Service Review*, Vol. 33, No. 3, September 1959.

[4]Wilbur Cohen, "Current and Future Trends in Public Welfare," *Social Service Review*, Vol. 29, No. 3, September 1955.

[5]Frank Adams with Myles Horton, *Unearthing Seeds of Fire: The Idea of Highlander* (Winston-Salem, N. C.: J. F. Blair, 1975).

took place in 1960 and, among other overdue conclusions, drew national attention to the disproportionate and growing number of aged persons in the small towns and farms of the midwest and south. Myrdal, and later Harrington, paraded poverty before an incredulous public—ghetto poverty and Appalachian poverty, tenement poverty and reservation poverty.[6] And from all these disparate sources came the same message: human problems, be they lack of resources, or growing old in isolation, or racial discrimination, or the prohibitive cost of medical care, or whatever, are common to the human condition. While the cities' numbers are greater, the rural incidence is often higher. The early 1960s took the American public back to Steinbeck and Caldwell's vision of rural. In this general awakening, social workers are not particularly prominent.[7]

But as the civil rights movement gained momentum and the War on Poverty started to take shape, many social workers began to return to the traditional concerns of disadvantaged populations. By the mid-sixties, rural social workers were active in various aspects of the Community Action Program and related Office of Economic Opportunity activities. However, because of the traditionally held image of the profession as clinical practice, some social workers were reluctant to enter into the rough and tumble of grass roots self-help programming, and many others were woefully unequipped for community development activities outside the more established bureaucratic structures. And quite suddenly, the truisms of generalist practice were rediscovered.

Just when the commonality of rural and urban problems reached programmatic acceptance, crisis in the cities, this time in the form of the "long, hot summers," again emerged. The plight of Watts, Newark, and the rest came dramatically home through television and, to many, rural problems seemed insignificant. But a core of professional leadership concerned with nonurban problems remained. As the Great Society became immersed in the Vietnam War and backlash to racial violence mounted, human service programs of all types took a backseat, both in general public interest and in budget priorities. Still, gains such as those represented by Medicare and Medicaid re-

---

[6] Gunner Myrdal, *Rich Lands and Poor: The Road to World Prosperity* (New York: Harper, 1958), and *Beyond the Welfare State* (New Haven: Yale University Press, 1960); Michael Harrington, *The Other America: Poverty in the United States* (New York: Macmillan, 1962).

[7] Theodore Schultz, "Our Welfare State and the Welfare of Farm People," *Social Service Review*, Vol. 38, No. 2, June 1964.

main. Many of the agencies which proliferated in rural areas during
the late sixties continue in some form.

While the new frontier and the Great Society promised massive programs, the New Federalism promised a return to local autonomy, a
prized value in rural America. The mechanism was to be revenue
sharing in various forms. But without categorical guidelines and
with funds geared to population density and tax base, there has generally been too little interest and too little money for social service program support. Initiatives undertaken with high hope have
withered, and there appears to be less local involvement in human
service programs in the revenue-sharing era than in its predecessors.

Another factor vitally affecting rural social work practice by the
early 1970s was the acceptance of the Bachelor of Social Work degree
as the level of beginning professional practice. Workers with the
B.S.W. degree were eligible for full membership in the National Association of Social Workers, accepted as professionals. Most significant in the 1970 decision was an acceptance by both NASW and the
Council on Social Work Education of the reality that M.S.W.'s would
never be plentiful enough and, perhaps more important, were not
needed to carry out many social work tasks. In rural areas, bacca-
laureate trained personnel had always been the mainstay of the major
service systems and the lack of "professional training" had regularly
been used to characterize rural practitioners. Now, with accreditation and a tight job market for B.A. graduates, many colleges and
universities saw the B.S.W. program as a means of attracting and
retaining students. By 1977, there were 113 undergraduate programs,
either accredited or in candidacy for accreditation, which were located in predominantly rural areas. The education in these programs
initially followed the urban graduate school mode. Soon, however,
both educators and students began to express their dissatisfaction
and look for new approaches. They found allies among the rural administrators who had been trying for years to point out the differences context makes in practice technology.

At the 96th Annual Meeting of the National Conference on Social
Welfare in 1969, the heretofore lonely, uncoordinated voices in the
rural wilderness found a spokesman in Leon Ginsberg, Dean of the
School of Social Work, West Virginia University.[8] His leadership
sparked renewed hope for laborers in such scattered vineyards as
Bozeman and Missoula, Montana; Columbia, Missouri; Knoxville, Ten-

---

[8]Leon H. Ginsberg, "Rural Social Work," *Encyclopedia of Social Work*
(New York: National Association of Social Workers, 1971), pp. 1138-
44.

nessee; and Madison, Wisconsin. In the South, work already begun by
the Southern Regional Education Board began to receive selective
national attention.

Momentum grew at the Council on Social Work Education's Annual
Program Meeting in 1973 in San Francisco, as a forum on rural social
work education was included for the first time since 1960. One outcome of that gathering, under the leadership of Dean Ginsberg, was
the establishment of a CSWE Task Force on Rural Practice with nationwide representation. Under Task Force auspices and the staff
direction of Joseph Sheehan, workshops and seminars for social work
educators were held beginning in mid-1973 in Indianapolis, Denver,
and Harrisburg, Pennsyvlania. Program presentations on rural social
work were offered at the 1974 National Conference on Social Welfare
in Cincinnati, and a book entitled *Social Work in Rural Communities*
was published by CSWE in February 1976. At each annual program meeting of the Council since 1973, there have been several sessions
focused on rural practice and/or rural education.

Through these channels, the work of Steve Webster (University of
Wisconsin-Madison), Paul Campbell (University of Alabama), Ed Buxton
and Dave Bast (University of Wisconsin-Extension), Louise Johnson
(University of South Dakota), Charles Horesji and Bob Deaton (Uni-
versity of Montana), and Edward Bates (Montana Division of Mental
Health) were first brought to national attention.

In addition, the CSWE thrust gave impetus to various colleges,
universities, and professional associations throughout the country
to begin developing workshops and programs centering on the nature
and technology of rural practice.

And so the dual pressures from practice and education have again
brought attention to the uniqueness of the rural environment and the
necessity of developing strategies, programs, and skills which meet
its peculiar demands. But the more we look for new directions, the
more we discover that we are on a well-trodden path. The fundamental social problems of rurality—economic insecurity, inadequate
medical care, fewer employment opportunities—are the same ones
addressed in 1908. The consensus among educators and practitioners
alike is that a generalist model is essential to rural social work
and many schools are now moving in that direction. But then Josephine Brown pointed that out in 1933.[9] Public assistance still runs
counter to the value of self-sufficiency, formal agency help is a
last resort, and personal or family dysfunctioning is indicative of

---

[9]Josephine Brown, *The Rural Community and Social Case Work* (New
York: J. J. Little and Ives Co., 1933).

moral weakness. And the social worker is still a somewhat alien role, not quite a tax collector but nevertheless an agent of external authority.

Much is left to be done in developing the philosophy, the rationale, the methodology of rural social work. But in 1978, there are more professionals focusing their talents on these tasks than ever before. But before going forward, it is imperative to look back upon and to appreciate where we have been.